BLACKS IN THE NEW WORLD
August Meier, Series Editor

A list of books in the series appears at the end of this book.

Black Leaders of the Nineteenth Century

Black Leaders
of the Nineteenth Century
Edited by Leon Litwack
and August Meier

UNIVERSITY OF ILLINOIS PRESS
Urbana and Chicago

Peter Humphries Clark illustration courtesy of the
Cincinnati Historical Society

William Henry Steward illustration appeared in Men of Mark *(1887)*
by Reverend William J. Simmons

Remaining illustrations courtesy of Moorland-Spingarn Research Center
at Howard University, Washington, D.C.

© 1988 by the Board of Trustees of the University of Illinois
Manufactured in the United States of America
C 5 4 3 2 1

This book is printed on acid-free paper.

LIBRARY OF CONGRESS CATALOGING-IN-PUBLICATION DATA

Black leaders of the nineteenth century.

(Blacks in the New World)
Bibliography: p.
Includes index.
1. Afro-Americans—Biography.   2. Afro-Americans—
History—19th century.   I. Litwack, Leon F.
II. Meier, August, 1923– .   III. Series.
E185.96.B535   1988   920'.009296073   87-19439
ISBN 0-252-01506-1 (alk. paper)

Contents

Introduction

This volume on Afro-American leaders of the nineteenth century supplements two earlier volumes published by the University of Illinois Press: John Hope Franklin and August Meier, eds., *Black Leaders of the Twentieth Century* (1982), and Howard N. Rabinowitz, ed., *Southern Black Leaders of the Reconstruction Era* (1982). The choice of individuals selected for treatment in this volume was based on a number of criteria: the importance and significance of the individual; the existence of adequate primary and secondary materials; the availability of scholars possessed of both time and expertise. Inevitably, space limitations also influenced our decisions. Readers may note the omission of people such as Prince Hall, founder of the black Masons; Nathaniel Paul, the early Baptist leader; James Forten, wealthy sailmaker and antislavery leader; William Still and David Ruggles, important figures in the Underground Railroad; Philip A. Bell, early spokesman for black migrants to the West Coast; Mifflin W. Gibbs, also a West Coast pioneer and later a Reconstruction politician in Arkansas; Isaac Myers, early labor leader and organizer; George Thomas Downing, successful restaurateur of New York and Newport and spokesman for black citizenship rights; Frances Ellen Watkins Harper, poet, feminist, and antislavery leader; Daniel A. Payne, after Richard Allen the most prominent bishop in the nineteenth-century African Methodist Episcopal church; Sojourner Truth, activist in antislavery and feminist circles; congressmen such as Jonathan C. Gibbs, Josiah Walls, Jefferson Long, and Richard H. Cain; influential newspaper editors such as Harry C. Smith of Cleveland and W. Calvin Chase of Washington, D.C.; and important late nineteenth-century accommodationists like J. C. Price of North Carolina and W. H. Councill of Alabama, to mention only a few.

To avoid overlapping with the essays in the two volumes mentioned above, we have given less space than we otherwise would have to Reconstruction leaders and to important figures like Booker T. Washington, T. Thomas Fortune, and Ida Wells-Barnett, whose careers spanned both the late nineteenth and early twentieth centuries. But we have included an illuminating essay by Eric Foner on black politics at the grass-roots level and the black political culture of

Reconstruction in the South, even though it lies outside of the format of the other essays. In addition, we have included three persons whose careers extended into the twentieth century and who illustrate both the rise of accommodationist leadership and the range of activism among turn-of-the-century black leaders: William H. Steward, Isaiah T. Montgomery, and Mary Church Terrell. Given demographic factors and the unequal opportunities for black activism in different parts of the country, the persons analyzed in this volume are largely from the Northeast and, after the Civil War, from the Southeast as well. Finally, it should be noted that religious and political leaders loom large among the individuals represented here. Ministers have always played a very important role in the black community, and in the nineteenth century the black church was far more prominent as a platform for leadership than it has been in the twentieth. Not only ministers but men who were not officially ministers, like William H. Steward, whose base was the Baptist organization of Kentucky, and Nat Turner, who functioned as a religious Messiah, played a striking role in all forms of civic and political activism. And politicians loom large in this volume, because of the unique opportunities provided by the era of Congressional Reconstruction.

In his essay on Frederick Douglass, Waldo E. Martin observes, "The central paradox of his leadership—and Afro-American leadership generally—consisted of the promotion of black integration into a nation dominated by whites who essentially despised and rejected black people." One can say, in fact, that as a group Afro-American leaders, like Douglass, struggled valiantly for the recognition of their people's human dignity and right to freedom and for full citizenship rights here in the United States. There were debates over whether this struggle should be undertaken with white allies, who sometimes acted in a condescending and paternalistic manner, or whether the struggle should be undertaken under black auspices in all-black organizations. Even larger debates took place over the desirability of looking toward Africa as the arena for securing freedom for American blacks, withdrawal from the United States based on a sense of Negro nationality, and identification with the black race rather than with a deeply flawed American nation, oppressive as it was in the face of its lofty Christian and democratic values.

The nationalist advocates were not consistent in their beliefs. At one time they had all focused their efforts on the attainment of full citizenship rights and acceptance into the mainstream of American society. Even when advocating emigration, they did not usually give up that struggle; they were at best ambiguous on whether or not all

American blacks should migrate to Africa, and in actuality they opted for a selective migration of a small number of skilled, educated, and dedicated Afro-Americans whose mission would be to end the slave trade and Christianize and civilize (i.e., Westernize) the inhabitants of the ancestral homeland. Most of the essays in this volume on nationalist figures make this point clear; though the essay on Henry Highland Garnet focuses almost entirely on his call for slave rebellion and his nationalism, all of this was also true of him.

In addition to the church, perhaps the leading platform for black activists during the nineteenth century was the convention movement. Inaugurated by northern free blacks in 1830, national and state conventions met periodically and spread to the South after the Civil War. They provided an arena for debate and discussion, as well as proposals for unified action, down to nearly the end of the century, when the movement was transmuted into the Afro-American Council, a more sustained effort that lasted into the early years of the twentieth century. The published minutes and newspaper reports of these conventions provide an extraordinary source for studying the thinking of the black leadership elite. It was at these conventions, and through the pages of the black press, that black leaders conducted their debates over ideology and strategy—over such issues as the use of violence, political activism, and emigration. While black leaders, given the power realities of American society, functioned chiefly as spokespeople, black officeholders during Reconstruction developed genuine political constituencies, usually among blacks but at times including certain elements among the white population.

Other spokespeople also had their own constituencies, largely among blacks but often including whites. White abolitionists provided considerable backing, even for independent black endeavors like Frederick Douglass's newspaper enterprises, though he alone among the major black abolitionists was of such stature as to be able to operate independently of either of the two major antislavery organizations in the decade prior to the Civil War. Even militant emigrationists-nationalists found themselves depending in part on white support, including Henry Highland Garnet, who headed the chiefly white African Civilization Society just before and during the Civil War, and Henry McNeal Turner, who accepted a vice-presidency in the American Colonization Society, detested though the A.C.S. was by nearly all other black leaders because most of its members were interested not in elevating blacks but in driving them from the country.

Many of the essays in this volume note the elitism of the black leaders and their frequent tendency to distance themselves from the interests of the masses. The causes of this virtually universal elitism among the Negro leadership class lay in egoistic motivations, class and color differences, and honestly held ideological views. The conflict between Douglass and J. Mercer Langston, for example, seems to have been based chiefly on rivalry for leadership positions in the conventions and other arenas, while Douglass's conflicts with Garnet were over genuine ideological matters. Moreover, ministers, politicians, fraternal officials, and leaders tended to be better educated, more well-to-do, and in other ways exhibited greater accomplishments and skills than the masses of people they represented. The motivations that led people to seek leadership positions involved both the desire for power and fame—mixed with a desire to retain one's position once it had been acquired—and frequently a genuine desire to help the masses. That the leaders' sincerely held ideas of what constituted racial elevation may not have been consonant with the needs of their constituencies should, of course, not be surprising. While agreeing with the authors of many of the essays in this book concerning the elitist nature of so much of black leadership, one would also have to say that such elitism was inevitable, being almost generic in the nature of leadership itself. After all, who was more elitist—yet more concerned about the problems of the black masses—than W. E. B. Du Bois?

AUGUST MEIER

Black Leaders of the Nineteenth Century

Albert J. Raboteau

1

Richard Allen and the African Church Movement

THE STORY is a familiar one. On a Sunday morning in 1792 or 1793, the black members of St. George's Methodist Church in Philadelphia learned to their surprise that they could not sit in the benches they normally used. Instead, they were ordered by the sexton to sit upstairs in the gallery recently added at the rear of the church. Though the situation was unfair—they had, after all, contributed like the whites to remodeling the church—they complied with the order. As the opening prayer began, one of the white trustees told Absalom Jones, a respected black parishioner, to get up and move from the front to the back of the gallery. Jones, a dignified man in his late forties, asked the trustee to wait until prayer ended, but the white man insisted he move immediately and motioned for another trustee to help him lift Jones from his knees. As soon as the prayer was over, Jones and the rest of the black worshipers stood and walked out of the church in a body.

The gallery incident at St. George's is undoubtedly the most famous event in Afro-American religious history. Because it is such a dramatic and clear-cut example of the racial discrimination that has constantly marred religious life in this country, the story has influenced historians to overemphasize white racism as the reason for the development of the black church. Dramatic and catalytic as the walkout was, it did not create the black independent church movement in Philadelphia. Long before the disruption Richard Allen had decided to settle in Philadelphia to "seek and instruct" his "African brethren," whom he described as "a long forgotten people." He had suggested a separate church for the black Methodists of Philadelphia, but his plan was rejected outright by the elder in charge and, at least initially, received little support from the black members of St. George's. Likewise, the leading black citizens of Philadelphia gave Allen no support in this project. They belonged to different denominations and had no interest in establishing a Methodist church. Disappointed, Allen continued to believe that a separate church for blacks was appropriate, as well as necessary. If, as the Methodists proclaimed, all people, regardless of status, were equal in God's sight, then blacks

1

should not only receive the gospel passively but, once converted, actively preach it. Who better could or should bring the gospel to the "African brethren" than an "African preacher"? Indeed, the failure of white clerics to evangelize blacks proved to Allen, and other early black preachers, that it was *their* calling to convert and pastor black people.

Allen's primary motive, then, for organizing a separate church was his desire to seek out and instruct "his African brethren," few of whom attended public worship at all. His dream preceded, by as much as six years, the trouble at St. George's. By 1792 the core of a black congregation had already formed out of the membership of the mutual aid association known as the Free African Society. Black religious independence arose from black initiative and not simply in reaction to white discrimination.

Richard Allen was born a slave in Philadelphia, on February 14, 1760, twenty years before the Pennsylvania legislature passed the first emancipation bill in America. He grew to manhood in the era of the Revolution. The rhetoric of individual rights, the spread of Evangelical Christianity, the formation of denominationalism, the gradual abolition of slavery in the North, and increased emancipation in the upper South all influenced the times, the life, and the career of Richard Allen.

As a child, Allen, his parents, and three siblings were sold by their owner, Benjamin Chew, the prominent Philadelphia lawyer, to Stokely Sturgis of Kent County, Delaware. Sometime before 1780 Allen experienced the profound inner turmoil and sudden release of religious conversion. By his own account: "I was awakened and brought to see myself, poor, wretched and undone, and without the mercy of God. . . . I cried to the Lord both night and day. . . . all of a sudden my dungeon shook, my chains flew off, and glory to God I cried. My soul was filled. I cried, enough for me—the Saviour died." Conversion led him to take two steps which would shape the rest of his life: he began to "go from house to house, exhorting" and he joined a Methodist class meeting.

Delaware, as well as nearby Maryland and Philadelphia, was a cradle of American Methodism. (Barratt's Chapel, erected in 1780 in Allen's own Kent County, was one of the first sites of Methodist organization.) Freeborn Garrettson, Joseph Pilmore, Thomas Coke, Francis Asbury, and other early Methodist itinerants observed that blacks were particularly receptive to John Wesley's heartfelt version of the gospel and urged them to respond to the call for conversion.

2

Blacks joined the first Methodist societies formed in New York City and at Sam's Creek near Frederick, Maryland, and added their names to the subscription lists for the first Methodist church, erected on John Street in New York in 1768. The direct appeal, dramatic preaching, and plain doctrine of the Methodists, their conscious identification with the "simpler sort," and especially their antislavery beliefs attracted Afro-Americans who were gathered into class meetings with whites or organized into all-black classes. Blacks constituted a significant percentage of Methodist growth in the cities of New York, Philadelphia, Baltimore, Charleston, and their environs during the closing decade of the century.

At the time of Allen's conversion and admission into the Methodist society, his master, Sturgis, though himself unconverted, permitted Allen and his oldest brother to attend Methodist meetings every two weeks. Allen later explained that he and his brother deliberately worked harder after conversion in order to disprove the old canard that "religion made worse servants." That piety and work were linked together remained a settled conviction in Allen's mind, no doubt because the combination of the two proved so successful in his own life. At Allen's request, Sturgis allowed Methodists to preach in his house. As a result of a sermon delivered by one of them, Freeborn Garrettson, on the text "Thou art weighed in the balance and art found wanting" (with appropriate application to slaveholders), Sturgis decided that slaveholding was wrong. One cannot help but wonder about Allen's role in Sturgis's conversion, since Allen had invited the Methodist preacher. At any rate, in January 1780 Sturgis signed a gradual manumission document agreeing that Allen could hire out his time until he raised sixty pounds in gold or silver or $2,000 in Continental currency to pay for his freedom. In 1781 Allen paid Sturgis $150 as a first installment; it took five more years to pay the last.

Licensed to hire out his time, Allen worked at a variety of jobs during this twilight period between slavery and freedom: he cut wood, did day labor, worked in a brickyard, and drove a salt wagon during the Revolution. All the while he exhorted and preached to those who would listen. After peace was declared, his preaching career began in earnest. Sometimes alone and sometimes in the company of white preachers, Allen traveled widely on the Methodist circuits, preaching, holding prayer meetings, and giving religious counsel to groups of white and black Christians in the small towns and rural settlements of Maryland, Delaware, Pennsylvania, and New York. According to one account, he ranged as far south as South

3

Carolina and even spent two months preaching among Native Americans. Allen's itinerancy between 1780 and 1785 brought him into contact with the founders and early communities of American Methodism. His religious travels gave him experience and a reputation in the developing network of this "plain" church, where a "plain" man could rise and achieve.

In 1785 Bishop Francis Asbury proposed that Allen travel with him on a regular basis, but he laid out certain conditions Allen found unacceptable. In slave counties Allen would have to avoid contact with slaves and would need to sleep in Asbury's carriage. The question of financial support also gave Allen pause. The bishop might remain unconcerned about temporal affairs, but Allen thought it imprudent for a black preacher to depend solely upon the generosity of others. Rejecting Asbury's offer, he traveled for a while on the Lancaster circuit in Pennsylvania. There he received a call from the elder in charge of St. George's in Philadelphia to preach to the black members of the church. Allen's ministry proved so effective that within a short time he had increased the number of black Methodists by forty-two. Initially he had figured on stopping in Philadelphia for only two weeks, but his success must have persuaded him—and the elder—that he should stay.

Philadelphia, when Allen settled there, had a black population of 1,600 (almost 6 percent of the city's total). An influx of migrants would increase this number significantly over the next decade, as free blacks and former slaves, like Allen, flocked to the city, primarily from the upper South, in search of work. Though a few blacks, like the sailmaker James Forten, rose to prominence and wealth in Philadelphia, the vast majority supported themselves, as had Allen, in the humbler occupations, as day laborers, teamsters, seamen, mechanics, chimney sweeps, cobblers, tradesmen, and domestics. It was this largely uneducated, poor, and unchurched community Allen sought to instruct. His rapid success at St. George's convinced him that the most effective means to reach them was a separate black church.

Initially Allen's plan for a separate place of worship attracted only three of the black Methodists of St. George's: Doras Giddings, William White, and Absalom Jones. When broached on the subject, the white elder ridiculed the whole idea to Allen's face in "very degrading and insulting language." Rebuffed, Allen and Jones continued to discuss the matter and in 1787 decided to organize a religious society. Motivated, as they put it, by "a love to the people of their complexion whom they beheld with sorrow because of their irreligious and uncivilized state," they intended this Free African Society

4

to function as a benevolent mutual aid organization as well as a nondenominational religious association. This dual aspect of the society was reflected in its rules, which required members to contribute regularly to the common fund for assisting the sick, the widowed, and the orphaned and at the same time obliged them to lead orderly and sober lives, distinguished by temperance, propriety, and marital fidelity.

Surprisingly, within two years Allen had quit the Free African Society. After he rejected several invitations to return, a standing committee formally dismissed him from membership on the grounds that he had stirred up discord by "rashly convening" meetings with members of the society. Allen's motivation for breaking with the society and the charges for dismissing him remain unclear. William Douglass, who abstracted the society's minutes in his *Annals of the First African Church* (1862), speculated that Allen left because "the current of religious sentiment in this Society was not flowing in the direction he desired." Very likely, the conflict occurred over religious preferences. Allen wanted to organize a separate black church, preferably Methodist. Apparently his efforts to do so among the membership of the Free African Society met with opposition from those who thought they had formed a nondenominational aid society and wanted to keep it that way. From their perspective, Allen's proselytizing threatened to introduce religious dissension into the society since its members belonged to different denominations and held different beliefs. Their bond of association was philanthropic and moral, "without regard to religious tenets."

After Allen's departure, the Free African Society did move step-by-step toward becoming an African church while avoiding the divisive issue of denominational identity as long as possible. In addition to guarding the morals of its members, the society began to take on the functions of a religious congregation. Members, for example, could choose to have their marriages solemnized in a wedding ceremony developed by the society, and in January 1791 the society initiated regular meetings for Sabbath worship. As they evolved into a church community, the members of the Free African Society came face-to-face with two practical problems: they needed a regular place for worship, and they needed to agree upon some form of religious discipline and doctrine. In search of a permanent meeting house, they turned to the prominent physician and philanthropist Benjamin Rush for assistance and advice. Rush not only sympathized with their desire for an African church but offered to draft for them a plan of church government and articles of faith general enough "to embrace

5

all, and yet so orthodox in cardinal points to offend none." In the summer of 1791 the majority of the members voted to accept Rush's outline of church organization. The transformation from aid society to congregation was, at least in theory, complete. All that was lacking was a minister and a building.

At this point the gallery incident at St. George's galvanized the black Methodists—indeed, the black community at large—into action. The walkout from St. George's made the need to erect a separate church not only apparent but also urgent. The Free African Society took the lead in the campaign to raise funds for the church. Though a few members refused to allow their dues to be used for this enterprise, the majority approved the transfer of their money from the society to a church building fund. Now that his goal was shared by the majority, Richard Allen joined the common task. He and Absalom Jones, William White, and William Witcherly, all active members of the Free African Society, constituted a committee assigned the task of finding property and raising more funds for a church building. Again with the aid of Benjamin Rush and of Robert Ralston, a wealthy white merchant, they quickly compiled a list of white and black subscribers. The Methodist elder opposed the project and threatened to dismiss all the black Methodists who did not erase their names from the subscription lists. Allen and the others replied that they had not violated the Methodist discipline and argued that the disgraceful treatment they suffered at St. George's more than justified their efforts to build a church of their own.

Though interrupted by the yellow fever epidemic that struck the city in 1793, the campaign succeeded and the committee authorized Allen to purchase a lot on the corner of Lombard and Sixth streets. After Allen had reached an agreement with the seller, the rest of the committee decided to buy a different lot on Fifth Street, leaving him personally responsible for the first lot, which would eventually become the site of Mother Bethel Church. As the originator of the idea of an African church, Allen was given the honor of breaking ground for construction. With the church building underway, the leaders of the church, called "elders and deacons" under their ecumenical plan of church government, faced the issue of denominational affiliation. According to Allen, the majority favored the Methodists, but the local elder continued to refuse to have anything to do with an African church. Methodist policy dictated that the ordinances of Baptism and the Lord's Supper could only be administered by an ordained elder or deacon. In 1793 the only black preacher in Philadelphia was Allen, but he was not ordained. To whom, then, could these blacks turn for full ministerial service and denominational legitimacy? The majority of the church leaders voted to affiliate with the Episcopalians. Perhaps their choice was influenced by the active concern of Rev. Joseph Pilmore, the Episcopal minister of St. Paul's Church, who had demonstrated his willingness to minister to black Philadelphians by presiding at their weddings and by assisting in the religious organization of the Free African Society. At any rate, only two leaders voted to remain Methodist, Jones and Allen. On August 12, 1794, the African Church of Philadelphia "consented and committed all ecclesiastical affairs to the Protestant Episcopal Church of America" and two years later incorporated as St. Thomas Episcopal Church with 246 members. Allen said he was approached about pastoring the church but declined because he was committed to Methodism. Absalom Jones, despite his Methodist sympathies, accepted the pastorate and eventually was ordained the first black Episcopal priest in the United States. Allen and Jones, denominational differences aside, remained friends and collaborated on several projects during the following years.

Although the majority, including his oldest supporters, Jones and White, affiliated with the Episcopal church, Allen remained single-minded in pursuit of his goal. On May 5, 1794, he and eleven other black Methodists met at his home to make final plans for a separate house of worship. They agreed to purchase a frame structure, a former blacksmith shop, and move it to the lot Allen had purchased at Sixth and Lombard. Carpenters were hired to make the building suitable for church meetings, and by July, Allen had the satisfaction of watching Bishop Asbury dedicate Bethel African Church. On April 9, 1799, the year before the Methodist General Conference approved ordination of blacks, Asbury ordained Allen as a local deacon.

Bethel increased in membership during its first decade, assisted by a general revival among Methodists in Philadelphia, which Allen reported to Asbury in February 1798: "Our churches are crowded, particularly Bethel. We are now making more seats, and think shortly we must enlarge the house. It is at Bethel the work is most general." In 1799 the Methodists reported 211 black members and 411 whites in Philadelphia; by June 1803 Allen informed an English correspondent that Bethel had 457 members. The frame church, no longer adequate, was replaced by a rough cast brick structure in 1805.

It took eight years, but Allen had realized his dream: the African Methodists had their own place of worship. His decision to stay with the Methodists, despite all obstacles, was based on his conviction that Methodist simplicity was better suited to the evangelization of an

7

unlettered people than the more "highflown" instruction offered by the Episcopalians and Presbyterians. From personal experience, as a convert and as a preacher, he felt certain that the plain gospel presented in spiritual (i.e., extemporaneous) preaching would warm many more hearts than would manuscript sermons, crafted in the preacher's study. Moreover, he prized the Methodist system of discipline as an effective method of reforming and ordering the lives of individuals and groups. By means of small class meetings, Methodists simultaneously encouraged individual participation and communal coercion. In this way values became internalized. The life that these intimate communities sanctioned was supposed to be simple, honest, modest, provident, and sober. This set of virtues, implied by the term "discipline," appealed to Allen personally and as a method for lifting a "lowly" people literally "up from slavery." Methodism offered the masses of black people a coherent pattern of values by which they could order their lives. The Methodist way provided a detailed prescription of how one should live, supplied communities to observe and encourage one's moral progress, and reinforced one's commitment to a virtuous life by emotional praying, preaching, and revival meetings.

Allen's own career demonstrated the value of Methodist doctrine and discipline for black people. The Methodists had preached the gospel which emancipated him spiritually from sin and physically from slavery. For Allen, piety, discipline, and freedom constituted a distinctive Methodist ethos, a gospel of equality for blacks and whites alike. Therefore, when he observed Methodist preachers dismissing black members from society without trial, for trivial offenses and on the basis of hearsay evidence, he accused them of acting "without discipline." Their racial prejudice and authoritarianism betrayed the Methodist faith. In his later years, looking back over the history of American Methodists, Allen remarked on their declension: "the simplicity of the Gospel that was among them is not now apparent" and their "discipline is altered considerably from what it was." He, and generations of African Methodists to follow, believed that it was the vocation of Bethel to preach the simplicity of the gospel and the discipline of Methodism, from which white Methodists had strayed. "We would ask for the good old way, and desire to walk therein," he confessed simply.

The most obvious example of Methodist declension was the retreat of the General Conference from firm antislavery legislation in the face of southern resistance. Closer to home, the efforts of white elders to control Bethel further alienated black Methodists from denominational authority. In 1796 Bethel had been incorporated under the Methodist conference, thus placing the church property under the control of the local elder appointed by the conference. Ezekiel Cooper, a white Methodist, drew up the papers of incorporation in this manner, despite the wishes of the Bethelites, because it was Methodist policy. The congregation first learned of the matter ten years later when James Smith, a newly appointed elder, demanded the church keys and books and forbade any meetings not called by him. When the Bethelites refused to comply and protested that the church was theirs, he told them that it belonged to the conference and threatened to dismiss them from the Methodist society. A quick appeal to an attorney revealed that Smith was right. But all was not lost, the lawyer informed them. A vote of two-thirds of the membership could amend the terms of incorporation. Accordingly, in 1807 the congregation, men and women, unanimously passed a supplement that gave the black trustees control of the church property and went even farther in granting them the right to nominate "any duly qualified person to officiate in place of the elder" in case the elder of St. George's neglected to minister at Bethel regularly. Finally, the supplement restricted the elder of St. George's from assigning anyone to preach at Bethel unless the majority of Bethel trustees concurred with his choice. A succession of elders at St. George's contested the legality of this "African Supplement." They ignored its provisions, overcharged for their services, neglected to supply regular preaching, failed to acknowledge the authority of Bethel committees to discipline their own members, and even attempted to put the church property up for sale. To pressure the congregation to yield, one elder forbade all preachers to serve Bethel under pain of dismissal, published a circular disowning the Bethelites as Methodists, and opened a rival African church to draw away members. When all these steps failed, the elder, Robert Roberts, insisted on taking spiritual charge of Bethel and announced that he would preach from her pulpit whether the trustees approved or not. On the Sunday he planned to preach, the congregation denied him access to the pulpit by blocking the aisles. Another elder tried a different approach: he sued for legal control of Bethel. After a long and expensive suit, the Pennsylvania Supreme Court decided in favor of the African congregation.

Black Methodists of Bethel Church in Baltimore, themselves locked in a similar struggle with white authorities, reacted enthusiastically to the news from Philadelphia. On January 21, 1816, their leader, Daniel Coker, preached a celebratory sermon comparing the victory of the Philadelphia brethren to the return of the Jews from captivity in

Babylon. Contact with Coker in Baltimore and reports of conflicts between black and white Methodists in several other locales persuaded Allen to issue a call for a convention of African Methodists to meet in Philadelphia to discuss their common problems. In April, delegates representing the black Methodists of Baltimore, Wilmington, Attleborough, Pennsylvania, and Salem, New Jersey, gathered in response to Allen's call. Sizable black congregations in New York City and Charleston, South Carolina, did not send delegations but followed the proceedings with interest. The convention delegates "in order to secure their privileges and promote union and harmony among themselves" resolved that the churches they represented "should become one body, under the name of the African Methodist Church." As the leaders of the two largest churches and as men of exceptional ability, Allen and Coker seemed the logical choices to lead the new denomination. Before a vote could be taken, Allen was called away from the convention on personal business; during his absence, the delegates elected him and Coker the first bishops of the A.M.E. church. Upon his return, Allen accepted the election of Coker but objected that the new church was too small to justify two bishops. The public would think them ambitious for status and power. Persuaded by his remarks, the delegates reversed themselves and elected just one bishop, Richard Allen. On April 11, 1816, seventeen years after Asbury had ordained him a local deacon, the fifty-six-year-old Allen was consecrated bishop by the imposition of hands of five ordained ministers, including those of his old friend, Absalom Jones.

The next step was to formulate the rules and structure of the new church. Allen, Coker, and James Champion, an officer in Allen's congregation, modeled the by-laws of the African Methodist Episcopal church upon the *Discipline* of the Methodists, with two exceptions. They abolished the office of presiding elder and restored the legislation prohibiting slaveholders from membership. To the first edition of the A.M.E. *Discipline* (1817) they added a historical preface which explained the cause of their separation from the white Methodists:

We have deemed it expedient to have a form of Discipline, whereby we may guide our people in the fear of God, in the unity of the Spirit, and in the bonds of peace, and preserve us from that spiritual despotism which we have so recently experienced— remembering, that we are not to Lord it over God's heritage, as greedy dogs, that can never have enough; but with long suffering, and bowels of compassion, to bear each other's burdens, and so fulfil the law of Christ. . . .

10

The A.M.E. convention of 1816 occurred within the context of general denominational ferment in the early nineteenth century. Federal and state disestablishment of religion created an environment of voluntarism in which church organization flourished. Between 1790 and 1810, African Baptists, Methodists, Presbyterians, and Episcopalians, concluding that religious freedom applied to them, too, founded churches, exercised congregational control where possible, and struggled with white elders, bishops, and associations to gain autonomy. The African Methodists were the first to achieve independent control of church property, finances, ministry, and governance on the denominational level. Between 1815 and 1821 they organized three separate denominations: the Union Church of Africans, organized by Peter Spencer in Wilmington, Delaware; Allen's African Methodist Episcopal church; and the African Methodist Episcopal Zion church, founded in New York City in 1821. From bitter experience, these black Methodists had learned that congregational independence was precarious as long as they remained under the ecclesiastical jurisdiction of whites.

Denominational structure freed Bethel from meddling white elders and at the same time burdened Allen with new responsibilities as bishop of a rapidly expanding church. In 1817 the A.M.E. church structure consisted of two annual conferences (regional districts), in Philadelphia and Baltimore, served by seven itinerant ministers. In 1826 there were three annual conferences, seventeen itinerant ministers, and ten circuits; and membership, which had stood at 6,784 in 1818, had grown to 7,937. (The total would have been 3,000 more but for the suppression of the A.M.E. church in Charleston after the discovery of the Denmark Vesey conspiracy.) By 1827 A.M.E. missionaries had crossed the Alleghenies to preach in Ohio, émigrés from Mother Bethel had established St. Peter's A.M.E. Church in Haiti, and four A.M.E. missions had been founded in Canada. In 1828 the sixty-eight-year-old Allen finally received some administrative help when Morris Brown, formerly pastor of the Charleston church, was consecrated as the second bishop of the A.M.E. church.

Interdenominational squabbles and church politics harassed Allen's entire ministry. Black Methodists in Wilmington and New York, for example, rejected his overtures and decided to go their own way. Though Peter Spencer, leader of the Wilmington church, participated in the Philadelphia convention in 1816, he never affiliated with Allen, perhaps because his own organization antedated Allen's by a year. In addition, Spencer disapproved of the A.M.E. church structure, particularly the episcopate. Black Methodists in New York organized a separate church in 1796 but failed to send representatives to Philadelphia, perhaps because of intercity rivalry between the two black communities. In 1820 several leaders of this New York Zion church began to negotiate with Allen in secret. But when Allen precipitously invaded their territory by sending one of his elders to organize a society in New York, the Zionites felt betrayed. Allen alienated them further when he refused their request to ordain some of their men unless they first agreed to place themselves under his conference. To the Zionites, Allen seemed ambitious and opportunistic. To Allen, no doubt, the Zionites seemed divisive, at a time when the strength of the black churches depended on unity. The New York Methodists could take some comfort, however, from the fact that a group of dissidents from Bethel set up a rival church only ninety feet from Allen's and proceeded to affiliate with the Zionites. When the trustees of Bethel and Wesley, as the new church was called, attempted a rapprochement and invited Allen to preach at the Wesley pulpit, a near riot ensued. As Allen preached, one of the Wesley partisans sat on the pulpit, interrupted the sermon, and even spat on the bishop. Eventually the two churches were involved in a lawsuit, which Bethel lost.

On the one hand, these internecine squabbles must have troubled Allen and distracted him from more urgent concerns. On the other hand, the tendency of black, no less than white, Protestants to "multiply by division" demonstrated the vitality and diversity of their church life and illustrated their determination to exercise religious independence. From one perspective, three distinct African Methodist denominations may seem redundant; from another, these church and denominational disagreements may be seen as part of the process by which free blacks organized their communities.

As a successful and respected figure, Allen aroused his share of jealousy and animosity. In 1823, for example, he was attacked in print by Jonathan Tudas, a disgruntled former member of Bethel (and leader in the founding of Wesley), who published a pamphlet charging that Allen mishandled church funds during his tenure as treasurer. Tudas also accused Allen of stirring up racial tension by publicly criticizing whites and suggested that the whole incident at St. George's had been invented, or at least misrepresented, for Allen's own purposes. On behalf of Allen the trustees of both Bethel and Wesley published a rebuttal, called *The Sword of Truth,* in which they portrayed Tudas as a malcontent who had stirred up trouble at St. Thomas's African Episcopal Church, created dissension at Bethel, disrupted Wesley, and finally quit the church to avoid trial for "seducing a poor white woman." Tudas's charges must have been particularly galling to Allen, since he had for years accepted no salary from Bethel and had, in fact, frequently paid church debts out of his own pocket. Tudas's attack had to be rejected in the strongest terms possible, not just because it defamed Allen, but because it defamed the A.M.E. church, which the public identified with Allen. Though the A.M.E.s had other leaders, like Coker and Brown, the A.M.E. church was the church of Allen; he was the founder. More important, his life exemplified the values and goals of the church: in a phrase, the independent Christian "manhood" to which the race should aspire.

Allen's leadership rested upon his role as pastor *and* on his status as a successful businessman. Ecclesiastical and civic authority were intertwined in Allen's career, but not because the church was the only civic institution blacks controlled. In his own thinking Allen made a direct link between freedom and piety, prosperity and morality. He had achieved freedom and prosperity, under God's providence, of course, by dint of honesty, industry, discipline, and responsibility. Just as these values had raised him from slavery, so they could raise the black race from poverty and degradation. Though born in bondage, Allen had prospered enough (as proprietor of blacksmithing, shoe-making, and chimney-sweeping businesses) to buy several income properties and to build a three-story brick house in which more than a few white bishops and elders enjoyed his hospitality. All the while he ministered to his flock, he also worked, so that with the help of his first wife, Flora, and his second, Sarah, he never had to depend upon the Bethel congregation for support. In fact, when it came time to die, he was able to leave his widow and six children an estate valued at $80,000. Allen was justifiably proud, as he remarked late in life, that "my hands administered to my necessities."

The social and racial dimensions, however, are what made Allen's ethic much more than a gospel of wealth. It was not enough to merely "refrain from debauchery, folly and idleness." It was not enough to provide for one's family. True Christians had to stretch out their hands beyond the circle of family and friends to comfort the poorer neighbor, the stranger, the widow, and the orphan. The corporal and spiritual works of mercy fulfilled Christ's most fundamental command and at the same time refined the spirit, freeing Christians from the weight of possessions. Individual acts of charity, however, did not suffice. Given the poverty and illiteracy of blacks in Philadelphia and elsewhere, charity needed to be institutionalized. Allen helped found the Free African Society, the Bethel Benevolent Society, and the African Society for the Education of Youth, precisely to institutionalize compassion. These self-help and moral reform societies also served as outlets of race pride and community action. Though he did not hesitate to ask white philanthropists, like Rush, for occasional help, Allen knew that blacks themselves had to cooperate to change the day-to-day conditions in which they lived. Racial progress depended upon moral reform and education. Without thrift, temperance, industry, fidelity, and responsibility, blacks could not climb out of poverty.

Allen also recognized that race advancement was blocked by white stereotypes about blacks. Statistics on crime, poverty, even disease in the free black community were used to argue that blacks were unfit for freedom. Therefore, blacks had to lead moral and sober lives in order to disprove racist theories of black inferiority.

> Much depends upon us [Allen proclaimed] for the help of our color—more than many are aware. If we are lazy and idle, the enemies of freedom plead it as a cause why we ought not to be free, and say we are better in a state of servitude, and that giving us our liberty would be an injury to us; and by such conduct we strengthen the bands of oppression and keep many in bondage who are more worthy than ourselves. I entreat you to consider the obligations we lie under to help forward the cause of freedom.

The antislavery cause required free blacks to organize for moral uplift in order to demonstrate that they were capable of freedom and were not innately inferior. Allen was well aware of the absurdity of trying to prove that persons were capable of freedom, especially in the city which had in his own lifetime declared that all people were equal and endowed with the inalienable right of liberty. He protested that white attitudes blamed the victim for the crime:

> The Judicious part of mankind, will think it unreasonable, that a superior good conduct is looked for from our race, by those who stigmatize us as men whose baseness is incurable and may therefore be held in a state of servitude that a merciful man would not doom a beast to; yet you try what you can to prevent our rising from a state of barbarism you represent us to be in; but we can tell you, from a degree of experience that a black man, although reduced to the most abject state human nature is capable of . . . can think, reflect and feel injuries. . . . We believe if you would try the experiment of taking a few black children, and cultivate their minds with the same care and let them have the same prospect in view as to living in the world, as you would wish for your own children, you would find upon the trial, they were not inferior in

mental endowments. . . . Will you, because you have reduced us to the unhappy condition our color is in plead our incapacity for freedom . . . as a sufficient cause for keeping us under the grievous yoke?

Allen was forced to protest again when prominent newspaper editor and publisher Matthew Carey attacked the black people of Philadelphia for their behavior during the yellow fever epidemic of 1793. Carey had written a pamphlet claiming that black Philadelphians profited from the epidemic by charging exorbitant fees for assisting the sick and by outright stealing from the homes of the deceased. Though Carey had praised Allen and Jones personally for their devoted service to the sick and dying, in their view he had libeled the black community. In their own *Narrative of the Proceedings of the Black People during the Late Awful Calamity in Philadelphia* they tried to set the record straight by recounting frequent instances of blacks voluntarily tending the ill and burying the dead even after it had been proven that black people were not immune to the disease, as had been thought. Carey's attack was not only wrong, it was dangerous because it fed white prejudice against free blacks.

A much more dangerous threat to the free blacks in Philadelphia and everywhere in the nation appeared in 1817 when the American Colonization Society was formed. The A.C.S., a reform society, was organized to support the emigration of free blacks from America to Africa. Its members believed that emigration would solve the problem of slavery by removing one of the major obstacles to abolition: the anomalous presence of free blacks in a country belonging to whites. Allen and other black leaders feared that the A.C.S. would pressure Congress into legislating the emigration of all free blacks, thus resolving the slavery problem by expelling the most vociferous opponents of the system. Two weeks after the organization of the A.C.S. a mass protest meeting was held at Bethel. Initially Allen did not oppose voluntary emigration for blacks. Indeed, along with James Forten, he supported the plans of Paul Cuffe, a black ship captain from Massachusetts and an early advocate of colonization in Africa. Moreover, the A.M.E. church supported missionary enterprise in Africa and the Caribbean. Daniel Coker sailed as a missionary to Sherbro, West Africa, on a voyage supported by the A.C.S. in 1820. Responding to Haitian President Boyer's invitation to U.S. blacks to emigrate, several members of Bethel, presumably with Allen's blessing, settled in Haiti in 1824. But Allen strongly opposed the notion that blacks must leave this land to find freedom. As debate over the desirability of emigration continued to divide the black community, Allen came to see colonization as a mistake and publicized his view in the November 2, 1827, issue of *Freedom's Journal,* the first black newspaper in the United States. First he questioned the colonizationists' plan to use Afro-Americans to civilize and convert Africans. Since American blacks were largely illiterate and uneducated, how could anyone argue that they were ready to convert or civilize others? They desperately needed education and religious instruction themselves. The real purpose of the colonizationists, he warned, was to remove free blacks from the country so that slaves would not see other blacks enjoying liberty. Furthermore, Allen wondered, if there were enough land and labor for the thousands of immigrants flocking to America each year, why send "the first tillers of the land" away? Finally, he appealed to patriotism: "This land which we have watered with our tears and our blood, is now our mother country and we are well satisfied to stay where wisdom abounds, and the gospel is free." If reformers were sincere about ridding the nation of slavery, they should abandon illusory schemes of colonization, support the education and advancement of blacks here, and oppose slavery in the South. Allen believed that well-intentioned blacks who supported colonization were flirting with catastrophe.

One of the strongest arguments against colonization in Allen's mind was the fear that the large-scale emigration of free blacks would effectively abandon the vast majority of American blacks to slavery. Without the activism of free blacks in the North, the antislavery movement would be weak indeed. The arrival of recently freed slaves from the South and of free blacks from South Carolina following Vesey's conspiracy reminded Allen and the Bethel congregation of slavery's harsh reality. The Bethel Church basement and the Allen home sheltered fugitive slaves enroute to points further North, out of reach of slave catchers. Allen himself was accosted by a slave catcher who swore that he was a runaway slave. But Allen had resided in Philadelphia for over twenty years and was so well known that the constable serving the warrant was embarrassed to ask him to appear before the magistrate. Allen sued the slave speculator, whom the magistrate remanded to jail when he failed to post an $800 bond. Three months in jail was long enough to teach the man a lesson, Allen concluded, and he dropped the charges. While Allen's prominence saved him from kidnapping, less famous blacks had more to fear.

In 1794 Allen published an *Address to Those Who Keep Slaves,* in which he attacked slavery and the arguments for it. Pointing out "the dreadful insurrections" slaves had mounted as proof that they were far from content, he warned slaveholders: "If you love your children, if you love your country, if you love the God of love, clear your hands from slaves, burden not your children with them." Turning to the slaves, Allen advised them to trust in God and avoid despair. Based upon his own experience of enslavement, he cautioned that impatience only led to emotional "darkness and perplexity." Religion could help the slaves in two ways. It might lead to a relationship of mutual regard between master and slave, a relationship that would tend to promote the liberty of the slave, just as it had for Allen. And in those situations in which reciprocity between master and slave was impossible, religion would instill in the heart of the slave a freedom no master could take away: the freedom of the children of God.

Fugitive slave laws, slave catchers, the American Colonization Society, and legal and customary discrimination clearly demonstrated to free blacks that their situation was tenuous and seemed to be worsening with each passing decade. They would have to organize some general protest, some national movement to fight back. At the initiative of Hezekiah Grice, a free black from Baltimore who had circulated a letter to black leaders calling for a national convention, Allen and the Philadelphia leaders issued a public notice of a convention to be held in 1830, the first of the national Negro conventions. Forty people attended the 1830 convention, whose sessions were held at Bethel from September 20 to 24, with Allen sitting as president and convenor. The convention organized the American Society of Free Persons of Color, whose purpose was to improve conditions for blacks in the United States and establish a settlement in Canada for those driven from their homes by discriminatory laws. In addition, the convention published an address to the free people of color, urging them to "pursue all legal means for the speedy elevation of ourselves and brethren to the scale and standing of men." To achieve this end the convention recommended racial unity, self-help, and a practical program encouraging agriculture and mechanical arts. Agriculture, black leaders reasoned, would lead to independence, and mechanical arts would "ennoble the mind;" both, they confidently predicted, would eventually "give us the standing and condition we desire."

When the convention met Allen was seventy years old; he died within the year, at the age of seventy-one. The convention represented a fitting conclusion to his career. From an unordained preacher struggling to start an African church and facing rejection from the leaders of black Philadelphia, Allen had become one of the foremost black leaders in the nation, the bishop of one of the earliest black denominations, and the president of the first black political organization. Allen had single-mindedly pursued his course and more often than not succeeded. How can we account for his record of leadership? Allen did not question that it was *his* responsibility to lead, to make pronouncements, to take positions on issues and publish them, to represent and defend the race. Though he was certainly not timid and could seem opinionated, his leadership, because it was basically religious, remained pastoral. One does not sense in Allen the pride or self-absorption of the autocrat. His prose style and his portrait reveal a straightforward, direct man who was assured, plain, sober, authentic.

An incident in Allen's youth reveals a key to his character. While living in Delaware he found a trunk filled with money and advertised for its owner, returning the trunk with its contents intact. Allen refused the money pressed upon him as a reward, and when the owner insisted on giving him a suit of fine clothes, Allen relented but only if the suit were made of plain cloth. The *Discipline* itself enjoined "extravagance in useless ornaments and unnecessary fashionable dress." Allen traced the declension of Methodism to the introduction of the ministerial gown, an affectation from the Church of England. His insistence on plainness and simplicity was an essential factor in his leadership and explains his ability, despite his prosperity and success, to remain close to the situation of his church members. Because he did so, the pattern of his life could remain an effective exemplar for them; his way seemed possible for them too. Thus Allen's life, as much if not more than his sermons, preached the plain gospel he saw as the essence of Methodism and the salvation of his people.

Peter H. Wood   2

Nat Turner: The Unknown Slave as Visionary Leader

Nat Turner was born a slave in Southampton County, Virginia, not far from the Great Dismal Swamp, on October 2, 1800. His master was Benjamin Turner, a successful farmer and practicing Methodist. His father, whose name is unknown, was the son of Old Bridget, a slave on the Turner farm; his mother was a young woman who had arrived in Norfolk aboard a slave ship from Africa during the 1790s. Turner had purchased her in 1799 and given her the name Nancy. A week before Nat's birth, a slave named Gabriel, the property of Thomas Prosser, had been arrested for organizing a major insurrection. Only a torrential rainstorm had prevented hundreds of slaves from capturing the city of Richmond during the last weekend in August. Nat was only five days old when Gabriel and fifteen accused rebels were hanged in the Virginia capital they had hoped to conquer. Stories—whether cautionary or inspirational—of this impressive design for a black uprising must have been told often among black and white Virginians during Nat's early years.

While the boy was still very small his father disappeared, apparently making a successful escape from slavery. At age nine Nat accompanied his mother and grandmother to the nearby plantation of Samuel Turner, the son of Benjamin. When Samuel's father died in 1810, he became their legal owner until his own death twelve years later. At that time Nat Turner, now twenty-two years old, was put up for sale along with his wife, Cherry. He was purchased for $400 by Thomas Moore and taken to Moore's farm near Flat Swamp in the western part of the county. His spouse, whether through good luck, general sympathy, or prior arrangement, was bought at a low price by Giles Reese, who owned the smaller farm next door. When Moore himself died six years later in 1828, fortune gave Nat yet another owner: he became the property of Moore's nine-year-old son, Putnam. By the end of the next year a local wheelwright named Joseph Travis had married widow Sally Francis Moore and moved onto the farm where she lived with her children and their slaves. So from the start of 1830, Nat found himself living under a new head of household and continuing to work on what now became known as the Travis place.

21

As of 1830 nothing distinguished Nat Turner from other Afro-Americans as an obvious leader. Among the 2,000,000 unfree Negroes in the southern states many, like Turner, had experienced the separations of parent and child brought on by slavery. Among more than 500,000 blacks within his own state, thousands besides Nat had been traded arbitrarily from one master to another. And among the 16,074 people of Southampton County (where 7,756 slaves and 1,745 free blacks outnumbered 6,573 whites) hundreds of enslaved workers were struggling, like Nat and Cherry, to raise small children while isolated on separate plantations. If the slave of young Putnam Moore possessed extraordinary personal qualities, as supporters and detractors would later claim, none of the attributes had commanded public notice as yet. In the late summer of 1831, when word suddenly flashed across the South that an individual named Nat Turner had led a violent slave revolt and still remained at large, it took Virginia's governor more than three weeks to obtain an accurate enough description of the man to publicize a reward for his arrest.

Governor John Floyd's proclamation of September 17, 1831, which offered $500 for apprehending "the contriver and leader of the late insurrection," described a man in his early thirties with broad shoulders, thinning hair, and a brisk walk. He had a distinguishing scar on his temple where he was said to have been kicked by a mule, plus another on his neck and "a large knob on one of the bones of his right arm near the wrist produced by a blow." He stood "5 feet six or 8 inches high—weighs between 150 & 160," though in fact Turner weighed considerably less by the time he was finally apprehended on October 30. Twelve days later he was dead—hanged by the neck on November 11 by order of the local court. Supposedly, county doctors later dissected his body; and, according to local lore, several whites retained physical keepsakes from this process. If so, their act prefigured the morbid regional custom, familiar in postbellum generations, of saving grim mementos after highly charged public lynchings.

Since Turner became known to the world only weeks before his death, it is not surprising that his outward appearance and, more important, his inner motivations, have remained highly elusive. In southern Virginia contrasting tales immediately sprang up around his name and persisted in local folklore. Some people claimed that his skull, when opened, proved misshapen and remarkably thick, and many parents—white and black—used violent stories of Nat's rising to frighten children into obedience. Other people, however, claimed that the tree limb from which he was hanged became cursed and died, that the soles of his feet revealed a dark letter "W" for "War," and that when his body was taken from the gallows he bore mysterious marks on his hands and feet that linked him to Jesus. Percy Claud of nearby Boykins, Virginia, born shortly before 1900, still recalled in the late 1960s what his mother had said about the "mission" of Nat Turner: "She told me that he was a man that was God's man. He was a man for war, and for legal rights, and for freedom."

The contradictions that appeared in local oral traditions emerged in literary and historical appraisals as well. From the beginning, most of these treatments (such as Harriet Beecher Stowe's 1856 novel, *Dred, A Tale of the Great Dismal Swamp*) drew wholly or in part on the firsthand *Confession* taken down by Thomas R. Gray before Nat Turner's trial and put on sale for twenty-five cents a copy by a Baltimore publisher less than two weeks after the hanging. Gray's own pamphlet contained seeming contradictions that could be used to feed contrasting views. On the one hand, he related — using some of the language and details of initial newspaper accounts — the "deeds of . . . barbarity" committed by fanatical "monsters" and "ruthless savages" out to gratify a "thirst for blood." The interviewer stated dramatically that when he looked at the "fiend-like face" of the leader, "my blood curdled in my veins." In introducing the horror tale to his numerous readers (Gray planned a huge first printing of about 50,000 copies), he predicted that "many a mother as she presses her infant darling to her bosom, will shudder at the recollection of Nat Turner, and his band of ferocious miscreants."

On the other hand, Gray expressed awe for the "calm, deliberate composure" of Nat Turner, "clothed with rags and covered with chains; yet daring to raise his manacled hands to heaven, with a spirit soaring above the attributes of man." He denied emphatically the idea in circulation that the prisoner was "ignorant and cowardly," a robber and drunkard: "it is notorious," the interviewer stressed, "that he was never known to have a dollar in his life; to swear an oath, or drink a drop of spirits. As to his ignorance, he certainly never had the advantages of education, but he can read and write, (it was taught him by his parents,) and for natural intelligence and quickness of apprehension, is surpassed by few men I have ever seen." When Gray had first asked him to relate the history of his motivations for revolt, Turner began by observing, "To do so I must go back to the days of my infancy, and even before I was born." He then summarized briefly his personal background and formative experiences in cogent detail, and the lawyer came away convinced that the uprising "was not instigated by motives of revenge or sudden anger, but [was] the results of long deliberation, and settled purpose of mind."

While proslavery forces worked to portray Turner as a deranged fanatic, abolitionists quickly heralded the same man as a prophetic freedom fighter whose only failing was to be too far ahead of his time. The former stressed his heathen beliefs, while the latter emphasized his Christian training. But both drew on Turner's *Confession* as printed by Gray for their arguments. After all, hadn't he admitted candidly to the lawyer that from an early age he had powers to prophesy the future and recall the past? His apparent ability to speak with spirits, interpret natural signs, and even heal the sick had given him influence over other slaves and affirmed his belief (and that of his mother) that he was destined for some great purpose. "I had a vision," he explained, "—and I saw white spirits and black spirits engaged in battle, and the sun was darkened—the thunder rolled in the Heavens, and blood flowed in streams." Not long after that Nat "discovered drops of blood on the corn as though it were dew from heaven," and he "then found on the leaves in the woods hieroglyphic characters, and numbers, with the forms of men in different attitudes portrayed in blood." Finally, when an eclipse of the sun occurred in February 1831, he took it as a sign; six months later when a heavy mid-August haze revealed dark spots on the sun (part of the largest sunspot activity in two generations), Turner believed the sign had "appeared again, which determined me not to wait any longer."

This person who showed evidence to some of being a demented heathen soothsayer struck his Christian admirers as something of a biblical prophet. Nat mentioned that as a boy he often saw his church-going master at prayer "with other religious persons who visited the house." He recalled that as a young man, "hearing the scriptures commented on at meetings, I was struck with the particular passage which says: 'Seek ye the kingdom of Heaven and all things shall be added unto you.'" Later, when he heard these words spoken to him again while "praying one day at my plough," he identified the voice as the "Spirit that spoke to the prophets in former days." On May 28, 1828, a date forever fixed in Turner's mind, the Spirit again appeared before him with the message that "the Serpent was loosened, and Christ had laid down the yoke he had borne for the sins of men, and that I should take it on and fight against the Serpent, for the time was fast approaching when the first should be last and the last should be first ." At this point Gray asked, "Do you not find yourself mistaken now?" And the man in chains answered with a question: "Was not Christ crucified?"

So detractors and supporters could each build arguments on the actions of Nat Turner and on the complex statement of motives read to the court and then published to the world by Thomas Gray. But the historical person behind these competing archetypes has remained hidden, a source of recurrent fascination for each new generation. "Who now shall go back thirty years and read the heart of this extraordinary man?" asked Thomas Wentworth Higginson in a Civil War essay on the insurrection. He observed that "Mrs. Stowe's 'Dred' seems dim and melodramatic beside the actual Nat Turner." Similar things were said, more vehemently, in 1967 when William Styron published his much-debated novel entitled *The Confessions of Nat Turner.*

Despite the commercial success of Styron's *Confessions* in a culture beginning to rediscover the fascination of "docudrama," many judged the Virginia novelist's work to be, in several senses, a cavalier presentation. Building on more than a century of competing traditions, both Styron and his critics made partial use of scarce evidence to fashion interpretations that had more to do with the shifting currents of the 1960s than with the historical record of 1831. The controversy surrounding the bestseller revealed how remarkably little most Americans knew about black history. (They would know somewhat more by the time Alex Haley's *Roots* appeared a decade later.) But when all the literary and political dust had settled, the life and heart of the actual Nat Turner still seemed as inaccessible as ever. It is hardly surprising that Twentieth-Century Fox, which planned to capitalize on the uproar with a lavish film starring James Earl Jones as Nat Turner, dropped the project abruptly in 1970.

The imbroglio over Styron's *Confessions,* revolving largely around issues of Negro family life and black militancy that infused the 1960s, reminded scholars how readily the historical record could be disregarded and misused. So they were encouraged in 1971 when another Virginian, Henry Irving Tragle, published *The Southampton Slave Revolt,* stating that the "primary purpose of this book is to resurrect the major segments of this record." By gathering newspaper clippings, trial proceedings, contemporary documents, and a dozen of the most influential later published accounts, Tragle opened up the search for Nat Turner to a new generation of participants and started them off with more source material than most of their predecessors had accumulated in a lifetime.

The record is still by no means complete. Indeed, as with the earlier and similar Stono revolt of 1739 in South Carolina, no one as yet has even matched contemporary charts and property deeds with detailed modern survey maps and aerial photographs to plot the exact course of the insurrection. Slavery scholarship by its very nature, even more than most historical work, remains a patient chore of surrounding a subject from all angles, sifting and weighing scant documentation rather than rushing to some predetermined conclusion. One must entertain as at least conceivable the most extreme previous views—that Turner was a blundering fanatic or a miraculous demigod—while steadily testing new interpretations and delving for further evidence. What one would not give for the special bundle containing "all the pages in relation to the insurrection in Southampton" which Governor Floyd forwarded to the Virginia House of Delegates on December 31, 1831, and which has never been located by modern archivists.

But even when new papers do not turn up, careful historians are always gleaning fresh insights from old sources. Occasionally an accepted portion of a standard narrative will be altered drastically by the reexamination of existent documents, casting the whole story in a different light. Within the last decade this is the case for Nat Turner. A regional historian working unobtrusively on a general history of Southampton County has discovered new information about the man who wrote down the original *Confessions* and hence, indirectly, about the possible nature of Nat himself. This seemingly minor revision in the traditional saga may open the way for a broader reappraisal of the historical Turner in the near future. But before this prospect can be suggested, it is necessary to recall in detail the sudden train of events and the dramatic repercussions that raised a rural fieldhand named Nat Turner to the controversial status of nineteenth-century black leader.

In the first hours of Monday, August 22, 1831, Nat Turner and six fellow slaves launched an insurrection in southeastern Virginia that would change the outline of American history. Turner himself, as he confessed to Gray, had been feeling the secret stirrings of a great design for at least half a dozen years, and with February's eclipse he knew, he said, that "I should arise and prepare myself, and slay my enemies with their own weapons. And immediately on the sign appearing in the heavens, the seal was removed from my lips, and I communicated the great work laid out for me to do, to four in whom I had the greatest confidence, (Henry, Hark, Nelson, and Sam)." They planned, by no idle chance, "to have begun the work of death on the 4th of July," but Nat "fell sick, and the time passed without our coming to any determination how to commence." They were still "forming new schemes and rejecting them, when the sign appeared again," in the shape of ominous sunspots on the afternoon of Saturday,

August 13. According to a later newspaper account, Nat told his compatriots "that as the black spot had passed over the sun, so would the blacks pass over the earth." They would commence the apocalyptic movement in the early hours of August 22. That date, perhaps through sheer coincidence, was forty years to the day after the famous secret meeting that launched the Haitian Revolution.

Shortly after midnight the men set out from their secluded gathering place at Cabin Pond on the property of Giles Reese, where they had met through much of Sunday. Turner knew the area well, for the pond lay between the Travis place where he resided and the Reese homestead where his wife lived with their several children. He had visited her recently to leave his crude maps and papers in her safekeeping. The men ignored the Reese home, perhaps because the owner was a powerful man who kept two large bulldogs, and proceeded instead to the house of Joseph Travis. Turner knew exactly where Travis, his current master, and twelve-year-old Putnam Moore, his legal owner, would be sleeping, and others in the group knew the dwelling and its inhabitants equally well. Hark (or Hercules) was owned by Mr. Travis himself. Mrs. Travis's twenty-six-year-old brother, Nathaniel Francis, owned two of the other men, Sam and Will. Among the remaining three — Henry, Nelson, and Jack — the last was married to Hark's sister.

The seven approached the Travis homestead about 2 A.M. and were met by several others. Some fortified themselves with a drink at the cider press while others armed themselves with axes; then they approached the house. Afraid that breaking down the door might awaken the family, Hark laid a ladder against the chimney and Nat, as he later explained to Thomas Gray, entered silently through an upper window, "came downstairs, unbarred the door and removed the guns from their places."

It was then observed that I must spill first blood. Armed with a hatchet and accompanied by Will, I entered my master's chamber. It being dark, I could not give him a death blow: the hatchet glanced from his head, he sprang from the bed and called to his wife. It was his last word — Will laid him dead with a blow of his ax, and Mrs. Travis shared the same fate as she lay in the bed.

The murder of his family, five in number, was the work of a moment. Not one of them awoke. There was a little infant sleeping in a cradle, that was forgotten until we had left the house and gone some distance, when Henry and Will returned and killed it.

Unknown to Turner, a young Travis slave had set out through the night for the farm of Nathaniel Francis, Travis's brother-in-law, with word of the attack. The first few homesteads in the rebels' line of march were taken wholly by surprise, however. To the six killed at the Travis place, six more victims were added at the next three farms; an overseer left for dead became the first white to survive. Having gathered six new recruits, nine horses, and a small supply of weapons, Turner's band moved northeast, hoping to swell their numbers through more surprise attacks and then to march quickly on the village of Jerusalem, just across the Nottoway River, where an arms supply could provide the means to consolidate and expand the revolt. By midday, after additional bloody raids, Turner and his troops had killed more than fifty persons without losing a man, and Nat's ranks, by his own account, "amounted now to fifty or sixty, all mounted and armed with guns, axes, swords and clubs."

Empty houses told Turner clearly that word of the uprising had moved ahead of him and the element of surprise had been lost. Moreover, not all of his recruits were dedicated insurrectionists, and some had to be guarded at gunpoint for fear they would escape and help spread the alarm. At James Parker's farm less than three miles from Jerusalem the insurgents met their first armed opposition: eighteen whites who broke ranks and ran. A larger militia unit quickly arrived with reinforcements; they managed to wound half a dozen rebels and force the others to retreat. According to Turner:

> Finding myself defeated here I instantly determined to go through a private way, and cross the Nottoway river at the Cypress Bridge, three miles below Jerusalem, and attack that place in the rear, as I expected they would look for me on the other road, and I had a great desire to get there to procure arms and ammunition. After going a short distance in this private way, accompanied by about twenty men, I overtook two or three who told me the others were dispersed in every direction. After trying in vain to collect a sufficient force to proceed to Jerusalem, I determined to return, as I was sure they would make back to their old neighborhood, where they would rejoin me, make new recruits, and come down again.

So far Turner had attacked only small farms, hoping that the brutal murder of whole families would terrorize other whites into fleeing the district and would mobilize fellow slaves who knew him personally. But now the appearance of local militiamen and the sure knowledge that further white reinforcements must be on the way obliged the

28

leader to alter his strategy. Cut off from Jerusalem, he doubled back toward the west, hoping to reach Bellfield in Greensville County. At the same time, in desperate need of new recruits, Turner shifted his attention to large plantations. His band numbered roughly three dozen by Monday evening, when it approached the extensive holding of Major Thomas Ridley, who owned 150 slaves. The militia had gotten there first, however, called in to protect the third largest planter in the county, and under those circumstances only four blacks were willing to defect. Having been awake thirty-six hours, Turner made camp for the night, but even as he slept half of his demoralized force disappeared into the darkness.

Of the score that remained on Tuesday morning, several rebels were killed or captured in an attack on Dr. Thomas Blunt's plantation; three more died in a later skirmish; and others deserted the failing cause. By ten o'clock the faithful had been scattered. Nearly undone, Turner dispatched his last four loyalists to seek out dispersed associates and fresh recruits for a rendezvous at Cabin Pond, where final plans for the uprising had been made on Sunday. By Wednesday evening Turner himself had returned to the deserted Travis homesite, but instead of black insurgents he saw only a white search party. "On this I gave up all hope for the present," he stated stoically. Appropriating provisions the following night, he holed up in a nearby cave and remained there for weeks while his compatriots were being apprehended, tried, and executed. Amazingly, he managed to elude an extensive manhunt for several months, until, by his own telling, a hound dog happened on his hideout in mid-October.

A few nights after, two negroes having started to go hunting with the same dog, and passing that way, the dog came in again to the place, and having just gone out to walk about, discovered me and barked. I spoke to them to beg concealment. On making myself known, they fled from me. Knowing then they would betray me, I immediately left my hiding place and was pursued almost incessantly until I was taken a fortnight afterwards by Mr. Benjamin Phipps, in a little hole I had dug out with my sword, for the purpose of concealment, under the top of a fallen tree. On Mr. Phipps' discovering the place of my concealment, he cocked his gun and aimed at me. I requested him not to shoot and I would give up, upon which he demanded my sword. I delivered it to him, and he brought me to prison. . . . I am here loaded with chains and willing to suffer the fate that awaits me.

From the time he first set out from Cabin Pond on August 22, Nat Turner had returned to the same vicinity within four days and had been apprehended in ten weeks. But the shock waves from the Southampton revolt spread across Virginia and the South within days and reverberated across the region for months and years. The initial reactions of southern whites involved sudden panic and swift reprisals. When news of the event reached Petersburg, the nearest sizable town to the north, the alarm bells rang throughout the night, and a rumor spread that 500 blacks were marching toward the city. Those guarding the bridge overheard a visiting bookseller from England remark that "the blacks, as men, were entitled to their freedom, and ought to be emancipated." The man was warned to depart and then was dragged from the stagecoach by a mob. They stripped him naked, lashed him severely while authorities looked on, and finally forced him to leave town unclothed and on foot. Further north, Richmond dispatched two volunteer units to Southampton and organized a temporary company of horsemen to patrol the city every night. Rev. G. W. Powell wrote on August 27, "*many negroes are killed every day:* The exact number will never be ascertained."

Word of the uprising spread southward into North Carolina on Monday afternoon, when a stunned survivor rode into Murfreesboro, followed by other refugees. Eventually 1,000 worried whites crowded into town for protection, and when a rumor spread that black rebels had been sighted only eight miles away, an old man supposedly died of fright. By Tuesday the news had traveled into neighboring Halifax County, and the town of Halifax became "literally a garrison," harboring hundreds of frightened women and children. Stories of a huge slave force in the area made local militiamen so edgy that they shot one of their own men by mistake. "Negroes are taken in different directions and executed every day," wrote a Halifax County resident on August 29. From Raleigh, Governor Stokes asked the secretary of war for a detachment of federal troops; at Chapel Hill students petitioned for weapons to protect the state university in case of slave insurgency; and in Hillsborough the local militia commander mustered out a company of cavalry. "Oh my Dear father," wrote young William Pettigrew from the Hillsborough Academy on September 3, "the negrows have been rising down in South Hampton, and have killed seventy white familys."

In North Carolina the most intense panic and reprisals occurred further south in the large slaveholding counties of Duplin, Sampson, and New Hanover. Earlier, in December 1830, a petition to the state legislature from that region had asserted that many of the slaves were out of control: "they go, and come as they please, and if attempts are made to stop them, they flee to the woods where they stay for months committing depredations" against white property holders. Word of the Southampton uprising heightened black assertiveness and white suspicion. In early September a Negro named Dave, owned by the sheriff of Sampson County, was accused of hatching a major conspiracy comparable to Nat Turner's. In confessions extracted through torture, slaves stated that on the morning of October 4, blacks in Duplin and Sampson counties were to rise up and march south on Wilmington. When false rumors spread on September 9 that a slave revolt was already underway, a Duplin County mob overpowered militiamen at the jail, shot Dave and another slave, and placed their severed heads on posts as a warning. Three days later, when night revelers fired off guns near Wilmington, hundreds of the town's white residents believed that the insurrection had begun, and bitter reprisals ensued.

From Wilmington this wave of fear among whites washed southward, breaking along the coast of South Carolina. Rumors reached Charleston of rebellions in Georgetown and Cheraw near the northern border, and the legislature approved a Horse Guard of 100 cavalrymen to protect the city where Denmark Vesey's plot had been uncovered only nine years before. Camden beefed up its patrols, and Columbia citizens offered a reward for the capture of anyone who spread inflammatory literature. In Union blacks were imprisoned without charges and white families were put under guard, while in Laurens two slaves were punished for stating what they would do if Prophet Nat and his rebels arrived in town. A white woman who grew up in South Carolina later recalled, "we had all our things put up in bags, so we could tote 'em, if we heerd they was comin' our way." Beyond the Savannah River in Georgia, white residents of Macon tumbled from their beds and rushed to a central building, guarded by militia, when word spread that armed Negroes were approaching. Similar rumors surfaced in Twiggs, Jones, and Monroe counties. In one incident "several slaves were tied to a tree, while a militia captain hacked at them with his sword."

Elsewhere across the South alarms sounded about supposed local plots. In Alabama, Columbus and Fort Mitchell heard rumors of a joint conspiracy involving slaves and Indians, reminiscent of stories that had swept the colonies on the eve of the Revolution more than half a century earlier. Citizens in Claiborne found a copy of William Lloyd Garrison's *Liberator* and immediately jailed scores of blacks.

"I remember when I was a boy," one Alabama native later told Frederick Law Olmsted, "folks was dreadful frightened about the niggers. I remember they built pens in the woods where they could hide, and Christmas time they went and got into the pens, 'fraid the niggers was risin'."

In Fayetteville, Tennessee, authorities claimed to have unearthed a plot by slaves, whose "object was to set fire to some building, and amidst the confusion of the citizens, to seize as many guns and implements of destruction as they could procure, and commence a general massacre." Many of the slaves, reported *The Western Freeman* in nearby Shelbyville, "have been *slashed with the severity which the iniquity of their diabolical schemes, so justly deserves.*" And in New Orleans a prophecy that had circulated across the South in the springtime—that the city's blacks "intended to rise as soon as the sickly season began"—seemed about to come true. In September handbills urging revolt were in circulation, as was the persistent rumor that a large cache of weapons had been found. Authorities called out four companies of regular troops, backed up by 500 citizens under arms. On November 14 the governor of Louisiana stated that while the wave of apparent insurrections was only "momentary," it had, "with much reason, excited the serious attention of most of the states of the south."

As word of the Southampton revolt swept across the South reactions were by no means uniform. Predictably, as with previous uprisings, some whites tried to minimize and suppress the story, while others inflated and publicized it. "Do not be alarmed," Emma Mordecai wrote from near Richmond on August 28; "it is not a proper insurrection but only a company of black robbers, committing such depredations as we have often heard of being committed by white ones. . . ." Yet on the same day a Richmond businessman, writing to the New York *Journal of Commerce,* reflected a different view. "We can now conceive that the murders at Southampton could not have been so much an affair of runaway negroes, as was at first supposed," he told the editors, "and the question now arises, if the slaves in that county, would murder the whites, whether they are not ready to do it in any *other county* in the State. . . . " He urged northern merchants not to ship items to Virginia for the moment, on the grounds that if slaves were to "attempt any harm in towns, they would most likely resort first to *fire* to aid them: and goods destroyed by such a fire would not be paid for by insurers."

Just as white interpretations differed, so did the reactions among blacks, whether slave or free. Some were heartened and inspired, hoping "Nat's Fray" would bring changes for the better; others were rightly fearful of the indiscriminate and harsh reprisals that would come down heavily on the black community. "In Nat's time," a black woman named Charity Bowery later told Lydia Maria Child, "the patrols would tie up the free colored people, flog 'em, and try to make 'em lie against one another, and often killed them before anybody could interfere." She recalled correctly that "they killed a great many at a place called Duplon," meaning Duplin County, North Carolina. "At the time of the old Prophet Nat, the colored folks was afraid to pray loud," Mrs. Bowery continued, "for the whites threatened to punish 'em dreadfully, if the least noise was heard. The patrols was low drunken whites; and in Nat's time, if they heard any of the colored folks praying, or singing a hymn, they would fall upon 'em and abuse 'em, and sometimes kill 'em, afore master or missis could get to 'em. The brightest and best was killed in Nat's time," the old woman concluded. "The whites always suspect such ones."

While roughly sixty white persons were killed by the insurgents themselves, probably twice that number of blacks, perhaps many more, died in the regional reprisals that followed. The process Charity Bowery recalled of extracting false accusations through torture cost many innocent lives, and the fact that "General Nat" remained at large for several months only added to the white paranoia. Moreover, it became clear even before his capture that Nat Turner had no previous record as a recalcitrant and had been regarded as a reasonably obedient and faithful man of God by his first victim, Joseph Travis. The evidence that even a trusted servant with no obvious immediate grievance could resort to organized violence brought consternation to planters across the South. Their reaction was only reinforced by Turner's later statement to Thomas Gray that Travis "was to me a kind master, and placed the greatest confidence in me; in fact, I had no cause to complain of his treatment to me."

In dozens of incidents during the late summer explicit punishments merged with indiscriminate retribution—a counter-terror intended to offset the panic aroused by the brutal rebellion and to shift the fear of awesome vengeance back onto the black population. When a North Carolina slave from near Ahoskie entered Murfreesboro heading north at the height of the alarm, he was summarily shot by the local guards, who rolled his body into a ditch and placed his severed head on a pole at a central intersection. It remains impossible to appraise the explanation sent to Governor Stokes, that the man "had procured a forged pass and made a bold attempt to reach the neighbourhood where the Massacre was committed in Southampton, having told a negroe, before he left home, there would be a war between Black & White people."

In a white society where racist dogma had held sway for more than 150 years, some found black rebellion inconceivable, while others saw all slaves as guilty by implication and deserving of harsh reprisals. Between the psychological extremes of complete denial, on the one hand, and belief in a universal antislavery conspiracy, on the other, there would emerge a growing sentiment among prominent southerners that the Southampton insurrection, far from being spontaneous, had deeper and broader roots than initial reports allowed. "From examinations which have taken place in other counties," wrote a correspondent for the Richmond *Enquirer* on September 6, "I fear that the scheme embraced a wider sphere than I at first supposed." According to court testimony against those accused of revolt, a slave named Isham told another worker on Saturday, August 20, "that Genl. Nat was going to rise and murder all the whites," and that even if he did not join the plot, the whites inevitably "would kill him if they caught him." Two days earlier Nelson, the slave conjure man who would take part in the final planning at Cabin Pond, had warned his overseer ominously "that something would happen before long—that any body of his practice could tell these things."

Even more revealing was the testimony of a young house servant of Solomon Parker named Becky, who claimed that in the week before the uprising she had overheard part of a conversation in a Negro cabin where Frank (a blacksmith) said that the master who had cropped his ears would himself be cropped "before the end of the year." She listened to several slaves announce that "if the black people came they would join and help kill the white people," a declaration she had heard from others in the neighborhood earlier in the year. Indeed, while attending a quarterly meeting in May at the Raccoon Meeting House (near the line between Sussex and Southampton counties northwest of Jerusalem), she had heard several men say, "God damn the white people they had reigned long enough," and they threatened that if she betrayed them, the whites would "shoot her down like a squirrel and would not bury her." On the opposite side of Jerusalem, toward Nansemond County and close to the North Carolina line, similar discussions apparently took place at Barnes's Methodist Church, where whites and blacks attended a revival service on Sunday, August 14. Slaves were present from as far away as Winton, North Carolina (between Murfreesboro and Ahoskie), and whites judged the behavior of many to be "disorderly." After the insurrection, some people maintained they had seen Nat Turner there preaching and recruiting, urging each sympathizer to show support by displaying a red handkerchief around the neck.

If the South's political atmosphere seemed charged by the ongoing tariff debate and the spreading conflict over nullification, the religious climate appeared heated as well. Revivals were in progress from Virginia to Georgia, and evidence continued to surface that religious meetings—where black and white, slave and free, could mingle readily— provided the best locale for spreading dissension and organizing resistance. During the last week in August a free black Baptist preacher named London Gee, who lived near Barnes's Church, was taken into custody in Murfreesboro along with Samuel Brantley from neighboring Northampton County, also a black Baptist preacher, and several other Negroes. Thomas Burland of Murfreesboro informed North Carolina's Governor Stokes that yet another black preacher, a man named Grimes, had put out word that a widespread insurrection would occur on the evening of the *last* Sunday in August, after he had preached at a funeral gathering, and only a breakdown in communication had launched the uprising a week ahead of schedule.

In Virginia an intercepted letter, sent from Chesterfield County on August 29 by a white named Williamson Mann to a black named Ben Lee in Richmond, illustrated a similar point for Governor Floyd. The author mentioned letters he had written to a wide network of slaves and servants, including instructions for burning Richmond, and he predicted the flames of revolt "are about to break out in Goochland and in Mechlenberg and several other counties very shortly." He passed the word to servants that "all must be in strict readiness," adding that "if there had never been an association—a visiting with free and slaves[—]this would never have been. They are put up by the free about their liberation." Mann had heard from the local barber that "a methodist of the name edmonds has put a great many servants up to how they should do and act by setting fire to this town. I do wish they may succeed[, for] by so doing we poor whites can get work as well as slaves or collord . . . so push on boys push on."

A different kind of letter was delivered to the Southampton post office later in the fall and passed on to Governor Floyd with a note dismissing it as "evidently a hoax, & no doubt from a white man." It came from someone using the pen name "Nero" who described himself as the son of a slave woman and a planter in southern Virginia. He claimed he had absconded to New England and joined an elaborate and disciplined black underground organization that was bent on fomenting a revolution of the slaves. His leader, Nero stated, also came from Virginia and had escaped "to St. Domingo, where his noble soul became warmed by the spirit of freedom." He boasted that the organizers possessed substantial funds and a ready printing press, that they had several dozen members training in Haiti, and that they already had "many a white agent in Florida, S. Carolina and Georgia." He invoked the genius of Haiti's Toussaint L'Ouverture and pledged—in the manner of a hardened and cynical vanguard revolutionary—that his comrades would play on the "prejudices and superstitions of the miserable" slaves, making them "think that their leaders are inspired, or that they are doing God's service," when they rise up against their masters. As for Turner's foiled rebellion, he claimed credit while denying defeat. "Do not flatter yourselves," he warned; "we did not calculate upon any thing of consequence—it was a mere feint . . . a starting of the machinery to see if it was in order." Besides, scarcely one "of the men you caught in the late bustle, had any knowledge of the great enterprize, that is in agitation."

Combined with other evidence this anonymous piece of bravado, whatever its actual origin or authenticity, had an effect on Governor Floyd. "In relation to the extent of the insurrection," he wrote on November 19, "I think it greater than will ever appear," and two days later he recorded in his diary his secret wish "to have a law passed gradually abolishing slavery in this State." A visit from Vice-President John C. Calhoun several weeks later may have dissuaded the governor from taking action. Nevertheless, in January the Virginia legislature launched an unprecedented discussion of the prospect of abolition, and the local newspaper dared to publish the debates. According to the Richmond *Enquirer,* "we now see the whole subject ripped up and discussed with open doors, in the presence of a crowded gallery and lobby. . . . And nothing else could have prompted them, but the bloody massacre in the month of August."

How swiftly the man named Nat Turner became lost in the storm clouds he helped to create. Henry Tragle, in preparing his compilation of sources on the Southampton revolt nearly two decades ago, found a pervasive tendency to treat the actual Nat Turner as a "nonperson," much the way problematical relatives are glossed over in a family genealogy. The most recent generation of slavery scholars, adept at tracing the broad curves of social forces and quick to avoid the simplified generalizations that can flow from "great man history," has done little to establish Turner's personhood.

If the historical individual is ever to emerge from behind the Turner of legend, polemic, and melodrama, then help must come from other quarters. One positive sign of how this process can work comes from the research of Thomas C. Parramore, a dedicated southern historian who recently wrote a local history volume entitled *Southampton County, Virginia.* In the process he discovered new and striking facts about the identity of a prominent individual whose story would be of little lasting interest if he had not also been the sole interviewer of a condemned slave. To rediscover Nat Turner we must reexamine first the man who published his *Confessions.*

Like others in the Turner saga, Thomas R. Gray has always been a shadowy figure. Tragle, scanning the census of 1830, surmised that Thomas Gray "was between 60 and 70 years old, childless, and with a wife who was between 30 and 40. He owned 19 male and 14 female slaves, practiced law in Jerusalem, and had served as appointed defense counsel for some of the insurgents," before drafting the *Confessions.* Some have suspected money as his main motive for the pamphlet. Others have seen him as grabbing at the coattails of history to secure personal fame. Most have viewed him as a hostile, if fascinated, questioner. William Styron went so far as to convert him into a full-blown southern caricature—the aging and paunchy backcountry lawyer who mixed courtroom jargon and cracker-barrel philosophy, "a fleshy, red-faced man—he must have been fifty or a little more—and his eyes were hollow and bloodshot as if he needed sleep."

Literary stereotypes aside, did the real Thomas Gray interview Nat Turner in order to bring some clarity to muddy water or to give it another stir with his own stick? Did Turner come clean to this inquisitive white man or engage in one final act of deception? Did the interviewer write down what he heard or what he hoped to hear and what he thought his audience wanted to read? Did Gray rush into print more to let the silenced rebel speak or to feather his own nest? The answers to these questions are important, for much of our understanding of Turner's person must hinge on the nature of Gray's *Confessions.* Despite its brevity, the pamphlet is so revealing and compelling that any reader, then or now, must feel an initial wave of skepticism. But the more we learn about Thomas Gray the less likely it seems that Nat Turner duped him or that he in turn willfully duped a gullible public.

The person who interviewed Nat Turner was not the old man identified by Tragle in the 1830 census. That elderly gentleman was Captain Thomas Gray, the son of a colonial planter-legislator of the same name, who owned a huge estate called Round Hill northeast of

Jerusalem and who ranked as the leading horse breeder in a county that had long been obsessed with horse racing. He had three children (whom Tragle apparently overlooked): a daughter called Ann and two sons, one named Edwin after his brother (an affluent member of Congress) and the other named Thomas. This son, Thomas Ruffin Gray, had been born in 1800, the same year as Nat Turner, and was destined to be his interviewer under the most strange conditions. According to Thomas Parramore, young Gray seems to have prospered effortlessly throughout his twenties, as one might expect the scion of a wealthy family to do. By 1829 he lived on an 800-acre estate worked by 21 slaves, and he graced suitable public offices, such as overseer of the poor, commissioner of Indian lands, and justice of the peace.

Within a year or two, however, things had started to go terribly wrong. Gray's wife disappears from the records, perhaps dying after the birth of their daughter, Ellen Douglas Gray. Thomas's debts mounted and his property began to dwindle, whether through drink, gambling, disillusionment, grief, or some less predictable cause. By 1831 he owned only 300 acres and a single Negro, and he had obtained a license to practice law in Jerusalem to help pay the bills. When the insurrection trials began in September, Gray was the court-appointed defender in only four of the early cases, at a fee of ten dollars each, while his colleague William Parker received most of the work. Then, at the height of the trials, during the second week of September, old Captain Thomas Gray died, only days after drafting his final will. When opened, the document excluded his son Thomas entirely, dividing the huge holdings equally between the planter's other two children and Thomas's infant daughter. "Should my son Thomas R. Gray . . . bring any claim against my estate whatsoever," the captain had stated emphatically, "it is my desire that the portion . . . bequeathed to my Grand Daughter Ellen Douglas Gray may be equally divided between my son Edwin and my Daughter Ann Gray."

Cut off from any inheritance, young Gray's fortunes went from bad to worse. Whatever income came from the wide sale of the *Confessions* must have gone to pay outstanding debts, for by 1832 all his land and slaves were gone. He owned only a horse, and his young daughter had been made the legal ward of attorney William Parker. In 1839 Gray moved to Portsmouth on the coast and died there from a fever in the summer of 1845. An unusually candid obituary notice made it clear that while the deceased had been free of malice and "worthy of esteem" in many ways, he had often troubled his friends by being "a scoffer at religion" who showed an "independence and fearlessness of mind, which disdained alike concealment and restraint." Whatever the deceased had "tho't on any subject," concluded his eulogist, "that he said," however troubling or "misdirected" Virginia's gentry might find his remarks to be.

So, we finally have a different and more accurate view of the outspoken person and troubled circumstances behind the *Confessions.* During the first three days of November, with both men caught up in terrible crises in their own totally different lives, "Nat Turner and Thomas R. Gray conspired to create the most compelling document in the history of black resistance to slavery." Whether or not one accepts Parramore's judgment of the *Confessions,* it is hard to ignore his surprising and cogent argument as to the origin of the pamphlet's power. "The source," Parramore concluded,

> of the pathos and grandeur of the portrait of Nat seemed unmistakable: on the face of the defiant black prophet, Thomas Ruffin Gray had read the mirror image of his own ravaged soul. Born in the same county and in the same year as Nat Turner, Gray must have understood only too well the sources of the turbulent emotions in the breast of the enigmatic black man. The same blind destiny that cast Nat into a life of slavery had robbed Gray of his patrimony, his wife, the affection of his father, his standing in the community. As with the narrator, so with the recorder, might the pattern of regulatory beliefs and devices of white dominion have appeared more as an enemy than an ally. Unwilling to acknowledge his affinity with the rebel, yet unable to escape it, the young attorney seems to have found in the recesses of his own heart a chord that responded vibrantly and in unison with . . . the slave.

Will a revised and authentic Thomas Gray eventually lead us any closer to the historical Nat Turner? Possibly, for now we may scrutinize the remarkable *Confessions* with renewed care and confidence. While acknowledging Gray's own deep ambivalence and obvious contradictions, we can accept as plausible the unique first part of the transcript in which Nat purportedly relates his important background experiences almost without interruption. (The latter portion of the manuscript, recounting the insurrection itself, can be corroborated from other sources and has never been so problematical—or important.) Rather than separating out the heathen soothsayer from the Christian prophet in this brief autobiography, we thus can begin to see these two sides of Turner as overlapping strands in a single story. What stands out in Nat's own account, but has been obscured by most later observers, is the fact that he was raised up with a dual heritage; he was clearly—like numerous first-generation Americans before and after him—the joint product of Christian and non-Christian cultures.

According to tradition Turner's mother (and perhaps his father's mother as well, if not his father, as some writers have claimed) was born and raised in Africa. Though guesses as to her exact origin will always remain speculative, there can be little doubt from the *Confessions* that she played a major role in shaping not only Nat's strong sense of self but also his complex understanding of the way the world worked. Yet it is equally clear that the intense exposure to evangelical Christianity that he received, first in the Turner home and later in the integrated revival meetings of Southampton County, also had a profound effect. More than either one of these traditions, it was the interweaving of the two over time into a single significant braid that gave Nat Turner his unusual perspective and intense vision.

Until recently, few scholars of American slavery have felt enough detachment from nineteenth-century Protestantism or enough interest in West African belief systems to examine both strands of this braid, separately or together, in a balanced way. But increasing interaction between historians and anthropologists, growing consciousness among Westerners of the complexities of non-Western thought, and expanding interest in the specific details of African cultural integration into the multiracial slave societies of the New World—all these things are now at last combining to make possible a reappraisal of Prophet Nat as a unique but meaningful representative of the first-generation African-American. Ever since he was hanged and cut apart in 1831, this unknown black leader has been largely shrouded from view, despite the best efforts of researchers. Perhaps soon they will be able to restore substantial flesh to the living bones of the historical Nat Turner. If so, we may yet "read the heart of this extraordinary man."

Benjamin Quarles   **3**

Harriet Tubman's
Unlikely Leadership

"**I** GREW UP like a neglected weed—ignorant of liberty, having no experience of it." The speaker, a short, spare, black-skinned woman of thirty-five, was being interviewed at her home in St. Catherines, Ontario, in the summer of 1855. "Now, I've been free," she added, "I know what a dreadful condition slavery is." The speaker's interviewer, Benjamin Drew, a Boston school principal and a part-time journalist, made "verbal alterations" (as he put it) in the broken English of Harriet Ross Tubman, but he caught the animating spirit that would give meaning and purpose to a long career then in its budding stages.

A rescuer of slaves, Tubman had achieved nearly mythic status within ten years after her own dash for freedom. Save for the white South, contemporary references to her invariably bore a eulogistic ring. The author and reformer Thomas Wentworth Higginson dubbed her "the greatest heroine of the age," in a letter (June 17, 1859) to his mother. "Her tales of adventure are beyond anything in fiction and her ingenuity and generalship are extraordinary. I have known her for some time—the slaves call her Moses."

A present-day scholar, Larry Gara, holds that "the legendary exploits of Harriet Tubman are undoubtedly exaggerated." But it is equally undeniable that Tubman has resisted being demythologized. One who lived into her early nineties, she proved to be a legend that would not fade in the memory of her contemporaries and a figure who would find a niche in folk literature ("a heroine in homespun") as well as on the pages of the more formally written histories.

Whence the source of Tubman's imperishable legendary status? As the premiere conductor on a legendary liberty line, the Underground Railroad, Tubman might elude the sniffing dogs of the slave catchers but she could hardly escape the legends that would attach to her name. Tales of derring-do inevitably cluster around those whose operations, by their very nature, have to be clothed in secrecy. Moreover, in the case of the tight-lipped Tubman, legend had to fill in for her ingrained reticence about her activities, a circumstance growing out of her experiences as a slave and as a rescuer of slaves. Even after the crusade against slavery and its death in the Civil War, Tubman's modesty kept her from recounting her role in either occurrence; a brief, passing mention on a rare occasion was the extent to which she ever unburdened herself as to those by-gone days. The Tubman legendry was also stimulated by her illiteracy, hearsay having to fill in for written records.

Contributing significantly to her fame, Tubman's legendary status played an important part in elevating her to a leadership level that she had not sought but did not spurn. Believing that her actions were preordained, she remained indifferent to whatever the sources of her power, whether stemming from her actual accomplishments or from a romancer's exuberance of spirit.

Even shorn of myth the existential Tubman compiled an impressive record, leaving her mark on our national history. This influence may be assessed by noting in turn her interrelationships with other blacks of her own day and time and her interaction with her white contemporaries, closing with a glance at her hold on the American mind since her death in 1913—an image that has not lost its luster.

Her basic story is readily grasped, furnishing background and providing us a glimpse into the Tubman psyche, her value system, and her vision of the world. Born in 1821 in Dorchester County, not far from the town of Cambridge on Maryland's Eastern Shore, she was one of the eleven children of Harriet Greene and Benjamin Ross, both slaves. Called Araminta as a baby, but later choosing the name of her mother, Harriet was put to work by the time she was five. For seven years she did general housework, including service as child's nurse and maid. Losing her house-slave status while still in her teens, Harriet then labored in the fields, a circumstance that would lead to her famed muscular strength and the physical endurance that belied her spare figure and habitually underfed look.

Two or three years after becoming a fieldhand, Harriet had an experience that marked her for life. She was struck on the head by a two-pound weight hurled at another slave, whom she was attempting to shield from a wrathful overseer. She never fully recovered from this nearly fatal blow. By swathing her head in a turban she could conceal the deep scar on her skull, but for the rest of her life she was prone to recurring seizures of deep, sudden sleep. She did regain her strength, however, and her capacity for manual labor rivaled that of a man by the time she was twenty.

Harriet's hard life in slavery was lessened a little by her marriage in 1844 to John Tubman. A free black, he lacked his wife's willpower and sense of mission and scoffed at her forebodings. Not fully reciprocating her deep affection for him, he did not join her after she made the dash for freedom; indeed, he soon took another wife. Losing the man, Harriet kept the name, even after taking a second husband in 1869.

One of Harriet Tubman's forebodings, the dread of being sold to the Deep South, took on a new intensity in 1849 upon the death of her master and the rumor that his estate would be broken up and his property dispersed. Impelled to delay no longer, she made her way to free-soil Pennsylvania. Upon her arrival she felt, she said, like she was in heaven.

Tubman's mood of exultation quickly gave way to a resolve to help others become free. As her schemes required money, she moved to Philadelphia and took work in a hotel, the first in a series of part-time jobs. After a year of penny-pinching frugality, she had saved enough to launch the first of her uniformly successful operations, a trip to Baltimore to rescue her sister, Mary Ann Bowley, and her two children.

To give a connected recital of Tubman's subsequent journeys into slavery locales is not possible. Insofar as she could, she operated in secret. Even had she been able to read and write, her sense of taking no unnecessary risks would have inhibited her from keeping a record of her movements. In some ten years of rescue work she made at least fifteen trips southward, personally escorting at least 200 freedom-bound slaves.

Tubman's traits of character and her methods of operation help to explain this extraordinary record. She was courageous, undeterred by the knowledge that there was a price upon her head. Her bravery was matched, moreover, by her coolness in a tight spot, her resourcefulness in a perilous situation. If the fugitives she led lacked her fearlessness, they were silenced by her blunt, no-nonsense manner. The rifle she carried while on rescue trips was not only for protection against slave catchers but also to intimidate any fugitive who became faint of heart and wished to turn back.

Her character molded by a deep reservoir of faith in God, Tubman felt that Divine Providence had willed her freedom and that a guardian angel accompanied her, particularly on her missions of deliverance. Gospel exhortations and spirituals came readily to her lips. When she was referred to as Moses, she did not demur.

If Tubman had complete trust in the Infinite, she also exercised great care in planning operations. She was unsurpassed in the logistics of escape—in anticipating the needs of her fugitive flocks, whether for food or clothes, disguises or forged passes, train tickets or wagons.

45

Every precaution was carefully considered, down to carrying pare-
goric for fretful babies whose crying might jeopardize the escaping
party. Well might she boast that she never lost a passenger.

Tubman was not a one-woman Underground Railroad, however, as
this secretive mode of passage required a concerted effort. Her careful
planning included full cooperation with others, and she worked hand in
hand with two of the most dedicated stationmasters, Thomas Garrett in
Wilmington, Delaware, and William Still in Philadelphia. Both assisted
her by providing shelter for the fugitives she conducted and by making
arrangements, if necessary, for their transportation further north.

Tubman's efforts to undermine slavery were redirected with the
outbreak of the Civil War, a development she had predicted. Viewing
this conflict as the climax in the struggle against slavery, she made
arrangements to go to the South Carolina seacoast regions, arriving in
May 1862. With Beaufort as headquarters for her roving operations,
she spent the next three years assisting the newly freed slaves, working primarily as a nurse and cook. Her hospital-oriented services
were punctuated by assignments with the Union army as a spy and
a scout. Regardless of their nature, her services were readily welcomed.
Wherever she went she hardly needed the glowing letters of recommendation that accompanied her, whether from civilian officials
or military officers.

The termination of the war did not bring to an end Tubman's
concern for the welfare of others. During the remaining half century
she was to live, she was always active on behalf of the less fortunate,
including such activities as raising money for schools for former
slaves, collecting clothes for destitute children, and giving assistance
to the sick and disabled. She assumed the complete care and support
of her parents, whose escape she had personally conducted in June
1857 and whom she settled in Auburn, New York, where she herself
took up residence the following year.

Tubman's management of fiscal affairs, although scrupulously honest,
was somewhat impulsive. According to a fellow Auburnite who knew
her well, her way of administering funds was "to give away all the
money she had on her at the moment and trust to the Lord to fill the
void." In doing charitable work, however, she was never discouraged
by the chronic lack of funds and the absence of any personal income
until she was over seventy-five. For her own wartime services she
received no benefits despite petitions to the federal government on
her behalf from prominent people. In 1890, however, she began to
receive a pension as widow of a war veteran, having in 1869 married a
Union soldier, Nelson Davis, who died in 1888.

Tubman died on March 10, 1913, appropriately enough in the Auburn home for the elderly that she had been instrumental in founding. Her passing elicited an obituary response from the *Afro-American Ledger* (March 15, 1913) that referred to her as "Queen of the Underground" and carried a piece entitled "In Many Ways She Proved Herself to Be One of the Foremost Women of Her Times." This high appraisal from the Baltimore-based weekly reflected the common sentiment among Tubman's black contemporaries ever since she had first emerged as a public figure. Esteem for her was practically universal among the blacks of her day, including high and low, young and old, male and female, and cutting across sectional lines. Her interrelationships with other blacks, along with the goals they shared in common, provide a clue to the chorus of praise that greeted her name in black circles. These fall into two major phases and periods: namely, the joint effort of both parties in the struggle against slavery in pre–Civil War days, and their mutual efforts in the work of racial uplift during the half century following the war.

To blacks of the antebellum period, North and South, the central theme was the abolition of slavery. Of all the ways to bring this about the most direct, short of insurrection or war, and hence the most satisfying, was the Underground Railroad—the cooperative work of assisting slaves to run away and then assisting them to get a fresh start as free men, women, and children. In matters relating to fugitive slaves, blacks had a personal and vital interest, a particular sense of responsibility toward one another. In the process of striking at slavery, a black Underground Railroad operator was also striking at the conjoined caricature of a free black as a shiftless ne'er-do-well and of the slave as a submissive Sambo.

In the operations of the Underground Railroad the conductors, those who ventured into slave terrain seeking out prospective escapees, were invariably black, and none was better known than Harriet Tubman. To Afro-Americans she personified resistance to slavery as did no other single figure of her generation. She symbolized courage, determination, and strength.

In slave circles her status was unexcelled. The folklorist Harold Courlander points out that in the isolated communities in which many slaves were located Tubman's name was hardly likely to have been a household word, and when some slaves sang "Go Down, Moses," they must have done so "in the belief that Moses simply meant Moses." True enough. Yet Tubman's name was likely to have been an inspiration to thousands she never met, slave communities having their own systems of communication. Thomas Cole, a runaway slave from Huntsville, Alabama, said that during his escape he "was hopin and prayin all de time dat I could meets up wid dat Harriet Tubman woman." Whether in the flesh or as a symbol, Tubman made slave property less secure.

Tubman's sway over the slaves she sought to rescue was unquestionably absolute. In her relationships with these fugitives her unconscious and unstudied inclination toward self-dramatization came into its fullest sway. Communicating with slaves was easy for her. In overcoming the barrier of their mutual illiteracy, Tubman was verbally resourceful to the point of creativity, an unpolished eloquence being second nature to her. She was nothing if not action-bent, but to accomplish the deed she did not scorn the word. Far from empty, her rhetoric came from a well-stocked mind. As a slave she had developed her powers of recall, memorizing recited passages from the Bible. Her visual memory was no less acute, enabling her to interlard her discourses with homely details of earlier sights and scenes. She had the gift of tongue, a trait much admired by slaves and one that made a lasting impression on them.

Tubman had a strong singing voice, adding to her hold on the fugitives. Her repertoire consisted of those spirituals that bore a barely concealed freedom ring, abounding in code words and double meanings, such as "Didn't My Lord Deliver Daniel?" As used by Tubman, whether to announce her presence in some secluded spot or to keep up the group morale at strategically timed intervals while on the road, such songs became part of slave rescue apparatus. To those she escorted to freedom, one spiritual inevitably came to acquire a special significance. It was first sung some forty years before Tubman's birth, and to the runaways it took on the aspects of prophesy now come to pass. Having lodged itself in their hearts, it came readily to their lips:

> Go down, Moses,
> Way down in Egypt land.
> Tell ole Pharaoh
> Let my people go.

Obviously, too, Tubman's profound religious faith impressed the fugitives. Themselves church-oriented, they quickly recognized in her a deeper sense of Christian commitment than was customary and a greater trust in Divine Providence. Praying frequently, spontaneously, and with obvious conviction and expectation, Tubman seemed to find it easy to communicate with the Deity, and sometimes she seemed to act as though she had received a direct reply. Hence, although the biblically knowledgeable slaves knew that God was no respecter of persons, they might sometimes have wondered whether this held for Harriet Tubman.

If the slaves and fugitives revered her, the free blacks held her in the highest esteem short of worship. In the South her free black admirers would have to speak her praises privately and in hushed tones, but blacks north of slavery sang her name in full voice, removing any doubt as to their acclaim. The black in the best position to appraise Tubman and her work was the Philadelphia-based William Still, second only to Tubman herself as the leading black figure in the Underground Railroad. As secretary and executive director of the General Vigilance Committee, Still assisted the runaways reaching Philadelphia. Every major northern city had a similar vigilance committee, but the group in Philadelphia had no equal, in large part because of Still's energetic and resourceful leadership. From his many years of working in concert with Tubman, in 1872 Still offered this assessment of her: "A more ordinary specimen of humanity could hardly be found among the most unfortunate-looking farm hands of the South. Yet in point of courage, shrewdness and disinterested exertions to rescue her fellow-men, she was without equal. . . . Her like it is probable was never known before or since."

A similarly belated appraisal came from Frederick Douglass, like Tubman an escaped slave from Maryland. In a letter he told her that he had "wrought in the day" and to public attention and applause, whereas she had "wrought in the night," her witnesses the midnight sky and the silent stars. But, he went on, "excepting John Brown—of sacred memory—I know of no one who has willingly encountered more perils and hardships to serve our enslaved people than you."

In referring to Tubman, her northern-based black contemporaries readily used the term "heroine." When in April 1860 in Troy, New York, she led a group of rescuers that overpowered the officers and assisted Charles Nalle, a fugitive slave, to escape to Canada, *The Weekly Anglo-African* (May 12, 1860) praised her "intrepidity," capping their assessment with a complimentary comparison: "She acted like a heroine." During the Civil War, when the young schoolteacher Charlotte L. Forten visited Beaufort, South Carolina, she was ecstatic about Tubman, an entry in her diary for January 31, 1863, expressing her admiration: "We spent all our time at Harriet Tubman's. She is a wonderful woman—a real heroine." This theme recurs in a later notation in the diary for the same day: "My own eyes were full as I listened to her—the heroic woman."

Many antebellum blacks linked Tubman's name with that of Sojourner Truth, the two having much in common. Both were deeply religious former slaves. Like Tubman, the unschooled Truth had a rude eloquence, but unlike Tubman, she was a familiar figure on the lecture circuit, her six-foot frame and deep, resonant voice not without their effects on an audience. Primarily a women's rights activist, Truth played only a minor role in the Underground Railroad. Apparently the first time the two reformers met was in Boston in August 1864, Truth then assuring Tubman that President Lincoln was "our friend," in an effort to allay the latter's doubts on that score.

The close of the Civil War meant that the relationships between Tubman and other blacks would take on a much less dramatic aspect, a calmer course. With slavery dead, the communal spirit it had helped to create in black circles would now be channeled into cooperative efforts to promote racial uplift and progress. Ever bent on serving others, and with little thought of self, Tubman could be counted on to engage in the work of racial self-advancement, however limited her finances or advanced her age.

Tubman's reciprocal relations with other blacks centered largely on efforts to help the poor and needy among them. The two major groups with which she worked were black women's organizations and the black church. Viewing racial liberation and woman's liberation as being inseparably linked, Tubman was a staunch advocate of women's rights. She was a delegate to the first annual convention of the National Federation of Afro-American Women, which met in Washington, D.C., in July 1896. When the other delegates learned that she was present, they halted the proceedings and passed a motion that all privileges and courtesies be extended to her. Tubman sought affiliation with these middle-class, more formally educated black clubwomen because their interests went beyond civil rights and liberties and embraced, as Gerda Lerner points out, "issues of importance to poor women, working mothers and tenant farm wives." Hence, when Tubman was asked to give a talk at this first meeting, her theme was characteristic: "More Homes for Our Aged." She kept in touch with the National Association of Colored Women, a merger of the two nationwide black women's groups, for its work in conducting hospitals, day nurseries, and homes for the elderly had an especial appeal to her.

When the time came the clubwomen did not hesitate to extend aid to Tubman herself. Learning in the summer of 1911 that she was in need, the Empire State Federation, an affiliate of the national body, held a linen shower for her, collecting "an abundance of good things."

Not stopping there, the organization voted to send "twenty-five dollars per month to further her comfort for the remainder of her life." The New York group also paid for her funeral and for the marble headstone over her grave.

The deeply religious Tubman also worked in concert with black churches. In her Underground Railroad days the black churches had provided overnight accommodations for the runaways she shepherded, lodging them in the pews. Through "donation festivals" these churches had raised money expressly for her rescue trips. In her postwar work of helping others the black church was not overlooked. She was a fundraiser for the local church she attended in Auburn—the Thompson Memorial African Methodist Episcopal Zion. "She took an active part in the growth of the Western New York Conference of the A.M.E. Zion Church," writes William Jacob Walls, a bishop of the denomination. In 1896 the black Methodist churches of Auburn appointed her as their agent "to collect clothes for the destitute colored children," as she wrote in a dictated letter asking for a contribution. It was an assignment for which she was well qualified by some thirty years of solicitation for those in need.

When in 1896 Tubman managed to purchase twenty-five acres of land adjoining her house, she had in mind a home for the old and poor to be operated by the local church. Lack of funds, however, prevented the incorporation of so ambitious a venture until 1903, when she deeded the land and her own home to the parent A.M.E.Z. Trustees. One of the key figures in raising the funds to pay the mortgage on the property, and thus make the transaction possible, was Robert W. Taylor, a zealous Zionite and the financial agent for Tuskegee Institute. Among other expedients to get the mortgage money, Taylor published a brief, hastily assembled biography, *Harriet Tubman: The Heroine in Ebony* (Boston, 1901), which bore a laudatory introduction by Booker T. Washington. On May 19, 1911, no longer able to take care of herself after having been an invalid for three months, Tubman herself entered the Harriet Tubman Home for Aged and Indigent Colored People. "It is the desire of the Home management to give her every attention and comfort possible these last days," wrote Edward U. A. Brooks, general superintendent of the home and a Zionist clergyman, in a letter dated June 7, 1911, to Booker T. Washington, asking for a "donation toward the maintenance of Aunt Harriet."

The church and the women's organizations had no monopoly on holding Tubman in high regard as a leader and as a person. It was an attitude held by blacks in general, finding such expressions as making a trip to Auburn to see her, as if on a pilgrimage, or naming something after her, as did the blacks in Boston who, in 1904, founded the Harriet Tubman Home, its purpose being to assist colored women. "Not many of us are animated with the idea which seems to have possessed Harriet Tubman throughout her eventful life—to lay out time, talents, and opportunities for God's glory, and the good of our fellow-men," wrote schoolteacher Pauline E. Hopkins in 1902 in *The Colored American Magazine.* It was an evaluation that few blacks of her day would have questioned. Who among them, in a single person, had demonstrated more of a physical courage amounting to bravery, had lived a life more dedicated to the service of others, had exhibited more traits of an impeccable character, or had a deeper faith in the working of a Divine Providence?

An appraisal somewhat less celebratory and expansive characterized the reaction to Tubman by her white reformist allies. While singing her praises, white admirers hardly viewed her in the capacity of a leader or role model. While ever cordial and devoid of the person-to-person tensions so characteristic among black and white co-workers in reform movements, Tubman's experiences across the color line were not free of racial overtones, reflecting something of the prevailing patterns in race relations and attitudes. Her earliest experiences with white people were hardly reassuring. As a slave she had been constantly overworked and often whipped, whether by her master or those to whom she was hired out. She could never forget the angry overseer who had marked her for life, and she would have no fond memories of a kind and indulgent mistress. As she later explained, she had "heard tell" that there were good masters and mistresses but had not come across any of them.

Locating in Philadelphia after her escape, Tubman came in contact with a white population many of whom were in sympathy with runaway slaves and would incur any risk in assisting them. In 1775 the first organized society against slavery was founded there, its lengthy title indicating its broad program: the Pennsylvania Society for Promoting the Abolition of Slavery, the Relief of Free Negroes Unlawfully Held in Bondage, and for Improving the Condition of the African Race. Tubman became acquainted with abolitionist whites through her association with the General Vigilance Committee, which, though headed by William Still, was interracial in composition. White Underground Railroad operators in Pennsylvania and Delaware reflected a strong Quaker influence, as Tubman quickly found out.

The single white with whom Tubman worked most closely was Thomas Garrett of Wilmington, Delaware, a lifelong member of the

Society of Friends. A key figure in slave rescue work along the mid-Atlantic corridor, Garrett gave much of his time and means and ran some risks to his personal safety, Delaware being a slave state. He provided shelter for the fugitives Tubman led and furnished her with the money to carry them on to Philadelphia and beyond. In August 1857, when Tubman's escaping parents were passing through Wilmington, Garrett gave them thirty dollars to pay their way to Canada. In soliciting funds for Tubman's trips, Garrett wrote to such well-wishers as the Edinburgh Anti-Slavery Society (Scotland), telling them of her exploits. "To our brave Harriet he often rendered most efficient help in her journeys back and forth," wrote Tubman's first biographer, Sarah Bradford. In a letter to William Still on the eve of the Civil War (December 1, 1860), Garrett made a typical reference to their co-worker: "I write to let thee know that Harriet Tubman is again in these parts. She arrived last evening from one of her trips of mercy to God's poor, bringing two men with her as far as New Castle. . . . "

Tubman's attitude toward white people was shaped by her contact with reformers like Garrett—men and women who raised money for her and also gave her a kind of affection and a measure of respect. As a rule, the reform-minded whites with whom she became acquainted liked her. The courage and daring of the runaways was a stimulus to the abolitionist crusade, and Tubman personified the heroic slave.

Whites also liked Tubman because in person-to-person contacts she did not make them feel uncomfortable, burdening them with a sense of guilt. Her language and manner were marked by an absence of bitterness. To whites she was nonthreatening, not pushy, not peer-basis-minded, not status conscious, and hence not given to self-pity or bent on upward mobility. In speaking in public she tended to be folksy, anecdotal, and given to reminiscence. "She spoke in a style of quaint simplicity," wrote a reporter in 1859. Tubman was not likely to pose questions a predominantly white audience would find awkward, such as Sojourner Truth's "Is God dead?" or the Frederick Douglass inquiry as to what the Fourth of July might or might not mean to the slaves.

By their financial support the white abolitionists expressed their kindly sentiments toward Tubman. In addition to raising money specifically for her slave rescue work, they assisted her in purchasing a home in Auburn, New York, for her parents. A befriender of Tubman's, Senator William H. Seward of New York, had sold her the home on liberal terms, and to pay for it she received unsolicited donations from other white supporters. At the annual meeting of the Massachusetts Anti-Slavery Society in 1859, its president, Thomas Wentworth

Higginson, asked for a collection to assist her in buying the house so that "her father and mother could support themselves, and enable her to resume the practice of her profession!" Higginson's observation was greeted by "laughter and applause."

In private, as in public, Tubman and her white associates apparently had little trouble adjusting to each other. In their homes, as in their public gatherings, Tubman expected to be hospitably received, and to a greater extent than any other antebellum black she was. Unlike some former slaves, the uninhibited Tubman seems not to have felt ill at ease in a white household, however educated or affluent the family might be.

No white reformer held Tubman in higher respect and esteem than John Brown, who made it a point to establish personal contacts with black leaders. He regarded her as a kindred spirit, and she fitted into his plans as the shepherd of the slaves he proposed to run off, by force of arms, if necessary. He was well aware that Tubman was not gun-shy (Who in abolitionist circles had not heard of the long rifle she carried on her slave rescue trips?). Brown was also aware that the Tubman name would help him raise money from her white admirers, particularly those in Massachusetts. During the eighteen months before his raid on Harpers Ferry, Virginia, in October 1859, Brown met with Tubman on some half dozen occasions, one of them lasting nearly a week. His opinion of her fortified, he called her "General" and, according to his confidant and biographer, Franklin B. Sanborn, "she was fully conversant with his plans."

Apparently due to illness, Tubman did not accompany Brown to Harpers Ferry. Immediately after the abortive raid Frederick Douglass fled to Canada to avoid being served an arrest warrant issued against him as a Brown accomplice. No such warrant was issued for Tubman; even had there been legally admissible evidence of her complicity, an arrest warrant would hardly have been practical for someone whose whereabouts were a mystery.

Brown's hanging impelled Tubman to give his life a scriptural interpretation. She promptly confided to Sanborn that she had "been studying and studying upon it, and its clar to me, it wasn't John Brown that died on the gallows. When I think how he gave up his life for our people, and how he never flinched, but was so brave to the end; its clar to me it wasn't mortal man, it was God in him." The hanged Brown never left Tubman's memory. In an interview in 1912, reporter Anne Fitzhugh Miller quoted her as referring to Brown as "my dearest friend."

Although not present at Harpers Ferry, Tubman came under fire during the Civil War, her battlefront services drawing official commendation from Union officers, including Generals David Hunter and Rufus Saxton, Colonel James Montgomery and Acting Assistant Surgeon Henry K. Durrant. Like John Brown, these white commanders had a high respect for Tubman. To say that they "never failed to tip their caps when meeting her" (William Wells Brown, *The Rising Son*) is somewhat sweeping but reflects their basic attitude toward her.

Although Tubman would subsequently revise her early opinion of Abraham Lincoln, she was critical of him during the opening months of the war, saying that "God's ahead ob Massa Linkum. God won't let Massa Linkum beat de South till he do the right ting. Massa Linkum he great man, and I'se poor nigger; but dis nigger can tell Massa Linkum how to save de money and de young men. He do it by setting de niggers free."

After the Civil War, Tubman's basic relationships with whites followed an established pattern. Retaining her interest in the feminist movement, she was a familiar face at the white-led women's rights gatherings. In April 1897 the New England Woman Suffrage Association held a reception in her honor, thus duplicating a similar action taken five months earlier by the Woman's State Association of New York at its convention in Rochester. Tubman had a long-lasting and cordial relationship with the suffragist pioneer and leader Susan B. Anthony, who in a private letter in 1902 reaffirmed her high regard for "this most wonderful woman—Harriet Tubman." When asked, late in her life, whether she believed that women should have the right to vote, Tubman replied, "I have suffered enough to believe it."

Tubman's most typical postwar relationship with whites was in the financial support she received from them, whether in helping her redeem the mortgages on her property, in taking care of her parents, or in supporting her efforts on behalf of the less fortunate. To raise money for her personal welfare white benefactors financed the publication of two biographies written by Sarah H. Bradford, an Auburn schoolteacher: *Scenes in the Life of Harriet Tubman* (1868) and a later, expanded version, *Harriet Tubman: The Moses of Her People* (1886). For two decades white supporters sought to secure for her a government pension for her three years of service during the Civil War. Unsuccessful in this, they fared better in obtaining a pension for her as the widow of war veteran Nelson Davis. To assist her in her wide-ranging charities white contributors sent trunks and bundles of clothes and packages of sundries, along with an occasional gift of cash.

Tubman's broad appeal, cutting across lines of race and class, age and gender, received public expression upon her death. The *New York Times* carried a two-paragraph obituary (March 14, 1913), and her funeral was attended by the local post of the Grand Army of the Republic. The city of Auburn, after a year's preparation, held a day-long memorial service in June 1914, unveiling a tablet in her honor. On that day many homes flew the Stars and Stripes, thereby demonstrating "that we are not forgetful of those who suffered for the cause of freedom," in the exhortatory accents of Mayor Charles W. Brister. At the evening exercises held in the city auditorium the featured speaker, Booker T. Washington, eulogized Tubman as one who "brought the two races together."

Beginning rather than ending with the observance at Auburn, the memorials to Harriet Tubman would continue over the years, taking a variety of forms and expressions. The national sentiment toward her was conveyed by agencies of the federal government. During World War II a liberty ship was christened the *Harriet Tubman,* prompting President Franklin D. Roosevelt to praise the U.S. Maritime Commission for having chosen so appropriate a name. In 1974 the Department of the Interior gave her Auburn home the status of a national historic landmark, and four years later the U.S. Postal Service issued a thirteen-cent Harriet Tubman commemorative stamp, the first in a "Black Heritage U.S.A. Series."

The mounting interest in women's history, a field sorely neglected until recent decades, has aided in keeping Tubman before us. Pointing out (in 1978) that black protest literature had focused largely on males, historian George P. Rawick advanced a corrective suggestion: "Why must we always use Nat as the name for the rebellious slave? Why not Harriet? The women's liberation movement has for some time used a poster that reproduces the image of Harriet Tubman with a long rifle. I think that might be a good symbol for the black struggle."

In keeping the Tubman name alive and aglow a host of creative spirits in literature, music, and the arts have exercised their creative talents. Poets expressing their admiration of Tubman include Margaret Walker (Alexander) and Langston Hughes. Focusing on her in his moving, free-verse "Runagate, Runagate," Robert Hayden pictures her as:

> woman of the earth, whipscarred
> a summoning, a shining

Some poets have reached out to the rhyme-minded juvenile reader:

> A snake said, "Hiss!"
> An owl said, "Whoo!"
> Harriet said, "We are
> Coming through!"

On concert tours baritone Paul Robeson introduced the spiritual "Go Down, Moses" by explaining that it was a protest song among slaves who had Tubman on their minds. To the tune of "Kansas Boys," folksinger Woodie Guthrie composed a "Ballad of Harriet Tubman." Robert De Cormier and Donald McKay wrote a cantata based on her life, "They Called Her Moses."

Keepers of the Tubman flame have included a number of visual artists. To black painters she was an obvious figure to portray. Among the Tubman-inspired paintings is a mural fresco by Aaron Douglass, a brooding portrait by Charles White "in Chinese ink and wash" entitled "General Moses," and a series of thirty pieces by Jacob Lawrence (many of which have been reproduced in *Harriet and the Promised Land* [1968]). Bent on knowing more about Tubman before beginning to paint her, artist Hughie Lee-Smith said that as a result of his investigations he "came to love this woman" and that she became "very real to me." Not everyone seeking to know more about Tubman might come to share such a sense of her personal nearness. In general, however, she was the type of person who seemed to improve upon better acquaintance.

Certainly it would seem sure that Tubman is destined to remain an established presence in American life, her fame undiminishable. With freedom as its motif, the Tubman theme would seem to be as enduring as the American theme, to which it is contributory and of which it is the essence. In her aftertime, as during her life span, Harriet Tubman could best be characterized as "coming through."

Waldo E. Martin, Jr.   4

Frederick Douglass:
Humanist as Race Leader

In 1848 James McCune Smith, a highly respected black medical doctor and abolitionist, wrote to Gerrit Smith, an influential white political abolitionist, regarding their mutual friend, Frederick Douglass. "Only since his Editorial career," Smith remarked, "has he seemed to become a colored man!" Having read the initial issues of Douglass's *North Star* carefully, he found "phase after phase develop itself as regularly as in one newly born among us." Douglass seemed increasingly aware of the complexity of his people's plight, particularly the tension between integration and segregation as well as racial and national identity.

Besides a heightened sense of racial awareness, Douglass's continuing maturation revealed a growing comprehension of the invidious impact of white racism on whites and blacks alike. The central paradox of his leadership—and Afro-American leadership generally—consisted of the promotion of black integration into a nation dominated by whites who essentially despised and rejected black people. With characteristic optimism Douglass believed that, through much time and effort, white racism could be alleviated and that blacks and whites would one day coexist as equals in the United States. His valiant attempt to use a humanist approach to undermine a racialist society reflected his perception of the international quality of both his people's struggle and his leadership. Paradoxically, he functioned as a race leader to help realize a nation where race was insignificant. He ultimately saw himself as a spokesman for his country and for humankind, not just for Afro-Americans. This catholic vision signified an enduring measure of his leadership.

Douglass's appeal as a leader derived from many factors, including his humble origins, his inveterate moral sensibility, and his grandiose vision of a singular humanity. As a former slave he relished the fact that his every achievement as a free man represented more evidence of self-made and extraordinary success. The larger significance of his personal triumph, however, was that it represented the potential and real achievements of his struggling people. Indeed, he saw his own life as symbolic of his people's inexorable progress from slavery to freedom. "Mine has been the experience of the colored people of America, both slave and free," he offered.

Much more than a drama of individual black achievement and inspiration, Douglass's life story exemplified the basic American emphasis upon hard work, perseverance, thrift, morality, and religiosity: values central to the society and culture. Douglass was an authentic American hero and a self-made man. Because his ascent began from such a low station in life and proceeded apace, in spite of seemingly insuperable odds, his achievements were that much greater and inspiring. His life gave meaning to the American success ethic. His appeal and accomplishments as the quintessential Afro-American leader of his day owed in large measure to his classic embodiment of deeply held cultural notions about pulling one's self up by one's bootstraps, obstacles notwithstanding, to solid middle-class respectability. For blacks, as for other racial and ethnic groups, this required assimilation and integration.

The pervasive moral tone of Douglass's leadership resonated among his fellow Americans whether they agreed or disagreed with his specific messages. Speaking cogently from the perspective of the oppressed, he skillfully addressed the American conscience. He repeatedly drew upon the nation's adherence to a moral and divinely ordered worldview and emphasized the nation's special mission as a beacon of liberty. Black liberation specifically, and social reform generally, signified justice and truth as well as right and good. The use of moral suasion as a liberation and reform strategy, however, betrayed serious shortcomings. Perhaps most important, the reality of immorality and amorality often undercut the ideal of ethical rule. Nonetheless, given the nineteenth-century American belief in a coherent moral universe, contradictions aside, Douglass's principled ethical posture often forced many Americans to ponder issues from a different, potentially enlightening perspective: that of the oppressed.

Douglass took very seriously the Apostles' Creed: the belief that in God's kingdom there exists only one human race. This belief, carried to its logical end, forced Douglass to subordinate philosophically the concepts of racial and national identity to a singular human identity. In actuality, however, as he understood so well, the ideal of one human family foundered on the rocks of racial (ethnic) and national divisions. Nevertheless, for Douglass assimilation and integration constituted a viable start toward alleviating what he viewed as ultimately meaningless yet presently determinative distinctions.

As a leader who never held elective office, and one who lacked an organizational base, Douglass's influence derived largely from his uncanny ability to articulate his people's needs and aspirations in such a way as to appeal to many whites as well as innumerable blacks. He achieved this by couching his people's struggle in the context of a quest for rights and privileges basic to American democracy, by stressing the inherent link between black liberation and the worldwide historical tradition of freedom struggles (including the American Revolution), and by viewing black freedom and advancement as an inseparable element in the march of nineteenth-century progress. This expansive view of his people's ongoing struggle reflected a dynamic tension between his humanism and race consciousness which necessarily exerted a powerful impact on his leadership.

Douglass's emergence as the prototypical Afro-American leader transpired in two interrelated phases. His prewar and wartime leadership (early 1840s to 1865) showed the activist and social reformer at his best. Then, between Reconstruction and his death in 1895, he aligned himself with the Republican party. The latter, in concert with his growing venerability, caused his leadership to assume a more symbolic and patriarchal character. Douglass captured the public imagination in the 1840s and remained a significant public personality throughout his life, critics and opponents notwithstanding, through the force of his charisma, drive, vision, and the representative character of his leadership.

Frederick Douglass's years as a Maryland slave (1818–38) revealed several qualities that foreshadowed his future leadership: an exceptional intelligence; an ability to interact with whites as well as blacks; a powerful drive to succeed; and a fervent commitment to his own and his people's freedom and elevation. Not only did he, as a child, devise various strategies to learn how to read and write—often with the witting and unwitting help of whites—but he also displayed a degree of insight and critical detachment unusual in a child. His early questioning of both the morality of slavery and the logic behind his own enslavement, as well as the significance of slave practices like drunken holiday sprees, suggested an uncommon lad. His precocity became increasingly evident after he was sent to live in Baltimore with relatives of Aaron Anthony, his master. This change from the less propitious rural setting of his early years on Maryland's Eastern Shore to the urban home of Hugh and Sophia Auld, and Thomas, their son, proved significant for seven-year-old Frederick. Not only did the wonders and apparent possibilities of city life captivate him, but Sophia Auld initiated his formal reading instruction. Even after her husband forced her to desist, Frederick surreptitiously continued to learn how to read and write.

The relatively freer atmosphere of Baltimore also heightened Douglass's understanding of and desire for freedom. Not surprisingly, therefore, the libertarian message of Caleb Bingham's patriotic anthology, *The Columbian Orator,* enthralled the thirteen-year-old, encouraging him to intensify his own efforts toward intellectual and physical emancipation. In fact, his future decision to employ oratory and the pen as weapons in the black liberation struggle in part grew out of the powerful lessons he gathered from *The Columbian Orator.*

Whites and blacks alike often saw in young Frederick a bright and precocious lad; consequently, many indulged him. Early acts of kindness toward him, especially by some whites—such as his mistress Sophia's efforts to teach him how to read—showed him that whites and blacks might warmly express their common humanity and contributed to his skill at working with supportive whites.

Frederick's desire to succeed was deep-seated, deriving in part from a need to overcome, or perhaps to compensate for, the unsettling nature of his family drama. Separated from his family at a tender age and haunted by the likelihood that the father he never really knew was his white master, young Douglass envisioned greatness as a way to create a fuller and more satisfying identity. Thus, Rev. Charles Lawson—surrogate father figure, confidant, and spiritual mentor—confirmed Frederick's deeply felt sense of his own uncommon destiny when the preacher, a free black, told the boy that the Lord had chosen him for a "great work."

Even as a Christian, Frederick found it increasingly difficult to resign himself to mere faith and hope regarding his eventual emancipation. God, he believed, demanded that he strike a blow for his own freedom: "God helped those who helped themselves." Frederick's fateful adolescent victory over Covey, the "Negro-Breaker," revealed his thoroughgoing adherence to that belief. After returning to the Eastern Shore, he had been hired out by his master to the notorious Covey to have his rebellious spirit subdued. Instead, the sixteen-year-old slave whipped Covey psychologically as well as physically. Douglass later maintained that this triumph "revived a sense of my own manhood. . . . It recalled to life my crushed self-respect, and my self-confidence, and inspired me with a renewed determination to be a free man."

Frederick thus rededicated himself to the emancipation of others as well as himself. He led at least two Sabbath schools, where he taught other blacks how to read and write. He also led an unsuccessful escape attempt involving his five closest friends, who had been pupils in his last Sabbath school. These efforts clearly illustrated his courageous and deep commitment to self-reliance in the cause of black liberation and elevation, foreshadowing his future leadership.

Frederick soon returned to Baltimore where his master hired him out as a caulker and promised to free him at age twenty-five. His growing involvement with Baltimore's free black community in the 1830s proved invaluable in his continuing efforts at self-improvement. Notwithstanding his slave status, Douglass became a very active member of the East Baltimore Mental Improvement Society, a secret debating club including his closest free black friends, where he further refined his rhetorical skills and engaged in the discussion of a wide range of issues. Likewise, much of his education in rhetorical techniques came from his involvement with several black churches, where he imbibed of the rich oratorical tradition among black preachers. These experiences presaged his strong involvement in the local politics of the black communities he first lived in once he came North and, again, reflected his profound commitment to self-elevation as basic to racial advancement. They also constituted important influences in his early development as a black leader.

Douglass's fervent abolitionism provided the platform for his rise to prominence as a leader. In 1838, shortly after his escape from slavery (following a heated dispute with his master), he and Anna, his first wife, settled in New Bedford, Massachusetts. He soon came across the *Liberator,* the most influential abolitionist newspaper in the United States and his introduction to the fiery abolitionist philosophy of its editor, William Lloyd Garrison. The newspaper's cogent espousal of immediate and unconditional emancipation struck a sympathetic chord with Douglass. It was not long before the *Liberator,* next to the Bible, became the basic text in his abolitionist education. Concurrent with his study of the *Liberator,* he participated in local black meetings, notably abolitionist gatherings. His status in the community rose to the point where on June 30, 1841, he chaired a meeting that denounced the efforts of the Maryland Colonization Society to force the state's free blacks to leave and encouraged them instead to protest against such a proposal. The group also went on record in opposition to the local steamboat policy of racial segregation.

Douglass first heard Garrison speak on August 9, 1841, at the annual meeting of the Bristol Anti-Slavery Society. He came away so impressed with the man and his message that he initially envisioned him as "the Moses raised up by God, to deliver His modern Israel from bondage." Three days later Douglass spoke to an antislavery meeting in Nantucket at the urging of William C. Coffin, a local Garrisonian who had previously heard Douglass speak in a local black schoolhouse. In spite of his uneasiness, he consented and gave a stirring account of his life as a slave. The speech mesmerized those present, including Garrison, who used Douglass's words as the basis for his subsequent address. The Garrisonians were so impressed with Douglass that they asked him to join their organization. After initial anxiety concerning his qualifications, he agreed and worked with them for close to ten years.

Douglass's years as a Garrisonian were central to his development as a leader. Under their tutelage he honed his rhetorical ability to the point where he soon became one of the leading orators in an age of great oratory. His association with the Garrisonians likewise enhanced his personal fame, among both blacks and whites. Furthermore, Garrisonianism as a philosophy of social reform, particularly abolitionism, exerted a profound impact on his life, contributing immeasurably to his ideological maturation. Douglass's growth into the leading black abolitionist of his day also owed significantly to the way in which his Garrisonian commitment enhanced his sense of racial awareness and responsibility. He joined those working to unite the traditions of black and white abolitionism, but the ubiquitous racial divide impeded such a synthesis. As a result, black and white abolitionists often pursued similar goals and employed similar strategies in separate organizations and meetings. The moral suasionist Garrisonian American Anti-Slavery Society and the politically oriented American and Foreign Anti-Slavery Society—the two major abolitionist organizations—had black members and blacks participated in their activities, yet both groups were mostly white in membership and white-dominated. Not surprisingly, then, Douglass's increasing participation in local, state, and national black conventions where blacks themselves articulated their own opposition to slavery and racial proscription also enhanced his ideological development, particularly his growing awareness of the need for an independent and a larger black voice in the movement.

Douglass's evolving abolitionist leadership espoused a constellation of beliefs common among black abolitionists and more perceptive white abolitionists. For them, the battles against slavery and antiblack prejudice and discrimination constituted part and parcel of a black freedom struggle seen, in turn, as an integral aspect of the progressive history of freedom struggles. Like nineteenth-century American abolitionism generally, Douglass's abolitionism traced its roots to evangelical Christian ethics and fervor, natural rights and romantic philosophy, and, even more specifically, the egalitarianism enshrined in the Declaration of Independence. For the true believer, like Douglass, abolitionism signified a religious and humanitarian crusade: the best of American ideals.

From Garrison, Douglass gained insight into the philosophical and tactical importance of moral suasion for the social reform cause, notably abolitionism. Moreover, the powerful ethical and religious element in nineteenth-century American culture meant that the belief in the efficacy of moral suasion as an abolitionist tactic was quite common even among those non-Garrisonians who viewed political action as a flawed strategy. Characterizing the Constitution as a proslavery document, however, the Garrisonians interpreted any political action against slavery under its aegis as a tacit endorsement of a proslavery national compact. Consequently, they advocated disunionism as the moral and logical alternative. They likewise advocated leaving proslavery churches in favor of antislavery ones, viewing proslavery churches and a proslavery interpretation of Christianity as immoral. As anti-Sabbatarians, they believed that each day of the week should be treated as a Sabbath. Both of these beliefs incurred Douglass's staunch support. Also, at first the Garrisonian stress on nonviolent protest against slavery found a supporter in Douglass, even though he found violence in the cause of self-defense justifiable. Furthermore, he found attractive the Garrisonian brand of universal reformism aimed at alleviating oppression and injustice in general. His Garrisonian commitment thus clearly strengthened his moral and humanist convictions.

The notion that slavery engendered antiblack prejudice constituted an article of faith among the Garrisonians. As a result, they endeavored to overcome their own racism with varying degrees of success. Douglass found the relative egalitarianism among the Garrisonians rather impressive and he, like most black and innumerable white thinkers, agreed that slavery represented the primary cause of antiblack prejudice. According to Douglass, who reiterated another common theme among black leaders and progressive whites, emancipation and black uplift were essential to the alleviation of this prejudice. Whites, in turn, ideally had to begin to try to view and treat blacks as equals.

Douglass's stature within the American Anti-Slavery Society grew dramatically and quickly. Even though he typically shared the platform with the likes of Wendell Phillips, "abolition's golden trumpet," he soon became a major drawing card and featured speaker, spreading the Garrisonian message throughout the North and Midwest.

Audiences saw in him a striking illustration of both black potential and a common humanity. Physically imposing, he looked the part of a great leader: six feet tall, broad shoulders, leonine head, long hair parted on the side, furrowed brow, piercing eyes, well-shaped nose, full lips. Innumerable contemporaries noted his charm and handsomeness. One observed that he was "a commanding person . . . of most manly proportions."

His charisma drew likewise upon his rhetorical flair as well as his deep, melodious voice. Naturalness and grace—rather than artificial gestures and declamation—characterized Douglass's oratorical style, which also included dramatic skill, notably mimicry. The wit, satiric bite, and pathos of his speeches combined with a poignant earnestness to mesmerize listeners. More specifically, the clarity and force of the plain statement of his own experiences and observations as a former slave proved riveting.

Speaking throughout Great Britain between 1845 and 1847, Douglass found his audiences enthusiastic and inspiring. Besides his abolitionist blasts, he spoke out forcefully in favor of temperance, Irish home rule, repeal of the corn laws, and the Free Church of Scotland returning money they had received from proslavery Southern Presbyterian churches. In addition, having always sought to fathom the broader dimensions of his experience and that of his people, his speaking tour of Great Britain enabled him to articulate more fully his expanding humanist perspective. Writing to Garrison in 1846 he explained, "I cannot allow myself to be insensitive to the wrongs and sufferings of any part of the great family of man." His humanist vision demanded that he use all of his influence "for the welfare of the whole human brotherhood." His perception of the lack of race prejudice in Great Britain, moreover, intensified his revulsion at the American contrast. It likewise reinforced his fundamental commitment to egalitarianism. Much of his future condemnation of American racism reflected a growing awareness of its absurdity and irrationality, which his British travels confirmed.

Over time Douglass's leadership spoke more and more to international issues. He supported the cause of the oppressed throughout the world, from the imported East Indian labor in the West Indies to the landless European peasantry. "Whatever tends to elevate, whatever tends to exalt humanity in one portion of the world," he argued, "tends to exalt it in another." His beliefs in the millennium and in America's mission as a beacon for freedom and democracy made a broad humanitarian concern imperative.

Douglass's grand reception in Britain necessarily forced him to reassess his role in the abolitionist movement. In particular, his ability to galvanize British opposition to American slavery enhanced his self-esteem and his perception of his influence. This singular appeal, for instance, enabled him to help augment British contributions to the annual Rochester (New York) antislavery bazaar after he moved there in late 1847. He increasingly understood that as the preeminent black American abolitionist he spoke with an authority and an emotional power that touched audiences in a way white abolitionists, even Phillips or Garrison himself, could not. As a result, he came to see that he could operate effectively on his own, outside the Garrisonian fold. This growing independence strengthened his charisma, especially among whites and blacks who found Garrisonianism too radical and among blacks who argued for greater self-reliance.

Upon returning to the United States, Douglass redoubled his resolve to do all he could to undermine his nation's pernicious system of racial slavery and proscription. Several British supporters had urged him to start an abolitionist newspaper which they promised to help underwrite. His Garrisonian cohorts, on the other hand, tried to convince him that his calling was to be an orator and that the newspaper business was too risky. After extensive reflection and at first deciding not to publish a newspaper, he changed his mind, and from Rochester on December 3, 1847, the first issue of his *North Star* appeared. This decision highlighted an intensifying compulsion to express himself more freely. Equally important, it revealed a growing desire for more personal recognition and status both within the abolitionist movement and as a leader in general. His Garrisonian cohorts correctly viewed his decision as evidence of a growing rift between them. Unfortunately, they tended to misconstrue his motivation and aim.

The dilemma Douglass confronted consisted of how to square the increasingly rigid confines of his Garrisonian tutelage with his expanding awareness of the need for greater black self-reliance, particularly strong black leadership. Several incidents plainly showed Douglass that the Garrisonians viewed him and, by extension, blacks generally as subordinates. In 1843 he and Charles L. Remond, a fellow black Garrisonian, quarreled with John A. Collins, their white cohort, over his attempt to introduce "communistic ideas" at what they believed to be an antislavery meeting. Several of their other white colleagues, especially Maria W. Chapman, interpreted the incident as an unfair attack on Collins. While they reprimanded Douglass and Remond for publicly airing a dispute the organization's opponents might exploit, they nonetheless forgave them. Similarly, several of Douglass's colleagues had worried about his trip abroad because they believed he might be seduced into joining the rival British and Foreign Anti-Slavery Society, which in opposition to the Garrisonians favored female exclusion and political action. Chapman, unknown to Douglass, had asked Richard G. Webb, an English associate, to look after Douglass and to keep him away from the rival camp. When Douglass, through Webb himself, learned of Chapman's behind-the-scenes overlordship, he vigorously chided her: "You betray a want of confidence in me as a man, and an abolitionist."

Douglass's eventual decision to go forward with plans to publish a newspaper greatly disturbed his fellow Garrisonians. They viewed his decision as impulsive and wrongheaded, suggesting that ambition and conceit had undermined his better judgment. On the contrary, Douglass contended that his decision did not show any "unworthy distrust or ungrateful want of appreciation of the zeal, integrity, or ability of the noble band of white laborers" in the cause. Instead, the central issue remained that "we must be our own representatives and advocates, not exclusively, but peculiarly—not distinct from, but in connection with our white friends."

Douglass's increasing emphasis on the necessity for greater black independence reflected his growing comprehension of race prejudice among white abolitionists, even Garrisonians. This prejudice, often evidenced by arrogance and paternalism, inhibited social interaction among white and black abolitionists as well as equality within the movement. Yet the more conservative political abolitionists, as well as the Garrisonians, were far more progressive than the vast majority of whites in their attitudes and actions toward blacks. Accordingly, the causes of the 1839–40 split between the two wings of the movement were fundamental differences over strategies rather than goals. While both groups remained ideologically committed to black freedom and equality, the political abolitionists rejected the Garrisonians' "broad platform," which linked abolitionism with other issues like women's rights and nonresistance, as too radical. The Garrisonians, on the contrary, viewed political abolitionism as collusion with a corrupt political system. Unfortunately, they could not countenance an independent Douglass because his rising stature only redounded to their benefit as long as he remained securely within their orbit.

In 1851, after much reflection and many discussions with Gerrit Smith and other political abolitionists, Douglass—who in Rochester found himself in a hotbed of political abolitionism—announced a stunning about-face. He now adhered to the viability of political action, in concert with moral suasion, against slavery and accepted an antislavery interpretation of the Constitution. Consequently, he disavowed disunionism, positing that concerted action by the free states was essential to emancipation. His shift outraged the Garrisonians and pleased the political abolitionists. The resulting dispute between Douglass and his estranged Garrisonian cohorts became quite bitter, at times assuming a vindictive and even slanderous character. What Douglass viewed as an honest change of mind, they viewed as apostasy. While he saw their motives as narrow and prejudiced, they saw his as misguided and selfish. The conflict reached its nadir in 1853 when Garrison publicly suggested that Douglass and Julia Griffiths—English abolitionist, friend, and newspaper assistant—were having an affair. Although Garrison soon recanted, Douglass's anger persisted and he lambasted his estranged mentor for spreading a vicious lie.

The heated controversy cooled only slowly over time. Garrison and Douglass apparently did not speak to one another for nearly twenty years. The break with Garrison had substantial ramifications for Douglass's maturation. He later acknowledged that their relationship had once been "like that of a child to a parent." His tutelage now formally over, he declared his ideological and personal independence. The intimacy of their interpersonal bond had clearly exacerbated the break. Nevertheless, he now felt more secure in his identity as a black man and, correspondingly, less compelled to compensate for his lost and presumably white patrimony. This expanding perception of his blackness as integral to his psychic well-being buttressed his continuing development as a leader.

Douglass's shift toward a more self-reliant posture likewise revealed increasing involvement with fellow black abolitionists. As a Garrisonian, he had moved largely in white circles and developed close ties to his mostly white colleagues. As a result, his growing involvement in the national Negro convention movement, from 1843 on, proved indispensable to heightening his racial consciousness and afforded him the invaluable opportunity to debate ideas and proposals regarding emancipation and uplift with other leading blacks. This kind of interaction, in addition to his participation in various local and state black conventions, helped to hone his insight into his people's plight and to impress further upon him the crying need for racial solidarity and self-reliance, which he diligently championed in the 1850s.

A distinguished career as a journalist also served to enhance Douglass's race consciousness and ideological development. He served variously as editor and publisher of the *North Star* (1847–51), *Frederick Douglass' Paper* (1851–60), *Douglass' Monthly* (1860–63), and the *New National Era* (1870–73). The pressure to produce a newspaper of

69

consistently high quality forced him, notably in the beginning, to improve his communication skills and to develop greater business acumen. The savvy and knowledge that he gained, moreover, made him a better orator. In addition, his newspapers provided an effective and widely disseminated written vehicle for his leadership.

Early on Douglass's leadership met rigorous scrutiny, and sometimes strong opposition, among his black colleagues. Samuel R. Ward and Henry Highland Garnet, important religious leaders, had forced him to reexamine his initial opposition to political action, and Garnet had rejected Douglass's early opposition to violent slave resistance. At the 1843 National Negro Convention in Buffalo, Garnet had led the support for a resolution calling upon slaves to strike immediately for their freedom, violently if necessary. Douglass had led the successful opposition to the resolution, which failed to pass by one vote. If the resolution actually reached the slaves, he reasoned, its impact most likely would be negligible, for it would also reach their masters, who would tighten their repressive control. At this juncture Douglass favored a nonviolent and moral abolitionist thrust. By the late 1850s, however, the perceptions of an increasingly violent slaveocracy, various discussions with John Brown (in addition to the ill-fated raid he led on Harpers Ferry in 1859), as well as the arguments of black cohorts, forced him to accept the likelihood that emancipation would require violence.

Douglas came of age as a race leader in the 1850s. The black and white press acknowledged his preeminence, and his growing stature within the national negro convention movement signified his strong influence among fellow black leaders. For example, the decade witnessed heated debate on a question vital to Afro-American identity: whether blacks should seek to integrate or separate from the American mainstream. This debate proceeded in several directions, two of which Douglass endorsed and led: to stay in the United States rather than emigrate elsewhere, such as West Africa or the West Indies, and to work for color-blind American institutions. On the other hand, the emigrationists, led by people like Martin R. Delany, concluded that blacks could never realize freedom, justice, and equality in a racist white America, so they advocated selective emigration to a black country. There they could not only promote that country's progress, but they could also work for racial justice in America. Nevertheless, the emigrationists continued to find American values and ideals attractive, as evidenced by their emphasis on Western notions of civilizing and Christianizing the host people and society. Indeed, emigrationism often combined Western cultural imperialism, missionary zeal, and militant race consciousness.

The deep-seated ambivalence toward the United States common among separatists or emigrationists simultaneously attracted to its democratic ideals and repelled by its undemocratic reality animated integrationists, too. The latter group, however, seemingly reflecting the dominant black attitude, retained at least a glimmer of hope that conditions would eventually improve. Furthermore, integrationists remained more firmly convinced of their fundamental Americanness, refusing to leave the land so inextricably bound with their sense of self and their history. Douglass always insisted that "the native land of the American Negro is America. His bones, his sinews, are all American." Widespread black opposition to the white American Colonization Society's efforts to resettle American blacks in Liberia also undermined general black interest in emigration.

Douglass concurred with the individual's right to emigrate to improve his or her situation, but he adamantly opposed a mass emigration. Recognizing blacks as a nation within a nation, he maintained: "Individuals emigrate—nations never." Yet while fully aware of the distinctive collective identity of black Americans, his vision of racial, or ethnic, nationalism remained subordinate to his vision of American nationalism. For Douglass the former actually enriched the latter. He firmly believed, nevertheless, that the Negro's sense of twoness—his or her often conflicting racial and national identities—could only be satisfactorily resolved in a humanistic commitment to the integrationist-assimilationist imperative of a more expansive political and cultural—rather than merely racial—nationalism.

Although he never saw sufficient evidence to necessitate massive black emigration out of the United States, on the eve of the outbreak of the Civil War, Douglass had planned to visit Haiti to survey prospects for black emigrants. The apocalyptic expectations spawned by the war forced him to cancel his trip to Haiti and to redouble his efforts to ensure an abolitionist peace. He apparently never again seriously considered the possible viability of extensive black emigration.

Consistent with the integrationist-assimilationist ethic his deep-seated commitment to the United States demonstrated, Douglass ideally opposed segregated, color-conscious, or complexional institutions. Racial caste, he contended, was "a relic of barbarism" and grew out of the erroneous notion of innate black inferiority and its corollary, white racism. Racial segregation, then, signified whites' efforts to separate themselves psychologically as well as physically from the blacks in their midst. "This shameful outrage upon the institutions of free, humane, enlightened, and Christian America" constituted a key aspect of the structural racism blacks battled. For instance, the poor education his own children confronted in segregated schools in Rochester gave a special urgency to his leadership in the successful prewar movement to integrate these schools. Likewise, after the war, when the Washington, D.C., branch of the Columbia Typographical Union refused to admit Lewis, his son, Douglass blasted their policy of black exclusion. In fact, given the intransigence of union racism, Douglass and other progressive black leaders typically supported black unions, or more often no unions at all, as a viable and expedient alternative.

Blacks generally embraced complexional institutions, such as black manual labor schools and black conventions, as a necessary and desirable response to discrimination in predominantly white institutions. Racial uplift, race pride, and self-reliance demanded black institutions in a white racist society. Yet a vocal minority, like the wealthy reformer Robert Purvis, disagreed, arguing that complexional institutions were a capitulation to race prejudice. Lewis Woodson, an influential minister, had argued in the 1830s, however, that "whenever a people are oppressed . . . distinctive organization or action, is required on the part of the oppressed, to destroy that oppression." Douglass agreed. Separate black conventions were imperative, he reasoned, because whites were already "in convention against us in various ways and at many important points. The practical construction of American life is a convention against us." Still, he and most black leaders envisioned separate black institutions as a transitional stage in the evolution of color-blind institutions. Indeed, Douglass has come to embody the integrationist and assimilationist traditions among black leaders as well as the optimistic vision of American life both traditions have demanded.

In spite of the vexing situation of blacks, Douglass did not succumb to despair and disillusionment. Whether during the especially trying times of the 1850s, the early war years, white "redemption" following Reconstruction, or the lynching terror of the 1890s, he never soured on American ideals and prospects, in spite of his searing criticisms of American reality. The inevitable triumph of enlightenment, progress, and moral law, he believed, plainly verified the ultimate success of his people's cause and America's mission. A firm grasp on reality, however, usually tempered his characteristic optimism and prevented it from veering too close to illusion or delusion.

Douglass consistently touted and, consequently, has come to personify the efficacy of resistance as against accommodation to promote racial progress. Throughout his life he actively fought public antiblack discrimination, often to the point of public protest or disturbance. In one of his most famous speeches, delivered at a West Indies Emancipation Day celebration in Canandaigua, New York, in 1857, he asserted that freedom demanded agitation: "If there is no struggle there is no progress." Furthermore, he explained, "the limits of tyrants are prescribed by the endurance of those whom they oppress." This emphasis on resistance reflected a basic understanding among innumerable blacks and their leaders, tactical differences notwithstanding.

Historically, the largely religiously inspired humanist idealism Douglass (essentially a secular leader) exemplified has been a significant feature of Afro-American leadership. Leaders like Daniel A. Payne, bishop of the A.M.E. church, in the nineteenth century and Rev. Martin Luther King, Jr., in our own, have typically identified their people's cause as well as their concern for America generally as reflective of a basic concern for humankind. A strong commitment to egalitarianism and human uplift led many nineteenth-century black leaders to embrace a plethora of social reform causes as integral to human progress and happiness. This active reformism formed a part of a larger reform ethos sweeping nineteenth-century America. Notions about the rule of moral law, human perfectibility, and progress undergirded a belief that social reform would eventually help to usher in the millennium. Douglass therefore engaged in a range of reform activities he understood as being interrelated. For him, clearly, social reform represented a critical means toward racial elevation. Although his work in the black struggle took precedence over everything else, he also participated in the campaigns for women's rights, temperance, free public school education, land reform, universal peace, prison reform, and an end to flogging in the navy. Speaking before an appreciative audience at a temperance meeting in Cork, Ireland, in late 1845, he explained that "all great reforms go together."

Douglass's pioneering work in the woman's rights movement exemplified the humanist, egalitarian, and moral qualities of his reform leadership. Elizabeth Cady Stanton, perhaps the most important American feminist of her generation, converted him to the cause in 1840. At the historic Women's Rights Convention in Seneca Falls, New York, on July 19–20, 1848, he gave strong support to the controversial resolution calling for women's suffrage, helping it to carry by a narrow margin. He also supported the convention's Declaration of Sentiments and its list of demands: a woman's right to personal and religious freedom, to equality in marriage, to her own children, to possess property in her own name, to her own wages, and to equal opportunity and training in the professions and trades.

Despite the public derision he faced, Douglass advocated women's rights because he sincerely believed the movement to be just and urgent. His appreciative understanding of the pivotal roles women played in the abolitionist campaign, in addition to his own life, forced him to grapple with women's plight. As a result, he comprehended with increasing clarity over time how male dominance warped women's lives and how racism, in addition, warped the lives of black women. Not surprisingly, then, the *North Star* featured the slogan "Right Is of No Sex" on its masthead and Douglass's newspapers generally covered significant meetings and developments in the women's rights movement. His commitment to women's rights enhanced his comprehension of human oppression generally, as well as racism, and of sexism and racism as interrelated and characteristically alike yet different.

The Civil War saw Douglass exercising his leadership at its best. He consistently strove to impress upon the Union and President Lincoln three positions. First, emancipation had to be made a primary war aim. Second, slave and free blacks had to be allowed to fight for the Union. Third, a true peace had to integrate blacks more fully into the mainstream of American life. Even before the Confederacy fired on Fort Sumter on April 12, 1861, Douglass persistently reiterated a growing national perception that "slavery must be all in the Union, or it can be nothing." For him and those he spoke for a slavery-ridden Union paled in significance to black freedom. They understood all too well that "slavery must be abolished in the South, or it will demoralize and destroy liberty in the North." Douglass also argued— and Lincoln ultimately agreed—that emancipation would drain away the labor supply of the Confederacy and thus undermine its productive capacity.

Lincoln's cautious prosecution of the war, his fascination with black colonization schemes, and his plans for compensating slaveholders for emancipation alarmed Douglass. Initially, moreover, the Union rejected the services of black soldiers. Avidly assuming the role of propagandist for a Union war effort more consistent with racial justice, Douglass saw the issues of the acceptance, use, and equal treatment of black troops as symbolic of his people's cause. Emancipation, he contended, could be better achieved through the employment of slave and free blacks as troops: a black liberation army. With emancipation as a major war aim, black troops would obviously have added incentive for a Union victory. Douglass adamantly maintained that "the Union cause would never prosper till the war

74

assumed an anti-slavery attitude, and the Negro was enlisted on the loyal side." Black troops, especially from the slave ranks, would represent a powerful political, diplomatic, and military thrust into the Confederacy's heart. Besides much-needed additional human resources, the use of black troops would signify Union commitment to a higher moral standard and an important step toward equal opportunity.

Douglass spoke to both his nation and his people. He excoriated the Union leadership and northern whites for the racist attacks against the use of black soldiers who, though typically discriminated against, had demonstrated uncommon valor in all of America's previous wars. The rejection of the black soldier exemplified white America's rejection of the black man. "Is he not a man?" Douglass inquired rhetorically. While trying to push the Union to accept black soldiers, Douglass had to keep up his people's morale and convince them that black soldiers would soon be asked to join in a war for black freedom as well as the Union. Rather than becoming disillusioned, blacks should "drink as deeply into the martial spirit of the times as possible." He urged them to "not only be ready on call, but be casting about for an opportunity to strike for the freedom of the slave, and for the rights of human nature." Political and military necessity—growing human resource needs and the unexpected persistence of the war—compelled both Lincoln's formal announcement of his limited Emancipation Proclamation and Union acceptance of black troops.

Now that the war had officially assumed an abolitionist character and black soldiers were being quickly readied and rushed into battle, Douglass continued to urge his people to expand their commitment to the Union cause. Like blacks in the broader society, black soldiers had to persevere in the face of enormous hardships. "We shall be fighting a double battle, against slavery at the South and against prejudice and proscription at the North," he explained to black troops, "and the case presents the very best assurances of success. Whoever sees fifty thousand well-drilled colored soldiers in the United States, will see slavery abolished and the union of these States secured from rebel violence." Besides enhancing their status as American citizens, black participation in the "ennobling and soul enlarging" emancipation war signified a racial responsibility. "Liberty won by white men," Douglass argued, "would lose half its luster."

As the chief advocate for the black soldier's cause, Douglass increasingly criticized the unjust treatment they often endured. This included poor training; their overuse in petty, demoralizing jobs; their use as shock troops; Confederate abuse and murder of black prisoners of war; the lack of competent white commanding officers for blacks as well as the lack of black commissioned officers; and the lower pay and bounties they received. The last problem proved especially galling and many black soldiers protested against it. In mid-1862 Douglass ceased his recruitment campaign until he could be convinced of some official attempts to resolve such grievances. In a late July audience with President Lincoln, he tried to get him to act to alleviate these problems. Lincoln responded that eventually black troops would get their proper pay and bounties and that he would sign any commissions for black officers that he received. The threat of further Confederate brutality, Lincoln maintained, prevented the Union government from retaliating for excessive Confederate brutality toward black captives. Even though Douglass found Lincoln's cautious and diplomatic response only partially satisfactory, he came away convinced of the president's sincerity. When a purported commission for Douglass failed to materialize, he refused to sulk. Instead, he redoubled his agitation to ensure an abolitionist and just peace.

Emancipation and the hopeful prospects it engendered for black advancement marked the apotheosis of Douglass's activist leadership. A "great life's work" had been achieved. He plainly understood that the contributions of innumerable individuals, black and white, had helped to make emancipation a reality. The valiant record of black soldiers proved particularly meaningful to him. As he had predicted, it appeared that "the black man, in arms to fight for the freedom of his race, and the safety and security of his country" had given his compatriots "a higher and better revelation of his character." Furthermore, Union victory and emancipation confirmed his wartime judgment that if the war provided any lesson for the American people, it proved "the vanity and utter worthlessness of all attempts to secure peace and prosperity while disregarding and trampling upon the self-evident rights and claims of human nature."

Douglass's position as the preeminent black spokesman continued after the war and emancipation. Forty-seven years old in 1865, he decided after much soul-searching that he could still best serve his people's cause through hard-hitting agitation as a leader rather than as an elected official. In fact, with increasing age, personal comfort, and venerability, Douglass's leadership often assumed a more moderate and emblematic quality that tended to overshadow its earlier, more activist and reformist quality. Time and experience helped to transform the angry young insurgent into "Old Man Eloquent" and the "Sage of Anacostia" (his last neighborhood in Washington, D.C.). Combining the roles of race leader, social reformer, and Republican party stalwart proved difficult in the tumultuous years between 1865 and his death in 1895.

During the war and the early years of Reconstruction, Douglass focused on the vote as essential to a full recognition of black Americans' citizenship, to their uplift, and to their protection. Black suffrage, he believed, would help to prevent black reenslavement and would undergird the call for equal opportunity in the "race of life." The achievements of black soldiers during the war gave additional support to the demand for black suffrage. In addition, Douglass believed that the Republican party—the party of emancipation and of Lincoln— represented the only logical choice for blacks. In a famous nautical metaphor he likened the Republican party to "the deck" and all others to "the sea."

During the early 1850s Douglass's emergence as a political aboli- tionist foreshadowed his shift to mainstream political involvement. The harsh realities of compromise and amorality sullied the political process, but over time he became convinced that only by working through conventional political channels could the process itself be improved and political progress transpire. In spite of his growing commitment to political action as critical to social reform, he still remained wedded to the primacy of moral suasion. Altering public sentiment, Douglass believed, required deep prodding of its heart: the moral conscience. The political conscience, on the other hand, often operated "in the rear of public sentiment." This paradoxical alliance between moral suasion and political action produced a curious and often unstable partnership. Its achievements were mixed at best.

Douglass generally supported the Reconstruction ideals and poli- cies of the radical phalanx of the Republican party, headed by Repre- sentative Thaddeus Stevens and Senator Charles Sumner. He thus favored punishing the former Confederacy for its transgressions against the national union and reconstructing the South in the image of the North. The tragic limitations of President Andrew Johnson's lenient reconstruction policy had been revealed throughout the former Con- federate states by the proliferation of repressive black codes; an alarming increase in white violence against blacks, notably murders, physical brutality, and intimidation; and the return to political power of former Confederate officials. On February 7, 1866, Douglass led a black delegation to discuss with Johnson race relations and Recon- struction. They sought unsuccessfully to show the president the falla- cies in his notions that blacks should be allowed to vote only where a white majority supported the proposal and that, in light of inevitable interracial antipathy, blacks should be colonized elsewhere.

The elaboration and protection of emancipation, Douglass believed, necessitated full civil and economic, in addition to political, equality, with social equality to evolve naturally. He vigorously supported the Thirteenth, Fourteenth, and Fifteenth amendments; the various supplementary civil rights statutes, like those of 1866 and 1875; the Freedmen's Bureau; and the Freedmen's Bank. Whereas Black Reconstruction found the freedpeople adjusting well to their novel status, especially given the enormous obstacles they confronted, most southern and many northern whites viewed the entire process with alarm. As a result, they denigrated the achievements and grossly exaggerated the mistakes of the period as a pretext for undermining Reconstruction and restoring white rule in the South.

Douglass's Reconstruction leadership betrayed a common and telling paradox. The advocacy of both self-reliant individualism and federal aid as critical to the former slaves' progress created a situation whereby the relative responsibility of the individual and the government for freedpeople's progress remained unclear. Cognizant that the former slaves themselves bore the primary responsibility for their future, Douglass likewise understood that without full-fledged and much-needed government assistance that future, given southern white efforts to control it, would be bleak. He therefore stressed to the former slaves that "a new condition has brought new duties." It was clear, he explained, that "no people can make more desirable progress or have permanent welfare outside of their own independent and earnest efforts." The crucial dilemma remained how to decide where self-reliance ended and government aid began—or more properly, how they might mesh.

Douglass stressed that the impossibility of equalizing any time soon the relative situations of blacks, particularly former slaves, and whites did not free the federal government from its responsibility to ensure a successful transition to freedom for the former slaves. In spite of fundamental ideological and political reservations among many about the nature and extent of the federal government's role, if any, in this process, Douglass joined those urging the government to help provide land and education as well as protection of the freedpeople's political and civil rights. Extensive reliance on voluntarism and private philanthropy, or charity, and a laissez-faire social welfare policy—notions consistent with the traditional belief in a limited national government—would not suffice. Federal aid signified a measure of atonement for national complicity in black slavery: a first gesture of justice and good will toward the former slaves. Full retribution, Douglass comprehended, was impossible. "The nearest approach to justice to the Negro for the past," he concluded, "is to do him justice in the present."

The freedpeople themselves saw land and jobs—economic self-reliance and security—in addition to education and political and civil rights as central to their liberty and considerations of justice toward them. Douglass, like most black leaders, rejected as too radical programs such as those of Stevens and Sumner calling for the confiscation of former Confederates' property and its redistribution among the former slaves. Instead, he called for a more moderate program whereby the government would purchase large tracts of land and sell it to the freedpeople on manageable terms. Such a program was not only consistent with the concept of the sanctity of private property but also posed a less direct threat to white property owners. "Thousands, I fear, will continue to live a miserable life and die a wretched death," Douglass forecasted, unless the government helped to provide land for the freedpeople.

Without land reform the postwar southern economy increasingly rendered the former slaves landless, and more and more often peons. Douglass argued that the most serious failure of Reconstruction had been economic. The overthrow of Reconstruction by bitter conservative whites also undermined the political and civil rights of southern blacks. The Compromise of 1877, which ended both Reconstruction and federal help for the freedpeople, gave the white South permission to reassert its hegemony under the guise of alleviating black misrule. This return to "normalcy" meant that the federal government was reneging on its moral as well as constitutional duty to protect the freedom of the former slaves. For the remainder of his life, as the oppression confronting southern blacks intensified, Douglass continually reprimanded his country and the Republican party, especially, for ignominiously betraying the freedpeople.

Douglass aligned himself with the Republican party as the best institutional vehicle for his people's continued advancement. The party, however, having wearied of the freedpeople's cause, constantly ignored its continuing rhetorical commitment to that cause. Indeed, the conflict between Douglass's race leadership and his allegiance to the Republican party fluctuated in intensity throughout his postwar career. He opposed the Liberal Republican insurgency within his own party in the early 1870s precisely because he saw that movement's emphasis on southern home rule as an abandonment of the freedpeople. Yet at the same time he supported President Ulysses Grant's proposal to annex Santo Domingo, having returned from an official trip there convinced of the resident population's support for the move and believing it would benefit both countries. His support also reflected a larger sense of loyalty which the party, fully cognizant of Douglass's stature, over time rewarded with several functionary positions. Thus he received presidential appointments to serve as U.S. marshal for the District of Columbia (1877–81), recorder of deeds for the District of Columbia (1881–86), and chargé d'affaires for Santo Domingo and minister to Haiti (1889–91).

When Douglass failed to criticize immediately the Compromise of 1877, some charged that "a fat office gagged him." He countered that President Hayes had assured him that the new departure would not mean abandoning the freedpeople. As soon as he realized that the compromise did undermine their situation, he forcefully criticized the new departure. Critics likewise alleged that he tolerated party insults aimed at him, such as Grant's failure to invite him to an official White House function for the Santo Domingo Commission—of which he was a member—and Hayes's removal of certain responsibilities from his job as U.S. marshal. Privately hurt, Douglass publicly dismissed such incidents as trivial. Party loyalty often seemed to require public rationalizations.

His prominence notwithstanding, during the postwar years Douglass faced criticism from his people on various occasions. In April 1870 he created a mild furor when he told an audience that he gave the major credit for emancipation to those who had labored for the cause. God received indirect credit because He, according to Douglass, worked through human intermediaries. This position reflected his religious liberalism, a perspective squarely at odds with the religious fundamentalism of most blacks. It also illustrated a conflict between his secular leadership and the pervasive religious leadership—often functioning in civil and political contexts—among blacks. One irate black man strenuously objected to Douglass's "covert infidelity." Such blacks obviously preferred a more God-fearing leadership.

Similarly, Douglass's association with the ill-fated Freedmen's Bank led to "an amount of abuse and detraction greater than any encountered in any other part of my life." Several months before the bank's collapse in mid-1874, he had assumed its presidency after officials assured him of its sound condition. His excitement was short-lived, however, because he soon discovered that the bank faced imminent collapse. Unfortunately, as an institution dedicated to teaching the freedpeople "sobriety, wisdom, and economy, and to show them how to rise in the world," the bank's failure meant tremendous financial losses as well as bitter disillusionment for the bulk of its depositors. Although Douglass had not been at all responsible for the bank's grave financial status, as the preminent black American and its final president he felt compelled to bear a large measure of moral responsibility for the tragedy of its collapse.

Douglass's opposition to the Exoduster migration represented an instance where he stood virtually alone among black leaders who typically supported it. This migration of southern blacks to Kansas mostly between 1879 and 1881 constituted a mass folk movement spawned by the lure of a better life in "John Brown's Kansas" and the growing economic repression, violence, and terrorism they faced in places like Texas, Mississippi, Louisiana, and Tennessee. Douglass's explanation for his opposition revealed several dubious arguments. The oppression the Exodusters fled was not, as he posited, "exceptional and transient." The increasing control whites exercised over the forms of black labor and the increasing exclusion of blacks from politics seriously undermined his view of the South as blacks' natural and logical home. He also underestimated the extent of white southern brutality toward blacks and overestimated the role of professional agents as a cause for the movement. His contention that it was the government's responsibility to protect southern black lives and property constituted his most cogent point. Given the government's indifference and hostility toward southern blacks, however, this protection never materialized.

Douglass's opposition to the Exoduster migration owed significantly to his basic opposition to a mass black migration. Over time, however, he modified that view. As a result of his southern travels in the 1880s he came to favor limited black migration out of the South to areas where blacks' civil and political rights would be more secure. Douglass's opposition to the Exoduster migration had revealed, and his southern observations confirmed, that he had lost touch with the plight of ordinary southern blacks. This dilemma also vividly betrayed a rift between the bourgeois world in which Douglass, like major nineteenth-century black leaders in general, moved and the peasant and working-class world of most blacks. Not surprisingly, this class cleavage sometimes contributed to disturbing results. In the early 1870s, for example, Douglass and other well-known black Republicans turned the National Colored Labor Union into a mouthpiece for party rhetoric, undermining it as a forum for black working-class interests. Such efforts diminished both the radicalism of his leadership and, among some, his popularity.

In the increasingly oppressive late nineteenth century, black leadership tended to give greater emphasis to the need for economic self-sufficiency and racial unity and pride than to the agitation of civil and political issues. Douglass, however, once again found himself at odds with many of his black colleagues over the necessity for civil and political agitation, which he continued to endorse, and racial unity and pride, which he thought some overemphasized. The latter concern engendered especially heated debate. In light of his humanism, his mulatto identity, his assimilationism, and his ambivalence toward race in general, it is not surprising that Douglass never espoused the fierce race pride associated with the likes of Delany. He believed racial pride and unity to be important, but he believed a more expansive belief in pride and unity on national and human levels to be more important. In 1889 he criticized "this everlasting exhortation by speakers and writers among us to the cultivation of race" as "a positive evil" and as "building on a false foundation." This overzealous race fixation, he maintained, bordered on "the thing we are fighting against"—"an assumption of superiority upon the ground of race and color."

"Bruce Grit," journalist John Edward Bruce, blasted Douglass's "bad advice." Douglass's assimilationist-integrationist dream, he charged, was a sham "which he nor his posterity will hardly live to see realized." Bruce suggested that "Douglass evidently wants to get away from the Negro race, and from the criticism I have heard quite recently of him, he will not meet with any armed resistance in his flight." Douglass countered that his lifelong dedication to his people's cause spoke for itself. He reiterated, moreover, that ultimately humanism and nationalism had to supersede race, or racialism.

In 1884, less than two years after the death of his wife, Anna, Douglass remarried. This time he chose as his mate Helen Pitts, a white woman. The celebrated interracial union engendered a mixed chorus of praise and condemnation. Blacks, especially, were divided in their reaction. Some saw it as a courageous strike against prejudice; others as an insult to all blacks. One black observer noted that "the colored ladies take it as a slight, if not an insult, to their race and their beauty." The apparent contradiction of the foremost black American leader marrying a white woman disturbed many blacks; indeed, some contended that the marriage undercut Douglass's popularity among his people. Nonetheless, Douglass saw his second marriage as a private matter having no bearing on his leadership. For him it signified a logical decision given his assimilationist-integrationist outlook and his humanism. "I do not presume to be a leader," he explained, "but if I have advocated the cause of the Negro it is not because I am a Negro, but because I am a man." Nevertheless, his interracial marriage had to contribute to his deemphasis on racial pride and solidarity in his later years.

Controversies and criticisms notwithstanding, Douglass's position as the major black American leader of his generation persisted. Indeed, even though his later years featured a more patriarchal style, the fiery determination still distinguished his race leadership. The adoption of the Fifteenth Amendment in 1870, for instance, had led to a serious rift in the liberal coalition of black advocates and women's rights advocates—the Equal Rights Association—over the amendment's exclusion of women. Douglass, quite understandably, stood firmly with those who saw the black man's right to vote as more pressing. While still fervently committed to women's suffrage as the next stage in the women's rights struggle, his primary commitment remained black advancement. Unfortunately, the bitter dispute rent the Equal Rights Association asunder and rendered it moribund in spite of continuing interracial efforts—which Douglass helped to lead—on behalf of sexual and racial equality. Not surprisingly, then, on the day of his death, February 20, 1895, he had attended the morning sessions of the pro-women's suffrage National Council of Women.

Throughout his later years, Douglass witnessed much that might have destroyed the hope and optimism of lesser men. The Republican party's growing indifference to his people's plight forced him to heighten his denunciations of the party's growing commitment to "money" rather than humanity. The shocking increase in disfranchisement, segregation, public and civil discrimination, economic repression, and brutalization which southern blacks endured deeply disturbed him. Especially appalling was the growing number of blacks lynched by whites. Douglass, along with other black leaders like Ida B. Wells, forcefully condemned this unconscionable phenomenon and demanded that the government take action to stop it. That the usual charge against the victim was a typically false accusation of raping a white woman clearly revealed the psychopathology of the ghastly practice. Similarly, it betrayed the psychosexual roots of white racism. Reinforcing racist stereotypes of black men as criminal, libidinous, and always lusting after white women, the rape alarm threw upon "every man of colour a mantle of odium" and scarred him with "a mark of popular hate." Douglass also explained that the rape hoax highlighted a cruel irony: a system of racist oppression that allowed, even encouraged, the rape of black women by white men and the emasculation of black men.

White indifference toward and support for the lynching disgrace proved extremely unsettling for Douglass. In addition to exposing the depths of antiblack prejudice, these attitudes betrayed two fundamental misconceptions: that the race problem constituted a black and southern problem and that blacks themselves were largely to blame for their own oppression. The race problem, Douglass countered, originated "not with the Negro, but with his white oppressors. It can be more properly called a white than a black problem, since its solution depends more upon the action of white men than upon that of black men." Indeed, the dilemma was essentially moral and national.

> The real question, the all-comanding question, is whether American justice, American liberty, American civilization, American law and American Christianity can be made to include and protect alike and forever all American citizens in the rights which . . . have been guaranteed to them by the organic and fundamental law of the land. It is whether this great nation shall conquer its prejudices, rise to the dignity of its professions, and proceed in the sublime course of truth and liberty. . . .

Douglass's leadership valiantly aimed to alleviate the challenge posed by that question. As a representative American he persuasively demonstrated that the core values, attitudes, and beliefs of all Americans and the black struggle for freedom and equality were inseparable. His singular ability to evoke the essential Americanness of blacks and their goals distinguished his leadership, resonated among blacks and sympathetic whites, and largely accounted for his preeminence. The considerable prewar and wartime influence that he exercised declined in the postwar years as the nation increasingly neglected blacks and Douglass himself became more moderate and venerable. Equally important, the rapidly changing national climate became less amenable to his aggressive moral and political leadership and more amenable to the accommodationist economic and social leadership Booker T. Washington came to epitomize. Ultimately, however, the humanism that characterized Douglass's leadership proved itself, in his time, and remains emotive and powerful.

84

Jason H. Silverman   5

Mary Ann Shadd and the Search for Equality

Educator, orator, reformer, and the first black woman editor of a newspaper in North America, Mary Ann Shadd worked throughout her life for the social and political integration of blacks. She first sought to achieve integration in the northern United States, but when that goal was thwarted by white legal maneuvering, especially after passage of the Fugitive Slave Act in 1850, she decided that integration could better be achieved outside the United States. Thus, along with thousands of "hunted blacks," as W. E. B. Du Bois described them, Shadd moved to Canada in 1851. Unlike other emigrationists, though, she constantly held to an idea of integration with white society and white institutions as the only means by which blacks could achieve racial parity. Her uncompromising insistence on integration occasionally set her apart from other black leaders in both the United States and Canada, and because of this her leadership of the black community proved to be less effective, but more widely known, than it otherwise might have been.

Mary Ann Shadd was introduced to the black quest for civil equality by her father, Abraham D. Shadd. In 1819 Abraham Shadd inherited not only his father's occupation as shoemaker but part of an estate valued at $1,300. He successfully continued in the trade and subsequently acquired some property in Wilmington, Delaware. It was into this well-to-do free black family that Mary Ann was born, the eldest child, on October 9, 1823. Abraham Shadd had become an active abolitionist, at least by 1830, representing Delaware at the National Convention for the Improvement of Free People of Color in Philadelphia in 1830, 1831, and 1832. As president of that national convention in 1833, he condemned the American Colonization Society for its support of black expatriation to Liberia. He stressed instead the need for the Society to aid in educating blacks, for he believed that education, thrift, and hard work would enable blacks to achieve racial equality. Starting in the mid-1830s he also covertly opened his home to fugitive slaves going further north via the Underground Railroad, believing that blacks must help themselves and each other if they were ever to achieve a better life.

Shadd had been forced to act on his self-help ideology seven years earlier, when he uprooted the family from Wilmington. In the 1820s Delaware had provided no educational opportunities for people of color. Consequently, the Shadds relocated in 1833 to West Chester, Pennsylvania, where they enrolled Mary Ann in Price's Boarding School, under the auspices of the Society of Friends. After six years of schooling, the sixteen-year-old Mary Ann demonstrated how profoundly she had been affected both by her denial of education in Delaware and by her father's attitude toward self-help when she returned to Wilmington to organize a school for black youth. For eleven years (1839–50) Mary Ann taught, first at the Wilmington school and subsequently at black schools in New York City and in West Chester and Norristown, Pennsylvania, everywhere echoing her father's views on black education, thrift, and hard work as the desirable means of achieving racial parity, and thus integration, in America.

Indicative of Mary Ann Shadd's views at this point in her career was a pamphlet on the elevation of her race that she published in 1849. *Hints to the Colored People of the North* pointed to the folly of black imitation of white conspicuous materialism and asserted that blacks would not profit or improve their condition by such a display of themselves. Following the legacy of her father's political activism, Mary Ann implored blacks to take the initiative in implementing antislavery reform without waiting for whites to provide their beneficence or support. By the age of twenty-six, then, Shadd had gained considerable recognition by articulating what would become her perennial themes: black independence and self-respect.

The situation for blacks in the United States significantly deteriorated by 1850, causing changes in black attitudes toward emigration. The passage of the Fugitive Slave Act, facilitating the return of runaway slaves to the South, suggested the precarious nature of black freedom in the North. Because of the increased risks, some black leaders, who until this point had largely eschewed emigration as a means to racial elevation, now became its vocal advocates. Lewis Woodson, a minister and teacher in Pittsburgh and a former slave, had written essays in the 1830s and 1840s calling for a national identity among blacks. He theorized that integration would not work in the United States and suggested as alternatives either the establishment of black communities, to be called Africanas, or emigration. These essays helped to promote the emigrationist movement of the 1850s, which was joined by Mary Ann Shadd and by such black illuminaries as Henry Bibb, Samuel Ringgold Ward,

James T. Holly, Henry Highland Garnet, Alexander Crummell, and Martin R. Delany. With black leaders encouraging emigration and finding freedom in the northern United States increasingly fragile, thousands of blacks emigrated to Canada seeking freedom, security, and equality.

What American blacks found in Canada, however, differed considerably from what they had anticipated. Canadians undeniably gave refuge to thousands of fugitives, but they did not necessarily do so for philanthropic or humanitarian reasons. As the number of impoverished blacks entering Canada increased, so too did Negrophobia on the part of white Canadians. This sentiment manifested itself in educational, social, and religious discrimination that permeated all levels of black life. Although slavery had been abolished in Canada on January 1, 1834, blacks still were kept out of white schools, experienced great difficulty traveling on public transportation, lived in segregated areas of towns and cities, obtained few jobs, and participated in the political system infrequently at best. In the end, the ostensible Canadian Canaan at times strangely resembled the antebellum United States North.

Nevertheless, along with her brother Isaac, Mary Ann Shadd departed for Canada. Arriving in Toronto in the fall of 1851, she participated in a convention of distinguished black leaders gathered to discuss emigration, the repercussions of the Fugitive Slave Law, and the new environment in which American blacks now found themselves. Eminent emigrationists Martin Delany and Henry Bibb attended this convention, where Shadd quickly learned that she would have to defend her deeply held integrationist posture. While Delany and Bibb advocated emigration, they also buttressed Woodson's concept of a separatist black identity. Partially advanced by the belief that integration would fail no matter where it was attempted, black separatists contended that blacks should maintain their racial identity based on a common black experience, culture, and worldview. Both Bibb and Delany espoused this philosophy, with Delany becoming the most outspoken proponent of "Africa for the Africans." Shadd, however, maintained the principles that her father had taught her: that full black equality could ultimately be achieved only by integration with mainstream white society. As secretary of the convention, Shadd's perceptive account of the proceedings soon appeared in both American and Canadian newspapers, earning her the reputation of a knowledgeable black leader.

Over the issue of segregation in Canada, Shadd soon found herself embroiled in a bitter and persistent struggle with Henry Bibb. Born a slave in Kentucky in 1815, Bibb had seen his family sold one by one. He ultimately became such an incorrigible slave that he was sold to six different masters after attempting to escape the same number of times. In 1842 Bibb successfully escaped to Detroit, and eight years later, when Congress passed the Fugitive Slave Act, he joined many of his fellow fugitives in crossing the border into Canada. He and his wife, Mary, settled in Chatham, where they quickly assumed the leadership of the black community in Canada West. Besides establishing the bimonthly newspaper *Voice of the Fugitive,* the Bibbs founded a separate day school, participated in the building of a Methodist church, and assisted in the creation of educational, temperance, and antislavery societies as well as a society devoted to greeting and aiding newly arrived fugitive slaves. An influential and popular figure among Canadian blacks, Bibb would strongly support separate and segregated institutions.

Shadd's challenge to Bibb's leadership in Canada West arose immediately over the issue of integration. When the Toronto meeting adjourned, Shadd continued on to the town of Windsor, located at the opposite end of Lake Erie. She chose Windsor as the place to begin helping elevate the immigrants because it was one of the most destitute black communities in Canada West. Believing like her father that literacy constituted the first step on the road to self-sufficiency, Shadd at once created a private school for those denied an education by converting an old military barracks into a classroom. Opposition, however, came from within the black community itself when Shadd announced that her school would not segregate black children from white. Mary Bibb led the attack by suggesting that the black community petition for a separate public school instead of supporting an integrated private one. Popular black opinion ran in favor of Bibb's separatism rather than Shadd's integrationism, but to a great extent the question was moot as the existence of public schools for white children ensured that few would attend a private school for black fugitives. Indeed, though blacks were legally entitled to send their children to public schools, neither white Canadians nor black fugitives preferred that arrangement. Nevertheless, the principle of integrated schooling mattered much to Shadd. She felt that caste institutions would only exacerbate racial discrimination and distrust. She also observed that whites often abused the black alternative of building separate public schools for, in practice, whites ensured that blacks attended segregated schools only. In the face of opposition Shadd opened her theoretically integrated classroom and operated the night school for only eight weeks before it disbanded. The day school continued, however, but as more and more blacks disclaimed the idea of integration, choosing instead Bibb's vision of a self-contained and insulated existence, Shadd sadly observed, "I stand alone in opposition to caste schools."

Viewing all segregated institutions with nothing less than contempt, Shadd openly condemned those blacks who willingly subjected themselves to that kind of second-class citizenship. She believed that separate black schools, black utopian or vocational communities such as Elgin, Dawn, or Wilberforce, and the Refugee Home Society alienated whites even further both by their economic failure and by their perpetuation of old stereotypes that identified blacks as incapable of living a life of freedom. In frequent letters to newspapers in the United States, Shadd relentlessly criticized the organized and isolated black communal experiments in Canada for leading blacks to a life of segregation instead of encouraging them to integrate into mainstream Canadian society.

Yet writing letters provided, at best, only a fragmentary and incomplete refutation of the separatist philosophies of Henry Bibb and his followers. To express her views more fully, Shadd published, in the summer of 1852, a pamphlet entitled *A Plea for Emigration, or Notes of Canada West, in Its Moral, Social, and Political Aspect.* To encourage emigration to Canada, Shadd presented salient statistics and information about life north of the border. She revealed where land was available and its cost and explained the electoral process with great emphasis on the absence of discriminatory laws. Admonishing her black brethren in the United States, Shadd concluded that it would be naive for them to hope for a miraculous overthrow of slavery. On the contrary, she surmised, more ground had been lost to the slavocracy in the wake of the Fugitive Slave Act. She asserted that black spirit and pride would better be served by a decision to emigrate peacefully than by "a miserable scampering from state to state, in a vain endeavor to gather the crumbs of freedom that a pro-slavery besom may sweep away at any moment." By providing detailed information about Canada West, Shadd hoped to show that the province, as well as Mexico, the West Indies, and Vancouver Island, compared favorably to the situation facing blacks in the northern United States.

Shadd also attacked the growing separatist philosophy of blacks in Canada. In *Notes of Canada West* she prevailed upon blacks to emigrate to Canada in order to integrate with all free people under the protection of British law. Throughout the pamphlet Shadd's assimilationist philosophies abound. Recognizing the fundamental problem with separation from mainstream Canadian society, she maintained that exclusively black settlements would tend to identify blacks with "degraded men of like color in the States". That, in turn, would induce white Canadian estrangement, suspicion, and distrust of the fugitives. Lamenting that some blacks in Canada made a broad line of separation between themselves and the whites, Shadd castigated those separatists as perpetuating black prejudices against whites. She observed how black separatists construed and transformed even casual white remarks into Negrophobia, thereby influencing the recently arrived fugitives into believing that separatism would provide them with a better way of life. Moreover, Shadd feared that because of separatism blacks would seldom attend schools, and the result would be the ascendancy of whites over illiterate fugitives.

Despite the widespread circulation of *Notes of Canada West,* Shadd still functioned at a disadvantage when it came to disseminating her beliefs. With increased vehemence in the wake of the publication of Shadd's *Notes,* Henry Bibb attacked her assimilationist philosophies in his newspaper, *Voice of the Fugitive.* Able only to respond through letters, Shadd lamented the helplessness she felt in reaching her people. Still working full-time as a teacher, the thought of planning and establishing a newspaper of her own increasingly appealed to her. At that time just a few white women had entered the press world, and they, for the most part, submitted articles and letters in much the same fashion as Shadd. Pittsburgh native Jane Swisshelm changed that tradition, however, in 1848 when she founded and edited the antislavery newspaper *The Saturday Visitor.* Following Swisshelm's example, Shadd would soon cross both sex and color barriers to become the first black woman editor of a newspaper in North America.

Such a move did not come easily, however. Bibb's criticism of Shadd in the *Voice of the Fugitive* escalated. Indirectly attacking her for race betrayal, Bibb categorized anyone who shared "the deluded sister['s]" integrationist beliefs as "vile traitors who give 'aid and comfort' to the enemies who attack us." In the aftermath of this vituperation Shadd found it particularly difficult to marshal support for her undertaking. But by early 1853, with the timely help of Samuel Ringgold Ward, another prominent fugitive slave who had left the United States, and a committee of local luminaries, Shadd published the first edition of the *Provincial Freeman.*

Proclaimed editor of this bold venture, Ward actually lent only his name to the paper to generate interest and subscriptions. An excellent orator, the "Black Daniel Webster" spent most of his time traveling extensively through Britain raising funds for various black causes. Although Shadd had taken no official title or position, she represented the driving force behind the new enterprise. She explained in the first issue the difficulties of Ward's titular editorship, noting that, because he was either traveling or residing elsewhere, he could not devote his attention to the paper. At no time, indeed, did Ward act as editor or invest his own money in the operation.

Staunchly assimilationist in tenor, the first issue of the *Provincial Freeman* appeared in March. Publication was then suspended for a year while Shadd traveled in the United States and Canada on a lecture tour to raise money for her fledgling endeavor. As a public speaker she blazed new paths. With the exception of Frances Ellen Watkins, very few other black women could, or did, take to the lecture circuit. Upon the completion of her tour, Shadd triumphantly returned to Canada as a foremost champion of black equality.

Now quite prominent in her own right, Shadd found sufficient support for the *Provincial Freeman* by early 1854 to resume publication. She chose Toronto as her new headquarters, most likely because of the large concentration of blacks there and the presence of several prosperous black businessmen who had expressed interest in her newspaper. In any event, in March 1854, with the motto, "Self-Reliance Is the Fine Road to Independence," the *Provincial Freeman* began appearing on a regular basis. Immediately directing her pen toward Bibb's separatism, Shadd stated uncategorically that the newspaper's raison d'être was to represent the intelligent choice of "Colored Canadians" for integration. Perhaps, though, the fundamental difference between Bibb and Shadd was more subtly expressed by the very titles of their respective journals. On the one hand, the *Voice of the Fugitive* described blacks as actual fugitives and implied their temporary relocation in Canada. On the other hand, the *Provincial Freeman* obviously used Canada as the point of reference, imparting the feeling of a more permanent move. Toward this end, Shadd urged her fellow blacks to contribute their energy and industry "to the weal of their adopted country."

Bibb's death in the summer of 1854 deprived Shadd of her primary nemesis. By autumn, with Ward's name expunged from the masthead, Shadd directed the fortunes of the *Provincial Freeman* with her sister Amelia. Bereft of any benefits accruing from association with Ward's reputation, Mary Ann Shadd again began lecturing in Canada and the United States to meet the newspaper's operational expenses. Returning to Toronto she unexpectedly met with public opposition to a newspaper run exclusively by women. Realizing that hers was the only black newspaper left in Canada, Shadd acquiesced and very reluctantly searched for a male editor to placate her opponents and prevent any disruption of her press. She settled on the Reverend William P. Newman, a rather innocuous individual, to act as nominal editor. Yet she sharply chastized her readership for their captiousness toward her as a woman editor. Cognizant of her own importance in breaking "the Editorial ice," she implored other black women to go into editing despite the obstacles.

The title of editor was all that Shadd surrendered. Her reputation as orator and equal rights champion firmly established, she journeyed to Philadelphia to attend the 1855 National Negro Convention, the first black woman to be admitted as a corresponding member to the colored convention movement. Her impressive address to that group moved Frederick Douglass to observe that she made "one of the most convincing and telling speeches in favor of Canadian emigration I ever heard." From Philadelphia, Shadd visited other areas of the United States generating interest in and subscriptions to the *Provincial Freeman*. When she again returned to Canada she moved the newspaper's offices to Chatham, a former Bibb stronghold, where a larger number of blacks had settled.

Shadd used her newspaper to comment on all aspects of black life in Canada, but she focused especially on problems of racial discrimination and segregation. Exposing discrimination wherever it occurred, Shadd publicized, much to the chagrin of many white Canadians, specific examples of their racist behavior. She described Wardsville, a town near London, Ontario, as a contemptible and disgraceful place because of the discrimination aimed at fugitives. As she did on numerous other occasions, Shadd warned blacks to avoid that area or experience "lessons in colorphobia."

So fervent an integrationist was Shadd that she had much difficulty comprehending why blacks should be subject to the peculiar detestation of white Canadians. In defense of her philosophy, she noted in an editorial the biblical precedent for leaving a land ruled by tyrants, comparing the black exodus from "the hell of the continent" with the departure of the children of Jacob from Egypt. Her most telling analogy compared the Puritans as fugitives of Europe with blacks as fugitives from the United States. She observed that both kinds of emigrants were fugitives from oppression and contended that skin color alone differentiated the two. She then tried to proselytize both white Canadians and black fugitives to accept integrationism.

To implement her assimilationist policy, Shadd encouraged blacks to strive for financial independence in Canada. The *Provincial Freeman*'s motto of self-reliance echoed her personal motto, as well as the lessons she had learned as a child about self-help. She wrote that the best way available to help the refugees was to employ such measures as would make them independent, self-sustaining laborers within the given social structure. Their success in this endeavor would thereby prove "the fitness of the slaves for freedom . . . and the perfect capability of the negro to live and to advance under the same government and upon terms of political and social equality with the anglo-saxon race or any other of the one great human family." Success would also facilitate the abolitionist cause by serving as an example to American slaveholders. Black progress in Canada, according to Shadd, would be a triumphant refutation to racial prejudice everywhere.

While the *Provincial Freeman,* by its very publication, continued to provide some service to the fugitives, by 1856 it seemed that the venture would cease due to insolvency. Shadd worried about obtaining the 3,000 subscriptions necessary to maintain publishing. In the summer, a planned thirty-day hiatus to equip a new office evolved into a four-month disruption in publishing because of the shortage of funds. Of course, most black newspapers faced a similar situation at that time. As Shadd struggled to resume publishing operations, she noted that *Frederick Douglass' Paper* had been greatly reduced in size yet much improved in appearance. She applauded Douglass's changes as sensible and wrote to a friend that black newspapers must survive even if reduced to the size of one's hand.

Regular publication of the *Provincial Freeman* resumed in the fall of 1856, but with many of its subscribers in arrears the financial state of the journal again rapidly deteriorated. Shadd's husband of two years, Thomas F. Carey, a Toronto barber, began selling lamps to supplement the newspaper's income. A widespread depression during the late 1850s, however, hastened the paper's demise. Shadd managed to publish it sporadically until 1859, at which time the financial burden became too debilitating.

In the wake of the *Provincial Freeman*'s demise, Shadd returned to full-time teaching at an American Missionary Association–supported school—an ironic twist of fate since Shadd had long been at odds with the A.M.A. With its money she had opened her first school in Windsor in 1851, but the A.M.A. withdrew its support in 1853, ostensibly because Shadd was not an Evangelical Christian. (Earlier a Roman Catholic, Shadd had joined the African Methodist Episcopal church but left it in Canada because of its segregated policies to become a Methodist.) The true reason the A.M.A. withdrew its support of her, Shadd believed, rested upon her sharp criticism of an association-affiliated project, the separatist Refugee Home Society, directed by her nemesis, Henry Bibb, and created to settle blacks on low-cost land in Canada. Shadd publicly accused all of the Society's agents of malfeasance, asserting that they cheated the fugitives by granting them five acres of land conditional upon the purchase of twenty more—clearly beyond the financial capacity of most blacks. She claimed the agents kept for administrative expenses between twenty and twenty-five percent of all funds solicited. By accepting the job at an A.M.A.-supported school, though, Shadd apparently went against her own idealistic rule of never allowing interest to become the master of principle.

No longer running her own enterprise freed Shadd to enter more actively into the abolitionist movement. With particular vigor she assailed those who sought to compromise in any way with slavery or who were prepared to allow blacks to accept temporary second-class citizenship. Singling out such abolitionists as Hiram Wilson, Josiah Henson, and the late Henry Bibb, Shadd opined in a letter to a friend that the antislavery cause consisted of too many "pretended leaders." Indeed, she predicted that all of their conventions and caucuses would be fruitless since they attended such meetings only for self-aggrandizement. As a Garrisonian, Shadd also had little use for John Scoble, secretary of the British and Foreign Anti-Slavery Society and manager of Dawn, a black community in Canada. Describing Scoble, Shadd wrote that his pomposity and petulance totally undermined his effectiveness. Nor did she have any kind words for the Canadian Anti-Slavery Society and its secretary, Thomas Henning. She recorded the hypocrisy of Canadian abolitionists and criticized "this disgusting, repulsive surveillance, this despotic, dictatorial, snobbish air of superiority of white people over [black], by Canadian anti-slavery people." Shadd repeatedly drew attention to those Canadians who verbally endorsed abolition but who never attended meetings, gave contributions, or assisted blacks in any tangible way. She thereby attempted to embarrass or harass them into changing their ways, but in that effort she succeeded only in proving her own self-righteousness. Her leadership at times seemed to consist only of carping criticism of those not meeting her expectations.

Shadd watched with great interest as the sectional crisis intensified in the United States. Her hope for the potential destruction of slavery by the impending conflict heightened upon John Brown's arrival in Chatham in the spring of 1858. Meeting with Brown, a group consisting of Shadd, her husband, her brother Isaac, and a friend, Osborne P. Anderson, became privy to the visionary's intended plans. So taken with Brown was Anderson that the young black joined him at Harpers Ferry and survived to record his memoirs in a volume entitled *A*

Voice from Harper's Ferry, edited and prepared for publication by Mary Ann Shadd. Shadd, who held Brown in highest regard, wrote the New York *Weekly Anglo-African* shortly after his death to eulogize the "plucky" abolitionist.

Through the early years of the Civil War, Shadd continued to teach in an interracial school in Chatham, but she also wrote letters in support of abolitionism to many American newspapers. Not surprisingly, the activist grew tired of watching the American Civil War from a distance, and, anxious to assist in the Northern war effort, she accepted an invitation from Martin Delany, in late 1863, to serve as an enlistment recruiter. Without hesitation, Shadd returned to the United States to participate in the recruitment programs of several states, ultimately obtaining a commission as a U.S. recruitment officer from Indiana's governor, Oliver P. Morton. That she succeeded in this effort came as no surprise to her contemporaries. William Wells Brown wrote that she raised recruits with as much skill, tact, and order as any government recruiting officer and that her men were always considered among the best recruited.

Shadd agonized over whether to remain in the United States after Appomattox. Still hoping for an integrated Canadian Canaan, she had witnessed a steady exodus of blacks from Canada following the Emancipation Proclamation. With seemingly safe conditions in the United States, thousands of blacks, fatigued with broken promises and Canadian racism, returned to search for friends, relatives, and freedom. Shadd concluded that she could best serve her people by remaining in the United States to educate and help assimilate the millions of newly emancipated blacks. Toward this end, in 1869 she obtained an American teaching certificate and taught for a while in Detroit; shortly thereafter she relocated to Washington, D.C.

"The capital," Shadd recorded, "is the Mecca of the colored pilgrim." Observing the numbers of recently freed blacks migrating to Washington, D.C., in pursuit of their fortunes, Shadd reflected that a great potential for racial equality now existed, if intelligence dictated action. And intelligence, to her, still meant racial uplift and advancement through education. This, of course, complemented her view that racial advancement should aim at and, in the end, produce acceptance and integration into the mainstream of American society. Toward this goal Shadd once again promulgated self-help in lectures to biracial audiences, for she felt that the greatest mistake blacks could commit would be to compromise themselves by relying on others' philanthropy. She had abandoned emigrationism but retained a belief that dependence on the benevolence of whites would emascu-

97

late the freedpeople and prevent them from integrating. In this she would recognize no middle ground.

The passage of the Thirteenth, Fourteenth, and Fifteenth amendments convinced Shadd that blacks would also have to be fully cognizant of the laws of the land were they ever to achieve equality in postbellum America. Hoping to serve as a role model, Shadd, at the age of forty-six, enrolled in the evening law school of the recently created Howard University—the first woman to do so. Intermittently she would study law, supporting herself by teaching, and would eventually receive her degree in 1883.

As she pursued her law degree, Shadd continued to write articles and letters to newspapers expressing her sociopolitical concerns. For example, she disparaged Reconstruction politics of both parties as tending to divide and exploit the black community. She noticed that white politicians, after adroitly pitting blacks against one another, complacently deprecated them for being so divided. Proposing a rather radical panacea given the times, Shadd encouraged blacks to unite in a boycott of discriminatory white businesses. They should demand that these prejudicial businesses allow black customers or else blacks would withdraw their patronage from all white businesses. The opinionated Shadd encouraged blacks to proclaim such a policy and then "stick to it like grim death."

Long recognized as a spokesperson for racial equality, Shadd increasingly turned her attention to gender equality. A fervent supporter of equal rights and equal opportunity for black women as well as men, she wrote often to Frederick Douglass's *New National Era.* In a series of articles in the spring of 1872, she chided black women for maintaining a frightened silence and by that silence condoning petty criminality and vagrancy in the black community. She noted that white women were gaining some power in the United States, and she implored black women likewise to speak out on social issues. One of a handful of black women leaders, Shadd felt that black women should establish a voice in those matters most directly affecting them.

Supporting rights for women, both black and white, Shadd actively participated in most women's rights conventions in and around Washington, D.C. Testifying before the House Judiciary Committee on behalf of women's suffrage, she praised the passage of the Fourteenth and Fifteenth amendments but declared that women all over the country still felt discriminated against by the retention of the word "male" in the amendments. After all, she reasoned, millions of women shared with men the responsibilities of freedom. She encouraged legislators to expunge any sexist references from the amendments as expeditiously as possible and provide women with the franchise. Arguing that women were taxed and governed in other respects without consent, Shadd simply requested that the principles of the founding fathers be applied to women as well as to men.

On March 19, 1874, Shadd put her theories about equal rights into practice. Along with sixty-three other women in the District of Columbia, she attempted to register to vote in an approaching election. Anticipating the refusal, the women, both black and white alike, demanded that the clerks provide sworn, notarized affidavits stipulating they had been denied the right to vote. Armed with what any attorney would consider incriminating documents, Shadd penned a series of condemnatory exposes for the local press.

Recognized by Susan B. Anthony and Lucretia Mott as a valuable member of the movement, Shadd, upon invitation, addressed the National Woman's Suffrage Association convention in 1878. Caught up in the zeal to obtain the franchise for women, she temporarily forsook her long-held preference for integration in favor of what appeared to be separatism. Shortly after addressing the National Women's Suffrage Association, and with its support, Shadd founded the short-lived auxiliary organization called the Colored Women's Progressive Franchise Association. The fledgling organization attracted many to its first few meetings by advocating that black men and women in the District of Columbia create labor bureaus, cooperative stores, banking institutions, printing establishments, and lecture bureaus for their mutual benefit. The organization declared that while it would tolerate no gender discrimination, women would nevertheless have the controlling power since they had the most to gain. Shadd's organization received cautious coverage from Washington's black newspapers. The *People's Advocate,* for example, reported that Shadd had stated "our leading men of color were always talking about providing for 'our boys' but never a word did they say of 'our girls.'"

As activity in her organization waned, Shadd took to the lecture circuit to engender interest in and support for equal rights. Commenting on topics that ranged from race pride to the Republican party, from women's rights to the Ku Klux Klan, she addressed audiences both north and south of the Mason-Dixon Line. Until her seventieth year Shadd maintained an active schedule. Finally, enfeebled by rheumatism and cancer, she died in the summer of 1893. In the twilight of his own life, Frederick Douglass commented that Mary Ann Shadd proved the mental capacity and dignity intrinsic in black women. By her lifework he felt she had demonstrated "the possibilities of her sex and class." And indeed she had. Shadd surpassed her father's role in the abolitionist movement to become not only a prominent abolitionist but an emigrationist as well. Her lifelong goal was to see equality achieved for all black men and women. To achieve this she was ready at various times during her life to endorse emigration and even separate institutions. Throughout her career, though, she always retained her basic belief that through education, thrift, and hard work blacks could achieve integration. At times her personality made her a less effective leader, able to persuade or to cajole and not to convince. Nevertheless, Shadd spoke for all oppressed men and women by her actions. She aired her views as early as 1849, when she was only twenty-six. She emigrated, and then facilitated the way for others by authoring her *Notes of Canada West.* She became the first black woman editor of a newspaper, writing scathing editorials on those she thought had betrayed the fugitives. She actively participated in the women's suffrage movement, agitating alongside white women for something in which she believed. She lectured, published, and rarely compromised, and in so doing Mary Ann Shadd assuredly made her voice heard and her ideas known.

William Cheek and
Aimee Lee Cheek

6

John Mercer Langston:
Principle and Politics

AT THE TIME of his death in 1897, after a multifaceted career
in black protest, politics, education, and the law, stretching over
nearly half a century, John Mercer Langston had attained prominence as a black leader second only to Frederick Douglass. Langston
was eminent as an orator but also served the black cause as organizer
and intellectual. A magnetic personality on platform and off, he
combined a democratic temperament with an aristocratic style. He
articulated and, to a striking degree, embodied an ideal of black
American manhood whose essential elements were self-reliance, self-
respect, and self-assertion. With black freedom and citizenship his
unchanging goals, Langston involved himself extensively in black
institutions and organizations, urging free people of the prewar North
as well as freedpeople of the postwar South to demand their rights. At
the same time, recognizing that the power to effect these objectives
resided in the larger white-controlled society, he engaged—longer
and more influentially than any other black leader of his day—in
conventional politics. While Langston pragmatically explored diverse
remedies for the intractable problems impinging on black Americans,
his leadership's central thrust was the attempt to reconcile the principle
of black equality with the politics of a profoundly prejudiced nation.

Childhood and youth furnished Langston with strong motives and
uncommon resources for leadership. Born free in 1829 in Louisa
County, Virginia, he was the son of Ralph Quarles, a white planter of
wealth and position, and Lucy Jane Langston, a freedwoman of
Indian and African ancestry. When both parents died in 1834, ending
an apparently loving liaison of some twenty-five years, John Mercer's
slaveholding father left him an inheritance that would pay for his care
and education. Later, husbanded by Langston into profitable investments in real estate, it would provide him with considerable financial
independence and the consequent freedom to pursue reform endeavors.

To escape Virginia's repressive conditions Gideon and Charles
Langston, John Mercer's older brothers and later black activists in

their own right, took the orphaned four-year-old to Ohio. The move was only the first disruption of Langston's boyhood connected to slavery and prejudice. A cultured white family (friends and former neighbors of his father) sheltered the child in their Chillicothe home and treated him like a son until, when he was nine, they decided to resettle in Missouri. At a last-minute court hearing, a judge ruled that Langston's inheritance and person would be in jeopardy in the slave state and separated him from his white guardian. Until this moment the light-skinned boy had been raised without conscious recognition of his mixed blood. Taught in the white-only public school, he had been treated at home as a "little Virginia gentleman," tutored in the courteous manners and aristocratic bearing that would distinguish his later conduct. After the hearing he boarded in a succession of households, both of white abolitionist New Englanders and of blacks with Southern roots; he worked as farmhand and bootblack, and intermittently he attended privately supported black schools. Through these experiences Langston gained an intimate knowledge of contrasting types of Americans, an appetite for hard work, and an appreciation of self-reliance. But his double orphaning, the second linked to his coming to racial awareness, could only incur large psychological costs. Langston was left with a gnawing need to prove his self-worth, as well as with a deep insecurity that surfaced at moments of particular emotional vulnerability during his career.

While still grappling with the grief of separation and the strangeness of the racial identity imposed upon him, the boy was moved to Cincinnati. The community, with large numbers of self-emancipated slaves in residence, was notable for combining white abolitionist teaching and organizing with black enterprise and cultural strengths. Shortly after Langston's arrival he was caught up in the large-scale riot of 1841. Even as the attack by white mobs terrified him, the bold, organized self-defense mounted by blacks stirred his admiration. In the riot's aftermath he settled into an extended family relationship in the hard-working black upper class. He experienced the communality of Negro churches and heard black orators defend black rights. The resilience of the community's leadership and institutions intensified his aroused sense of kinship to black people.

At the age of fourteen a diffident but resolute Langston began what became more than eight years of study at Oberlin College. Here he was educated, as he put it, "soundly in politics as well as morality." Evangelical, abolitionist, and democratic in outlook, Oberlin pioneered in higher education without regard to sex or race. Langston subsequently would judge the school and community freer of prejudice "than any other place in the country." Though he had never previously had a white friend of his own age, he forged close relationships at Oberlin with students of both races and sexes. By dint of natural aptitude and the arduous preparation that became a lifelong habit, the black scholar learned he could compete successfully with white peers. Comprehensive formal training and participation in student debating societies developed his skill and confidence as an orator. Langston earned A.B., M.A., and theological degrees at Oberlin. His college years stimulated his wide-ranging curiosity, encouraged his philosophical turn of mind, and supplied him with a fund of interest, assurance, and purpose that he would draw on gratefully throughout his life.

A man of large pride and ambition, Langston contended not only with his inner stresses but with those societal forces designed to deter the gifted and black. When at nineteen he received his bachelor's degree in 1849, as Oberlin's fifth black graduate and one of a handful in the country, he was determined to become a lawyer and to labor for black advancement. Yet he confronted a situation that he would characterize as "dark as night." His legal aspirations were ridiculed; his applications to law schools were rejected.

At mid-century racism was as omnipresent in the North as slavery was omnipotent in the South. Ohio, in law and custom, was no exception. The state constitution of 1802 barred blacks from voting, while other measures, together known as the Black Laws, required black settlers to register and post bonds, forbade black testimony in cases involving whites, and excluded blacks from juries, public relief, and the state militia. Some change did occur in 1849, just months before Langston's graduation, when a small contingent of abolitionist Free Soilers wielded its balance of power in the state legislature to wring concessions from the proslavery Democratic plurality, including repeal of the restrictions on immigration and testimony. Legislation in 1848 and 1849 also ended the long debarment of blacks from the system of public education. No gains could be effective, however, without the cooperation of local officials who, except in such abolitionist pockets as Oberlin, often acted to impede black rights. Enforcement was likewise arbitrary when it came to the judicial decisions that light-skinned Negroes, whose ancestry was more than half white, were entitled to the civil and political rights of white residents. Overall, in public institutions, public accommodations, and economic opportunities, segregation and discrimination prevailed.

In response, black Ohioans banded together for self-help and protest. Early efforts in Cincinnati, Chillicothe, Columbus, and other areas of significant black settlement produced a state black civil rights movement with an organizational structure featuring state conventions. From 1837 to 1860 black Ohioans held at least twenty-one such conventions, more than in any other Northern state. A small but enduring group of leaders propelled the movement. These men, either through the state central committee or on an ad hoc basis, arranged the conventions and implemented policies. Predominantly southern in origin, both slave and freeborn, and uncommonly literate, they were mainly artisans and businessmen and were possessed of reasonable means. Their reform philosophy, as revealed in convention and out, was rooted in a dynamic mix of evangelical Christianity, abolitionist principles, and the democratic-republican values of liberty, equality, and self-government—the very ideology inculcated in young Langston by upbringing and education.

Langston channeled his energies, idealism, and indignation into the Ohio black movement throughout the prewar decade. He was only eighteen when he attended his first national black convention in Cleveland in 1848 and, encouraged by presiding officer Frederick Douglass, made a speech condemning those who refused to help fugitive slaves. The following January he participated in his first Ohio state black convention. Modest but assertive, eager to impress, the articulate young man was much in evidence, so much that a teasing colleague at the 1850 proceedings dubbed the twenty-year-old "Senator Langston." Headlong in his enthusiasm for black protest, he was also sporadically caustic in his criticism of black churchmen and others he deemed too conservative. Nonetheless, movement leaders, his brother Charles H. Langston prominent among them, choosing to employ his talents rather than resent them, regarded him as a favorite son and promoted him from the start. Their democratic orientation, willingness to delegate responsibility, and pragmatism were qualities that Langston would incorporate into his own leadership.

As early as the 1849 convention Langston, torn between hope and doubt, had begun to formulate the ideas about black identity that composed the nucleus of his leadership philosophy. He staked his claim in the words of the Roman slave Terence: "I am a man, and there is nothing of humanity, as I think, estranged to me." Blacks themselves must demand respect and rights. "The spirit of our people must be aroused. They must feel and act as men." Yet he held that blacks could not enjoy full human dignity without the privileges of citizens, and he feared that, even should slavery be abolished, prejudice would still preclude the Negro's ever attaining an American "nationality." Pleading the eventual necessity of black mass emigration,

106

he bitterly averred, "Dearly as I love my native land, I am willing to go wherever I can be free."

The passage of the Fugitive Slave Act and other objectionable political developments, in combination with repeated rebuffs of his attempts to study law, seemed to confirm his forebodings. At the Ohio black convention in January 1852, over which he presided, Langston joined his brother Charles in proposing black emigration as an expression of political disillusionment and black nationalist pride. In the course of the full-dress debate, John Mercer Langston argued that "mutual repellency" between whites and blacks, innate in the relationship between oppressor and oppressed, prohibited their living together on terms of equality. Inspired by European liberation movements, while seeking to promote a black pride untainted by notions of racial superiority, he urged a black nationality as the means for attainment of the Negro's fullest human potential. Despite the solid rejection of emigration by the convention, Langston and fellow advocates helped to stimulate a major black movement of the decade. By the fall of 1854, however, when Martin R. Delany launched his own emigration proposals, embracing many features earlier put forth by Langston, the Ohioan had changed his mind. He informed the Delany-inspired convention in Cleveland that he no longer considered white American prejudice impregnable. National events in conjunction with local politics and Langston's rising personal hopes had persuaded him that black Americans might find liberation and "nationality" in their own country.

Even before this conversion Langston, prompted by his concern for black self-assertion, and by the immediacies of black need, had plunged into reform. Despite the legislative gains of 1849, the free blacks of Ohio both chafed under remaining restrictions and came under constant threat of new oppressive enactments. To defend and extend their rights, through demonstrating black resolve and building white support, black Ohioans undertook numerous enfranchisement drives during the prewar decade. Langston spearheaded these campaigns in state conventions and in the field. As a twenty-year-old novice in 1850 he traveled the state for the better part of a year, boarding with black colleagues, conferring with community leaders, speaking wherever he could find an audience, gathering signatures on petitions. During this tour he spent several weeks with the visiting Douglass, profiting from the chance for close study of the famous black abolitionist's techniques. Both men narrowly escaped a white mob in Columbus, an experience that lent particular force and urgency to Langston's speeches.

The young orator soon made a name for himself. He impressed

others with his moral earnestness as well as his emotional appeal, with his well-trained command of both formal and extemporaneous speaking styles, and with his reliance on "stubborn facts"—extensive historical and legal documentation to which he added firsthand observations of black life footnoted by statistics of his own collection on black property holding, taxpaying, and education. Boston black reformer William C. Nell, teaming with Langston in mid-decade during an Ohio black suffrage drive, called him "a walking and talking encyclopedia" of black American achievements and potential. Nell further credited Langston as the individual most responsible for promoting black enfranchisement in Ohio. Although that state would not grant black suffrage until ratification of the Fifteenth Amendment in 1870, Langston and his Ohio colleagues had reason for self-congratulation in the knowledge that they had helped to stave off new repressive measures.

Concurrently, Langston worked to buttress black public education. Since his own years of teaching during Oberlin's winter vacations, begun as the fifteen-year-old master of a privately supported black country school, the legislative reforms of the late 1840s had made public funds available for black schools. It soon became apparent to Langston, however, that Negro parents would have to be rallied not only to organize their schools, as some already were struggling to do, but also to demand that hostile or indifferent local white officials fulfill their legal obligations. In the fall of 1851 he organized a student society at Oberlin to supply teachers and set out to mobilize black communities, traveling around the state periodically over several years. The unofficial superintendent of the colored schools, as a state legislator called Langston, achieved some impressive results. By 1857 he, like other knowledgeable observers, remarked upon the beneficial influence of the black common schools. "In our literary qualifications," he asserted, "we compare favorably with other inhabitants of this commonwealth." The assessment may have erred on the side of optimism, but not too much, in a state where public education was still rudimentary and white school attendance modest. Its positive tone, in contrast to the despairing pessimism or scolding paternalism of some northern black leaders, was characteristic of Langston's appeal to his people, not only in youth but throughout his career.

Langston and other black Ohioans struggled to build the black constituency for the civil rights movement. Judging from the good response to the numerous petition drives, the attendance at local protest meetings and state conventions, and the masses of black Ohioans who turned out annually for the First of August celebrations

108

of emancipation in the British West Indies—frequently featuring Langston as orator—he and his fellows were able to attract support that, if wavering under political reverses, was nonetheless widespread. Langston appealed with most effect to men who were restless and willing to risk themselves to obtain relief: the artisans and self-employed businessmen; the small group of educated ministers and teachers; the independent farmers residing, as did the majority of black Ohioans, in the countryside. Egalitarian regarding sex as well as race, Langston also appealed to women, especially those with some formal education and those in skilled trades.

An actual statewide black organization, though attempted by nearly every Ohio black convention from 1850 onward, continued to elude the black leadership. Then, in the fall of 1858 a sizable force of black and white rescuers, mainly from Oberlin, descended on nearby Wellington to wrest a fugitive slave from his captors. The Oberlin-Wellington Rescue and the federal prosecution that ensued attracted national attention. Charles Langston, one of the two rescuers actually sentenced, would become famous for his impassioned courtroom plea. Just after the rescue both Langstons helped to establish the Ohio State Anti-Slavery Society. It was dedicated, like earlier abortive black organizations, to the abolition of slavery and the attainment of black rights. Black women were accorded full membership privileges, and membership also was open to whites. Langston and other Ohio black leaders balanced a commitment to racial integration against a conviction that blacks must prove themselves by independent action. Thus, they invited whites to their meetings but conducted their own business. For his part Langston cooperated with white abolitionists of diverse outlook, speaking at important gatherings; Oberlin whites, at least, did participate in the local chapter of the Ohio State Anti-Slavery Society.

John Langston served as president and chief traveling agent of the Anti-Slavery Society, while Charles, as secretary, managed the central office in Cleveland. By capitalizing on the black emotional response to the Oberlin-Wellington Rescue, and later to John Brown, and by applying the organizational skills he had gained, Langston, alongside his long-term allies, managed to build a statewide black organization with auxiliaries in various localities. At a time generally portrayed as one of growing demoralization among northern blacks, the Anti-Slavery Society's first annual meeting in January 1860 was a spirited affair. In welcoming the delegates the thirty-year-old Langston, as presiding officer (the third time he had served as president of an Ohio state black convention), could well regard the gathering as the culmination of a decade of organizational efforts.

During the 1850s Langston's involvement in radical party politics was consonant with his dedication to black advancement. Entering the political arena in Oberlin as early as the autumn of 1852, he worked successfully with radical whites to get the Free Democratic party (the label adopted by most Free Soilers by 1850) in Ohio to endorse black suffrage. In the indignation over the Kansas-Nebraska Act, he campaigned on the Reserve for formation of a new political coalition—soon to be known as the Republican party—which triumphed in the Ohio congressional elections in the fall of 1854. The victory elated Langston, who had thrown his talents into the winning campaign of an Elyria lawyer with whom he was studying law. That September a judicial panel reluctantly ruled that Langston's light skin entitled him to the rights of a white man and admitted him to the Ohio bar. But the first Negro lawyer in the West was uncertain of his ability to attract clients and set himself up as a farmer in rural Brownhelm, an otherwise all-white township near Oberlin. The following spring, as the Free Democratic candidate, Langston won election as township clerk. With this the conversion of the one-time black nationalist-emigrationist was complete. The first Negro elected to public office in the United States, he jubilantly informed Douglass: "What we so much need just at this juncture and all along the future is political influence, the bridle by which we can check and guide, to our advantage, the selfishness of American demagogues."

Langston was married in 1854 to Caroline Matilda Wall, the daughter of a slave woman and a wealthy white North Carolinian. An Oberlin student at the time of their marriage, Caroline, who would bear Langston's five children (one of whom died in childhood), shared her husband's intellectual bent and reform interests. "Some one must take the lead in very advanced steps as to the capability of the Negro," she would advise him in the late 1880s, with neither in doubt as to whom she meant, "but who will dare to take the lead? It cannot be a coward."

The young family moved to Oberlin in 1856. During a fifteen-year residency Langston built a reputation as an adroit attorney and a competent public executive. Though his practice flourished he regretted his inability to attract black clients, a failure he attributed mainly to their fears of the prejudicial effect of his race in a hostile legal system. Finally, in early 1861, a black Oberlin man sought his services. As Langston prepared his case, a rival white attorney who had previously monopolized the black legal business warned the client that the "nigger lawyer" would betray him. Langston retaliated on his white antagonist with kicks and blows and unrepentently paid the token fine of five dollars levied by a sympathetic town court. The black lawyer thereafter enjoyed a proportionate share of the black patronage, a result all the more gratifying if an at least subconscious motivation for his attack was the desire to prove himself to other blacks. Though Langston's emotions were usually under tight rein, and his preferred weapons were his tongue and his wit, his resort to violence on several occasions expressed an anger over denigration of his race and personal and professional honor that, though selective (in that his outbursts occurred within the relatively protecting confines of Oberlin or of Western Reserve courtrooms), was nonetheless profound.

Elected repeatedly to local office in Oberlin, Langston served on the town council, handled the township's legal affairs for several years, and helped direct the progress of Oberlin public education for more than a decade. Instrumental in persuading local and county Republican conventions to support black suffrage and other radical measures, he stumped the district for local, state, or national Republican candidates in every year up to the Civil War. Despite its shortcomings on racial questions, Langston supported the Republican party as antislavery's surest political vehicle to date. "If the Republican party is not anti-slavery enough," he counseled black Ohioans, "take hold of it and make it so." He proved adept at merging the roles of radical party propagandist and black protest agitator. He exploited the 1856 presidential canvass, carrying the joint message of "Fremont and Freedom" and Ohio black suffrage around the state. After the Oberlin-Wellington Rescue he used print and platform to stoke public outrage. He seized upon the rescue to illustrate his major antislavery theme: white and black Americans shared identical interests since the Slave Power imperiled the freedoms of both. When Republicans staged a giant protest rally at Cleveland, Langston, surrounded by such party dignitaries as Governor Salmon P. Chase and Joshua R. Giddings, was the sole black speaker. The rescue agitation helped to redirect the Ohio Republican party from its recent skid toward conservatism onto a more radical course.

Langston's pronouncements crackled with militance during these months. He urged the 1858 Ohio black convention to resist oppressors "by force of arms" where feasible. Further, he speculated to a biracial gathering in Oberlin early in 1859 that upholding American freedom might require war with the slaveholders. Not only did blacks demand the right to fight, but he himself yearned to take the field, "as a common soldier or in a more exalted rank," and "strike" for his country. Still in this frame of mind when later solicited by John Brown's son, Langston came to the support of the Harpers Ferry movement with funds and—by encouraging two Oberlin black men to join Brown's band—with recruits. He led the next Ohio black convention in praising Brown and his compatriots as "Heralds and Prophets of that new lesson, the lesson of Insurrection."

Langston's prewar organizational exertions in Ohio bore fruit during the war years. When Massachusetts undertook the first Northern black recruitment in early 1863, Langston's oratorical and executive skills, as well as reputation, made him a natural choice to head recruitment in the West. Working with white and black recruitment agents and involving local black leaders, he succeeded in recruiting large numbers of Negroes from Ohio and several other midwestern states for the Massachusetts Fifty-fourth and Fifty-fifth regiments. Thereupon, the same Ohio governor who previously had refused Langston's offer to raise an Ohio black regiment asked him to do just that. Langston accepted gladly.

Although Ohio, unlike some other Northern states, did not furnish black volunteers either bounty payments or support funds for their families, Langston hoped to raise compensatory private contributions while remaining confident, in any case, of black Ohioans' willingness to enter the fight. But as recruitment commenced, the national government divulged a payment policy that reneged on earlier assurances of equal recompense and treatment for black soldiers. Privately, Langston protested to prominent Republicans that Negroes were "asked to take an inferior position as soldiers." Publicly, he appealed to the moral and physical courage of black Ohioans. "Pay or no pay," he entreated, "let us volunteer. . . . Let us not be disgraced, but let honor distinguish our conduct." Langston drew on the black movement's organizational capital throughout a nearly five-month recruitment drive, conducted with less public funding than the raising of any other Ohio regiment. In state convention and local meetings blacks rallied to his summons. By early November 1863 Langston had recruited 800 black Ohioans for the U.S. Fifth Regiment.

Gratified though he was by black fortitude and valor, Langston's personal ambition to evince the black man's capability for command would be thwarted. He applied in the spring of 1865 for a colonel's commission, in the hope of leading an all-black regiment recruited by himself and staffed by officers chosen from experienced black ranks. Ohio congressman James Garfield, noting that his fellow radical from the Reserve had "probably done much more" to recruit black soldiers "than any other Colored man in the U.S.," heartily recommended the appointment. But the war ended before it could materialize.

Although Langston's prewar and wartime activities gained him attention, his role in Reconstruction elevated him to national prominence. He worked at first independently through a black organization he directed and afterward under the various auspices of the federal government, the Republican party, and Howard University, in pursuit of a Reconstruction based on equal opportunity and a redistribution of political and economic power. Langston acknowledged that the vote, land, education, civil rights, and the development of social and moral character all were essential to free blacks' elevation, but he understood the need to tailor demands to time and circumstance. His program evolved roughly in three stages, the objectives in each being related and overlapping. From 1864 until the onset of Congressional Reconstruction in 1867, Langston emphasized his enduring goal of equality before the law, seeking to persuade white politicians to institute black suffrage and working to prepare the freedpeople to exercise citizenship rights. Once the political mobilization of blacks was underway with the election of delegates to state constitutional conventions in the fall of 1867, Langston began to expand upon economic issues and integration. Protection of the freedpeople, always a major question, became even more crucial in the 1870s, when Langston also stressed black political appointments and training blacks for leadership.

Langston held that equality before the law must be the first priority. In opposition to some white abolitionists' belief that the educational and moral advancement of free blacks should take precedence over suffrage, Langston maintained his prewar argument that no gains could be secure without enfranchisement. Further, the demand for equality must be entered in the national ledger without delay, while a segment, at least, of the northern public seemed willing to acknowledge its black war debt. As early as December 1863, before a Washington audience, Langston argued that the battlefield contributions of black Americans confirmed their inherent claims to the vote. The national black convention at Syracuse in October 1864 ratified a black agenda for reconstruction drafted by the committee that Langston chaired. Its goals were "immediate and unconditional" abolition of slavery, racial unity and self-help, and equality before the law. The convention created a new black organization, the National Equal Rights League, and elected Langston president.

As head of the National Equal Rights League until early 1868, Langston shaped the first viable national black organization. The league foreshadowed in several respects the National Association for the Advancement of Colored People. It functioned through state and local auxiliaries and national conventions and employed such techniques as petition drives, lobbying of public officials, and civil rights litigation, while publicizing, on the one hand, black accomplishments and, on the other, southern white obstructionism. But from the outset of his presidency Langston confronted the same kind of personal, ideological, and sectional differences among the northern black leadership that had disrupted previous attempts at unity. His tactic for minimizing such conflict was to eschew public exchange of charges and countercharges. For example, when members of the proposed league executive board failed to attend meetings, Langston merely renewed his pleas for united effort. Meanwhile, with two secretaries conducting the league's routine business from a central office in Philadelphia, Langston took its message directly to the people. Throughout 1865 and into 1866 the league president, usually at the invitation of and in cooperation with local black groups, went into the upper South as well as the West and the Northeast. With black enfranchisement always the major object, Langston himself waged vigorous suffrage campaigns, not only in Ohio, but also in Kansas and Missouri. On the platform and in private, Langston sought to translate his people's rising hopes for freedom into an organized political force for black rights.

Blacks responded gradually. In the North leaders of prewar civil rights drives joined with men who had come to maturity during the war to set up local leagues and elect delegates to conventions where state leagues were formed. In the South self-emancipated and free-born blacks, including northern-educated teachers of the freedpeople, joined with black Union army veterans and others to lead such efforts. James H. Harris in North Carolina, a former slave, and J. Milton Turner in Missouri, slave-born but emancipated in childhood, both of whom had known Langston in Oberlin, sparked leagues in their own states. Through the league and his later Reconstruction activities, Langston formed close associations with emerging black leaders in the South and West, many of whom he subsequently introduced to white politicians in Washington. By war's end nine state auxiliaries already had been established; some twenty months later Langston could boast of state leagues nearly everywhere.

Langston and the National Equal Rights League represented black political aspirations in Washington. In the first days of Andrew Johnson's administration, Langston, who several months before had spoken in the Tennessee statehouse and met the presiding governor, secured an interview with the president. Diplomatically remarking that Johnson's "past history gives us full assurance that our liberty and rights will be fully protected and sustained," Langston, speaking for the league, articulated the black demands: "complete emancipation and full equality before American law." The league petitioned Congress in September 1865 for a constitutional amendment, based on the guarantee of a republican form of government for every state, that would prohibit "any legislation based on race or color." As Johnson's southern policy unfolded, Langston and league representatives set up lobbies in Washington in 1866 and 1867 and increasingly sought out white radicals. In January 1867, on the eve of Congressional Reconstruction, Langston helped to organize a forceful presentation of black "grievances and wants." A league-sponsored national black convention drew more than a hundred black delegates from seventeen states, nine of them southern, to Washington. In a cogent appeal to Congress, Langston, as league president, asked for a Reconstruction grounded upon "impartial justice, one that brings safety and peace to the loyal white American, happiness and prosperity to our common country, while it is the shield and buckler, the strong defense of the American freedmen."

For Langston the principle of black equality and Republican politics converged in the spring of 1867. Congress placed the South under military rule and authorized the enrollment of an electorate that for the first time included black males. Langston accepted dual appointments, prompted by Chief Justice Chase, as educational inspector for the Freedmen's Bureau and Republican party organizer of black voters in the South. As bureau inspector of schools in 1867 and 1868 he traveled from Maryland to Texas, urging black parents and children to acquire education, counseling teachers and principals on their duties, and investigating the black condition. He scrutinized the bureau's performance and often found it wanting. Bureau-supervised labor contracts between planters and freedpeople, for example, were "hard—too hard" on the latter, having a "very important bearing not only on [their] material prospects" but on their "educational and moral condition as well." Many of the bureau's subcommissioners, agents, and school superintendents Langston singled out as incompetent or indifferent and called for their replacement. By contrast, the young northern missionary teachers, black and white, won his approval as a dedicated and "generous" band who imparted "liberal and Christian" ideas to the freedpeople. Langston pressed Freedmen's Bureau officials in Washington both to seek clarification of the laws respecting free blacks' civil rights and to move quickly to set up the schools already authorized. Despite its shortcomings, Langston consistently supported continuation of the bureau as an "educational and political instrumentality."

Langston acted in a signal role for the Republican party. Building on the foundation laid by the National Equal Rights League, he organized Republican Union leagues across the South, through which, particularly in Virginia, Mississippi, and North Carolina in 1867, he instructed and encouraged freedpeople to register and to vote. Once black voters in Georgia and Louisiana had succeeded in electing some Negro representatives to their state constitutional conventions, he advised them on strategy and programs. In Louisiana he persuaded Oscar Dunn, a talented young black man, to run as a Republican for lieutenant governor, the post to which Dunn later was elected. Langston's encouragement of Dunn typified his belief that qualified blacks, while allying themselves in the Republican party with loyal white southerners and carpetbaggers supportive of equal rights, should assert their own claims to office.

Most conspicuously Langston delivered addresses in defense of Reconstruction policy before huge audiences, usually composed of both races, in almost every southern state. The style and substance of three powerful native traditions—black, evangelical, and democratic—that had helped to make him a popular orator in the prewar North proved equally attractive in the postwar South. He extracted such common values as self-reliance, pragmatism, optimism, fairness, and a belief in ordinary people to fashion speeches designed to reach intellect, emotion, and conscience. Courteous yet bold, earnest but with an affecting wit and warmth, Langston articulated radical principles in a reasonable tone, employing unthreatening language and assuming a generous and hopeful posture. His strong, musical voice, finished rhetoric, and arresting presence combined to charismatic effect.

Langston based his appeal to blacks on self-reliance, self-respect, and self-assertion. He insisted upon suffrage and all other rights of citizenship and expounded upon the concomitant obligations. Southern blacks were responsible for the institution of "loyal constitutions" and a "proper reconstruction" in their states. "Who shall bring the state back into the Union?" he queried an audience of Virginia free blacks. "You," he answered. He urged them to work hard to acquire education, property, and wealth, to "secure character and influence," and to use "these moral levers to elevate yourselves to the dignity of manhood and womanhood."

Langston's appeal to whites rested on enlightened self-interest. He extended a flattering, conciliatory vision of the southern role in the American past and its possibilities for the future and spoke in tactful, even empathetic terms of its "present temporary depression and distress." Aware that the self-help advice he directed to blacks spoke also to white concerns about a reliable work force, he assured them that blacks asked no special favors and needed only a "fair opportunity." He asked "nothing for the Negro because he was black, but because he was a man, he would ask everything for him that other men had." Interracial cooperation, based on justice and legal equality, would, he predicted, lead to an "unexampled prosperity and a superior civilization."

In 1868, following his address to a huge, racially mixed crowd in the hall of the Georgia constitutional convention, a member of the audience asked if the Negro was not too ignorant to vote. Drawing himself erect and folding his arms, Langston replied: "Your slavery has been very hard upon us; it was a fearful thing; it has terribly scarred our backs and limbs; it has kept us in ignorance; it closed our mouths; but it taught us to think, and to catch the words that fell from the white man's lips." Candor, courage, and civility characterized Langston's discourse.

With the free blacks enfranchised, Langston pressed his views on labor, land, and integration, while persistently urging governmental protection. He insisted that the terms of government-supervised labor contracts be "liberally and fully met." In an address to the Louisiana constitutional convention in December 1867 Langston put forward a taxation plan designed to shift landownership and economic power toward loyalist whites and blacks. He called for a levy on the property of former Confederates to defray the costs of the war; in cases of noncompliance, the government should appropriate the lands and sell them to pay the debt. In the wake of the 1868 elections, Langston and fellow black members of a newly constituted National Executive Committee tried to persuade Congress to throw open public lands in several southern states through homestead legislation and simultaneously entreated business leaders and benevolent homestead associations to extend loans to Negroes for land purchases. Langston proposed an integrated public school system, first to framers of the Louisiana constitution and again in the Alabama and Georgia state capitals in early 1868. "I demand, in the name of the poor degraded white," he told a vast crowd in Montgomery, "that every school in the land be opened to him, and that to the poorest black, the school be likewise opened." He conceived of integrated schools as the bedrock of black Americanization. "This is no more a white man's country and government than it is the country and government of the black man," he declared, " . . . it is the country and the government of the American people."

Langston's political performance in the South drew plaudits from nearly every quarter. Conservative whites, uncertain of the course of Reconstruction, offered such praise less as a tribute to his oratory than as a token of their own designs of winning the new black electorate. But loyal whites appreciated Langston's moderate sounding approach and a program that promised their political, economic, and educational advancement. The free blacks, harboring their own dreams of landownership and independence, warmed to his example, his lack of condescension, and his vision of the educated, property-holding, dignified, enfranchised black American. Conservative white newspapers painted him as a responsible partisan, their radical counterparts as a bold advocate of their doctrine. State and local Republican leaders, white and black, lauded his persuasiveness with both races. White northern party organizers in the South, like the ubiquitous Thomas Conway, respected their black colleague as a motivator who could impel blacks to be "bolder for the right" and as a negotiator who could smooth factional differences within the southern party. In fact, Langston's moderating intervention in a Virginia dispute so impressed one leading white southern Unionist that he proposed the black Republican should be the party's candidate for vice-president in 1868. In a similar vein, the quality of his black leadership inspired black Congressman Josiah Walls of Florida, three years later at a southern black convention, to risk the Republican party's disfavor by nominating Langston to be President Grant's running mate in 1872.

Langston emerged from his southern tours more than ever persuaded of two fundamental needs for black advancement: "an equal and impartial education" and an understanding of the law. Howard University, in the fall of 1868, offered him the opportunity to forward these aims. During a six-and-one-half-year tenure as professor and later dean of the law department, and from December 1873 to July 1875 as vice-president and acting president of the university, Langston set out to construct an educational institution on the Oberlin model, open to both races (though preponderantly black) and both sexes and with rigorous academic standards. The law curriculum that he inaugurated emphasized classical as well as professional training, moral and social concerns, and a thorough grounding in oratory. Law students, black and white, gained practical experience and supported themselves through jobs that Langston, tapping his political associates, found for them in offices of the Grant administration. Langston communicated the potential of the law to his students, a number of whom went on to combine legal careers with civil rights activism: he made them feel, one afterward remarked, "the grandeur of responsibility." Just as in Oberlin, where Langston had paid marked attention to young black men and women, inviting them to his home and providing them (as well as white students) with scholarships, he

118

similarly encouraged and assisted students at Howard, among whom he attracted a wide following. Youthful race leaders, educated at Howard, Oberlin, and elsewhere, constituted an important element of Langston's national constituency.

His strong record at Howard notwithstanding, its board of trustees dealt Langston the first major defeat of his career. He made a bid to assume the presidency in his own right in the spring of 1875, and although the board, dominated by Congregationalist church members with close ties to the American Missionary Association, had honored him a year earlier, it now rejected him on a strictly racial ballot. Alarmed at the spreading northern disenchantment with Reconstruction and the proportionate dwindling of financial support for A.M.A. projects in the South, white trustees were considering downgrading the popular law department and other professional studies and otherwise redirecting Howard on a more accommodationist course. They deemed Langston—black, egalitarian, and, despite his theological training, a non–church member—ill-suited for this task. Angry and embittered, he was gratified when the entire law faculty resigned in protest. Further, he and Frederick Douglass called on July 4, 1875, for a black "Declaration of Independence" of organizations that treated blacks as less than equal.

Though Douglass rose to Langston's defense on this occasion, their relationship already showed signs of strain. Douglass and some other eastern black elders, with whom Langston had enjoyed amicable, if distant, associations in the prewar black struggle, had never been known for easy tolerance of competing claimants to racial allegiance. The close proximity of black notables in politically charged, gossipy Washington, where Langston took up permanent residence in 1871, promoted rivalry and discord. Under the pressures of national leadership, moreover, Langston's earlier proud modesty too often tended to dissolve into defensive vanity, particularly when black critics baited him. By 1873 a black journalist suggested that the one or two black men whose leadership stature was comparable to Langston's—obviously alluding to Douglass—considered him insincere and pretentious, more absorbed with "exaltation of self" than with advancement of race. While Langston praised Douglass on countless occasions as the greatest black American, the press engaged in unremitting speculation as to their respective claims to the title, advertising any controversy between them. In 1884 Douglass made an unkind remark concerning Langston's youngest son, who had shot and killed a man; and this, on top of earlier differences that were more personal than political, caused Langston to break with him.

In the meantime, Langston functioned as the Republican party's most active and, except for Douglass, most consequential black spokesman. No ranking Republican made a more concise estimate of Langston's political worth than President Grant, who said that Langston, "a gentleman of liberal education and high standing . . . has much influence with the people of his race." The party made heavy use of his talents, dispatching him in the 1872 presidential election alone to ten states, evenly divided between North and South, to deliver more than sixty speeches. Gratitude, self-interest, and patriotism dictated black support for Republicans, Langston argued, even though the party had "much room for improvement" in its treatment of Negroes. Utilizing his access to both moderate and radical Republicans, he pressed for patronage for blacks. The administration's response to such urgings as his 1871 call for a "very prominent and influential federal position" for a black man was limited to a modest number of mainly low-level black appointments, usually cleared through him. One of the more substantial was the naming of Langston himself to the Board of Health of the District of Columbia in 1871, where he served for six and one-half years. Despite determined resistance on all sides, Langston, in the sensitive position of finance cochairman, and the four white board members managed not only to avoid entanglement in the widespread governmental corruption but to improve the quality of life in the capital while forwarding the revolutionary concept of public responsibility for private health. Langston, serving as legal counsel, drafted the sanitation code for the district.

During the 1870s Langston displayed mounting concern about the defense and expansion of black rights. In interviews with President Grant he pushed for protection from the Klan and other extralegal organizations, and at Grant's request he undertook a southern tour in 1871 to document the growing violence and intimidation directed at black and radical white voters. In his major effort to secure black equality before the law, Langston, at the behest of Massachusetts senator Charles Sumner, drafted the bill that—shorn of the integrated school provisions Langston considered fundamental to the ultimate resolution of the race problem—would become the Supplementary Civil Rights Act of 1875. During the five-year interim between the bill's introduction and its passage, Langston, through speeches, memorials to Congress, and organized lobbying efforts, urged the legislation as the means to attain "peace and good order" and to promote "the welfare of our entire nation."

Langston's egalitarian vision and the relative progress of free blacks nonetheless increasingly came into sharp, deadly conflict with white supremacy. As late as September 1870, on an inspection tour of the South, he had been impressed by the Negro's generally improving condition. His major criticism concerned the drinking, fighting, and quarreling among many blacks during elections. In the next years, however, black advancement was checked and then halted. By the end of the seventies Langston offered a considered judgment of the essential flaws in the Reconstruction process. The behavior of the freed people, "in the main," had been "moderate and manly," but the North had never been committed to their elevation, either morally or politically. The government should have settled black men and women on lands specifically appropriated to them; provision for their education should have come earlier and been more thorough. There had been too much "political excitement and agitation," too many "incompetent" governmental officials in the South, and too often the legislatures had been composed of "largely ignorant, unqualified, impecunious whites and blacks." Most important of all, the "former master class," with a "hatred intense and seemingly implacable," had waged "systematic warfare" on Republicans, white and black, from 1865 onward, "growing steadily worse" until at times the "violence, intimidation, and murder" seemed to threaten "utter destruction."

The widespread condemnation of Republican Reconstruction confronted Langston in 1877 with an all but impossible choice between principle and politics. The New Departure policy of Rutherford B. Hayes—calling for conciliation of the South and pacification of the country—threatened the abandonment of free blacks. In interviews with the new president, whom he had known since the mid-1850s, Langston pressed for and received assurances that Hayes would honor his pledges to protect and promote black Americans. Further, in addition to his public pleas for respect of black rights, Hayes made two major promises to black delegations: if his southern policy did not prove beneficial, he would change it; he would appoint Langston and Douglass to "conspicuous positions." Heeding the demands of practicality and personal ambition, Langston led the black leadership in endorsement of the New Departure. Yet by the fall of 1877 it became apparent that the president, however sincere his intentions might have been, had to conform to an atmosphere wherein prosperity and peace drawn to southern specifications took precedence over Negro citizenship. Only two years later Langston pronounced the condition of free blacks in the South "practical enslavement" and called for black emigration to the North and West. The exodus, he argued, was the Negro's chance to throw off "utter dependence upon the old slave-holding class . . . and thus secure to himself the fact as well as the consciousness of real freedom." His disillusionment with Hayes did not stop there. The appointment tendered to Langston, rumored for months to be the influential post of commissioner of agriculture, had turned out to be one previously held by a black man— minister to Haiti.

Langston served in Haiti for eight years, most of that time as dean of the diplomatic corps, and performed with characteristic efficiency. Nevertheless, in 1882 a Democratic-controlled House of Representatives, rebuking Langston for vigorously campaigning for the election of President Garfield, reduced his salary by one-third. Three years later when Langston, as a Republican loyalist, resigned his post at the start of a new Democratic administration, he contended that the House had acted illegally because it had failed to repeal the original salary-setting enactment, and he presented the government with a demand for back pay totaling nearly $8,000. The Supreme Court upheld his claim, in a precedential decision. It was expressive of Langston's abiding sensitivity to racial slights that his suit was undertaken as much for personal vindication as for recovery of the money due him.

Returning to his native state in 1885, Langston hoped to spark a black political resurgence in the face of Democratic consolidation of power across the South. The ensuing struggle to uphold the principles he had defended over a lifetime—liberty, equal rights, and black American manhood—would call forth all his resources of character, skill, and experience.

Langston found a political base in Virginia's heavily black Fourth Congressional District. At the invitation of Virginia Republicans he headed the state college for Negroes in Petersburg, the district's urban center, for almost two years. His efforts to make Virginia Normal and Collegiate Institute a showcase of black capability met heavy resistance from the Democrats now in control of the state, who forced his resignation in the fall of 1887. In January 1888 Langston announced his intention to run for Congress. The obstacles were formidable: William Mahone, the beleaguered Republican boss, had no wish to surrender his party's sole remaining stronghold to a black man; black voters were beholden to the Mahone machine for the few favors they had received over the years; and Democrats controlled the state election machinery. Despite Langston's endeavors to win over Mahone, including the intercession of such prominent Republicans as presidential aspirant John Sherman (whose nomination Langston seconded at the Republican National Convention), the "boss" remained adamant. Mahone manipulated the party apparatus to block Langston's nomination by the district Republican convention, forcing him to run as an independent. Langston did succeed, however, in neutralizing the Republican National Committee's official attitude toward the dispute, an important factor in the final outcome.

Langston conducted a ten-month campaign to organize and reeducate the black electorate. Relying heavily on a cadre of educated, property-holding, politically experienced black professional men, soliciting the services of local black leaders and ministers, drawing on the zeal of former students from Virginia Normal, and bringing in women as equal partners, he thoroughly organized the district. He bought a campaign headquarters that also served for rallies, supported a newspaper, employed numerous campaign workers, and flooded the district with printed materials, spending at least $15,000 of his own money. In speeches, usually of at least two hours' duration, the black "bolter" reiterated Republican policies. But his most profound entreaty was for his people's aid in his "desperate struggle to establish the manhood, honor, and fidelity of the Negro race."

Blacks locally and around the country offered ardent support. A significant exception was the alienated Douglass. At Mahone's request, Douglass furnished a broadside charging that Langston was exploiting the race issue for selfish reasons: "No encouragement should be given to any man whose mad political ambition would imperil the success of the Republican party." Douglass's action drew general condemnation. Langston invited him to write another letter "and the gods shall have my election sure beyond a doubt."

Langston elaborated an election day strategy to circumvent the obstruction posed by Democratic control of the electoral mechanisms. Several hundred paid workers fanned out across the district to record the names and addresses of those who voted for Langston or were prevented from doing so. When the predictable fraud, intimidation, and bribery occurred and the Democratic candidate was declared the victor, Langston used these records to challenge the election. After a strenuous and protracted fight, involving an additional cost to the black challenger of some $10,000, Congress finally voted in September 1890—almost two years after the election—to seat Langston. Within days he was back in Virginia campaigning for reelection. Though he believed he won handily, the Democrats repeated their 1888 performance. This time the new Democratic dominance of the House of Representatives ensured that Langston's defeat was final.

In the three months he served as a lame duck congressman, Langston put into the national record his ideas on popular suffrage and higher education for blacks. His maiden address was an extemporaneous argument for nearly an hour in favor of a federal election bill aimed at establishing a free ballot and a fair count. In a further effort to forestall the disfranchisement of Negroes and white Republicans in the South, he introduced a resolution for a constitutional amendment to require literacy tests of all voters in federal elections, to reduce each state's representation in proportion to the number allowed to vote as compared to the whole number of males twenty-one years of age and older, and to give Congress the power of enforcement. Langston hoped to curtail southern influence in Congress and secure federal supervision of voting, while undercutting white complaints of Negro ignorance. Moreover, he remained confident of his people's impressive strides toward literacy. To enhance black educational opportunity he introduced a bill to create a national industrial university for Negroes. The proposal, reflective of contemporary enthusiasm for industrial education, contemplated not a mere trade school but an institution providing collegiate and professional training as well as instruction "in any special industrial occupation or trade." The long-time proponent of an integrated education bowed to reality in delimiting his scheme to black students, male and female. While voting restrictions applied equally to both races and industrial education for blacks were also aspects of Booker T. Washington's program, Langston—unlike the younger man—never endorsed the "separate but equal" philosophy, never blamed blacks for their condition, and never retreated from insistence on political and civil rights.

Throughout his remaining years Langston continued to interweave black protest, politics, education, and the law. While maintaining a voting residence in Petersburg, he practiced law in the District of Columbia, wrote his autobiography, *From the Virginia Plantation to the National Capitol,* and carried on a vigorous speaking schedule, frequently appearing at black colleges. In the early 1890s he tried to persuade Republican officials to protect black lives and voting rights and, at the same time, pursued appointment as a federal judge. In these fruitless efforts he jockeyed in Virginia for the favor of warring party chieftains, his old archenemy Mahone included, and wielded his prestige with the black electorate, stumping the North for Republican candidates in 1891 and 1892. When the Republicans went down to defeat in 1892 Langston charged it to their studied neglect of black interests and, though remaining an active Republican himself, advised blacks to vote in the future for the candidate or party that defended them. Even as Langston witnessed the beginnings of legal disfranchisement and segregation, he held to his faith that the principle of black equality could be reconciled with politics. "One day," he predicted in

1894, "the white and colored will join hands and abolish these evils." A year before death he advocated that "our strongest, most promising sons" study for the bar. "For it is in the courts, by the law," he added, in words that adumbrated the major direction of black protest for well over half a century, "that we shall, finally, settle all questions connected with the recognition of the rights, the equality, the full citizenship of colored Americans."

As Langston reflected on the significance of his congressional victory he could only conclude, as one of his most devoted students commented, that it demonstrated that "the Negro has organizing ability, and that there is race cohesiveness among our people when the necessities of the situation demand it." With his people's help Langston had won his campaign and then, however briefly, had forced his party to adhere to principle. He was convinced his victory would stand as a validation of the "justice and philosophy of equal rights."

Despite the sweep of Langston's achievement, he has been little remembered. It may be instructive to compare Langston in this regard with Douglass, his great contemporary. While each made distinctive contributions to the black struggle for freedom, equal rights, and human dignity, Douglass, already deemed the foremost black American of his day when Langston was still a schoolboy, was enshrined in the abolitionist movement, a cause of enduring respectability even after the freed men and women themselves had been forgotten. By contrast, Langston came forcibly to national attention during Reconstruction and its aftermath through radical politics rooted in equal rights, an ideology largely discredited and disowned by its former white adherents even at the time of his death. Deprived of the white sponsorship that was key to the national memory, Langston also exerted a more fragile hold on the black imagination than did Douglass. "The people respected and appreciated Langston as they appreciated Sumner and [Wendell] Phillips," a black journalist observed in 1933; "they loved Douglass as they loved their deprived selves." Douglass left a large body of writing, personal papers, and notable autobiographies. Most of Langston's papers were destroyed. The autobiography he published in 1894 with the idea of cementing his reputation had the ironic consequence, as Afro-American editor T. Thomas Fortune anticipated, of doing it "permanent damage." Hastily written while the defeats of his political hopes for himself and his people were fresh and his needs for justification strong, it was grandiloquent, boastful, and seemed self-serving, though in fact it omitted many of his accomplishments.

An examination of the record, however, begins to reveal why

Langston's generation of Americans, black and white, held him in such high esteem. It may reestablish the legacy that is suggested in a story told by Langston Hughes, the Harlem folk and revolutionary poet who was Langston's grandnephew. During his congressional term, Langston customarily rode to the Capitol from his residence near Howard University in a "sleek black rubber-tired carriage, drawn by two snow-white horses, with a coachman at the reins"—one of the "sweet chariots of this world." His route took him through a section inhabited by whites who "did not relish seeing a Negro ride in such style," and one day Langston found a wooden barricade blocking his passage. On a subsequent day, after legislative hours, the congressman stopped off at a hardware store on Pennsylvania Avenue where he purchased an ax. When his carriage arrived at the barrier, he dismounted, handed his gloves to the coachman, took the ax, and proceeded with all deliberate speed to chop it down. Thereafter, unimpeded, Langston "rode behind his snow-white horses through the streets of Washington, the ebony spokes of his highly lacquered carriage wheels gleaming." John Mercer Langston, his kinsman recollected, "did not believe in barriers."

A Last Stern Struggle:
Henry Highland Garnet and
Liberation Theory

AT LEAST ONE generation of Garnets had died in Maryland slavery and two more, by the time of Henry Highland Garnet's birth in 1815, faced that possibility. Indeed, oppression in the Garnet family was aggravated as births and deaths took place, leaving an influence on Henry that he later drew on in formulating his strategy for making slaves aware of the consequences of continued degradation in slavery. His grandfather had gone through the whole process of captivity in Africa, the middle passage, and enslavement in America, where he also saw his offspring, Henry's father, enslaved. On the death of their owner, the threat of imminent division of the family led the father, using the pretext of attending a funeral, to secure passes for the family to travel from the plantation. With his wife and children at his side he drove a covered wagon from the plantation and, traveling mainly on foot, escaped from Maryland into Wilmington, Delaware, where contact was made with Thomas Garrett, a Quaker noted for assisting slave runaways. With Garrett's help the Garnets moved on to Pennsylvania before reaching New York City in 1825. Thus, in a single act of daring, under George Garnet's leadership, the cycle of oppression in slavery was broken for the Garnet family.

To New York blacks Henry Garnet's father gave no evidence in bearing or appearance that he had ever been a slave. Alexander Crummell, whose parents lived next door to the Garnets, had rarely met anyone more grand or stately in character and stature, "a perfect Apollo, in form and figure; with beautifully moulded limbs and fine and delicate features; just like hundreds of grand Mandingoes I have seen in Africa; whose full blood he carried in his veins." The absence of servility in freedom suggests an earlier refusal by George Garnet to accept in spirit any notion of inherent inferiority, which resulted in part from the character of his own father—he was said to have been a chief—with whom he apparently lived for some years and whose fate, together with his own, might explain his sober demeanor. A certain reticence on matters of slavery in the presence of youths, however, was common for former slaves, which could account for how little is known of the Garnet family in Maryland. The principal source is Crummell, who knew Henry's parents well, but not well enough to elicit from them information about their lives as slaves.

Not long after their arrival in New York, George Garnet led the family in a ceremony that was carried out on countless occasions in antebellum America and following emancipation in 1865—a "baptism to liberty." He spoke directly to each member of the family, beginning with his wife: "Wife, they used to call you Hennie. . . . But in future your name is Elizabeth." Touching his daughter: "Your name is not Mary any longer, but Eliza." Then he took Henry on his knee: "And my dear little boy . . . your name is Henry. My name is George Garnet." This ceremony, a conscious effort to reclaim an identity—a certain power of definition for the family—could scarcely have occurred in a more propitious place, for it was said that blacks in New York took pride in their African heritage "and hesitated not to refer to themselves as free Africans." It would seem that George Garnet, though he had not known freedom before, entered among them with a high level of consciousness, able to meet enormously difficult challenges, which more than any other factor inspired Henry's faith in the utility of self-exertion.

The Garnets were not in New York for more than two years when a frightening incident hastened Henry's maturation and left him poised to fight, possibly to kill, for freedom. A relative of Colonel Spencer, the former owner of the Garnets, had traced them to their doorstep and asked for George Garnet, which led the father to leap from a window twenty feet above ground to the Crummell yard. Though he escaped, his daughter was later apprehended but released after convincing the authorities that she was not a runaway. Away at sea as a cabin boy, Henry returned to discover his family scattered and living in various residences on Long Island. For some time, infuriated, he walked the streets of New York with a knife as protection if approached by slave catchers. Such developments reminded the Garnets, along with other free blacks, of the continuing bond between them and slaves. From that time on, Crummell thought, Henry bore the responsibilities of a man.

The spirit of nationalism was strong in the religion of New York blacks and reflected in mutual aid societies such as the New York African Society for Mutual Relief, the New York African Marine Fund, and the Clarkson and Wilberforce benevolent societies—all of which were prominent in the opening decades of the nineteenth century. Around the banners of such organizations, with the New

York African Society for Mutual Relief in the lead, thousands of New York blacks, including young Henry and many of his friends, gathered on July 5, 1827, to celebrate Emancipation Day in New York State. James McCune Smith, a participant in the parade, left a record of the day: "The side-walks were crowded with the wives, daughters, sisters and mothers of the celebrants representing every state in the Union, and not a few with gay bandanna handkerchiefs, betraying their West Indian birth: neither was Africa itself unrepresented, hundreds who had survived the middle passage . . . joined in the joyful procession. The people of those days rejoiced in their nationality and hesitated not to call each other African or descendants of Africa."

African interaction was recognizable in New York, Pennsylvannia, and New England from the mid-eighteenth century throughout the slave era and was essential to the formation of a single people out of a multiplicity of African ethnic groups in the North as well as the South. Indeed, ethnic interaction was common in black America and did not go unnoticed by observers of the times. What caught their eye at celebrations such as Emancipation Day—the variety of African peoples—was perhaps no less noticeable and hardly less consequential than when blacks had contact with each other in the normal course of events. In any case, apart from his links with Africa through members of his family, the presence of such disparate groups of Africans provided Henry with a broader conception of the possibilities for African unity in America and in the world.

Henry was twelve at the time of the parade and, though he understood little of the culture of those parading, the experience for him and the other participants had the effect of heightening whatever sense of oneness they possessed. A principal source of his nationalism, it appears, was rooted in that awareness, in the knowledge that he and his family were of African descent and *of* those in the parade. Related to the cultural interaction of participants in the parade in ways not fully understood was the assumption by black leaders of responsibility for their people everywhere. In the First African Baptist Society of Albany, New York, Rev. Nathaniel Paul, immediately after Emancipation Day, stated the prevalent thesis of black leaders regarding enslaved Africans: "The progress of emancipation, though slow, is nevertheless certain. . . . I therefore have no hesitation in declaring from this sacred place, that not only throughout the United States of America, but throughout every part of the habitable world where slavery exists, it will be abolished."

A measure of the potential for sophistication of New York blacks was the society of Garnet's classmates at the New York African Free

School, established by the New York Manumission Society, whose membership included Alexander Hamilton. But the circle of Garnet's associates was charmed in its own right, for seldom had so talented a group of young black scholars been assembled in America, among them Crummell, who became an eminent pastor; Ira Aldridge, who gained fame abroad as a Shakespearean tragedian; Thomas S. Sidney, a precocious young scholar who died at an early age; and Samuel Ringgold Ward, who established a reputation as a logician of liberty. In youth they formed, together with others of talent, a network of relationships in which Garnet was at the center, one that in due course, given his uncommon ability, all but guaranteed him a place of leadership in black America. Moreover, Theodore S. Wright, the distinguished black Presbyterian minister who baptized and took Henry under his wing, helped direct the youth toward a path of future distinction and probably had some influence on his desire to become a minister.

Following their matriculation at the African Free School, Garnet, Sidney, and Crummell continued to study together. On invitation in 1835 from Noyes Academy, they traveled some 400 miles to Canaan, New Hampshire. It was a particularly trying time for Henry, who was suffering from a lame leg, for rarely would a hotel or an inn sell the youths food, and nowhere could they find shelter. Shortly after their arrival at Noyes—on the Fourth of July—a group of farmers from a wide region of New Hampshire resolved to put an end to the school, and they did so the following month, seizing the building "with ninety yoke of oxen" and dragging it "off into a swamp about a half mile from its site." This violent act led Henry and his band of friends, including eleven other blacks in attendance, to prepare for an expected attempt on their lives. Under Henry's leadership—he was then nineteen—they moulded bullets and, as night fell, waited in darkness. The pain of a bad leg burned steadily in Garnet's consciousness, compounded by his recollection of the long tension of his escape from slavery and his return from sea to find his family scattered by slave catchers. Such ruminations, even as he attempted to cheer up his classmates, ended as one swift rider passed their boardinghouse, firing at it as other lawless elements held back in the dark, an assault rebuffed as Garnet's shotgun "blazed through the window."

When the black students left Canaan, the mob gathered on the outskirts of the village and fired a cannon at the departing wagon. For his part Garnet had drawn strength from his past as he had from the blast of fire that halted the raiders that night in New Hampshire. Inheritance and experience were forming a leader in whom thoughtfulness and a willingness to take risks were present in fine measure, which helps to explain his readiness, within a decade of his experience at Canaan, to call slaves to resistance.

On hearing that the Oneida Institute in Whitesboro, New York, was open to black youth, Garnet repaired there and remained for three years, studying under Beriah Green, a fine teacher of "intellectual and moral philosophy" who believed in the capacity of blacks for scholarship. Garnet also studied Greek, logic and rhetoric, the sciences of government, and the New Testament. Despite the opportunity for systematic study, poor health prevented him from availing himself of it. At Oneida he was largely thrown back on his own intellectual resources, cultivating an original cast of mind, the most striking feature of which was a certain prophetic quality. Related to that was a quality of intuition, wrote Crummell, "by which, without any labored processes of reasoning, and free from all metaphysical verbiage, he invariably reached, as by a straight and sudden dash, the clearest conception of his argument." As early as his African Free School days, Henry's brilliance apparently set him apart from even the brightest students around him.

Garnet's association with abolitionists through the African Free School (thanks to the New York Manumission Society), Noyes Academy, and the Oneida Institute had a powerful effect on him, leading him to accept some whites as allies in the struggle, all the more since he had met Thomas Garrett, whose role in his family's escape to freedom had been indispensable. But that meeting and his attendance at the African Free School had been arranged by his parents, the one a factor in his freedom, the other enabling him to begin his formal education, and both making it possible for friendly whites to come into his life without him seeking them out. Yet something of the suffering of blacks in the North as well as the South was witnessed by the Garnets, within the context of white American indifference, for Henry to see the negative aspects of black-white relations more than balance those that were positive. His awareness of an antislavery white minority and a proslavery majority was an argument for the view that the oppressed must take responsibility for liberating themselves, which was the continuing example of his father, who sometimes preceded him as a speaker on abolitionist platforms—on which Beriah Green was also present—in the late 1830s.

At a meeting commemorating the seventh anniversary of the American Anti-Slavery Society, Green arranged for his former student to address leading white abolitionists on the question of slavery. At roughly the same time Garnet came to the attention of the national black community as a theorist of black liberation during a nationalist-integrationist debate over the proper strategy for effecting liberation. In *The Colored American* he warned William Whipper and other advocates of integration—the spirit of which "ran all over the free states"—that one day they would realize that blacks have a better understanding of their cause than others and, therefore, if the work is to be done they must do it themselves. Using the pseudonym "Sidney" in response to Whipper's argument that only color-blind leadership could win freedom for blacks, Garnet declared self-exertion "the great law of our being." No matter how hard white abolitionists worked, the condition of his people would "remain the same ... unmitigated, until we awaken to a consciousness of a momentous responsibility. . . . We occupy a position, and sustain relations which they cannot possibly assume. They are our allies—*Ours* is the battle."

The history of all liberation movements, including the American Revolution, Garnet argued, confirmed the wisdom of the position that the oppressed must free themselves. It would not be otherwise for his own people, a view widely supported by blacks in the antebellum period but one to which Garnet gave special resonance in his exchanges with Whipper. Not only did he agree that "who would be free themselves must strike the blow," but he found the strength to do so self-generative, its sources in his people. In the most comprehensive terms he affirmed self-exertion as "the course hallowed by the efforts, and prayers, and benedictions of receding age, and the living energy and undying fervor of youth—the mode in which our best men, the living and the dead, have labored—not ineffectually—for years, in behalf of the rights of the people."

Garnet was pastoring in Troy, New York, when he pointed out in a speech before the Liberty party in 1842 that profound obligations to assist in the liberation process rested with whites. The efforts of the Liberty party and its abolitionist supporters were in fact contributing to the slaves' sense that "their claims to liberty and happiness" might be *established by law,* which leaves in doubt how blacks could win the battle through a legislative process dominated by whites. Nevertheless, western abolitionists with their belief in political action based on the Constitution as an antislavery document, in contrast to the Garrisonians who thought their efforts were doomed to failure, gave the slaves reason to believe they would one day "sit under their own vine and their own fig tree." The slaves knew they had "friends in the North in whom they may *confide* in case they are driven to desperation." Prefiguring in almost precise detail a conclusion that Frederick Douglass would draw a few years later, Garnet argued that it was that safety valve that prevented "a general insurrection of the slaves from spreading carnage and devastation throughout the entire South." But more powerful forces ruled out the "deliverance" of slaves by violence: "No, the time for a last stern struggle has not yet come (may it never be necessary.) The finger of the Almighty will hold back the trigger, and his all powerful arm will sheathe the sword till the oppressor's cup is full."

Why he changed his mind so quickly is unclear, but within a year Garnet had embraced a revolutionary stand. Impatience with the pace of racial progress, despite the relatively short lapse of time between the Liberty party speech and his "Address to the Slaves of the United States," was perhaps a factor, but the pace had been slow all along. A more decisive influence, it is likely, was his reading or rereading of David Walker's *Appeal,* issued in Boston in 1829 and widely banned in the South, for there he met a stern God whose sword, if not flashing, was ready to be unsheathed. Perhaps reading the *Appeal,* in which Walker's criticism of the oppressor is unflinching, caused Garnet to call the slaves to resistance. In doing so, though only twenty-eight, he spoke with the authority of an older man, legitimizing that authority by invoking the ancestors.

His address, delivered at Buffalo, New York, in 1843, at the National Colored Convention, has not received the attention it deserves, which makes it the more regrettable that we do not have a text either of Douglass's response or of Garnet's response to Douglass, which lasted an hour and a half and which some contemporaries have called Garnet's greatest speech. One suspects that there has been so little analysis of the address because scholarship generally holds that any major revolt would have been crushed, its chances of success having been almost nonexistent. When one considers, however, the fear that raced through the white South as a result of Nat Turner's revolt (though the revolt helped to cut off debate over the possibility of emancipating Virginia slaves), the fear in white Charleston that attended the Vesey conspiracy (though the conspiracy was brutally suppressed), and the fear that Walker's *Appeal* sent coursing through the white South (leading legislatures to ban its entry into a number of states), one can better appreciate Garnet's rationale in urging slave resistance. Moreover, the adoption of his views on slave resistance as those of the convention, with some obligation to circulate the document, would have strengthened black radicalism at the time and, it is likely, hastened the day of Douglass's adoption of a more militant strategy of black liberation.

Garnet himself, before his leg was amputated in 1840, had planned to go south to foment revolt. In any case, it was clear to him, from the revolts and conspiracies of the antebellum period, that a rising of thousands of slaves might not have been required to achieve his purpose; that resistance of the Nat Turner variety in three or four sections of the South simultaneously or in some degree of succession might have been a warning against slavery so stark as to force renewed debate, and possibly action, on slavery in Virginia and elsewhere. Indeed, Garnet allowed for such a possibility by invoking the names of Vesey and Turner as well as that of Toussaint. His exhortations were premised on the belief that the slaves' failure to bring a halt to their oppression guaranteed their offspring being heir to it, a subject considered in his earlier response to William Whipper:

> We behold our ancestors in the earliest situation in the country subjected to the most cruel wrongs and inhuman severities. Tracing their condition through successive generations, each and every succeeding one receiving to itself the accumulated sufferings and indignities of all the preceeding.... We come down to our times and find ourselves enfeebled in soul, power and capacity, with minds without culture ... with such an amount of oppression upon us as to awaken a bitter sense of consciousness ... of that oppression which is destroying with fearful certainty and unerring precision.

His concern with consciousness, with the need for slaves to realize in the clearest manner possible the master's dependence on them and therefore the absurdity of slavery, was brilliantly developed by the time he called on slaves, if need be, to die for freedom. The burden of that concern was the continuing and mounting cost of slavery, a concern that became more compelling with time, for the longer slavery persisted the more acute the consciousness of those who grasped the nature of their suffering, the more intolerable, therefore, their condition. Such a conception of consciousness recognized, crucially, that the source of African disaffection was originally an interior one: "Two hundred and twenty-seven years ago, the first of our injured race were brought to the shores of America. They came not with their own consent, to find an unmolested enjoyment of the blessings of this fruitful soil."

The effects of oppression built in collective memory from the time blacks were wrenched from the African homeland. This was Garnet's meaning when he reminded slaves that their ancestors had come "with broken hearts, from their beloved native land, and were doomed to unrequited toil and deep degradation. Nor did their bondage end with emancipation by death." Just as a profound sense of oppression was retained by many slaves, their sense of freedom before enslavement was retained as well; together they were combustibles of liberty, as in the Garnet family's encounter with slavery. Garnet's father was born on the same plantation as his son, inheriting the condition of *his* father, who before being taken prisoner in a tribal war had been free in Africa. "But the fires of liberty were never quenched in the blood of the family; and they burst forth into an ardent flame in the bosom of George Garnet, the son of the native African warrior."

The experience of the Garnets was not unique; rather, it was Henry's ability to formulate it in spiritual and psychological terms that led him to argue at Buffalo that "years have rolled on, and tens of thousands have been borne on streams of blood and tears, to the shores of eternity." Since the passage of time only multiplied suffering, death as a consequence of seeking freedom might result less from a lack of forethought, as Thomas Jefferson argued, than from recognition that the alternative might be a life of never knowing freedom, of which Garnet was deeply conscious. The whole cycle of spiritual pain and unrest was captured in a single sentence: "Succeeding generations inherited their chains, and millions have come from eternity into time, and have returned again to the world of spirits, cursed and maimed by American Slavery." That perception was a source of Garnet's demand: "You had better all die—*die immediately,* than live slaves and entail your wretchedness upon your posterity. If you would be free in this generation, here is your only hope." He continued: "But you are a patient people. You act as though you were made for the special use of those devils. You act as though your daughters were born to pamper the lusts of your masters and overseers. And worse than all, you tamely submit while your lords tear your wives from your embraces and defile them before your eyes. In the name of God, we ask, are you men? Where is the blood of your fathers? Has it all run out of your veins?" Garnet added: "Awake, awake; millions of voices are calling you! Your dead fathers speak to you from their graves."

Douglass's opposition to Garnet's address was the decisive factor in its rejection. That the two were engaged in discussion of the merits of slave resistance added to the importance and dramatic tension of the debate, to which both brought impressive skills. Douglass could hardly have been better prepared to present the case for moral suasion, having spent two years in the company of abolitionists of the stature of William Lloyd Garrison and Wendell Phillips. He argued for moral suasion "a little longer" in opposing Garnet, in whose person and address he found "too much physical force." He wished to avoid the insurrection that would occur if the advice "either of the address or the gentleman Garnet be followed." However, two years after the address at Buffalo,

Douglass wrote: "But for these Holidays the slave would be forced to the wildest desperation; and woe betide the slaveholder, the day he ventures to remove or hinder the operation of those conductors! I warn him that, in such an event, a spirit will go forth in their midst, more to be dreaded than the most appalling earthquake."

Although Garnet's economic views were more fully developed at a later time, they had begun to flower as he entered public life earlier in the decade and help to explain the urgency of his plea for a slave revolt. In laying the foundation of much of the nation's wealth, the slaves demonstrated how much the master needed them. In fact, the basis of all that the master class valued, including its leisure, was made possible by slave labor. It was precisely their labor that "contributed greatly in supporting the science and literature of the South." It was absurd, therefore, for whites to argue that blacks were not prepared for freedom: "We are told that the slaves could not take care of themselves if they were free . . . when now they take care of themselves, and their masters too, and that under the blighting influence of slavery." Consequently, Garnet also encouraged slaves to demand wages, which was tantamount to a call to insurrection.

Despite the fact that his was perhaps the most genuinely creative mind in the cause of black liberation, Garnet was never able fully to consolidate his political influence in the national black community because radicals, no matter how deep their thought and broad their sympathies, lack strong political standing if not supported by large numbers of the rank and file of their people. Without such support their very strength leaves them vulnerable in some respects. Such is the reality against which Garnet's attempts to foster slave resistance and black autonomy generally in the 1840s must be viewed—the period during which his independence, as it would later, cost him politically and materially.

No leader of the black masses emerged anywhere in the North. The opposition blacks faced, together with the relative thinness of the black population, made the notion of a genuinely mass movement essentially a fiction. Not only were all branches of the federal government opposed to black liberation, but all except a handful of northern whites embraced the prevailing notions of black inferiority. Few black leaders, however, were more effective than Garnet in relating to ordinary blacks on most matters. Despite his learning, as teacher in the colored school in Troy, as minister there and in New York City and Washington, D.C., as abolitionist, and as spokesman for causes ranging from temperance and peace to that of the Liberty party, he did not hold himself aloof.

Whatever the subject under discussion, Garnet was said to have treated it with such lucidity that no one listening "could go away mystified or in doubt as to the cause which had been advocated," an approach that contributed to his effectiveness in winning a following among former slaves wherever he had contact with them. At Troy not a few joined his church and remained there rather than continue their journey along the Underground Railroad into Canada. A contemporary of his observed that every refugee and fugitive "was welcome to his board, and could command his purse." Such a combination of qualities later contributed to a level of popularity in New York that placed him at the head of the black community as its spokesman, especially during the 1860s, in matters affecting his people. And there as elsewhere the young of both sexes were drawn to him and spent many "long hours in the joyous converse he would pour out sparklingly, hour after hour, amid his friends."

The inspiration of David Walker contributed to Garnet's ability to relate to his people. He was so impressed by Walker's *Appeal* that he made a pilgrimage to Boston to meet Walker's widow and to see firsthand where and how Walker had lived, reporting that Walker had deliberately chosen a life of austerity out of concern for the less fortunate. Walker's selfless devotion to the liberation of his people was the stuff of revolutionary spirits, and from available evidence it seems clear that he served as an important model for Garnet. In his personal life Garnet, like Walker, hated "avarice" and opposed wealth. Crummell said of him: "The great fault in his character was in that direction.... There was a princeliness in his largeness which not seldom landed him into poverty."

The publication under Garnet's editorship of Walker's *Appeal* and his own *Address* in a single volume in 1848 represented an effort by Garnet to reassert the need for slave rebellion at a time when growing militancy in the black community, inspired in part by his stance at Buffalo, coincided with growing sentiment in Europe favoring rebellion of the oppressed. With the republication of his *Address,* what was thought incendiary five years earlier was no less so, given the conditions of the times and especially the impact Walker's *Appeal* might have in combination with it. Still, it was as though the moment was somehow lost, as Garnet's delivery of the precise address at a Troy, New York, meeting of the Colored National Convention in 1847 also indicated. In a sense there is about the Troy speech the suggestion of a scene from the past being rehearsed, or so it seems to us today. But such was not the case then, considering the intensity of emotions the speech engendered.

In Douglass's view Garnet became his antagonist some years after the Buffalo encounter, probably sometime in 1847 or the following year. But it appears their differences were rooted mainly in the Troy encounter and, circumstantial evidence suggests, in Garnet's revival of his call for slave resistance. In this regard it is well to note that Douglass's attitude toward Garnet was radically different a few years earlier. In October 1845, while lecturing in the British Isles, Douglass called Garnet "the most intellectual and moral colored man that is now in our country." And they were on cordial, even confidential terms when Garnet, sometime in 1847, in speaking to Douglass of John Brown, lowered his voice to a whisper. But that subject could hardly have failed to revive memories for both men of the Buffalo convention and the narrow margin by which the Garnet blueprint for slave resistance was rejected.

Over a period of years the nature of the relationship between the two changed as each grew in stature and commanded larger followings. By 1847 Garnet and Douglass were almost peerless among black leaders generally. Under such circumstances their differences over questions of pivotal import all but assured some hostility between them, especially since, whether by design or not, they were contesting for leadership of their people. And though he apparently did not say so in print, Garnet had every reason to resent the influence Douglass exercised among blacks in opposing his calls for slave resistance, all the more since that opposition was approved in influential white abolitionist circles. That so many of the theses Douglass had so brilliantly advanced were derivative must have been a source of irritation to a man of Garnet's cast of mind and character, coloring his estimate of Douglass, who challenged black leaders while admitting to "something like a slavish adoration" of the Garrisonians.

Douglass's role at Troy caused Garnet, perhaps as never before, to wonder about him. It was then, on the second day of the convention, that Garnet read "an eloquent and impressive Address to the Slaves of the United States," apparently with no less conviction than at Buffalo four years earlier. The issues raised by him were referred to a Committee on Abolition, headed by Douglass, which was to consider "the best means of alleviating Slavery and Caste in the United States." The committee's report affirmed moral suasion and denounced violence. That Garnet was the object of the report's attack was hardly disguised; his language—"rather *die freemen, than live to be slaves*"—answered with "this great nation is thundering in the ear of our enslaved fellow countrymen the terrible fiat, *you shall be slaves or die!*" With that as background, the committee proceeded to attack advocates of violence in purely contemptuous terms, finding slave insurrection "the perfection of folly, suicidal in the extreme and abominably wicked." Arguments for such a course were "absurd, unavailing, dangerous and mischievous ravings." It was the sort of statement, decisively influenced by Douglass, that Garnet had in mind when he referred to "poison" emanating from a lofty source as far as influence and ability were concerned.

But the pages of Douglass's *North Star* remained open to Garnet, as in 1848 when he addressed the concerns of humankind as a whole, advising that the highest good in society is found in educating colored and white, rich and poor, in the same institutions—a repudiation of both racial and class privilege and a move in the direction of a more general leveling of peoples. Conscious of revolutionary currents of the time, and certainly prepared for them, Garnet spoke in explicitly radical terms: "This age is a revolutionary age, the time has been when we did not expect to see revolutions; but now they are daily passing before our eyes and change after change, and revolution after revolution will undoubtedly take place until all men are placed upon equality." That revolution must be economic as well as political was an ideal that was being explicitly affirmed in German and French radical circles through efforts to change the social order of those countries.

Garnet was no less influenced by the thought of white intellectuals in the economic than in the political sphere, but he made his own analysis and formulated a position applicable to his people and to whites as well. Like Walker he put the authority of God behind his belief in economic equality, asserting that when revolutions have run their course, "then and only . . . then, will all enjoy that liberty and equality that God has destined us to participate in." Economic determinism leading to equality was for him predicated upon Divine sanction, an equality as much the will of God as the political equality grounded in the Declaration of Independence. His celebration of such an ideal marked him off from most abolitionists of the period and illustrated his desire for fundamental economic change.

Shortly after his remarks on revolution in the *North Star,* Garnet elaborated upon his views concerning economic justice, defining the relationship between white workers and African slaves and between those workers and blacks with the advent of emancipation. His observations on the subject were elicited by an attack from Sidney Howard Gay, editor of *The National Anti-Slavery Standard,* on Gerrit Smith, an abolitionist of considerable standing in white and black America and Garnet's close friend. Gay accused Smith of being a land monopolist and charged that he did not believe in antislavery as much as he claimed—in fact, that "the overthrow of the monopoly of which he is so distinguished a representative is the first and real road to the destruction of the monopoly of laborers." Garnet argued that Smith had sought "to break every yoke":

> His language is, "I regard Land Monopoly, *take the world together,* as a far more abundant source of suffering and debasement, than is slavery." Take the world together, and you will find this remark to be true. In many parts of the world, where there is no chattel slavery, there do the iron heels of Land Monopolists grind out the life of the suffering poor. Behold Ireland! her mournful history records volumes. There is no slavery there, but the oppressions of Land Monopolists have engendered a lank and haggard famine, and the famine has swept away its thousands.

Garnet did not think his people could be completely free as long as whites were under the control of monopolists. The monopoly in land and labor of slaveholders had to be shattered as the first step toward freedom for blacks in America. Slavery was the most extreme expression of monopoly, one attended by efforts to control the whole being, physical and psychological, of slave men, women, and children: "Look around you, and behold the bosoms of your loving wives heaving with untold agonies! Hear the cries of your poor children! Remember the stripes your fathers wore. Think of the torture and disgrace of your noble mothers." Formerly "property," Garnet found in slavery a powerful reason for opposing monopolists. While he did not refer specifically to capitalist control of labor, that had more to do with the language of the times and the stage of capitalist development in America than with want of personal distaste for the capitalist ethic. In any event he argued that blacks after slavery, under the yoke of monopolists, would still be grievously oppressed. And since he understood that the interests of those whose labor was controlled by monopolists would be interrelated following as during slavery, he would hardly have differed with Marx's assertion, in *Capital,* that "labor in the white skin can never be free so long as labor in a black skin is branded."

With a concern for the whole of humankind that was emblematic of most antebellum nationalists, Garnet argued that "the chains of the last slave on earth may be broken in twain and still, while the unholy system of landlordism prevails, nations and people will mourn: But the moment that this widespread and monstrous evil is destroyed the dawn of the gospel day will break forth, and the world will have rest." The agony of economic oppression was worldwide and tied to

142

spiritual unrest and thus a central problem confronting the Christian world. "The history of the human race is but one continued struggle for rights," Garnet had declared in 1841, before either Hegel or Marx had come to the attention of American intellectuals. And that struggle was an outgrowth of the need for spiritual as well as physical liberation, spiritual liberation resulting from forcing the oppressor to respect one's humanity, which would lead an irresistible current to sweep away "time-sanctioned oppression and aged tyranny."

That the exploitation of one segment of humanity by another constituted the main source of the world's problems followed from Garnet's thesis that only with the cessation of such practices would the world know peace, a genuine religious life for humankind beginning at that point. It is precisely this view one must keep in mind if one is to understand Garnet's attitude toward the African Civilization Society and its efforts, in the 1850s, to initiate commercial ventures in a capitalist world. One must also note that Garnet would have stood little chance of bettering the economic lot of blacks in America and elsewhere through attempting to destroy capitalism. Unprepared spiritually to accept the fruits of capitalism for himself, he sought to bend the means of capitalism to the needs of his people. In dealing with the world as it was, he sought to transform it from within through the African Civilization Society and its effort to destroy the market for American cotton, and from without through slave uprisings aimed at destroying slavery and with it billions of dollars in "property."

Garnet's conception of the source of prejudice against blacks— formed before racism in America, some believe, had taken on a life of its own—seems strikingly modern in its possibilities for class analysis but modern also in the degree to which he underestimated racism as a force in its own right. From as early as 1841, and for sometime thereafter, he held that the condition of his people, not their color, caused whites to discriminate against them, a view in some respects contradicted by the realities of race confronting blacks of talent that led some to seek a home in Europe or in Canada rather than remain in so racist a country.

Garnet also had in mind a fundamental distinction between types of oppression and their relationship to color. Talking to free blacks after the war, he said: "You know it is better to work for Mr. Cash than Mr. Lash. . . . The more money you make, the lighter your skin will be. The more land and houses you get, the straighter your hair will be." He was, in part, speaking symbolically and understood that free labor, even though enslaved by the cash-nexus, is freer than slave labor. While among the first to sympathize with those suffering from economic exploitation in Europe and North America—he was considered a friend of white workers in New York—he nonetheless knew that the total physical enslavement of blacks in the Americas was without parallel in modern world history. Moreover, in bourgeois society physical characteristics do take a back seat to money. Much like a radical labor leader in our time, Garnet saw little alternative to fighting for better wages and living conditions for his people.

Though David Walker, in attacking avarice, laid the basis for compatibility between nationalism and socialism within the nationalist tradition, Garnet brought the two together in language that seems more modern than that of Walker. Unlike Walker, whose opposition to greed was applied specifically to the exploitation of people of color, Garnet's treatment of the subject was more easily applied to the oppressed of whatever color or circumstance and for that reason was more flexible theoretically. His formulation that exploited whites and blacks have similar interests, while insisting on the right of blacks to help determine the destiny of the country, contributed to liberation theory for all because it maximized possibilities for cooperation across racial lines without sacrificing the souls of black people. In that light Garnet had gone far toward reconciling the claims of nationalism and socialism with respect to America.

The gaining of independence by Liberia was probably responsible for Garnet favoring emigration by 1849. As with a number of questions of ideology, he formulated a distinctive position on emigration that later became the cornerstone of his African Civilization Society. While the argument that blacks could never be free in America without significant emigration was conventional among black emigrationists, Garnet argued that blacks could win freedom in America with or without emigration, a position based on a conception of struggle on two fronts, the one at times reinforcing the other. But in some sense his support of selective movement out of America was evidence of growing disillusionment with racial conditions in America, for shortly thereafter he visited England and for a while considered remaining there.

The occasion of his departure for England drew a cutting attack from Douglass in the *North Star.* He charged Garnet with hypocrisy for urging violence at home while asking England for "moral aid" in the fight to abolish slavery—as if morality, as Garnet later pointed out, were inconsistent with a revolt of slaves. Another thrust was designed even more specifically for Douglass's English readership: "The man whose convictions do not go with his words is not fit to plead this cause. . . . his feelings towards us so far as we have been able to learn them, are those of bitter hostility. His cause here has been that of an enemy. . . . We prefer an open enemy to one in disguise."

Still, there was one respect in which Douglass's opinion of Garnet had not changed despite the lapse of years. When in Ireland he had said that Garnet had "no taint of European blood" to lead whites to assume his ability derived from other than African sources. Later, as if to prove that the anger directed at Garnet was somewhat extreme, Douglass lamented that no one of Garnet's ability was around to advance the cause. Douglass was not surprised by James McCune Smith's estimate of Garnet's performance abroad: "Here was a gentleman of splendid physique, polished manners, extensive learning, well up, especially in English poetry, ably filling the pulpits of their best divines, and bearing all the laurels in eloquence, wit, sarcasm, interlarded with soul-subduing pathos . . . and this gentleman an African of pure lineage, with no admixture of Saxon blood as the source of his unquestionable talent and genius."

Garnet did not hesitate to call for moral aid, urging England to cease purchasing the products of slave labor. Such a boycott might have delivered a deathblow to American slavery if similar articles were produced by free labor in Africa and Australia. Moreover, Garnet attacked the American Colonization Society, explaining that the men who complained that the laws of the land were against blacks and that blacks should leave America "would be first to transport them!"; and that no agent of the society would "attempt to appear at a meeting of coloured people in any city of the free states." He assured his audience that "whoever asserted that the coloured people or their true friends entertain any other sentiments than the deepest contempt and abhorrence for colonizationists asserts that which is entirely false." It was an argument consistent with his beliefs since youth and remained so years later when he headed the African Civilization Society and insisted, in contrast to leaders of the American Colonization Society, that blacks could indeed achieve freedom and equality in America.

The temptation to remain in England was not strong enough for Garnet to resist an opportunity, which came in 1852, to do missionary work in Jamaica on invitation from the United Presbyterian Church of Scotland. By going to the West Indies his return to the United States was practically assured, though he remained in Jamaica somewhat longer than he must have anticipated. For some time he had moved among West Indians in New York, and in Cuba he had seen African slaves unloaded at the port of Havana. But the Jamaican stay provided Garnet with his first opportunity to live and work among West Indians over a sustained period of time, which contributed to his sense of the possibility for unity among people of African descent first inspired by his experiences as a youth in New York and as a cabin boy at sea. Illness ended his stay in Jamaica, and he returned to America early in 1856 to recuperate. Shortly thereafter Garnet succeeded Theodore Wright as pastor of Shiloh Presbyterian in New York City.

The period following his recuperation was one of intense activity. As Garnet established himself in his new post at Shiloh he discovered that black leaders generally had embraced views he had helped pioneer. Not only were the forces of black nationalism gaining strength among them but emigration sentiment, despite opposition from Douglass, was much stronger with Martin Delany, whom he came to respect, at the helm. Predictably, Garnet clashed with opponents of emigration, having in fact lived that creed in Jamaica and having been, by the time of his most serious debate over the subject, an emigrationist for nearly a decade.

A particular need to defend emigration resulted primarily from a cruel accusation against Garnet at a Boston abolitionist meeting in the summer of 1859 that he was a colonizationist. The charge prompted J. Sella Martin, in introducing him in Boston a few weeks later, to call attention to his "twenty-five years of sacrifice to the cause of the colored people in this country" and to note that he "now comes to remove the aspersions cast upon him in the late New England convention and to vindicate by his own statements, the position he occupies with regard to this movement."

It seemed, at the very start, like history coming full circle. Challenged from the audience by a black abolitionist objecting to meetings of colored men, Garnet was reminded of similar challenges twenty years before and expressed the belief that "we are in an age of progression" when colored people meet. "I tell you, my friends that we have been too long depending upon other people. Years have passed away and we have been looking to the Abolitionists to raise us. . . . I believe that God has a certain work for them to do, and that is to prepare the public mind for the full and free discussion of the subject. . . . the rest of the work we have to do ourselves." Denying that he was a colonizationist, Garnet counterattacked: "Any man that says I am behind my back is an assassin and a coward; any man that says it to my face is a liar, and I stamp the infamous charge upon his forehead! I have hated the sentiments of the America Colonization Society from my childhood." But he had not abandoned his faith in the value of emigration to Africa which would lead to the establishment of a Negro nation. He had long since, for that matter, resolved to express his honest convictions on those subjects, as he later put it, "if taken to the stake." In a rare personal reference to his material circumstances Garnet concluded:

> It was said by a Boston friend, who has often taken me by the hand and sat by the same fire-side, and walked with me on the streets, and mused with me in sacred places: "I knew Garnet when he was poor and had not a cent in his pocket." I would say to him that if he knew me twenty-five years ago, when I was poor, he knows me today as the same poor man. And I expect to be a poor man till slavery is abolished. If slavery is not abolished before I die, I shall die a poor man. But in all my poverty my house has been open to the flying fugitive . . . and I have never received a penny for what I gave them, but divided with them my last crust.

He was on the side of the worker as well as the slave, as his final remark that evening indicated: "I care not a straw for the Scribes, Pharisees, and hypocrites; the common people will hear me."

In the fall of 1859, before John Brown's raid at Harpers Ferry, Garnet predicted that the freedom of his people was near: "I believe the sky is brightening, and though I may not live to see it, the day is not distant when, from the Atlantic to the Pacific, from Maine to California, the shouts of redeemed millions shall be heard." An ability to grasp the shape of things before they were palpable to others gave him an edge as a thinker and leader. Something of that quality enabled him to know that blacks, in the presence of land and labor monopolists, following emancipation, would be "heavy-laden with an up-hill course before them." Garnet understood that as well as any leader of his time in this country or abroad. And his solution to the fundamental problem that confronted his people remains no less relevant to the one confronting their descendants in our time.

Martin R. Delany: Elitism and Black Nationalism

LIKE MOST nineteenth-century black leaders, Martin R. Delany's influence did not flow from the usual prerogatives of leadership. He could not reward his friends with patronage jobs or call out the militia against his enemies. His leadership lay instead in his ability to express what many Afro-Americans believed. As an abolitionist writer and lecturer in the 1840s and early 1850s, he insisted that blacks deserved the American citizenship they were denied. But as racial discrimination worsened in the 1850s and increasing numbers of Negroes contemplated expatriation, Delany acted. Prizing black self-reliance, he refused white American philanthropy, traveled to Africa, signed a treaty permitting Afro-American immigration, and called for a black nation with black men to govern it. Although the Civil War rekindled Delany's faith in this country, and he ended the war as a major in the U.S. Army, he was not able to translate his impressive credentials and symbolic leadership into political power during Reconstruction. His last organization was an emigrationist venture that failed. After his death in 1885, he remained virtually forgotten until his resurrection three-quarters of a century later as the father of black nationalism and the epitome of proud blackness.

The black revolution of the 1960s recast the study of Afro-American history by reaching for antecedents of the sentiments and movements that arose in that decade. Shunting aside the decorous, light-skinned integrationist idols of Negro history—the Booker T. Washingtons and the Ralph Bunches—men and women who considered themselves black nationalists rushed to find ancestors who, like modern black revolutionists, turned their backs on white America and spoke for their African nation in both America and Africa. Black college students found Martin Delany, prominent abolitionist and emigrationist, an ideal ancestor, for not only had he concretely advocated black American emigration to Africa, but he had also studied at Harvard.

Any examination of the career of this symbol of black pride and racial integrity exposes contradictions between the man of the 1840s, 1850s, 1860s, and 1870s and his role in the late twentieth century.

True, Delany strenuously rejected any notion of black inferiority on racial grounds, and in the 1850s and 1870s he proposed emigration rather than submission to racial humiliation. But beyond his willingness to consider expatriation to Africa, which he came to see as a solution for only a select few, Delany's thinking about race, class, and "elevation" was thoroughly American and right in step with that of his Afro-American peers; and, with the important exception of his repudiation of racial inferiority, it was as conventional as that of Henry Grady, white southern apologist for the aggressively capitalist New South vision of the 1880s.

As a black leader Delany was not alone in embracing American ideals like leadership by elites—(e.g., W. E. B. Du Bois's Talented Tenth) or in his faith in private enterprise that also appears in the thought of Booker T. Washington. As with Washington and Du Bois, and his friend Frederick Douglass, the secret of Delany's leadership lay in his eloquent espousal of purely American ideals purged of racism and racial subjugation. Delany spoke for men and women who considered themselves the best of the race, fitted through relative wealth and education to lead the black masses. As long as the class interests among black Americans did not seem to differ, Delany's conviction that what was good for black elites was also good for black masses held up. But when class interests diverged, as in Reconstruction South Carolina, the foundations of Delany's claim to leadership of all blacks crumbled.

Happily for the reputation of Martin Delany, his misadventures after the Civil War were ignored by the black nationalists of the 1960s, and the elitism of his brand of black nationalism did not attract scrutiny. Without knowledge of Delany in Reconstruction, black nationalists of the 1960s could read their black nationalism, centered on the masses, into Delany.

Martin Robison Delany was born in Charles Town, in what is now West Virginia, on May 6, 1812. He claimed that his paternal grandfather was a Golah (Angolan?) chieftain, a captive of war enslaved and transported to Virginia; his maternal grandfather was, he said, a Mandingo prince, also a war captive, who, after a period of servitude in this country, somehow gained his freedom and returned to Africa. Thus Delany boasted not only pure African ancestry but noble blood as well.

Delany's mother, Pati (Peace) Delany, was free; his father, Samuel Delany, a slave. The Delany children were bright and learned quickly, and their mastery of reading produced threats from whites that forced

Pati to move with them to Chambersburg, Pennsylvania, in 1822. Samuel purchased his freedom and joined them the following year.

In Chambersburg and later in Pittsburgh, where he moved in July 1831 at the age of nineteen, Martin Delany pursued his education at the Reverend Louis Woodson's school for Negroes and later in the offices of abolitionist medical doctors. A trip down the Mississippi River to New Orleans, Texas, Louisiana, Mississippi, and Arkansas in 1839, made under circumstances that are not known, constitutes a curious chapter in Delany's larger education. By his own admission Delany had something to say about everything, yet he never elaborated on his journey into the slavocracy. Neither slaves, slaveholders, nor the institution of slavery seems to have impressed him in a concrete way. In his abolitionist writings of the 1840s all three remained abstract entities, as they would in the mind of a writer who had never observed them firsthand.

As a well-educated young black man in Pittsburgh, Delany joined voluntary associations promoting temperance, gentlemanly culture, and antislavery. He served as recording secretary of the Temperance Society of the People of Color of the City of Pittsburgh, secretary of the executive board of the Philanthropic Society, which helped fugitive slaves to freedom in the North and Canada, and was one of the founders of the Theban Literary Society. In 1843 Delany married Catherine Richards, the daughter of one of several relatively prosperous and educated blacks with whom he associated in church and antislavery work. By then he had completed enough medical study to qualify as a cupper, leecher, and bleeder and could make a comfortable living as a medical practitioner. But given his interest in public affairs, he was fortunate that his wife was skilled as a seamstress. Catherine supported the family by sewing when Delany gave more of his time to public activities than to medical practice, which was often the case.

Delany's mentor in antislavery work in Pittsburgh was John B. Vashon, a well-to-do barber, veteran of the War of 1812, and, until his death in 1854, a friend and supporter of William Lloyd Garrison. With Vashon's encouragement Delany began publishing the *Mystery* in 1843, the first black newspaper west of the Alleghenies. In 1847 lack of money forced him to suspend publication of the abolitionist paper, but he was not long out of journalism. At the end of the year he joined Frederick Douglass as coeditor of the newly founded Rochester, New York, *North Star.* Delany traveled throughout the mid-Atlantic and midwestern states, speaking and raising money for the paper, reaching a national audience for the first time.

Delany's letters to Douglass, printed in the *North Star*, analyzed all he encountered. He criticized racists and praised whites who helped him; he enumerated the property holdings and business ventures of successful blacks and castigated those content in domestic service, encouraging and admonishing his readers by using the people he visited as object lessons. Echoing the Jacksonian ideal of the self-made man, which was also a staple of the contemporary black convention movement, Delany rejoiced when he found prosperous black communities of farmers and tradespeople. Business, not domestic service, he repeated, held the key to success for the colored people as a whole. Delany's formulas for racial uplift reappeared in his books written in the 1850s and 1860s, as did the elitism that characterized his thought throughout his life.

Delany believed that blacks deserved liberty as a human right, but he also believed in "elevation," which a people had to earn. He exhorted blacks to elevate themselves so as to close the gap between themselves and whites, by becoming skilled workers and landowning farmers. Elevation, which was one of Delany's favorite concepts throughout his life, meant more than mere material success and upward mobility. He defined elevation to include the acquisition of gentlemanly culture and correct speech, of upright morals, independent thought, and "manly" religion (as opposed to religiosity, which he disdained as servile). Elevation meant achievement that would earn the world's applause, such as owning a successful business or governing a prosperous nation. Delany wanted for his people the sort of collective self-respect that he thought only education, wealth, and recognition would secure.

Elevation offered a self-reliant strategy for racial improvement, for Delany despised what he saw as his people's dependence on whites. Though writing primarily to free northern blacks, he included southern slaves in his self-reliant vision. Just as northern blacks must earn their elevation through success in business, enslaved blacks must "dare strike for liberty." Only by acting on his own behalf would the American slave rise up "disenthralled—a captive redeemed from the portals of infamy to the true dignity of his nature—an elevated freeman." The alternative for Delany was retrogression, a sinking "inevitably down to barbarism and obscurity, worse by far, if possible, than the present."

Even though he was a member of the African Methodist Episcopal church, Delany castigated Afro-Americans for trusting in religion too fully. He believed that human affairs were regulated by three immutable, invariable "laws of God": the Spiritual, the Moral, and the Physical.

Black people erred by turning spiritual means toward moral or physical ends, Delany said, but they should instead borrow a leaf from whites, who used wealth, not prayer, to improve life on earth.

In the *North Star* letters Delany denounced Liberia as the creation and ward of the American Colonization Society, a white organization. Like most of his black contemporaries, he accurately judged the society and its scheme to remove free blacks from the United States so as to make slavery more secure, thereby serving the needs of slaveholders, not free blacks. From the society's founding in 1816 free blacks had condemned colonization as forcible exile, and Delany, too, saw the society's aims as degrading to blacks.

Afro-Americans were part of this country, Delany argued, and instructed them in American politics. He condemned the annexation of Texas, which he said made slave territory of what had been a land of freedom (slavery had existed in what became Texas before annexation, however), and he warned against southern expansionists' ambitions in Cuba. At the Free Soil convention in Buffalo in 1848, which nominated Martin Van Buren, Delany helped block the nomination for vice-president of a judge who had convicted Underground Railroad workers for aiding fugitive slaves to freedom.

Participating in the political ferment of the 1840s as an editor of the *North Star* suited Delany perfectly, but the Douglass-Delany collaboration suffered from financial and intellectual strains. Despite Douglass's prominence and Delany's untiring fund-raising tours, the *North Star* ran short of money. In June 1849 Delany resigned as coeditor, although he continued to lecture for some months. The parting reflected a growing philosophical divergence between Delany and Douglass, for Douglass welcomed the support of white abolitionists while Delany criticized them for racial prejudice and preferred that blacks help themselves. Although Delany's views were not unique, Douglass's position was more popular among American blacks in the late 1840s.

Delany grew discouraged in 1849–50. He had done his best to ameliorate the condition of his people, yet he did not feel appreciated. "I have labored for naught and received nothing," he wrote in the fall of 1849; indeed, he believed that he had borne more than his fair share of sacrifice for the elevation of his race. Political events compounded his sense of frustration. In September 1850 Congress tightened the Fugitive Slave Act to include fines and prison sentences for anyone aiding fugitives. Now the burden of proving free status fell on blacks, not on those attempting to reenslave purported runaways. Delany declared his hostility to the act, swearing that he would shoot anyone entering his house in pursuit of a fugitive slave. While continuing to help fugitives reach Canada, Delany pulled back from full-time public service and returned to medical study and practice. He also applied to several medical schools, only one of which admitted him.

Delany's application to the Harvard Medical School was supported by eight positive letters of recommendation, some signed by medical doctors, others by ministers. All agreed that he was an intelligent man of unimpeachable moral and religious character, a leader of the Pittsburgh community. His application reached the medical school at the same time as those of two other black men, sponsored by the American Colonization Society and destined to practice only in Liberia, as well as that of a white woman. The female applicant bowed to pressure and did not enter Harvard, but Delany and the other black men began attending lectures in November 1850. They became a source of controversy when several students demanded their removal. After other students rallied to their support, the brouhaha became the issue. Dean Oliver Wendell Holmes decided that the controversy was distracting to education and asked the black students to withdraw at the end of the winter term. Delany left Boston in March 1851 and reentered public life in Pittsburgh.

The early 1850s saw a heightening of racial feeling in the North. Hundreds of free and fugitive blacks, including the abolitionist Henry Bibb of Detroit, emigrated to Canada to escape the slave catchers' grasp, and slaves continued to escape from the South. Crowds in Boston, Detroit, Chicago, and other cities tried to prevent the return of fugitives, making the enforcement of the Fugitive Slave Act impossible without federal troops. Sectionalism increased with the publication of Harriet Beecher Stowe's *Uncle Tom's Cabin,* in serial form in 1851 and as a novel the following year. Objecting to Stowe's paternalism and to her use of colonization to solve the race problem, Delany decided to write his own book. On a trip to New York City he hurriedly summarized his thinking on citizenship, race, emigration, and racial destiny, including much that had appeared in the *North Star* in the late 1840s. In the spring of 1852 he published in Philadelphia *The Condition, Elevation, Emigration, and Destiny of the Colored People of the United States, Politically Considered.* The book suffered from the haste in which it was written but nonetheless presented the first full-length analysis of the economic and political situation of blacks in the United States. It is remembered today for its nationalism and its advocacy of emigration to Africa.

Delany assumed that black Americans were not uniquely oppressed. Every society contained an oppressed group that the dominant population considered inherently inferior, an imputation that grew from the condition of oppression, not from any natural, inherited defi- ciency of Afro-Americans or any other subordinate people. Delany argued that instead of being inferior, blacks were a superior people of especially resilient African stock who could function well under conditions in America that debilitated Europeans and Indians. Thus blacks had been foremost among the original developers of what became the United States. Afro-Americans had earned United States citizenship by having invested their blood and sweat in their native land, but should these investments not suffice, Delany listed scores of examples of prosperous, educated blacks who further reinforced the race's claims.

This vindication of the race is the book's central purpose. Delany pursued his logic, arguing that although Negroes were willing and able to play a constructive role in the affairs of their country, racism denied them a part in American nationality. Not recognized by whites as citizens and subject to kidnapping and reenslavement, free blacks now had no more rights than slaves—an intolerable predicament. Taking a sober look at race relations in the United States, Delany concluded that Afro-Americans should emigrate to Central or South America or to the Caribbean Islands, where they could become useful citizens and create a United States of South America. Develop- ment of tropical America was therefore the "great and glorious work" destined for the colored people of the United States, an opportunity to reach their final goals of elevation and self-respect.

Delany's central arguments seem commonplace today, but ideas he mentioned in passing continue to resonate. The famous phrase, in which he called black Americans "a nation within a nation . . . really a *broken people,*" appears only in an appendix in which he explained his plans to forge a true Afro-American nation in Africa, which contradicted the call for emigration within the Americas in the book's main text.

In *The Condition of the Colored People* Delany's main concern was elevation rather than nationalism, and his argument resembles what came to be known later in the century as Zionism. Contending that a successful (i.e., prosperous and commercially developed) black nation would elevate its own citizens and also free the slaves of the American South, he formulated an argument made famous half a century later in Theodor Herzl's *Der Judenstaat* (1896), which argued that Jews would only be able to defeat anti-Semitism in Europe through the establishment of a strong Jewish nation-state. Delany's vision of a black nation depended on a vanguard, and as his first step toward implementing his national project, he called a secret national convention of colored men "of the highest grade of intelligence." He assumed that such men would adopt his plan to send commissioners to explore Africa and locate a suitable place to settle, despite the obvious and influential example of Frederick Douglass, who flatly opposed emigration. Delany made no provision for antiemigration or for any other divergent opinions.

Having formulated what he took to be the single intelligent course of action, Delany supposed that the correctness of his views would silence dissent. Not only would the convention of intelligent colored men accept his emigrationist remedy, but all black Americans would in turn follow the commissioners' advice. He never questioned his assumption that the most intelligent of the race—however defined—should decide what the masses should do, and he saw unquestioning acceptance of "intelligent" leadership as the duty of the masses. As a prime example of colored intelligence, Delany saw his role as instructing the rest of the race.

"Intelligent" was the most common adjective in Delany's vocabulary, and, like many other educated mid-nineteenth-century Americans, he used it to connote common sense, leadership, education, cultured deportment, and independence of mind, the same qualities that characterized a people who had achieved "elevation." Intelligence was the means of acquiring elevation on the individual level; it was the psychological precondition for elevation. Intelligence and elevation ensured respect that gained the respect of others, which Delany valued tremendously. By 1852 he had come to see emigration as the only way in which Afro-Americans might gain world respect, for as poor and oppressed as they were in the United States, elevation at home was unlikely. As conditions worsened in the 1850s, increasing numbers of Afro-Americans agreed with Delany, but his position was never accepted universally among black Americans.

In the early 1850s emigration was a controversial solution to the race problem because many blacks associated emigration with colonization, which they opposed as forced expatriation. Delany himself opposed colonization. Even those who drew the distinction between expatriation and exile, like Frederick Douglass, still thought that the United States was the best place for Negro Americans.

During the 1850s Delany deepened his involvement with emigration, moving from advocacy to actual planning. One of the conveners of the first emigrationist convention in Cleveland, Ohio, in 1854, he wrote a pamphlet, *The Political Destiny of the Colored Race* (1854), depicting American race relations as hopeless enough to prompt emigration. Meeting shortly after Douglass's convention in Rochester

156

had denounced emigration, the Cleveland meeting did not attempt to convert non-emigrationists. All delegates were required in advance to support emigration, but none could advocate settlement outside the Americas at the meeting.

Two years later Delany called a second emigration convention in Chatham, Canada West (now Ontario), where he had moved with his family earlier in the year. He had visited Canada in 1851 at the invitation of Henry Bibb, a fellow emigrationist and editor of the Windsor, Canada, *Voice of the Fugitive.* Delany had resisted emigration to Canada for several years, but by 1856 he was ready to sacrifice his standing in the Pittsburgh black community and his established medical practice. Joining the 50,000 to 60,000 black Americans who moved to Canada before the Civil War, Delany left the city that had been his home for a quarter of a century.

In Chatham, Delany was immediately recognized as a leader. He contributed regularly to the local newspaper, took part in politics, and voted for the first time. Although the Delanys called Chatham home for eight years, Martin was there for only three years at a stretch in the late 1850s. Enjoying an unusually long stay with his family in Canada, he did not withdraw from the public activities that he saw as serving the interests of his race.

In the spring of 1858, John Brown visited Canada West and Delany arranged a one-day convention of blacks to hear Brown present his antislavery "Provisional Constitution and Ordinances for the People of the United States." The convention elected Brown commander-in-chief of guerrilla forces, then Brown went on his way. When his actual raid occurred the following year, Delany was in Africa. Before departing, however, Delany wrote the first half of his only novel, *Blake, or the Huts of America;* he completed the second half after his return from West Africa and Great Britain. The novel appeared in serial form in the *Anglo-African Magazine* in 1859 and in the *Weekly Anglo-African* in 1861–62.

Blake, the fourth novel written by an Afro-American, featured a Delany-like hero, Henry Holland/Henry Blake/Henrico Blacus, a free Afro-Cuban who had been kidnapped and taken to Mississippi. "Intelligent," manly, handsome, and educated, Blake is one of only two slave characters in the book who speak Standard English. The other is Blake's wife, Maggie, who like Blake represents Delany's racial ideals. Blake is of pure African ancestry; the equally dignified and "intelligent" Maggie is a beautiful mulatto. Both are Christians, but neither participates in the slave religion instilled by the oppressors.

When Maggie and Blake's master sells her to Cuba, Blake decides to organize an insurrection in the whole American South and Cuba. He travels throughout this country and even to the west coast of Africa, painstakingly constructing what novelist Sutton Griggs later called an *imperium in imperio*—an underground government ready to take control of a black American nation—after Blake and his fellow revolutionaries have overthrown slavery and killed all slaveholders.

The book ends before the revolution begins, but it is already clear that the insurrectionist leadership includes women and men of every stratum of the Negro race. They are black, mulatto, and quadroon; slave and free; rich and poor; Muslim, Catholic, and Protestant (no animists, however); creole and African-born. They constitute a vanguard party reminiscent of John Brown's band, and they plan an uprising "for the sake of our redemption from bondage and degradation." As in *The Condition of the Colored People,* the aims of collective action are abolishing slavery, establishing self-respect, and gaining the respect of others for people of African descent.

Delany's insurrectionist blacks are unified, well-organized, and thoroughly independent in their thinking. They formulate their own solutions, cooperate among themselves in the interests of the race, and are free of even the slightest hint of prejudice or ill feeling. They are dignified in demeanor and have a native sense of good taste. Delany shows them as revolutionaries with the lofty goals of elevation and racial redemption. In their gatherings, he explains, "there was no empty parade and imitative aping, no unmeaning pretensions." This was Delany's vision of enslaved blacks, nature's noblemen and noblewomen poised to claim their own freedom. Such people would rather leave the land of their birth than succumb to prolonged degradation. In his own life Delany found in emigration a practical form of insurrection.

At home in Chatham, Delany helped organize the third emigration convention in 1858. By this time he was the leading advocate of emigration. The convention identified him with Africa, and on his own recommendation he was designated a commissioner to investigate that continent. Delany's decision to explore West Africa represented a shift in his views. In 1852 he had advocated settlement in eastern Africa for reasons he did not explain, but it is likely that during the 1850s he realized the tremendous distance and logistical problems that would face organizers of emigration to East Africa. While West Africa was far more accessible, Delany faced competition there that probably persuaded him to act immediately. In 1858 the Reverend Henry Highland Garnet of New York, also a black abolitionist, had joined with several wealthy whites, including Benjamin Coates of

Philadelphia, who was associated with the American Colonization Society, to form the African Civilization Society, whose aims were similar to Delany's. Delany criticized the African Civilization Society's reliance on whites and objected particularly to whites associated with the suspect colonization society. The rivalry intensified when the African Civilization Society announced plans to explore West Africa. Delany would have to act quickly or be overtaken. He sailed to Liberia on a ship owned by three Afro-American emigrants, arriving in July 1859.

Delany had long criticized Liberia's relationship with the American Colonization Society and its dependence on American whites. Yet he shared the fundamental premises of this settler society, did not perceive Afro-American immigrants as oppressors of native-born Liberians, and enjoyed himself in Liberia as the contented guest of the Reverend Alexander Crummell. Delany delivered several well-received speeches that ambiguously urged both selective emigration of black Americans and the emigration of all free blacks. In Monrovia he argued that as a small minority of the population of a country in which the majority rules, blacks in America could never become a political force, even with the demise of slavery. He favored the immigration of northern free Negroes to Africa, where they would join the native population, "their degraded brethren, [and] assist to elevate them." This black nation in Africa, led by Afro-American settlers, would exert what Delany called a "reflex influence upon America" that would improve the lot of the blacks who remained, whether slave or free.

Delany accompanied Alexander Crummell fifty miles up the Caballa River to his Cape Palmas mission school, which for Delany represented Crummell's civilizing mission in Africa, a prime example of racial redemption and elevation. Delany reported that the school had changed the pupils from "dirty, ragged, barefooted black boys, feeding on nothing but rice and palm oil, eating on the ground, sleeping on naked mats on a bare floor—*because they would have it so,* and no teacher could prevent it—to that of cleanly, well-dressed, polite young gentlemen, assembling in the ordinary at meal time, and occupying neat and comfortable bed-chambers."

Crummell's mission and Delany's projected black American settlement in Africa were very similar. Both were thoroughly elitist and based on a supposed mandate to propagate civilization (i.e., Western civilization). Although Delany sometimes envisioned a mass emigration of Afro-Americans out of the land of their oppression, by the late 1850s he stressed "a select migration of intelligent persons (male and female) of various vocations." These chosen few would eventually effect the "regeneration" of Africa, morally, religously, and educationally. But more immediately, and for Delany more importantly, Afro-Americans would develop Africa and make it prosperous.

As in his articles of the 1840s, Delany saw commerce and farming as the means of regeneration. His settler nation would grow cotton for export, with black Americans supplying the management and Africans the labor. Intelligent Afro-Americans would make all the decisions, political and economic. When Delany called for "Africa for the African race and black men to rule them," he did not imagine that Africans would rule themselves. This was a paternalistic, not a democratic, scheme.

Although his settlers would be identified racially with the indigenous population, in other respects Delany's notion of an African nation differed little from those of British settlers in East Africa or Jewish settlers in Palestine. In all three cases settler spokespersons took for granted that their presence meant development and subsequent prosperity that would automatically benefit the local people, who in turn would appreciate the arrival of foreign settlers without resenting the loss of independence. The locals, it was assumed, would understand that they were degraded people and would welcome the opportunity to be civilized, and in West Africa, Christianized, trading their autonomy for a cash economy.

Leaving Liberia in November 1859, Delany traveled to Lagos (since 1960 the capital of the Republic of Nigeria) and Abeokuta. He probably picked Yorubaland because its people already lived in cities, which he would have seen as proof that they were further civilizable, and because of Alexander Crummell's ties with the African Anglican missionary Samuel Crowther. Crowther would provide Delany an opening to the local aristocracy that he would have lacked elsewhere.

In Abeokuta, Delany met his fellow commissioner, Robert Campbell, for the first time. Campbell, a twenty-seven-year-old, light-skinned Jamaican, taught science at the Institute for Colored Youth in Philadelphia. Together Delany and Campbell visited the other Yoruba cities of Ijaye, Oyo, Ogbomoso, and Ilorin; by himself Delany also went to Iwo and Ibadan. The climax of the expedition came on December 27, 1859, at Abeokuta, when Delany and Campbell signed a treaty with the *alake* (king) of Abeokuta and several nobles. Samuel Crowther and his son, a surgeon, served as witnesses.

The treaty permitted Afro-Americans associated with Delany and Campbell to settle unused tribal lands in exchange for sharing their skills and education with the Egba (part of the larger Yoruba people). The Afro-Americans, among themselves, were to be subject to their own laws, but in cases concerning both Egba and Afro-Americans, commissions of equal numbers from each side would settle the differences, the laws of the Egba to be respected by the settlers. Delany was satisfied with the treaty, although it did not envision his Afro-American hegemony and commercial expansion, which the *alake* most certainly would not have accepted. For Delany the specific wording of the treaty was less important than the very existence of a signed agreement between representatives of Negro Americans and African rulers. No one questioned him closely on the incongruity of his plans for Afro-American exploitation of African land and labor and the treaty provisions of respect for Egba land and laws.

The cordial welcome that he and Campbell received in Yorubaland delighted Delany, for the king of Ilorin called them "his people" and the king of Oyo lent his "kinsman" a special guard of honor. These and other signs of friendship reinforced Delany's conviction that black Americans were destined to play a special role in Africa. Happy with his contacts and findings, Delany departed for Britain in April 1860, ready to put the second half of his plan into place.

Like British and American advocates of free trade, supporters of the free produce movement, and his rivals in the African Civilization Society, Delany assumed that the cotton produced in his African-American nation would undercut slave-grown cotton from the American South in European markets. He imagined that African production costs would be lower because land would be free, the growing season would be longer, and that free labor would naturally prove more efficient than slave labor. In Glasgow he spoke with cotton dealers and international merchants; in London he met with philanthropists and businesspeople interested in supporting the implantation of Christian colonies in Africa to compete with the slave South. His findings encouraged the founding of the African Aid Society, which would have lent two-thirds of the money needed by the first group of settlers, who were expected to leave the United States for Yorubaland in June 1861. A phenomenal success in Great Britain, Delany had realized all his goals.

Before returning to Canada he unintentionally chagrined white Americans at a meeting of the International Statistical Congress, at which he had been invited to present a paper on his African explorations. In Britain, Delany attended social functions and the meeting of learned societies where aristocrats treated him with respect. But his presence at the Statistical Congress disturbed his fellow Americans. When Delany was introduced to the congress, the American delegation, led by Augustus Baldwin Longstreet, president of the University of

South Carolina, walked out. The matter became a public issue in Britain and finally reached the columns of the American antislavery press. Frederick Douglass drew the contrast between race relations in Britain and America: "Delany, in Washington, is a *thing!* Delany in London is a *man.*"

Abraham Lincoln's election and the beginnings of secession did not instantly convert emigrationists from their belief that Negro Americans would be better off outside the United States. With American race relations still dismal, the Reverend J. T. Holly, a black abolitionist, continued to advocate emigration to Haiti; Alexander Crummell toured the country to stimulate interest in immigration to Liberia; and Martin Delany wrote his *Official Report of the Niger Valley Exploration Party* (1860) and gave lectures on Africa while dressed in Yoruba robes. But as secession provoked hostilities, Delany's attention gradually turned from West Africa to the United States. He cancelled the departure of the first group of settlers.

In 1862, after the War Department reversed its refusal to enroll black volunteers in the Union army, Delany became a full-time recruiter of colored troops for the state of Massachusetts, which organized two black regiments, the Fifty-fourth and the Fifty-fifth. One of the Fifty-fourth's first recruits was Toussaint L'Overture Delany, Martin Delany's oldest son. (Delany had named each of his seven children after famous black figures.) During the rest of the war he also recruited for Rhode Island and Connecticut, which appealed to him in terms of both racial destiny and business sense. (Recruiters received a bounty for each man enrolled.) Delany felt he was performing a service that only he and a few others were suited to provide. "[I]ntelligent competent black men adapted to the work [of recruitment] must be the most effective means of obtaining Black troops," he wrote in 1863, "because knowing and being of that people as a race, they can command such influences as is required to accomplish the object."

After the Confederacy considered the use of black troops early in 1865 Delany wanted to broaden the use of blacks in the Union army. He proposed to Secretary of War Edwin M. Stanton that he be permitted to organize a black army with black officers (with the exception of the Louisiana Native Guard, existing black regiments had white officers). Such a force would "penetrate through the heart of the South, and make conquests, with the banner of Emancipation unfurled, proclaiming freedom as they go, sustaining and protecting it by arming the emancipated, taking them as fresh troops, and leaving a few veterans among the new freedmen ... keeping this banner unfurled until every slave is free...."

This was the grand gesture Delany had wished for in *The Condition of the Colored People,* a realization of Henry Blake's insurrection, an action that would command the respect of the rest of the world. After nearly four years of bloodshed Delany's idea appealed to the secretary of war and to President Lincoln, who endorsed the plan. On February 26, 1865, Delany was commissioned a major in the Union army, the first Negro American field officer, and he began to compile his list of officer candidates. Before taking up his duties in South Carolina he visited Wilberforce, Ohio, where he had moved his family in 1864. But before he had been in South Carolina long, the war ended.

Delany remained in South Carolina, where, as in Chatham, he was immediately recognized as an important public figure. His three and a half years of government service proved controversial, beginning with a speech delivered shortly after surrender, as he began his work with the Bureau of Refugees, Freedmen and Abandoned Lands (Freedmen's Bureau). He was already known as a popular public speaker when St. Helena blacks invited him to speak at the Brick Church there on July 23, 1865. The Army considered him sufficiently provocative to warrant planting informers in the audience, and one of them, a white Army officer, reported to the War Department and the commander of the Freedmen's Bureau in South Carolina that Delany was encouraging the freedpeople "to break the peace of society and force their way by insurrection to a position he is ambitious they should attain to."

Delany had told his audience of freedpeople that they would not have been freed "had we not armed ourselves and fought for our independence." In warning them not to believe the northern teachers and planters in the Sea Islands, he said "believe none but those Agents who are sent out by Government to enlighten and guide you" and seemed to be telling freedpeople to trust only blacks, not northern whites. Such phrases, applauded by the freedpeople, initially earned Delany a reputation as a race agitator. One informant called him "a thorough hater of the white race [who] excites the colored people unnecessarily." But Delany's antiwhite reputation subsided quickly, as he gained the grudging respect of the planters by proving himself a skillful arbitrator between workers and employers in the South Carolina low country. Before long a planters' newspaper praised him for being "on the right track" and cited his "wonderful influence for good over the freedmen. He tells them to go to work at once; that labor surely brings its own reward; and that after one more good crop is gathered, they will find their condition much better than at present."

A Freedmen's Bureau report reached similar conclusions, calling his advice to the freedpeople "sensible" and entirely in agreement with the bureau's own policies. Delany had not changed his views. He simply shared the economic assumptions of many southern planters and white northerners in South Carolina, the same ideas that had informed his plans for Afro-American settler nationality in Africa. In South Carolina, however, the laborers in question were freedpeople, not Africans.

Like many nineteenth-century Americans, Delany thought that all classes of society shared a common interest and that in a properly adjusted social order everyone's needs would be met equally. He did not believe in the inevitability of social or class conflict and was well disposed toward the planters he met in the low country, whom he took to be the region's natural leaders. They impressed Delany as being anxious to develop what he called "our common country—the South." To bring prosperity back to the area he proposed a system that was essentially sharecropping on thirds: one-third of proceeds to labor (freedpeople), one-third to landowners (planters), and one-third to capital (northern furnishing merchants). He called this a "Triple Alliance" that would bring all parties into a fair-minded partnership, for he believed that "a union of the whites and blacks is an essential industrial element for the development of the wealth of the South."

Delany saw no contradiction between his belief in the need for black/white and labor/employer unity and his ability to represent his race, most of whom worked for others and at whose expense such unity would be achieved. Without realizing it he took a class position that soon put him at odds with large numbers of blacks. As early as 1865, according to a biographer who worked closely with him, he noticed that freedpeople were beginning to think that "he was opposed to their interest and in that of the planters" and that "his advice to them only served to arouse their suspicions." To Delany, their distrust merely proved that slavery had made them incapable of taking good advice when it came from a Negro. When freedpeople disagreed with him, he concluded that they were dupes of white planters or white carpetbaggers. Throughout his stay in South Carolina, Delany took a patronizing view of southern freedpeople, who failed to measure up to his idealized black folk in *Blake.* He never hesitated to tell freed-people what was good for them and what they should do. But the longer Delany remained in South Carolina, the more clearly his views of what was proper for freedpeople coincided with the convictions of the "better class" of the state, who were also likely to be employers.

Delany's work with the Freedmen's Bureau—overseeing contracts, handing out blankets and clothes to freedpeople and white refugees— ended in early 1869, marking a watershed in his career. Leaving

Hilton Head to seek a new career at the age of fifty-seven, he failed to realize his ambition of becoming the first black minister to Liberia. (Not until 1871 did President Ulysses S. Grant appoint a black to that post, J. Milton Turner, a lawyer from Missouri.) Without a federal appointment Delany returned to South Carolina, while his family remained in Wilberforce.

Settling in Charleston, Delany went into the real estate business. He was an active Republican, and the governor appointed him one of seven lieutenant colonels of the South Carolina militia. In 1871 he received an appointment as jury commissioner of Charleston County, and in 1872 he served as a member of the state Republican executive committee. Yet he grew increasingly disaffected with Radical Reconstruction, criticizing Republican officeholders for corruption, carpetbaggers for demagoguery, freedpeople for disorderliness, and the Republican party for withholding offices from blacks. Conditions in South Carolina, he said, were "most disgraceful . . . all in the name of Republicanism."

By the early 1870s Delany had soured on Reconstruction, which he thought had ruined race relations and divided blacks among themselves. He wrote a bitterly accusatory open letter to Frederick Douglass which said that southern colored people used to be "polite, pleasant, agreeable, kindly common people, ever ready and obliging . . . proverbial for their politeness." But now they were "ill-mannerly, sullen, disagreeable, unkind, disobliging. . . . seemingly filled with hatred and ready for resentment . . . these people are despoiled of their natural characteristics and shamefully demoralized." Delany laid the blame squarely on white carpetbaggers who had misled the blacks and turned them against the intelligent colored people—like Delany—who ought to have been their leaders. It did not occur to him that carpetbaggers might have been saying what the freedpeople wanted to hear or that he was a carpetbagger himself. Instead Delany summed up the influence of carpetbaggers in South Carolina as "menacing, threatening, abusing, quarreling, confusing and frequently rioting."

He also accused blacks of serious errors: prejudice against different shades of color—the lighter refusing to associate with the darker—and discrimination against northern blacks by southern blacks. Delany called these distinctions a "shameful evil" that weakened the race even more than white demagoguery. Douglass also regretted divisions within the race, but he chided Delany for his other criticisms. "Were you not M. R. Delany," Douglass retorted, "I would say that the man who wrote thus of the manners of the colored people of South Carolina had taken his place with the old planters." Delany would not

165

have analyzed his thoughts in that way, but Douglass discerned the drift of his friend's sentiments.

Increasingly estranged from Republican Reconstruction and its constituency of poor blacks, Delany came to prefer what he called intelligence, respectability, and honesty. In his shift from the Republican camp of the freedpeople to the Democratic camp of the planters, Delany joined a small but prominent group of politically active blacks in several southern states (as well as some prominent white Republicans who saw themselves as reformers). In Louisiana this tendency was called "Southernizing," as black conservatives criticized carpetbagger-Negro-scalawag Reconstruction regimes and softened on Democrats. P. B. S. Pinchback of Louisiana, W. A. Pledger of Georgia, and the Reverend Richard H. Cain, Francis L. Cardozo, and Joseph H. Rainey of South Carolina all joined Delany in deploring the corruption they thought characterized Republican Reconstruction.

Southernizers advised black voters to alter their habits, turn unscrupulous Republicans out, put honest southern men into office, or be disfranchised. Lamenting the split of the electorate along racial and partisan lines that isolated blacks from their fellow southerners, Southernizers argued that carpetbaggers had never done anything for blacks. Southernizers advised freedmen to overcome their suspicion of Democrats and vote for those who represented the wealth and intelligence of their state—the elites who had ruled before and during the Civil War, conservative Democrats for the most part. This line of reasoning, based on what Delany saw as an identity of interest, represented an elaboration of the views he espoused in his "Triple Alliance" of the immediate postwar years.

For Delany "it was easy to see that it was [in] the interest of both races to go hand in hand together," because whites monopolized the land and education in South Carolina, blacks the ability to work. He envisioned a one-party political order without dissent, convinced that unless black voters broke with their enemies (carpetbaggers) and sided with southern white elites, blacks would lose their civil rights. By 1874 Delany was prepared to go beyond the rhetorical phase. He resigned his position as customs inspector and entered the gubernatorial campaign.

Delany ran for the office of lieutenant governor on the Independent Republican ticket, which represented less a party than a coalition of moderate and conservative Republicans who were distressed by the corruption and taxation policies of the regular Republicans or who had lost battles over patronage, and moderate Democrats who accepted black suffrage. (The Democratic party did not field a slate in South Carolina in 1874.) The Independent Republican ticket represented several strands of long-simmering opposition. In 1871 and 1874 taxpayers' conventions had denounced the state's mounting debt and the new basis for calculating representation in the state legislature. (In 1868 the constitutional convention had apportioned seats according to total population only, whereas the antebellum legislature had keyed representation to white population and amount of taxes paid. In Reconstruction, people, not wealth, were the sole basis for representation, which annoyed some of the well-to-do.) Besides issues of taxation and apportionment, several prominent individuals had denounced the corruption of the Reconstruction government for several years. Some Republicans, like Robert B. Elliott, a black congressman, leveled their criticisms from within the Republican fold. Others, like Delany, moved to the opposition.

Delany's gubernatorial running mate was Judge John Green, a Democrat who had held office before the war. Due to Green's poor health most of the burden of campaigning fell on Delany, who spoke throughout the state on themes he had voiced since 1871: Republicans had done nothing for the freedpeople; Republicans had arrayed blacks against whites and divided blacks against each other. Delany attracted other black supporters like Congressman Richard H. Cain to the Independent Republicans, but his campaigning in the largely white up-country attracted more attention. In Spartanburg and Chester, he spoke to mixed meetings that welcomed him enthusiastically. Blacks remarked upon a dark-skinned black man who spoke like a gentleman; whites marveled at the combination of Delany's blackness and his support of conservative positions. A Democratic newspaper praised his good work in "strenghthen[ing] the cause of Honesty and Reform."

Despite defeat at the polls, Delany was delighted with the company he was keeping. Assuming that his nomination meant that whites of the better classes honored and respected him, he flattered himself that they had proven their good intentions toward Negroes in general by taking him in. In the following electoral campaign, Delany felt justified as a black man in supporting the Democratic gubernatorial candidate, Wade Hampton III, the richest man in the South before the Civil War and a former Confederate general. Like Delany, Hampton was not experienced in the everyday give-and-take of democratic politics and believed in the identity of interest of all the people, whom he promised to serve equally.

Delany, like Hampton, disregarded the armed rifle clubs that were using violence and intimidation against black voters in the name of the Democratic party; he also paid more attention to Hampton's words, which resembled his own. Both men espoused what Delany termed *"a union of the two races,"* in which black as well as white civil rights would be respected *"in one common interest in the State."* Both men deplored racial hostility, and Delany repeated his warnings of the early 1870s that unless harmony were restored between the races, blacks would have "but one terminal destiny, political nonentity and race extermination."

Delany supported the Democratic redeemers in 1876 for what he saw as the good of his race and all South Carolina. He was convinced that a union of blacks and southern whites, under the Democratic banner, would produce a state government "that would have respectability, and possess the confidence and respect of the people." This was particularly important in the depression of the 1870s, for Delany— among others—believed that government by the best people would ease hard times by reestablishing peace and prosperity.

Seeking to attract northern capital, Delany reasoned in 1876 much as did the New South spokespeople of the following decade, and for many of the same reasons. His was the New South formula in which native white elites would lead a united following of blacks and whites, respect everyone's civil rights, and know best how to serve their state and region. This apolitical, elitist, Southernizing/New South position attracted many respectable blacks in the South. But Delany discovered on the campaign trail that his identity-of-interest argument did not fit every reality. On Edisto Island he encountered workers on rice plantations whom hard times had brought into conflict with their employers.

The rice plantations of the low country south of Charleston were the scene of labor disturbances during the depression of the 1870s, when rice planters, short of cash, had taken in 1876 to paying their workers in what they called "checks," or scrip, redeemable in goods at plantation stores that charged exorbitant prices, or in cash in 1880. Useless as a medium of exchange, checks provoked a strike by plantation workers who were also staunch Republicans. Their employers, the rice planters—including at least one black—were Democrats.

Being a Democrat in South Carolina in 1876 meant not only opposing corruption and prizing prosperity but also identifying oneself with the interests of planters and employers. In addition, hard times aggravated existing racial and partisan tensions, as planters and other employers pressured employees to proclaim themselves Democrats in order to get or keep jobs. Many strikebreakers had bowed to this pressure and called themselves Democrats, so that being a Democrat meant even more than being pro-Confederate and pro-planter in the low country; it meant being a scab as well. Ignorant of these conditions and unaware of the nexus of class, race, and partisan bitterness he would encounter, Martin Delany went to Edisto Island in support of Wade Hampton, a Democrat, for governor.

As soon as he mounted a wagon to speak to a crowd of blacks, they beat their drums and refused to listen to what they called a damned "nigger Democrat." As men marched away, women pressed around Delany to call him names and threaten him. Order returned after half an hour, and Delany began to scold his audience. He told them that "he had been in the presence of the nobility [of] many countries and black as he was he had never been insulted as he had been to-day by the people of his own race." With his speech frequently interrupted by jeers, he "reminded them of the fact that he had come to South Carolina with his sword drawn to fight for the freedom of the black man; that being a black man himself he had been a leading abolitionist. . . . He was a friend of his own race, and had always held the position that it was the duty of those who had education to teach them that their best interests were identical with the white natives of the State."

The following day Delany spoke alongside several white Democrats in the village of Cainhoy, ten miles inland from Charleston and, like Edisto, in the low country. Black Republicans again gave Delany a hostile reception. When the Negro militia and other Republican partisans fired on the speakers, Delany and his white comrades sought refuge in a white church. After Edisto and Cainhoy, Delany left the campaign. He did not speak for Hampton again, not even in ward meetings in Charleston, where he retained a measure of popularity. Despite his foreshortened campaigning, Delany was rewarded with the office of trial justice after Hampton's victory, a position he kept until the South Carolina legislature elected Hampton a United States senator in 1879 and purged black officeholders throughout the state. By this time Delany was sixty-seven years old, and he had identified himself once again with emigration.

As Reconstruction ended and white Democrats quickly consolidated their position in South Carolina and the rest of the region at black expense, many Afro-Americans doubted their future in the South. As in the trying 1850s, West Africa seemed to offer a field in which black men and women could work out their destinies. For many Afro-Americans in 1877 emigration extended a last hope for true freedom, and Liberia fever swept through the Deep South.

That spring Harrison Bouey of Edgefield and George Curtis of Beaufort had persuaded the Reverend B. F. Porter of Charleston to join them in organizing black emigration from South Carolina to

Liberia. Porter accepted the office of president of the Liberian Exodus Joint-Stock Steamship Company, and by the end of the year Delany had joined the company's board of directors, with the charge of negotiating with the Liberian government for land grants for Afro-American settlers. Enthusiasm for emigration outstripped the company's planning, however, and thousands of would-be emigrants converged on Charleston early in 1878. The company hastily acquired a ship and carried more than two hundred immigrants to Liberia in a passage plagued by delay, deaths, and unexpected expenses. As chairman of the committee on finance, Delany was responsible for sorting out the company's debts, but he failed to raise the $5,000 owed in early 1879 and the ship was sold at auction.

The Liberian Exodus Joint-Stock Steamship Company's legal and financial problems persisted into the mid-1880s, but by that time Martin Delany had left South Carolina. In the early 1880s he still cherished dreams of taking his family to Africa or of securing a government position in Washington or of managing a fruit plantation in Central America or of realizing a profit from his last book, *Principia of Ethnology: The Origin of Races with an Archeological Compendium of Ethiopian and Egyptian Civilization.* After a lecture tour selling *Principia of Ethnology,* Delany went home to Wilberforce in late 1884. He died in January 1885, nearly seventy-three years old.

Leaving no papers, money, or fashionable ideas, Delany seemed to disappear after his death. A few historians, like Carter G. Woodson, knew of him and discussed his work. But with this scholarly exception Delany's only memorial for decades was a Pittsburgh drill team called the "Delany Rifles," organized by a black veteran of the Spanish-American War. Then, in the 1960s Delany reemerged as a symbol of black nationalism, but transmogrified to fit the tastes and politics of the mid-twentieth century.

Because the black nationalism of the 1960s and 1970s was egalitarian and democratic, inspired by anti-imperialism and emphasizing self-determination for ordinary black people in the United States and Africa, many assumed that as a black nationalist Delany must also have held ordinary black people in high regard. Few of his twentieth-century admirers realized that his nineteenth-century black nationalism was an elitist, not a democratic, creed. His chosen constituency was what he called "intelligent colored men and women," and he saw the masses as no more than a mute, docile work force to be led by their betters—their *black* betters, but their betters nonetheless.

Delany could not conceive of policies that would benefit one group of blacks but not others, and he never understood why he had offended working-class black audiences in 1876. He saw always one entity, the colored people, with one true course, and he did not realize (nor did Wade Hampton) that his thinking was class-bound. He did not see that as a medical doctor, real estate agent, and trial justice his concerns were not those of the great mass of freedpeople, who were landless plantation workers. As one of the intelligent, he thought it his duty to point out what was right, whether or not his truths were popular. But when his views were unpopular, he concluded that the masses were wrong, not that they might have been reasoning from different premises.

Delany's outspoken love for his people, his praise of unmixed blackness, and his Pan-Africanism made him a leader in the nineteenth century and an attractive figure in the twentieth. But some of his convictions have been jettisoned by his twentieth-century admirers, such as his embrace of the settler ideal, which has caused such bloodshed in Algeria, Zimbabwe, and the Middle East and which now seems more to resemble these examples of colonial mentality rather than an enlightened plan to regenerate a homeland. Also forgotten is his insistence that everyone follow him or a small handful of designated, not elected, leaders, which now seems more authoritarian than philanthropic.

A claim to leadership in his own times lay in Delany's eloquence and activity in pursuing his ideals, which many other blacks shared. His was not the most popular position, but he never stood alone. Delany's unquestioning elitism was typical of his times, as was his patriotism. Before the Civil War his allegiance was to a nation of race; after the war his field broadened and his elitism and patriotism enfolded all the people of South Carolina, black and white. As a nationalist, he could not tolerate internal conflict, whether the "nation" in question was an Afro-American settler society in West Africa or the biracial commonwealth of South Carolina. Never seeking material gain in politics, he lived up to his ideals of a gentleman in public life.

David A. Gerber

9

Peter Humphries Clark: The Dialogue of Hope and Despair

I do not forget the prejudice of the American people; I could not if I would. I am sore from sole to crown with its blows. It stood by the bedside of my mother when she bore me. It darkens with its shadow the grave of my mother and father. It has hindered every step I have taken in life. It poisons the food I eat, the water I drink and the air I breathe. It dims the sunshine of my days, and deepens the darkness of my nights. It hampers me in every relation of life, in business, in politics, in religion, as a father or as a husband. It haunts me walking or riding, waking or sleeping. It came to the altar with my bride and now that my children are attaining their majority, and are looking eagerly with their youthful eyes for a career, it stands by them and casts its infernal curse upon them. Hercules could have as easily forgotten the poisoned shirt which scorched his flesh, as I can forget the prejudices of the American people.

THESE ANGUISHED, angry words were spoken by Peter Clark at an Emancipation Day celebration at Dayton, Ohio, in 1873. He argued on that occasion for northern black protest and political independence against those who, perceiving that white prejudice was deepening and Reconstruction was dying, urged a strategy of caution and loyalty to the Republican party. That Clark reached down into his own experience to make a political point is emblematic of the emotional and intellectual processes that gave him both moral energy and rhetorical force as a leader of black people. He showed a remarkable ability to elevate a deep sense of personal grievance into a political statement about the withering effects of oppression on the human spirit—and a statement, too, so universal in its feelings that blacks of all groups and classes (and also some whites) saw in him a man of moral authority worthy of their attention. People did not always agree with Clark, but they knew his views had to be taken seriously. These same strengths suggested Clark's limitations as a leader. The personalism that was so vital a part of his style of leadership usually made it impossible for him to separate private and public selves sufficiently to shield the former from assaults made upon the latter.

173

Peter Clark (1829–1925) was an educator and politician widely acclaimed for the practical leadership he brought both to the development of the segregated black public schools of Cincinnati and to the creation of postenfranchisement northern black political strategy. That Cincinnati's segregated black schools were among the best facilities in the nation after the Civil War was largely attributable to Clark's work. Moreover, for years and on his own time after the end of the school day, Clark himself trained several generations of black teachers who worked in segregated systems throughout the Ohio Valley well into the twentieth century. His political work did a great deal to make the black vote an acknowledged force in Ohio politics, and as a result it helped to pave the way for passage of civil rights and school desegregation legislation in that state.

While respected for these accomplishments during his middle years, in 1886, as a consequence of his political activism, Clark suffered the loss of the teaching position he had held for a quarter century. He fell quickly into an obscurity so profound that it enveloped the last four decades of his long life. That Clark suffered such a fate is not entirely surprising. His career was so paradoxical and quixotic that it has seemed both bizarre and uninterpretable, and it continues to puzzle historians. To his contemporaries, black and white, the controversial, outspoken educator seemed high-strung and mercurial, at times even unstable, though always brilliant. His political commitments eventually encompassed almost all the major ideological tendencies and partisan affiliations available to anyone in his day—and in no steady or predictable progression. Particularly at the height of his public career in the 1870s and 1880s, Clark frequently changed affiliations and ideologies. And what was true in his public life was true as well in the complex composition of his own identity and in his deeply committed religious life, in which widely divergent attitudes and beliefs mingled in apparently unrationalized profusion.

Always willing to account for himself, the articulate Clark made a good case for every position he held. Yet in him we sense something deeper at work at the center of his being which created intolerable strains, impelling him toward complexity, diversity, and contradiction, and thrusting a personal, though by no means unique, grievance into the public sphere as a generalized indictment of racism and all oppression. Realist and idealist; integrationist and defender of separate institutions; militant and accommodationist; Socialist, Liberal Republican, Republican, and Democrat; Unitarian and African Methodist—both the public and the private man were engaged in a ceaseless struggle to break free of the dialogue between hope

174

and despair that characterized his thought and to escape to a stable and consistent activism from the ambivalence, confusion of identity, and frustrated ambitions that plagued him. Clark's public career and private self may thus be seen as a complex tragedy of a society that, in its obsession with race, mocked his ambitions, thwarted his creativity, and wasted his talent, while ruining the lives of many of his people.

The intricately woven chain of events that placed Peter Clark in Cincinnati, the city of his birth, suggested the interpersonal tragedies created by the nation's system of racial subordination. Clark's father, Michael, was the natural son of Major William Clark, who achieved fame accompanying Merriwether Lewis on an expedition to the uncharted Pacific Northwest. The major, who at the turn of the nineteenth century lived near Lexington, Kentucky, and owned slaves, had five children by his mulatto slave Betty. Fearing that he would not return alive from the expedition to the West and anxious over the fate of his Afro-American family, William Clark, on the eve of his journey in 1804, resolved to free Betty and the children and settle them at Cincinnati. The settlement there of Afro-American blood kin by slaveowners was not uncommon in the antebellum period because of the city's convenient, commercially strategic position on the border between the sections. The same factor accounts, too, for the migration of large numbers of escaped slaves and southern free blacks to the area. By 1850 the city had one of the North's largest black populations—3,900 people.

In her new home Betty eventually married a dark-complexioned man, John Isom Gaines, who was, among local blacks, unusually affluent because of a successful steamboat provisioning business. He also served for years as clerk of the city's black schools. They began another family. Here, too, Michael came of age, married, and had his own family. This complex lineage was a significant part of Peter Clark's background. Light-complexioned, like his father, Clark possessed a darker family of half uncles, half aunts, and half cousins to serve as a reminder of his ties to a distant African ancestry. Yet his own near-white color symbolized ties to white America and to Europe, whose cultures and intellectual traditions he would make his own, and to one of the nation's eminent families. His middle name, Humphries, suggested such ties, too, though more ambiguously: it was the family name of William Clark's white, Irish-American wife, Ann. What Peter Clark made of this complex past with its multiple meanings we cannot say with certainty. Though he alluded with some frequency to his own general circumstances, he never spoke in public about any particular aspect of his personal history. But he was much too sensitive a man not to have given that history due thought, and there are indications it helped frame the ambiguity of identity present in his adult personality.

Clark was correct, though not literally so, when he stated that prejudice had stood by the bedside at his birth. If not at the bedside, it was certainly not far off. His parents' lives were no more secure or less influenced by racial oppression than those of other Cincinnati blacks. In 1804, Betty and her children came to Ohio, the legislature began to enact a series of laws requiring blacks migrating to Ohio to post $1,500 bond and present two character references as guarantees of good behavior and self-sufficiency. The intention was to discourage migration from the South of people poorer than Betty but, like her, black. Other state laws would eventually bar blacks from voting, testifying against whites, serving on juries and in the militia, and marrying whites. When a public school system was created by the legislature, blacks would be excluded from attending, though their property was taxed for the support of education. The legislature and the courts ultimately eased some of these disabilities. In 1849 a segregated system of black public schools was created. Also, the courts ruled that Afro-Americans with a large preponderance of white ancestry could vote. And the laws impeding black migration proved largely unenforceable. Yet the disabilities had their impact, particularly in southern Ohio, where the impoverished southern background of many white settlers and the continuing influence of southern culture and politics produced bitter prejudice and anxiety about black competition and hence persistent demands for repression. In 1829, the year Clark was born, Cincinnati whites rioted. Alarmed by black population growth and angered by failure to enforce antisettlement laws, they attacked black people in the streets and chased large numbers permanently out of the city.

Custom supplemented statutory discrimination and proved even less tractable especially in the southern counties. Riots against Cincinnati blacks broke out again in 1836, 1841, and 1862. Segregation grew evermore comprehensive and by 1860 eventually encompassed schools, churches, cemeteries, transportation, public accommodations, and neighborhoods. Blacks were largely restricted to the Queen City's poorest, most congested areas, where they lived in decaying, overcrowded tenements and shanties. It was in these neighborhoods that police allowed vice to thrive. Yet they certainly enforced other laws, for blacks made up a disproportionate number of those arrested: in 1870 one white in twenty-five was arrested, and one black in ten. The black economic situation was especially bleak. The discrimination blacks encountered in the crafts and in industry escalated in direct proportion to their ultimately hopeless competition with increasing numbers of German, Irish, and British immigrant craftsmen then settling in the city. By 1860, 42 percent of black wage earners were engaged in domestic and personal service occupations, waiting on whites, cutting their hair, changing their linen, and caring for their homes and children. Another 30 percent labored in unskilled positions, especially on the Ohio River docks, where as longshoremen they were able to profit from the great expansion of river traffic. But with the rise of railroad carriers in the 1850s and 1860s waterborne commerce declined, and by 1870, 54 percent of black wage earners were working in service and approximately 15 percent on the docks. The concentration in low-paying, petty employment was forcefully suggested by the fact that in 1860 the 3,900 blacks in Cincinnati (2.4 percent of the population) owned only 0.4 percent of its property. Perhaps as many as 90 percent of the blacks owned no property at all.

These conditions touched the Clark family's struggle for a decent life. William Clark had provided for training Michael in a trade and had secured for him an apprenticeship with a painter-paperhanger. But it was extremely difficult for blacks to sustain a position in such crafts, and Michael spent the last decades of his life running a barbershop, one of the few opportunities for proprietorship and one of the few skilled trades open to blacks. His son's efforts to find a dignified, challenging occupation were for a number of years filled with disappointment and clashes with racial discrimination, which left him with a deep distrust of whites but a profound identification with oppressed peoples. (He later remarked that the education in the ways of the white world he received in Cincinnati made him "tenderhearted toward all men who suffer.") Peter resolved that, unlike his father, he would never cut hair, finding it servile, demeaning work that could never challenge his mind. While still a student he showed sufficient intelligence to obtain a teaching position in 1846 in the city's then still privately financed black schools. But these schools could pay little, and Clark fastened his hopes on becoming a printer, the one trade that would bring him close to his first love—the written word. In 1848 he began an apprenticeship with a white stereotyper, to whom he gave $200 for training in the craft. Within a year, however, just as Clark was to attain journeyman's status, his boss left for California and sold the business to a man who refused to hire and train blacks. Clark then became a grocery clerk but was soon rehired to teach in the black schools, which had recently been absorbed into the public school system and thus seemed able to promise a secure livelihood. Yet because the all-white Cincinnati Board of Education sought to challenge the 1849 state law establishing black public education at the taxpayer's expense, Clark was not paid after his first three months on the job. The matter was tested in the courts, which took two years.

During this controversy Michael Clark died. Lacking an income, Peter had no choice but to take over his father's barbershop, no doubt a low point in his young life. He resolved to break with local custom and run an "equal rights" shop, which would cater to both white and black men. This led to a bitter confrontation with a white customer, after which Clark decided never to cut hair again. Reflecting on his failed bid for dignity, he now despaired of ever leading a decent life and fulfilling his quest for intellectual work in America. In this mood he decided to emigrate to West Africa, where John McMiken, a wealthy Cincinnatian who was a prominent colonizationist, had founded a settlement for free blacks on the Liberia–Sierra Leone border. To whites like McMiken, who sympathized with blacks but refused to disturb social peace by assaulting the color line, and to growing numbers of despairing blacks like Clark, who believed white Americans would always be racist, colonization proved attractive as a panacea for troubled race relations. But Clark got no further in this quest than New Orleans, for he refused to cross the ocean in the filthy schooner McMiken had commissioned for the party of some one hundred blacks. For the next two years, while the Afro-American pioneers struggled in West Africa and 90 percent died of fevers, Clark worked as a clerk for the municipal government of uniquely cosmopolitan, multicolored New Orleans. Such a position would have been unobtainable for a black man in northern Cincinnati, with its implacable color line. These experiences left a deep impression on Clark. They bred in him a strong dislike of emigrationism, which put him in conflict in the 1850s with the growing number of its black supporters. He also acquired a renewed understanding of the depth of northern racial prejudice.

Clark returned to Cincinnati in 1852 to work in the black public schools, which had won their court battle for public funding and were now hiring faculty. Except for 1853–58, he would be employed in these schools until 1886, first as a teacher, then as a teacher-principal in the pride of the black system—the high school. While his employment was not without its tensions, the black schools would be Clark's most assured and constant institutional base as a race leader. Though deeply involved in politics, his political affiliations shifted too often and unpredictably for him to emerge as a political boss. Under any circumstance Clark did not wish to be a political leader. There is little evidence that he sought to win blacks' loyalties through controlling such political resources as patronage. His practical claims to leadership lay elsewhere. He shared with his people a commitment to self-improvement, racial self-help, and overcoming the obstacles whites placed in their path; and like his people Clark possessed a profound faith in the power of education. It was in education and in teacher training, then, that Clark applied most consistently his substantial intellectual resources. Through his educational work and his powerful and morally vitalizing oratory, he also earned the authority to win the attention of blacks when he spoke out on political questions.

Nineteenth-century black educational and intellectual leadership of the sort Clark personified may best be understood if placed in the context of the race's self-help efforts. Excluded by prejudice and discrimination from the organized life of the general community, Cincinnati blacks, like free blacks elsewhere, responded by organizing themselves into a community and by creating, at times with white moral support and philanthropic assistance, their own institutions to further their aspirations for improvement. By 1860 six churches, seven fraternal and sororal lodges and mutual benefit societies, and an orphanage had been established. Blacks also founded an antislavery society, and numerous literary societies, and from time to time they organized cooperative businesses to expand black employment and generate capital for use within the race. The public schools to which Clark returned in 1852 had begun as private elementary schools. There were six of these schools by 1844 when a black high school, founded by an English clergyman, was established. The black schools had been maintained through contributions, tuition, and student musical performances, until they were absorbed into the public schools as segregated units. The products of considerable community activity and an investment in the future of children beginning life with such burdensome disabilities, the schools were a living embodiment of the self-help tradition. Because they continued to be managed largely by black administrators and taught only by blacks after becoming public, there remained considerable community pride invested in them. As a hardworking administrator, conscientious teacher, and a role model for black children, Clark became a voice for and a symbol of all the hopes and aspirations blacks looked to the schools to fulfill. In addition, as a persistent lobbyist in the schools' behalf, he was largely responsible for their political defense. Mostly through Clark's efforts, spending per capita on black education came in the 1860s to exceed

179

that for white education—a long overdue attempt by city school officials to make up for years of neglect.

The black schools nonetheless remained inferior to their white counterparts, as Clark himself sadly admitted in the 1870s, in equipment, curriculum, and convenience of location. A continuing challenge to Clark, they would also pose a cruel dilemma. By the 1870s Ohio blacks came to realize that only integration would bring their children equal educational opportunities. Clark understood this and agreed. Yet he could not contend for integration without threatening both his lifework and his career and those of the teachers he had trained. It was highly unlikely that black teachers would be hired to teach in integrated schools in color-conscious southern and central Ohio, where the majority of the state's blacks resided. Moreover, the inferiority of the black schools must have reminded Clark that whatever his own considerable ability as an educator, society would always place limits on him. That he felt frustrated and bitter at times with these limited circumstances was inevitable. After all, as a black biographer said of him in 1887, "A white man of his ability and learning would be president of a state college or governor of a state."

Career and political tensions had deep roots in Clark's life and character and resulted in dualisms that constantly plagued him. On one level they involved the pull of duty to a beleaguered, oppressed people and the simultaneous attraction of the wealthy, powerful white world, with its venerable intellectual traditions and its countless opportunities. Both had claims on Clark. On a less obvious level these tensions were instrumental in shaping Clark's most fundamental spiritual and philosophical orientations. As a committed Christian and a humanistic intellectual he hungered after a universalistic, inclusive vision of humanity, freed of the parochialism of race and race feeling. But in the everyday world he was always reminded of his "place" by American racism and by his own abiding sense of obligation to black people. Throughout his life, for example, Clark remained a loyal Mason and served at times as an officer in the order's highest ranks. He was attracted to Masonry, he said, by its idealistic vision of the unity of humankind. But Clark knew only too well that Ohio Masonry was segregated and that the state's white Masons for years had campaigned to establish the illegitimacy of black Masonry in the public mind. In the end it actually proved easier for the black Masons of Ohio to gain recognition, as they did in the mid-1870s, from lodges in Peru, Germany, France, Italy, Hungary, and the Dominican Republic than from white Ohioans.

The same tensions in Clark's life were even more apparent in religion. For many years he found himself torn between two very different denominations and theologies. Sometime in 1852 or 1853, after a decade of being buffeted about in his search for dignity and a career, Clark was converted to Unitarianism. So strong was the spiritual awakening accompanying his conversion that religion entered his teaching. He was dismissed promptly for this proselytizing and not rehired until 1857. It is not difficult to discern what Clark found attractive in the entirely white, liberal offshoot of New England Congregationalism. Although there is no evidence that he actually belonged to a Unitarian congregation, such membership was possible for blacks. The few Ohio blacks attracted to the faith were usually accepted without incident by a church. As an opponent of the color line, Clark was enabled through Unitarianism to breach one racial barrier. As an intellectual committed to reason and to letters, he found both a rationalistic theology and the opportunity for intra-denominational intellectual communion, in print, with the finest, white American minds of the age—Emerson, Lowell, Longfellow, Channing, and others. A humanitarian, he found a faith encouraging benevolence and service to the poor and handicapped of all races. A man inclined toward brooding and distrust, especially of whites, Clark found an optimistic belief in human decency and perfectability. And finally, a man straining against limits and parochialism, he found a faith that rejected predestination, embraced free will and personal responsibility, and came ever closer in the nineteenth century to espousing a doctrine of universal salvation.

Less clear than Clark's attraction to Unitarianism is how for many years, while holding these views, he also had a strong commitment to the African Methodist Episcopal church. In the early 1860s the A.M.E. congregation in suburban Walnut Hills regularly held religious services in Clark's home; and Clark, at times, spoke publicly like a committed African Methodist. The church's doctrines were quite different from those of Unitarianism. It shared with white Methodism an anti-intellectual, otherworldly orientation, which manifested itself in emotionalism, revivalism, pietism, and the absence of a social gospel. It, too, rejected predestination, but unlike Unitarianism it saw humanity as depraved and in need of a lifelong, soul-wrenching struggle against sin and for faith.

Yet Methodism had powerful nontheological, cultural, and political attractions for Clark. He explored them in a major oration in 1874 during the fiftieth anniversary celebration of African Methodism in Cincinnati. Reviewing the story of the church's origins, he praised it as a continuing, inspiring symbol of refusal to accept second-class spiritual status. In addition, said Clark, blacks had molded Methodism into a true manifestation of Afro-American culture. White Methodism's decorous, preacher-directed worship, with a trained choir in the background, did not suit "the ardent temperament we inherit from our African ancestors." By allowing for group participation and spontaneous individual religious expression during worship, however, blacks had made Methodism their own. Clark said with evident emotion, "No man can tell the Father for us, our hopes, our wants, our fears; no man or choir of men, can replace for us the privilege of announcing by the loud shout, the resounding hallelujah, and the triumphant hymn, the stream of joy which fills us, when the blessing is felt pouring like a flood into the soul." Clearly a part of Peter Clark identified in a powerful, emotional way with black culture as it was expressed in black religion. Participation in this supportive, enveloping culture through the A.M.E. church helped, moreover, to lessen the distance between him and the people he aspired to lead.

In the same address in which he praised black Methodism, however, Clark revealed his ambivalence, his longing to express the other part of his nature, which strove for universalism and desired to be part of a larger world beyond race. At the end of his oration Clark spoke of the future of African Methodism. He did not say that the future of the church would be secure as long as there were Afro-Americans and Afro-American culture but only as long as racism persisted. There was, he said, a need for the A.M.E. church until white prejudice was dead and black equality acknowledged. On this occasion Clark allowed for the possibility of such a transformation of the race's status. He suggested that some young people in the audience might "live to see that day when dissolution of the church will be a proper and wise thing" and when they might unite with white Methodists "in the rejoicing which will mark the event."

That Clark was pulled in so many, often conflicting directions at once placed him under considerable strain. After emancipation and enfranchisement the situation became increasingly intolerable for him and resulted in years of unstable activism. Clark's leadership was certainly not without its benefits to blacks during this time, but eventually his political position among Cincinnati blacks became so untenable that his status as a race leader was compromised.

Why did these complex tensions become so burdensome just at the historical moment when the prospects for Afro-Americans seemed more hopeful than ever before? Clark's distrust of whites and his acute sensitivity to evidence of white betrayal and manipulation led him often to distrust the race's new allies as much as its enemies. He feared that an undignified and self-defeating political dependence on the Republican party would replace slavery as a form of racial subordination. Furthermore, his personal quest for recognition and achievement continued to be frustrated even as new opportunities became available to the race. One such new opportunity—school integration—proved to be a personal disaster for him.

To understand this complex patterning of Clark's life at the dawn of the new era of race relations, one might compare his response with that of most of his peers to crucial events in the race's history between the mid-1850s and 1870: the emergence of an antislavery Republican party; the election of Abraham Lincoln; the defeat of the slaveowners; emancipation; reconstruction of southern society and politics; occupation of the South by federal troops; and the securing of federally protected civil and political rights for blacks. While these developments fell far short of full racial equality, the nation undeniably had come a long way in a very few years. From such hopeful signs northern race leaders of Clark's stature became optimistic that the day was not too distant when blacks would be integrated as equals into society.

That Clark shared such long-term hopes for the race is evident in his 1874 address on African Methodism. Yet almost from the start of these years of change, when it came to evaluating events then swirling around him, he evinced more caution than enthusiasm and a proclivity for seeing the underside of all positive trends. In the 1850s Clark was a leading organizer and participant in the black convention movement at both state and national levels. Many of his colleagues in the convention movement welcomed the founding of the Republican party. Clark, however, was far from enthusiastic. At a state convention in 1858, for example, there was a debate about whether the electoral decline of the proslavery Democrats and the rise of the Republicans was a hopeful sign. Clark was the only speaker to say it was not. He argued that the Republicans would make slavery more secure, because in their quest to become a national party they would seek to obtain southern votes. After the war Clark's belief that racial justice ranked low among Republican priorities combined with his personal distrust of whites to produce a continued lack of faith in the Republicans and, by extension, in the majority of the northern electorate, which was the bulwark of the party. While most black leaders measured the Republicans by how far they had come, Clark dispassionately examined their motives, which he found to be governed by considerations other than justice, for initiating progressive changes in race relations; and he emphasized how far they had to go. He regretted, Clark told a black audience in 1873, "that the motive which prompted the gift of freedom had not more kindly feeling toward the Negro in it." Emancipation had not been "done from any original impulse . . . to benefit us" but rather had become necessary to preserve the Union. And what more could one expect from a party founded by those "who felt no moral hatred of slavery" but merely judged it as an "inefficient" economic system and were most interested in "preserving the virgin soil of the West from the polluting step of the Negro, bond or free?"

After enfranchisement, when the overwhelming majority of black leaders believed, along with Frederick Douglass, that "the Republican party is the deck; everything else is the sea," Clark continued to press his criticisms of the Republicans for half measures and indecisive advocacy. In the early 1870s Republicans dragged their feet for some time before uniting successfully behind a national civil rights bill which would guarantee blacks equal access to public accommodations. In Ohio the party failed to give blacks anything but token patronage at any level of government and thus, Clark felt, bore responsibility for stifling black aspirations for symbolic recognition of the race's citizenship and for social mobility and economic security. The party helped sustain a system of inferior, resource-starved black schools in many central and southern Ohio towns and cities where it was in power. In light of these facts and the party's history of reluctant or inadvertent support for substantive change, Clark concluded by 1873 that it was little more than "a sentimental whine" to repeatedly tell blacks they should vote Republican out of gratitude and hope.

While distrust of even relatively progressive whites placed Clark at odds with much of black opinion in the 1870s, his own frustrated and ambivalent ambitions created other difficulties for him. Above all else there was the strain placed on him by his career in increasingly unpopular segregated schools, which he knew to be inferior. He could only contend for integration at the expense of all that he and his colleagues had worked for and accomplished over the years. Furthermore, Clark was not without personal political ambitions. He wanted a patronage position that carried with it prestige and a good salary. He desired recognition and inclusion in the ranks of those who mattered in America. He knew himself to be much more able than many of the whites regularly appointed to office. The position he did receive from the Grant administration in 1873—pensions agent—was a minor sinecure that increased his income, especially since he did not have to stop teaching, but was demeaning for a man of his intellect and aspirations.

184

Clark's growing frustration, blocked personal ambitions, public pessimism, and political ambivalence help to explain more than a decade of restless public activity which began in the early 1870s. Throughout these years his basic political problem was that no matter where he turned his allegiance, by his own criteria no party or group truly seemed to represent the promise of full citizenship and equality for blacks. In fact, some of the allies he made had no particular commitment to making black people's needs a paramount political issue.

His criticisms of the Republicans led him down some unconventional political paths other black militants were loathe to traverse. In the early 1870s Clark sided with white, anti-Grant Republicans, who would be the core of the Cincinnati Liberal Republican movement, because he agreed with the low-tariff and anticorruption views of these men. But above all he was attracted to their stand on the southern question, which the large majority of black leaders strongly rejected. Distrusting the Republicans as he did, Clark had reached the conclusion that the party was maintaining Reconstruction, through federal occupation of some southern states, only to enhance its power and out of no particular concern for blacks. Blacks were caught in the middle: used by northern white Republicans, who wanted their votes, and violently attacked by southern white Democrats, who rejected federal occupation and Republican rule. As a result of this view, Clark came to share with the Liberals the belief that continued federal occupation was accomplishing little more than increasing white racism and provoking antiblack violence. In place of the biracial Republican coalition that governed a declining number of states and localities with the support of the U.S. Army, Clark and the Liberals were willing to see the South returned to the leadership of the upper-class Democrats who had been among the leaders of the Confederacy. These patricians were believed to be the most willing, among all indigenous Democratic forces in the South, to accept the race's newly acquired freedoms and to end the violence. The basis of this belief was that the patricians often publicly expressed a paternalistic regard for blacks, which was actually rooted in their nostalgia for the prewar plantations, and they made ambiguous statements that appeared to indicate acceptance of blacks as citizens. While advocating this essentially accommodationist position, Clark strongly criticized Ohio Republicans for temporizing with local racism. For their part, his Liberal colleagues had no position on race in Ohio beyond acceptance of basic civil and political rights already mandated by the recent federal constitutional amendments.

Clark's acceptance of the Liberal position was a mark of his despair.

The violent situation in the South must not be allowed to continue. Yet, especially as the northern commitment to protect southern black rights waned, there seemed to be few promising alternatives. The patricians themselves proved unworthy of Clark's hopes. In fact, much of the antiblack violence during the postwar years was orchestrated by them. Once these same men attained power as Reconstruction ended in state after state, violent repression of black voters continued. As a result, Clark soon surrendered his alliance with the Liberals and returned to the G.O.P., which at least still supported federal occupation and protection of blacks from white terrorism in a few southern states.

His next years in the Republican party were troubled ones. At a well-publicized race meeting at Chillicothe, Ohio, in 1873, Clark called upon blacks to assume an independent position within the party: they must be willing to leave the party when it was indifferent to their welfare. Such independence, he promised, would persuade the Democratic party to compete for black support with patronage, nominations, and legislation. The success of the Chillicothe strategy depended upon black willingness to vote Democratic. But neither Clark nor the young black politicians, angered at the patronage situation, who attended the Chillicothe meeting were ready to do this. Though in 1871, with their "New Departure," Ohio Democrats had accepted the constitutional changes brought by the war and Reconstruction, they were still allied with southern racists and many of their own leaders still engaged in race baiting. The only practical result of the Chillicothe movement was that Columbus Republicans, perhaps disturbed by the attention Clark was receiving in central Ohio, nominated a black man for state representative, the first time this had been done in the state. He lost, as did Clark himself, who had been nominated as a delegate to the state constitutional convention.

Clark struggled with his political dilemma until 1877, when in the midst of the devastating economic depression and the great railroad strikes he announced himself a socialist. There can be no doubt of the depth of his commitment, his knowledge of Marxism, or his concern for the working class. The speeches he gave as the Workingman's party's losing candidate for state school commissioner in 1877 and for Congress in 1878 bristle with outrage at the assault on the living standards of workers by many depression-shaken capitalists. Clark denounced the self-help credo, which most black leaders embraced, as little more than an ideological hoax, and he called for an activist welfare state. Yet while satisfying some of his personal needs, this affiliation isolated Clark from black people. The Ohio Workingman's party was largely composed of immigrant German craftsmen, whose trades and unions were closed to blacks. The party voiced sympathy for the race but was ideologically conditioned only to assimilate the grievances of a skilled artisan class, which blacks had never been allowed to enter. Clark's socialist commitment did allow him an opportunity for leadership on the highest levels of a movement of white men possessing a universalistic ideology broad enough to encompass all humanity. But he soon wearied of the fierce intraparty ideological contentions and decided that he was not doing blacks any good as a socialist. The latter point loomed even larger in his mind because Cincinnati blacks had successfully defended his job when it was threatened by local white school officials angered by his radicalism.

The 1879 fall elections found Clark once more a Republican. But again, change was imminent. In 1882 he entered the Democratic party, and he and his son Herbert began publishing the Cincinnati *Afro-American* in the interests of the party, which provided large subsidies to the widely circulated newspaper. The editorial theme was Republican treachery, especially when it came to giving Ohio blacks the patronage promised them at election time. But the Clarks did not urge blacks to become Democrats. Their position was more in line with the Chillicothe strategy of a decade before. They argued that racial dignity and interests demanded more independent voting. On the southern question their views both harkened back to the Liberal Republicans and prefigured Booker T. Washington. They urged blacks to accommodate themselves to white Democratic power and to cultivate the bourgeois virtues of self-help, thrift, and enterprise. Not only did Clark thus give dramatic evidence of having drifted away from his socialist stance, but he again displayed a curious combination of militance on northern and accommodation on southern racial affairs.

Clark's reasons for becoming a Democrat were complex and inevitably both political and personal. They also involved discontents that were national and local in focus. Clark was bitter at the lack of Republican patronage, and not the least of his grievances was that President Garfield had declined to appoint him minister to Haiti. Also, President Arthur had adopted patronage policies inimical to the interests of southern black Republicans. In 1883, moreover, a Republican-dominated Supreme Court had struck down the Civil Rights Act of 1875. On the national level, therefore, Republicans seemed as willing as ever to betray blacks while asking for their votes every two years in the name of gratitude. By contrast, northern Democrats seemed considerably more attractive than in the past. During the 1870s, large numbers of once antislavery Republicans had switched parties because of new issues like the tariff and monetary policy. They took into the Democratic party liberal ideas about race, which might lead to reform in the North and perhaps even a softening of the views of the party's southern wing. Clark was not alone in seeing that blacks might benefit from this political transformation. Such eminent northern blacks as T. Thomas Fortune, a New York City editor, and George T. Downing, a Rhode Island businessman, now found Democrats as attractive as—or at least no more repellent than—Republicans.

All of the elements of this transitional and potentially beneficial political situation were quite apparent in Ohio in the 1880s. The titular heads of the two major parties seemed to symbolize changing political forces. George Hoadly, a Cincinnati Democrat who was a candidate for governor in 1883 and 1885, was a friend of Clark, a former antislavery Republican and long-time racial liberal. Joseph B. Foraker, Republican candidate for governor in 1883, 1885, and 1887, was said to have left college because of the admission of a black student, and it was well known that he had successfully defended the school superintendent of Springfield, Ohio, in a desegregation case brought to federal court by a black minister. But even had Hoadly been less attractive, Clark undoubtedly knew the time was right from a strategic point of view for playing the parties off against each other. From 1873 to 1885, in both presidential and gubernatorial elections, Ohio politics were unusually competitive and volatile. Winning majorities were small and fluctuated unpredictably between the parties. The situation was the same in other northern states, and in all of them some black politicians were quick to point out that the black vote, if set free of its Republican moorings, could constitute the balance of power. If that happened the parties would have to shower favors on blacks to win their votes. Increased patronage was usually mentioned as a goal, as was state civil rights legislation to replace the now-dead federal statute and school desegregation, probably the most difficult goal of all because of the depth of white resistance to interracial mingling.

Competition for the black vote did grow intense. Clark could legitimately claim much of the credit for the situation, though he was not alone in profiting from it. Hoadly attributed his narrow 1,318-vote majority in 1883 to the division of the black vote. While it is not at all clear that such a division took place, the argument had a life of its own. Hoadly moved to stake his claim to future, hopefully greater, black support by increasing the scope and scale of black appointments and liberally rewarding the two Clarks, whom Democrats saw as their chief contacts in black politics: Herbert got a clerkship in a state agency, while Peter became the first black trustee of Ohio State University. In his inaugural, Hoadly called for the passage of a law guaranteeing racial equality in public accommodations. He was ahead of his party on this issue, and the law the Democratic Assembly passed was weak. Black Republicans, now especially anxious to embarrass the Democrats, were quick to point this out in the black press. As a result, a stronger law was passed with bipartisan support. Hoadly then came out for school integration. However, he called for not wholesale desegregation but local option by blacks, in deference to Clark's concern for the future of black teachers. A bill embodying this proposal cleared the House but failed in the Senate.

The 1885 contest again pitted Foraker against Hoadly. Foraker did all he could to win black support, appearing before black audiences to clear his name and denouncing southern Democratic outrages against blacks. He called for school integration and repeal of Ohio's antebellum law banning interracial marriages. He also promised to better Hoadly's patronage record. When Foraker was elected by 18,000 votes, black Republicans claimed that he owed his victory to the race and had better follow through on his promises. Foraker appointed more blacks to office than any previous Ohio governor, and in 1887, with the aid of a Republican-controlled General Assembly, he achieved both repeal of the marriage law and a comprehensive school integration law. Many blacks did not share Clark's high regard for the local option provision because they feared whites would manipulate it to preserve segregation. Regret was expressed for the fate of black teachers, but most blacks felt that the opportunity to achieve racial integration in the schools was too important to the race's future to be passed up. The Republican majority gave them exactly what they wanted—integrated schools of the sort still only enjoyed by blacks in a few largely northeastern states. Of course, the political competition set in motion primarily by Clark was not alone in achieving integration. It mattered, too, that separate schools, even though inferior, were increasingly expensive; that the Ohio black population was still sufficiently small and scattered to constitute little threat to the interests of the state's whites; and that a good deal of racial liberalism continued to coexist with its opposite in the state. But certainly Clark must get some of the credit for this achievement. However tortured, his contribution helped to attain one of the most significant racial reforms in the North at the time.

Clark soon became the victim of his greatest triumph. In 1886 Republicans took control of the Cincinnati school board and charged the black educator with having offered a bribe to a witness in a political corruption case to save some of his new Democratic allies from going to prison. The evidence was strong and Clark was fired. Though he had alienated many Ohio blacks by his nonconformist politics and advocacy of local option, which were perceived as self-interested in nature, a number of Cincinnati blacks came to his defense. He had made too many enemies in Cincinnati, however, and he was finished there. At first he worked selling textbooks. Then he became principal of the segregated State Normal and Industrial School at Huntsville, Alabama, replacing William H. Councill. But soon Councill began efforts to regain his post; moreover, Clark could not accept the constraints placed upon him by southern caste relations. In 1888 he moved to somewhat more congenial St. Louis, where he taught in the black public schools until retiring in 1908.

After leaving Cincinnati, Clark seldom spoke out on public issues. So completely did he disappear from the public eye that on the few occasions when word of his work in the St. Louis schools or of his presence at some family celebration reached the black press in Ohio, people were surprised to learn that he was still alive. It was as if, after so many years of troubled activism, he had reached a point of exhaustion and had come to the opinion that there was no party or ideology left to turn to. Certainly he grew no more hopeful about race relations, for in 1908 he wrote the newly elected president, William Howard Taft, that white antipathy toward blacks seemed ineradicable to the extent that it vindicated the views of the black emigrationists of the previous century. Clark made no public statements in behalf of emigration or any other strategy or ideology, however. Perhaps he took solace in books and religion. But world-weary though he was, he did not forget the bitter world that had made him what he was or the price it had exacted from him in his quest for dignity. When he died in 1925, at age ninety-six, he willed his philosophy books to a St. Louis library, but he gave his beloved collection of volumes of poetry by blacks—and only these volumes—to a Cincinnati library. It is impossible not to believe that Peter Clark was making a final point.

Howard N. Rabinowitz   **10**

Three Reconstruction Leaders: Blanche K. Bruce, Robert Brown Elliott, and Holland Thompson

Emancipation and Reconstruction transformed the nature of black leadership. To be sure, there was significant continuity between the antebellum and postbellum years, symbolized by the continued predominance of the northern-based Frederick Douglass among black leaders. And, as before the war, many leaders did not hold either party or public office. This was true of some national figures and particularly so of local leaders, not only clergymen or prominent businessmen, but often illiterate farmers in the countryside. Yet during Congressional (or Radical) Reconstruction initiated in 1867, black leadership became centered in the South rather than the North, and despite continued contributions by non-officeholders, public and party officials were now the most important figures. Although there would not be a black congressman from the North until the 1920s, twenty-two southern blacks, including two senators, served in Congress between 1870 and 1901. Countless blacks served as state legislators and city councilmen and in other offices throughout the South.

Much controversy has surrounded black political leaders of the Reconstruction. Southern white opponents and even some northern whites at the time viewed them as illiterate, poverty-stricken, corrupt, and totally dependent on handouts from white Republicans, who allegedly controlled their votes. Early generations of scholars under the influence of Columbia University professor William Archibald Dunning and other critics of Reconstruction helped ingrain such views in history books. Woodrow Wilson, then a Princeton political scientist, concluded that during Reconstruction "unscrupulous adventurers" and plunderers, mostly from the North, manipulated "inexperienced blacks" in "an extraordinary carnival of public crime under the forms of law." Thirty-six years later, in 1929, Claude Bowers, in his best-selling book, *The Tragic Era,* viewed black leaders as lazy, ignorant, and childlike, managed by carpetbaggers and scalawags who preached hate and distrust of the former Confederates. The Mississippi legislature was "one of the most grotesque bodies that ever assembled.

A mulatto was Speaker of the House, a darker man was Lieutenant-Governor, the Negro Bruce had been sent to the Senate, a corrupt guardian was in charge of the public schools, a black, more fool than knave, was Commissioner of Immigration."

Yet a revision of this traditional approach was already underway. Begun by black participants in Reconstruction, the reevaluation of that era would include black and white liberal scholars and reflect the changing racial climate, capped by the civil rights movement of the 1950s and 1960s. It is now clear that no "Africanization" of southern politics occurred despite the unprecedented number of black office-holders at all levels of government. Even during the height of Reconstruction no black was elected governor or mayor of a major city, no large town had a black majority on its city council, and only in South Carolina did blacks constitute a majority in a state constitutional convention or legislative chamber. With regard to the backgrounds and qualifications of black leaders, the contrast with the traditional view is most vivid in places such as New Orleans and Charleston, S.C., which had contained significant antebellum free Negro communities; but throughout the South the first generation of Negro leaders was remarkably qualified for its new responsibilities.

On the basis of studies of individual congressmen, local leaders, and collective biographies it would seem that these black leaders tended to be relatively young, in their late twenties or early thirties, when the state constitutional conventions met in 1867 and 1868. Most were native-born and literate. One study of early Reconstruction leadership in New Orleans, for example, found that over 98 percent of these men were literate. The figures are about the same not only for the equally settled and cultured Charleston black community but for Raleigh, N.C., as well, where all twenty-five of the city's Negro councilmen between 1868 and 1901 were literate and all but one was born in North Carolina.

The leaders in Reconstruction were mostly artisans and petty tradesmen, with the addition, especially as the years passed, of an occasional lawyer or teacher, although ministers were especially important in Georgia. Significant numbers were property holders. In New Orleans 52.8 percent of the politicians had been skilled laborers and another 44 percent were businessmen and professionals in 1860–61; 25.3 percent of them had between $1,001 and $2,500 in assets. Few, if any, other groups of black leaders could match these figures, but the extent of property holding among them also was far greater than once acknowledged. For example, in 1870 the median wealth for the 174 delegates to the Reconstruction constitutional conventions of 1867–69 for whom such information has been found was $650.

Although many of the leaders were dark-skinned and most probably former slaves, there were disproportionate numbers of mulattoes and those with free antecedents. The latter two groups were again most significant in Louisiana and South Carolina, where there had been significant miscegenation involving upper-class white males and free and slave Negro females. In New Orleans over 91 percent of the leaders were mulattoes and over 97 percent had been free before the war; in Charleston the respective figures were 63 percent and 77 percent. More typical percentages were found among the delegates to constitutional conventions in which mulattoes and free Negroes had a slight majority, though individual conventions varied, with Louisiana and South Carolina having the largest number and Texas, Mississippi, and Georgia the fewest. Even in postconvention Georgia, however, where the influence of dark-skinned leaders and former slaves was perhaps the greatest in the South, among those state legislators for whom we have information, three of nineteen were mulatto and eight of twenty had been free before the war.

Southern black leaders were clearly an elite. Representing a largely unskilled, illiterate, rural constituency of dark-skinned former slaves, they were an ambitious group of young, skilled, educated men, often with urban connections, who were far more likely than their supporters to be mulattoes and to have free Negro antecedents. In his study of 255 Negroes elected to state and federal offices in South Carolina between 1868 and 1876, Thomas Holt concluded that most of them were literate, "a significant number" had been free before the Civil War, many owned property, and most worked in skilled or professional occupations.

The traditional view of black leadership concentrates on the alleged corruption, racism, and vindictiveness of black leaders and their manipulation by new white masters. The reality was quite different. Most black leaders supported amnesty for the former Confederates, opposed confiscation of rebel lands, and urged moderation in dealing with whites. Few of them called for "social equality" with whites. What they wanted for their people was land, education, and civil rights that included suffrage and equal access to public accommodations and public conveyances. Few black leaders called for integration. Initially, at least, they were satisfied to join their white allies in bringing about a shift from the exclusion that had characterized the previous policy toward blacks in schools, asylums, streetcars, and the like to a new policy of separate but equal access. By taking such stands, blacks helped produce the most democratic constitutions and responsible state and local governments ever found in the South. And while a few leaders came to favor black emigration as they began to despair over the undermining of Reconstruction by white economic intimidation, physical violence, and political fraud, most continued to seek the improvement of conditions for blacks within the South.

The relationship between the black leaders and their white allies was more complex. No doubt some were under the control of whites, whom they supported in return for jobs, money, or other favors; only a handful rose to power by defying whites of both parties; and few leaders were completely free from the need for white assistance. Nevertheless, black leaders followed their own instincts and sought to act in a way that would aid their people and also help their own careers. Although some leaders were placed in office by whites, most were elected or were attractive to whites because of their ties to the black community. Such basic institutions as the union leagues, churches, fraternal associations, and schools provided a training ground for black leaders that could be easily transformed into a power base.

White leaders who needed blacks as much as blacks needed them were often dismayed at black displays of independence. State and local Republican parties throughout the South were torn by factionalism that pitted white carpetbaggers, scalawags, and blacks against each other. But divisions were not simply on the basis of race, for blacks themselves were often divided. Sometimes divisions were based on color or antebellum status; at other times they were due to patronage or policy disputes, or simply competing ambition. In the end these divisions, as well as those between black and white Republicans and among white Republicans, made it easier for white Democrats to overthrow (or "redeem") the Reconstruction governments and severely restrict the power of those comparatively few blacks who remained in office.

The careers of three representative black leaders of the Reconstruction Era—Blanche K. Bruce of Mississippi, Robert Brown Elliott of South Carolina, and Holland Thompson of Alabama—help to illustrate the diverse nature of southern black leadership. Although no small sample can do full justice to the spectrum of that leadership, together these three men provide a revealing cross section in terms of their backgrounds, policies, and levels of political participation.

Senator BLANCHE K. BRUCE was the nation's most famous black officeholder. Although his less important fellow black Mississippian Hiram Revels had served briefly in the United States Senate in 1870, Bruce was the only black elected to a full term prior to the election of

Edward Brooke of Massachusetts in 1966. Bruce owed his success to close ties with influential whites and his skill at political infighting. He was a compromiser, or accommodationist, who favored gradual change and sought to avoid taking strong stands on controversial issues.

Though born a slave in 1841, Bruce grew up in Virginia, Mississippi, and Missouri as the playmate of his master's only son. He was taught how to read and write, did little work in the fields, and was further set apart from the other slaves by his light skin. Despite the outbreak of civil war and the proximity of freedom, Bruce initially chose to remain with his master. He eventually fled, first to Lawrence, Kansas, where he founded a school for former slaves, and then in 1864 to Hannibal, Missouri, where he established the state's first school for blacks. In 1866, after briefly working in a local newspaper office, he left to attend Oberlin, but a lack of funds forced him to return to Missouri. Soon after Bruce returned to his native South in the hopes of benefiting from the implementation of congressional plans for Reconstruction, which provided for Negro voting and officeholding. First he tried Arkansas, then Tennessee; with a friend he eventually moved to Mississippi, where blacks enjoyed a majority of some twenty thousand over whites at the polls. He found the Delta especially promising given the absence of an indigenous group of black leaders among its predominantly Negro population, coupled with the economic promise of the rich bottomlands.

Bruce first came to the attention of whites as a speaker during the 1869 elections and was appointed a voter registrar in Tallahatchie County following the wholesale Republican replacement of Conservative (a party name used interchangeably with Democrat in many southern states) officials. But Bruce already had a higher office in mind. Journeying to Jackson for the inauguration of the new administration in 1870, he impressed Governor-elect James Alcorn with his dignified manner, eloquence, and knowledge of government. With Alcorn's support Bruce was selected sergeant at arms of the state senate over several white candidates. Office quickly followed office, usually because of white support. Alcorn appointed Bruce tax assessor of the Delta's Bolivar County. With the help of a white carpetbagger named H. T. Florey, the boss of Bolivar County, Bruce was elected sheriff and tax collector in 1871. Soon after, the Republican state board of education appointed him county superintendent of education. Now the only black in the state to be both sheriff and superintendent of education (few blacks held even one of the jobs), Bruce broadened his power when he was appointed to the board of levee commissioners for a three-county district.

195

The key to this rapid rise seems not to have been the support of the black masses with whom he had little contact but rather of the white planters who continued to dominate the economy and therefore the politics of the area. Bruce was considered safe—a dignified and educated mulatto who did not identify himself with threatening issues. He became even more palatable when he, too, became a landowner, first by buying several town lots in the new county seat and then by purchasing 640 acres of swampy but fertile land which he developed into a plantation. More land followed, and by the 1880s he was a wealthy man, raising cotton with black labor.

Bruce performed effectively in office. His decisions as sheriff and assessor met with general acceptance by local whites, and there was no taint of scandal or corruption. No doubt he kept the tax rates quite low, especially after he himself became a landowner. His most impressive contribution came as superintendent of schools, taking a faltering system and turning it into one of the healthiest in the state. By the end of 1872 the county had twenty-one schools with more than a thousand students. Shortly before his resignation the next year, Bruce reported that "there are no longer difficulties besetting my progress in the future administration of the school system in this county, which energy and time will not remove." He had accomplished much by following a policy that did not offend local whites. As elsewhere in Mississippi and almost everywhere in the South, the schools were segregated, expenditures were kept low, black teachers replaced potentially "meddling" northern whites, and education was aimed at providing reliable workers and reducing crime. The prevailing attitudes and the continued power of the planter class over blacks and even white Republicans would have permitted little more. Still, by helping to establish the county's first school system and by assuring blacks a place within it, Bruce had furthered his own interests as well as those of his race.

At this point Bruce's relationship to his black constituents becomes clearer. Although he depended heavily on white allies, he was chosen for office to appeal to and provide recognition of a primarily black constituency. Black voters in turn could support Bruce for a number of reasons. Many blacks were grateful to him for giving them and their children an opportunity to get an education, no matter how limited. Others were thankful for patronage positions or personal favors that might range from an occasional small loan to a visit or a kind word. Still others no doubt voted for Bruce because they were paid to do so. But arguably the largest number of blacks supported him for symbolic reasons. To a certain extent they lived vicariously, taking pleasure in seeing one of their race, even though an "outsider," in positions of power and influence normally reserved for whites. What he did for them with that power was of less importance than its trappings.

Bruce's horizons continued to broaden as he now sought statewide office. In order to succeed he had to confront the white scalawags and carpetbaggers who controlled much of the patronage, as well as other ambitious blacks who sought to replace the recently deceased James Lynch as the state's most powerful black leader. It helped that Bruce was already known outside the Delta, having attended the state Republican convention in 1871 and having served as secretary to the Mississippi delegation at the 1872 Republican National Convention. He was further aided by the fact that he had not aligned himself with either Republican faction—the moderates led by Alcorn or the radicals led by Senator Adelbert Ames—in their bitter struggle to control the state. His policies in Bolivar County made him attractive to the Alcorn wing, while his failure to support moderate opposition to a strong state law against racial discrimination in public accommodations left him acceptable to the Ames wing.

During the critical 1873 campaign Bruce finally had to chose between the factions. The moderates under now Senator Alcorn and Governor Ridgley Powers were initially dominant, but their indifference to black rights and their cultivation of white southern Conservatives had alienated many Republicans. Courted by both wings at the state convention, Bruce was more receptive to radical entreaties for his support because he wisely realized that the moderates were losing influence. The radicals offered him the position of lieutenant governor. Adelbert Ames had left the Senate to become the Republican party's gubernatorial nominee, but he planned to return after gaining control of the governorship for the radicals, which meant that Bruce would soon move up to the governor's office. Nevertheless, he rejected the offer and instead asked for the Senate seat for himself. With Ames's support in the white-dominated legislature, Bruce subsequently defeated two white carpetbaggers by a comfortable margin and entered the Senate at the age of thirty-four, in March 1875. When his former patron, Senator Alcorn, refused to escort him for the swearing-in ceremony, Bruce fittingly attracted still another white sponsor in Senator Roscoe Conkling of New York, who stepped forward to do the honor. He repaid Conkling with his votes. And with the New Yorker's assistance Bruce was appointed to the standing committees on pensions, manufactures, and education and labor.

Bruce did not have an illustrious Senate career. Given the racist feeling in the chamber and the overthrow of Reconstruction in Mississippi in 1875 and throughout the South within two years, this should not be surprising. But he was a conscientious and capable representative of Mississippi and of his race. Like black officeholders at all levels of government he served constituents of both races in a number of mundane but necessary ways, such as introducing private relief bills. Bruce was also an especially strong advocate of Mississippi's interests as a member of the Senate Select Committee on River Improvements and as an ardent supporter of favorable railroad legislation.

His service in the Senate was most distinguished by his role as race spokesman. Although the first bill Bruce introduced called for desegregation of the U.S. Army, he normally took moderate stands and sought "to cultivate and exhibit . . . a courtesy that would inspire reciprocal courtesy." This time his strategy was less effective than it had been on the local level. Sometimes his low-profile approach frustrated him. Following the refusal of President Grant and other Republicans to aid Mississippi Republicans during the infamous 1875 political campaign and the subsequent overthrow of Governor Ames's regime, Bruce uncharacteristically lashed out at the failure of the national Republican party to protect southern blacks against Conservative violence and intimidation. Similarly, he condemned fellow Republicans for not seating P. B. S. Pinchback, the former black lieutenant governor of Louisiana, who claimed victory after a contested senatorial election. Like other black leaders Bruce defended the granting of civil rights to blacks and warned that southern white violence would rob blacks of the benefits of Reconstruction. "Violence so unprovoked, inspired by such motives, and looking to such ends," he declared in his maiden speech, "is a spectacle not only discreditable to the country, but dangerous to the integrity of our free institutions."

Like most freshmen legislators Bruce became more active midway through his term. He argued against a Chinese exclusion bill and for a more humane Indian policy, no doubt mindful of the effects that exclusionary treatment of other minorities might have on policy toward blacks. Although he briefly chaired the committee on river improvements, his most visible role was as chairman of the committee that investigated the failure of the Freedmen's Bank, which had cost thousands of blacks much of their life savings. The committee report blamed mismanagement by its white directors, but Bruce failed to secure congressional reimbursement for black depositors. Finally, symbolizing his conservative inclinations and belief that blacks could in fact receive fair treatment in the South, he opposed the Exoduster migration of the late 1870s. Thousands of blacks, the largest numbers from Mississippi, were fleeing the South to seek a better life in Kansas. Although Bruce warned Conservatives of the need to treat blacks better, his own need for black laborers and voters, the desire of white planters, and an evidently sincere belief that blacks would suffer greater hardships by making the journey led him to side with the majority of black leaders who opposed the migration. Nevertheless, Bruce made a valiant though unsuccessful effort to secure direct federal aid to destitute migrants in Kansas. He expressed even stronger disapproval of a proposed back-to-Africa movement, claiming that since the antebellum period the Negro had secured personal, civil, and political rights. Furthermore, whites were so dependent on black labor and blacks were such a potent political force that if the black man had patience and worked hard, "he will live to rejoice over a condition of society in the communities of the South in which he can entertain independent political opinions without prejudice, and to assert and exercise all the rights without hindrance and without danger."

Such pronouncements were less important in assessing Bruce's effectiveness as a political leader than were his actions within Republican party politics. By 1878 Bruce, together with two other Mississippi Negroes, James Hill and John R. Lynch, had wrested control of the state Republican party from the white-dominated moderate faction that had regained power following the "revolution of 1875." Hill, a former secretary of state under Ames, and Lynch, former speaker of the Mississippi House and three-term congressman, handled affairs in Mississippi while Bruce sought to protect the "triumvirate's" interests in Washington. The coalition's primary aim was patronage, which it remained in charge of until the 1890s. Although Bruce succeeded in getting President Hayes to appoint Hill collector of internal revenue in the state, the three men trod carefully, recommending only a handful of blacks for office, thus assuring continued white acceptance of their power, which in turn encouraged Hayes to turn to them on patronage decisions.

Bruce had solidified his position within the state Republican party, but by the time his Senate term was over, Democrats controlled the legislature and there was no hope for reelection. While maintaining his interest in state politics, Bruce settled in Washington, where he shifted his attention to national Republican affairs and the pursuit of appointive office for himself. He supported Secretary of the Treasury John Sherman and later former president Grant in their unsuccessful quests for the Republican nomination in 1880 but then campaigned loyally for the nominee, James Garfield. As a reward he had hoped for a cabinet position; instead he was offered a post as minister to

Brazil or as assistant to the postmaster general, both of which he declined. He asked instead to be appointed register of the treasury, and with the active support of his former Senate Democratic colleague, L. Q. C. Lamar, he won Senate confirmation to the highest appointive position given a Negro up to that point. He lost the position when Cleveland was elected president. Before returning to politics in 1888 to campaign for Benjamin Harrison, Bruce went on a national lecture tour to promote racial harmony and better treatment for all minorities. In return for his part in Harrison's victory he was appointed recorder of deeds for the District of Columbia. Again out of office following Cleveland's victory in 1892, Bruce contented himself by supervising his more than one thousand acres of fertile Delta land, dabbling in state politics, serving as a trustee of Howard University and a member of the local school board, and awaiting the return of the Republicans to power. With McKinley's election in 1896 he was again made register of the treasury, which, since his initial appointment, had been reserved by Republicans for prominent blacks. Four months later Bruce died of diabetes at the age of fifty-seven.

Prominent men of both races attended his funeral. The *New York Times* called him next to Frederick Douglass "the foremost man of his race." The *Washington Post* was more perceptive, noting that he was not "especially beloved by the masses of his colored fellow-citizens" but "was admired by the judicious and respectable among the whites and blacks alike." In a sense Bruce had always been cut off from the black masses (ironically the very people white slate-makers had used him to appeal to), first as a favored mulatto slave, then as a successful planter, and finally as a prominent national politician. Blacks voted for him for local office in large numbers, for reasons already noted, but there is no evidence that he was closely associated with any of the basic black institutions in Mississippi. And while black legislators helped elect him to the Senate, they comprised a minority of the Mississippi state legislature. Even in Washington he lived in a largely white world, married to a wealthy mulatto, primarily entertaining white guests (in addition to leading blacks like Douglass and Lynch) and belonging to a white church, the First Congregational. Although he was not a "race-first" man, like some leaders, he was not ashamed of being a Negro. Indeed, he was proud of it. "The Negro of America," he declared, "is not African, but American," and in his view assimilation into American society held the greatest prospects of success for him and his race. Like marginal people everywhere who are the products of a minority culture but feel equally or more comfortable within the dominant culture, Bruce served as an intermediary between the black and white worlds of nineteenth-century America, and in the end he came to prefer the latter.

For less fortunate blacks Bruce urged hard work, self-help, and the value of education. It was familiar and useful advice but increasingly less credible in the New South. Bruce knew that conditions did not favor black advancement. He protested the treatment of southern blacks and in 1890 urged federal aid to education and protection of black voting rights, but basically he believed that once southern whites came to appreciate the loyalty and ability of their black neighbors, conditions would improve. Meanwhile, Bruce discouraged emigration to Kansas and Africa, extolled black skills (as in his capacity as director of black exhibits at the Industrial Cotton Centennial Exposition in 1884–85), urged patience, and held out the vague hope that blacks would be assimilated into American society on the basis of equal, if at times separate, treatment. Such hopes made sense to him. After all, he had flourished within American society despite his humble origins. Yet to the mass of blacks mired in poverty and losing their political and social rights, Bruce's life-style, opposition to the exodus, failure to help on the land issue, and entreaties to hard work and patience had little relevance. It was easier to identify with Booker T. Washington on the basis of his darker color, his decision to remain in the South, and, above all, his more visible evidence of power among whites.

As a wealthy mulatto planter who had especially good relations with whites both within his state and the nation, thanks to his moderate policies and compromising nature, Blanche Bruce could not have been more different than ROBERT BROWN ELLIOTT, South Carolina's controversial black lawyer and congressman. The dark-skinned Elliott was a racial militant, anathema to most whites; though not above dealing with white politicians, he owed most of his success to a strong black base and his own forceful presence. Rather than a compromiser, he was an ardent practitioner of confrontational politics. And in whatever he did, neither he nor others ever forgot that he was a proud black man.

During Reconstruction, South Carolina offered more opportunities for black leadership than any other state. With 60 percent of its population black, it was the only state other than Mississippi with a black majority; and its blacks did a better job of capitalizing on their numbers than did those of Mississippi. Only in South Carolina did blacks comprise a majority of the delegates to the conventions called to draft constitutions for the first Reconstruction governments.

Although no black ever held the governorship, between 1868 and 1877 there were three black lieutenant governors, numerous other statewide officers, a two-to-one black majority in the House and a clear majority on joint ballot of the House and Senate. In short, South Carolina was just the kind of state to attract an ambitious carpetbagger like Elliott, even though, unlike Mississippi, it already had a cadre of indigenous leaders centered around the talented antebellum free Negro elite of Charleston.

Elliott was definitely an interloper, but his origins are shrouded in mystery. He claimed that he was born in Boston in 1842 of West Indian parents and had been educated in private schools in Boston, Jamaica, and England, including Eton College, from which he allegedly graduated with honors. He then briefly read law with a noted legal scholar before returning to the United States in 1861, soon after to join the Union army. Contemporaries and most historians have accepted his account, but his most recent biographer convincingly argues that except for the birth year it was all a fabrication. It seems instead that Elliott was actually born in England, educated in English schools (though certainly not Eton), trained as a typesetter, and served only in the Royal Navy. He might have jumped ship in Boston Harbor in 1866 or 1867 and decided to seek his fortune in America, without, however, taking out citizenship papers.

What is certain is that as of March 1867 Elliott was associate editor of Charleston's *South Carolina Leader,* a Republican newspaper edited by Richard Cain, a forty-two-year-old Negro clergyman from Brooklyn, New York, and a future state legislator and congressman, sent by the African Methodist Episcopal church to proselytize the freedpeople. One of Elliott's friends called Elliott "commanding in appearance," and his biographer describes him as "a full-blooded black of medium height with close-cropped hair and a neatly trimmed mustache." A *New York Times* reporter, however, provided a more common view among contemporary whites, describing him as "very black, very well spoken and bitter as gall." Indeed, throughout Reconstruction, whites would view Elliott as a talented orator and a forceful leader but also a racial militant who personified black resentment of second-class treatment. Under his leadership Cain's paper rejected its gradualist approach and adopted the slogan "Equality and Union," which Elliott championed throughout his short but spectacular political career, often to the dismay of allies and enemies of both races.

During the almost ten years of Radical rule in South Carolina, Elliott emerged as the major black spokesman in a state unsurpassed in the quantity and quality of its major black leaders. Elliott's importance and power is reflected in his impressive list of public and party offices. Although he arrived in South Carolina after the pivotal Colored People's Convention of 1865, which produced so many of the state's leaders, he was one of the seventy-one black delegates to the 1868 constitutional convention, which drafted the most democratic constitution in South Carolina's history. Though nominated for lieutenant governor at the Republican convention of that year, he dropped out of the race after finishing third on the first ballot. The next month, when he was already the only black on the five-man board of commissioners in Barnwell County, Elliott was elected to the state House of Representatives, where he finished second in the balloting for speaker. Following his selection as chairman of the powerful Committee on Railroads and his appointment to the vital Committee on Privileges and Elections, a Charleston paper claimed with some justification that he was one of eight men (four of them black) who controlled state government. Adding credence to this assessment was his appointment as assistant adjutant general of South Carolina, which placed him in charge of organizing a militia. In 1870 Elliott was elected to Congress over a white lawyer from a district that had only a slight black majority. He handily won reelection two years later but resigned near the end of the term to run again for the state House. Easily victorious, he served as speaker from 1874 to 1876. He was then elected state attorney general in 1876 but was among the five Republican officeholders removed following the Democratic triumph of that year. Elliott wielded even more power within the party itself. He attended three Republican national conventions (twice leading the delegation), served as state party chairman during much of the 1870s, and was usually permanent chairman of the state nominating conventions. In the latter two positions he played a decisive role in determining party policy and choosing candidates.

Whether in the constitutional convention, state legislature, or Congress, Elliott aligned himself with the Republican party's radical faction. At the convention he successfully led the fight against articles requiring a literacy test for voters and a poll tax that would be used to fund public education. In each case he correctly predicted that the measure could be used by future hostile administrations to disfranchise blacks and undermine the gains of Reconstruction. He was equally adamant in calling for the invalidation of debts contracted for the purchase and sale of slaves. In the legislature he strongly supported a successful bill to ban discrimination in public accommodations and public conveyances. As a congressman he gave a celebrated speech in favor of federal suppression of the Ku Klux

Klan, voted against the amnesty bill to remove political disabilities from former Confederates, and vigorously debated former Confederate vice-president Alexander Stephens over the merits of the proposed civil rights legislation that eventually became the Civil Rights Act of 1875. Fittingly, and as a sign of his growing national reputation, Boston blacks in 1874 invited Elliott to give the oration at ceremonies to honor the memory of the Radical U.S. Senator Charles Sumner.

Given Elliott's considerable power, visibility, and outspokenness on controversial issues, it is not surprising that he became the object of frequent Democratic attack and even opposition within his own party. What is surprising was the viciousness of the attacks and the extent to which he was singled out for abuse. There was, in fact, much in his record that Conservatives chose to ignore. Elliott occasionally lent support to white Democrats, in one instance supporting a Democrat for a circuit judgeship and in a second helping to remove the political liabilities of a Democrat who subsequently became his law partner. Despite his reputation as a racial militant, at the constitutional convention he coupled his support for a public school system and compulsory attendance with opposition to integration. Similarly, in a state so dependent on a black labor force, Elliott did little to threaten the economic status quo. Although he served as president of a state labor convention in 1869, he had favored a permanent halt to confiscation of planter land at the convention and never seriously interested himself in the plight of rural or urban black workers. And even some Democrats admitted that he took a more moderate view of the role of the militia than did Governor Robert Scott, who sought to use it as an offensive rather than a defensive force.

There was also the strong strain of self-help ideology that permeated Elliott's speeches. Like the more conservative Bruce, he was a firm believer in the value of public education. Then, too, he frequently reminded black audiences of the responsibility they had in South Carolina since they were the majority. In a nationally reported speech in 1874, following his triumphant civil rights speech in Congress, Elliott told a Columbia audience of the need to clean up state and party government because blacks were being judged by a different standard. Obsessed with fears about the fragility of the Reconstruction governments, conscious of the fact that "revolutions may go backward," Elliott called for federal support of southern blacks. But at the same time he argued that blacks themselves had their destiny within their own hands and should rise to the challenge.

Nevertheless, Democrats insisted upon seeing Elliott as an irresponsible hater of whites and a troublemaker. "Able, audacious and unscrupulous," one Democratic paper called him. To support such assessments white Carolinians, including some Republican enemies, claimed that Elliott was one of the state's major "corruptionists." This, of course, was a common charge against both black and white Radicals during Reconstruction. No doubt corruption existed, just as it did in the North, especially in such solidly Democratic cities as New York. Yet historians have amply demonstrated that even in the South white Democrats participated in much of this corruption during Reconstruction and often surpassed their Republican predecessors during the post-Reconstruction years. Among Republicans, South Carolina's white politicians, including carpetbaggers like Governors Robert Scott and Daniel Chamberlain and U.S. Senator John Patterson, and scalawags like Governor Franklin Moses, Jr., engaged most often in financial irregularities and received the largest share of the spoils. Black politicians were generally left with the crumbs, often in the form of petty bribes. Contemporary and later critics of Elliott exaggerated the extent and seriousness of his alleged corruption; his recent liberal biographer minimized it in an effort to present a favorable picture of him, other black leaders, and Reconstruction itself. The record, in fact, is not all that clear, but it does seem that while Elliott was resistant to small bribes and other minor enticements, he was not above reproach. He benefited financially from at least one suspect railroad deal, drew excessive legal fees as assistant adjutant general, received state and party funds for lobbying efforts (including $6,000 to prevent the impeachment of Governor Scott), and liberally distributed public and private money during election campaigns. As a result, despite a series of unprofitable law partnerships, he was able to live in fine style and purchase a number of city lots and an elegant three-story house in Columbia. But the corruption of a Moses or Scott was more blatant, and Elliott was never indicted for any crime, unlike several of his black and white contemporaries. The attention given to him seems to have been based on his considerable power and his color, not on any conclusive evidence.

Yet more than color, power, and positions were involved. Elliott was singled out in large measure because of his style and lack of deference toward whites, whether friend or foe. To one Democratic newspaper he was "as big a rascal as can be found anywhere within the ranks of Radicalism and is besides, *supremely insolent, arrogant and arbitrary*" (italics added). Sometimes blacks experienced his wrath or his acerbic tongue. During debate in the legislature, Elliott referred to future congressman Robert De Large as "a pigmy who was trying to play the part of a giant" and was "elocutionizing himself into

205

a perspiration which stood out upon his skin like warts." It was more disturbing to Conservatives when he showed the same disrespect to whites. During debate on the civil rights bill, for example, Elliott sarcastically concluded that the Negro "aims at a higher degree of intellect than that exhibited . . . in this debate" by a Virgina congressman who had claimed that blacks were racially inferior. Elliott verbally attacked all three Republican governors, calling Chamberlain, who was admired by many Democrats, a liar and a crook. Elliott could also be vindictive, as when he led an unsuccessful attempt to impeach Chamberlain's leading black ally, state treasurer Francis Cardozo, and in his unremitting opposition to Chamberlain's renomination in 1876. While other blacks might object to segregation in public accommodations, only Elliott could boast that he had a white federal employee fired for noisily leaving a normally segregated Washington restaurant when Elliott was permitted to eat there. Blanche K. Bruce, of course, never gave whites such ammunition.

Elliot owed much of his reputation for being "uppity" and a "race first man" to his key role in reversing the practice in South Carolina of blacks deferring to whites over nominations to major offices. At the 1868 nominating convention he had been reluctantly among those blacks who urged a go-slow policy that gave the four congressional seats to whites and settled for a black in only one state office. By 1870, however, as chairman of the nominating convention, Elliott was instrumental in placing blacks (all free before the war) in three of the four congressional seats, gaining the lieutenant governorship and in general expanding black influence in the party. Both white Republicans and Democrats seem never to have forgotten this. Nor did they overlook Elliott's continued role as a kingmaker in switching his support over the years from Governor Scott to Governor Moses and finally, and quite reluctantly, to Governor Chamberlain. The faction-ridden Republican politics of South Carolina, with its racially mixed slates of bolters and constant friction even among regulars, defies description in a short essay. Suffice it to say that Elliott, as chairman of the nominating convention and party chairman, rarely backed a loser in nomination fights, and his influence, especially as the sole designator of credentials committees, was often decisive.

This did not mean that Elliott was all-powerful or even able to promote his own interests to the extent he desired. In 1872, for example, he lost his fight for the U.S. Senate nomination. Dismayed by the lack of patronage given to blacks by the incumbent senator Francis Sawyer, and no doubt impressed by his own considerable qualifications, Elliott sought to take the nomination from Sawyer.

Despite his obvious strengths Elliott had a number of liabilities, which even in a fair fight might have meant defeat. Many whites were fearful and blacks envious, his sharp temper alienated others, and some simply believed that South Carolina's and the party's interests could be best served by a white man. When Sawyer dropped out of the contest the wealthy railroad magnate John Patterson emerged as the white frontrunner. Not taking any chances of being overlooked, Patterson liberally distributed bribes to legislators that allegedly averaged about $300. The other white candidate, former governor Scott, averaged $100 a vote. Elliott, who had no funds, gave out no bribes, though he readily admitted he would have done so if he had had the money. Patterson even offered Elliott $15,000 to remove himself from consideration. Elliott refused and Patterson won the nomination in the state Senate by offering $2,000 to a Scott man to switch his vote. Meanwhile, in the House, many blacks ignored appeals to vote their race and deserted Elliott, and so he lost by a count of twenty-seven to seventy-three. Clearly, whites rather than blacks tended to draw the color line, and with his liabilities and lack of resources Elliott had gone as high as he could.

Elliott hoped that his election as attorney general in 1876 would prove a stepping stone to the governorship, but time was running out for him and his party. As in Mississippi the previous year (and explicitly drawing on that example), white Democrats used violence, economic intimidation, and fraud to overthrow the Republican administration. Fraudulent returns from two northwestern counties produced a disputed election in which both sides claimed victory. For almost five months South Carolina had two state legislatures and both the Democrat Wade Hampton and the incumbent Daniel Chamberlain had themselves inaugurated as governor. Also in dispute were the state's electoral votes, which in 1876 assumed a critical importance. To win, Rutherford B. Hayes, the Republican presidential candidate, needed the votes of South Carolina, Florida, and Louisiana, the only southern states still in Republican hands. In the end the electoral votes went to Hayes; but in South Carolina, Democratic threats forced a favorable decision from the Republican-controlled state supreme court that produced a Democratic legislature and the installation of Hampton as governor. Chamberlain's fate was sealed when Hayes ordered federal troops, called out during the election, to return to their barracks. Elliott and five other executive officers who had been duly elected were subsequently removed by Hampton, an action upheld by the compliant supreme court. By the end of 1877 the Democrats had forced the resignation of numerous Republican legislators, a process made easier by the rifts within the Republican party.

As state chairman Elliott had been in charge of the 1876 campaign. Unlike the more cautious Bruce, who in Mississippi feared inciting whites as well as for his own safety, Elliott spoke throughout the state. He remained chairman, but in both 1878 and 1880 he successfully urged that the Republicans not run a statewide campaign. He believed that the lack of Republican opposition would lead to dissension among Democrats, just as the absence of Democratic challengers had earlier produced divisions among Republicans. By 1880, however, Elliott had become increasingly discouraged about prospects for the future. The following year he led a delegation of blacks to see President-elect James Garfield. Addressing Garfield, he listed the various examples of discrimination against southern blacks in the courts, voting precincts, schools, and public accommodations and warned that without federal help blacks would join the growing exodus. He was particularly interested in securing federal aid for education. Garfield answered with little more than platitudes.

Personal misfortunes fueled Elliott's despair. In 1879 dire financial straits forced him to close his law office. A minor patronage job as special inspector of the customs in Charleston at $144 a month helped, but he was soon required to sell his house to settle debts. His wife's medical problems and his first bout with malarial fever compounded his difficulties. He returned to the limelight as a delegate to the Republican National Convention in 1880, but he failed to see his choice, Secretary of the Treasury John Sherman, selected. Blanche K. Bruce remained optimistic about the Negro's eventual assimilation into American life because of his own experiences; Elliott, on the other hand, was pessimistic, particularly as his health, political power, and financial status declined. There followed other bouts of fever and an unwanted transfer to New Orleans, a move probably intended to separate a potential troublemaker from his power base. After eleven months in his new job as special agent of the treasury, Elliott's criticism of his boss and his decision to back a losing political faction cost him his job. A new law firm did not do well, his health worsened, and in August 1884 Elliott died of malarial fever at the age of forty-two.

Unlike Bruce, Elliott was not given an elaborate funeral, though his death was national news. Frederick Douglass penned a tribute, and some favorable obituaries appeared in northern and Negro newspapers. But the *Charleston News and Courier* more accurately represented the view of southern whites and most subsequent observers by headlining its report, "Another of the South Carolina Thieves Gone

to His Account." Elliott was clearly a charismatic leader who provoked outrage among whites and enthusiasm among blacks—unlike
Bruce, who did neither. He had his faults—among them a notorious
temper, vindictiveness, and, at best, amorality—but what outraged
critics was his racial pride and insistence on *demanding,* not asking,
for his rights and the rights of his people. By calling persistently for
the unprecedented expansion of national power to guarantee the
fruits of Reconstruction, while at the same time urging blacks to be
more worthy of the freedom they had won, Elliott was a precursor of
many twentieth-century black leaders. Yet despite the attention given
to him as a proponent of racial politics, Elliott was always an ardent
party man and, like Bruce, believed that a strong Republican party
and Union were the blacks' best hope for equality. As a result, while
whites such as Governor Chamberlain could attempt a rapprochement with Democrats and seek to deny office to black Republicans,
Elliott, even after opposing men like Chamberlain within the party,
could campaign vigorously for them in the general election. Had
more South Carolinians, black and white, been as devoted to party
unity and racial justice, perhaps the Republicans would not have
been as easily ousted.

Despite differences in style and policy and Bruce's greater prominence, both Bruce and Elliott were nationally known black leaders.
This was not true of HOLLAND THOMPSON of Montgomery, Alabama.
No one knew of him outside his state, historians have rarely mentioned
him, and he has been almost totally forgotten in his hometown. Not a
single Montgomery public facility immortalizes his memory, his death
went unrecorded in all but two local newspapers, and there were no
tributes from national leaders. Information about him is more fragmentary than in the case of Elliott or Bruce, and there is no known
photograph of him. He is thus representative of the large number of
forgotten local black leaders; but more than that, a study of his career
reminds us of the complexity of Reconstruction Era politics and the
hazards of labeling politicians as militants or accommodationists,
radicals or Uncle Toms.

Thompson was born a slave in Montgomery in 1840. His parents
had been brought from South Carolina in the 1830s by a South
Carolinian named William Taylor, who became a moderately wealthy
planter in Montgomery County. At the end of the Civil War, Taylor
still owned Thompson, who was working as a waiter at a local hotel.
After emancipation Thompson, who had learned to read and write as
a slave, opened a grocery that became one of the most prosperous

Negro firms in the city. By 1870 he owned city and rural real estate worth at least $500 and personal property worth $200. Unlike Bruce and Elliott, Thompson depended for his living on a black clientele. Thompson was more firmly rooted in the black community in other ways as well. A fundamentalist Baptist who advocated temperance and bible study, he was one of the founders of the First Colored Baptist Church and the Baptist State Convention and head of the local and statewide Baptist Sunday School Association. He also served as president of the association appointed to oversee operation of Swayne School for blacks (run by northern white Congregationalist missionaries), as chairman of the Union League's Lincoln Council (an all-black political club that struggled for parity with the city's two all-white Republican clubs), and as a member of the advisory board of the local branch of the Freedmen's Bank. In these various capacities and others he made himself further known through a steady stream of speeches and letters to local newspapers.

Montgomery was a good place for a young, ambitious, and able former slave who was a fine orator and, as a local paper described him, physically impressive—a "pure African, nearly as black as they are ever made, six feet high and with a rather good natured expression." In 1870, 49 percent of the city was black, more than 55 percent in Thompson's home base of the Fifth Ward, site of his church and store. Although Republicans had only a tenuous hold on the Alabama state government, losing control temporarily between 1870 and 1872 before finally being permanently overthrown in 1874, few cities in the South could match Montgomery as a Republican stronghold. Between 1868 and 1875 its mayor was a Republican, and for all but two years Republicans controlled the council. Montgomery County was also under Republican rule until 1877, and no Democrats were sent to the state legislature until the following year. Blacks were especially well represented in the state legislative delegation, and there were always two blacks on the twelve-man city council. Thompson was the city's most prominent black officeholder. Beginning in 1868 he served four terms as city councilman, three as board of education member, and two as state legislator. He was also one of the handful of blacks on the first state Republican Executive Committee. Although he clearly became a factor in Montgomery politics because of his work in black educational, religious, and political affairs, Thompson also benefited from the support of several key white leaders, including scalawag mayor Thomas Glasscock and two carpetbaggers, Sheriff Paul Strobach and U.S. Senator George E. Spencer.

How did Thompson wield his power? On the one hand there is

ample evidence to rank him as a moderate or even a conservative. In the immediate aftermath of emancipation he urged blacks to help themselves rather than look to federal support, or as he told an 1866 Emancipation Day rally, "The colored race . . . must not stand waiting for others to push them along." Blacks, he argued in 1867, had to work industriously, educate their children, avoid whiskey, and cease "bickering" among themselves. He also asked blacks not to join military companies because such groups angered whites. He spoke out against confiscation of white-owned property, asked blacks to end hard feelings toward "our conservative friends," and called only for civil and political rights, since social rights "will work [themselves] out in good time." As councilman he was instrumental in setting up a segregated public school system. Rather than seeking to integrate the local cemetery, Thompson called for the establishment of a separate black graveyard; rather than seeking desegregation of the city hospital, he sought to improve facilities for black patients there. As a state legislator he accepted segregated railroad cars and a separate state agricultural school for blacks. On a personal level he seems to have named his oldest son after his former master.

There was another side to Thompson, however. He fought hard for several measures of special concern to blacks, including a branch of the Freedmen's Bank for Montgomery, equal pay for black streethands, a city public defender, city soup kitchens, and taxation that did not unfairly affect the poor. In August 1866 he called upon blacks to combat the conservative policies of Andrew Johnson's administration. Unlike many black leaders he placed the highest priority on making the new southern homestead law a more effective means of providing land for the freedpeople. Both as state legislator and councilman, Thompson unsuccessfully fought against efforts to limit black political power through laws requiring registration and other tightened voting procedures. And in another personal matter he named a second son after Wendell Phillips—the famous white abolitionist.

Particularly noteworthy was Thompson's success in getting black policemen appointed for the first time in the city's history and keeping roughly half the force black during most of Reconstruction. When a leading white Republican proposed that black police be appointed only if they were restricted to arresting blacks, Thompson said that that would be all right if white police could only arrest white criminals. The white Republican withdrew his proposal and—to the chagrin of many whites—interracial arrests became a fact of life in the city. Thompson unsuccessfully sought to end enforcement of a state law barring racial intermarriage, and he split with the Congregationalist missionaries over their failure to use black teachers in Swayne School. While accepting segregated access to schools, graveyards, agricultural colleges, and railroad cars, Thompson, like so many other black leaders, sought to move a resisting white South from the antebellum system of exclusion to segregation—and in Thompson's case, not simply segregation, but separate yet equal treatment, in those days by no means a conservative proposal. Indeed, as a councilman and school board member Thompson saw to it that throughout Reconstruction per capita expenditure for black and white schoolchildren was at least equal.

Nor did Thompson back away from challenging the white Republican incumbent in a race for Congress. This came in 1872, when at the age of thirty-two, with four years of experience in the state legislature and the city council and a strong base among urban blacks, Thompson felt it was time that the roughly one-half black district had a black congressman. Yet he faced two major obstacles: Charles Buckley, the white incumbent, and James T. Rapier, a black planter and a more formidable and popular member of the pro-Negro wing of the party. In the end, Rapier triumphed.

Thompson's failure reveals much about the recruitment of blacks for higher office and the interaction of white and black politicians. He was initially at a disadvantage because he had weakened his own position with potential supporters. In a recent nominating convention he had been chosen chairman since he was thought to be neutral in the intraparty strife between the forces aligned with carpetbaggers Strobach and Spencer and an opposing faction. When he sided with Strobach and Spencer in a number of critical decisions, he earned the emnity of the losers. This came at a time when he was taking increasingly militant stands in the state legislature. He had also become embroiled in church politics. Charged with financial irregularities, he was temporarily expelled from his church, something that no doubt seriously weakened his black base of support. One of the white Congregationalist missionaries who had done battle with Thompson over hiring Baptist as well as black teachers for his school gleefully reported, "Holland Thompson is rapidly losing his influence and a more generous and liberal spirit is coming in its stead." Unlike Blanche K. Bruce, Thompson failed to avoid involvement in factional disputes; unlike Robert Elliott, he had lost control of his black base.

Even if Thompson had not weakened his own case, there remained the redoubtable Rapier. Struggles among blacks for power were common in Montgomery and throughout the South, and Thompson was no stranger to such conflicts. During his rise he had, for example, withstood challenges from a successful black farmer named Hales Ellsworth, who represented the interests of country blacks in Montgomery County. He had also crossed swords before with Rapier, who had defeated him for the presidency of the state Colored Labor Convention. But this time the contest was clearly a mismatch. As a successful planter from Lauderdale County, Rapier commanded a larger following in the rural districts; he also enjoyed the support of several prominent Montgomery blacks. Although Thompson held two important elective offices, Rapier's position as assessor of internal revenue had much greater political impact in terms of the favors and patronage he could dispense. Finally, Rapier was less threatening to white leaders of the Spencer-Strobach faction and to whites in general. In vivid contrast to the slightly younger Thompson, Rapier was a former free Negro, a mulatto, and well-educated in Canadian schools. The fact that his stands on racial issues were moderate buttressed the view that, if there had to be a Negro congressman, the more "refined" and "polished" Rapier was the man. In a state where white support was more critical than in Mississippi or South Carolina, the fact that Thompson was more a product of the local black community than someone like Bruce or Elliott actually proved to be a liability.

Thompson lost more than the congressional nomination. Shortly thereafter he was denied renomination to a third term in the legislature, evidently because of Strobach and Rapier, whom he had called thieves and fools. According to a Democratic newspaper the "carpetbag crew" wanted to destroy Thompson's influence among blacks because of his "independent ideas." Yet Thompson proved resilient. He repaired fences within his church and party, edited a Republican newspaper, and, with Senator Spencer's help, was appointed deputy collector of customs. In 1873 he was elected to a fourth term to the city council and was chosen orator of the day at the annual parade and banquet of Grey Eagle No. 3, the city's only black fire company. But the tide of change was apparent. In 1874 Democrats permanently returned to power in the state government; the next year a combination of fraud, intimidation, manipulation of voting requirements, and intraparty Republican strife enabled the Redeemers to triumph in Montgomery. Thompson did not stand for reelection and in the ensuing years participated only occasionally in party politics. He seems to have spent his time trying to bolster his declining grocery business, teaching young blacks to read, preaching, and helping to establish the Dexter Avenue Baptist Church, which Martin Luther King, Jr., would make famous. He also briefly served in 1881 as vice-president of the Industrial State Fair Association (Colored), which organized a Negro fair. Part of this withdrawal from politics was due to the limited opportunities for black political leadership following the overthrow of Reconstruction, but other black Montgomerians did remain active. More important in Thompson's case were a series of personal tragedies, including the death of his first wife in childbirth, the death of several of his children, and his own declining health. His last public appearance came in 1885 when he gave one of the eulogies at a service held to honor the memory of former president Grant. Two years later Thompson died of cancer at the age of forty-eight.

Thompson's political career had essentially ended in 1875 at the age of thirty-six. In a brief period that lasted no more than ten years he emerged from slavery to forge an impressive public career built on close association with the basic institutions of black life. He gained additional access to black voters through his relief activities as a councilman and the operation of his neighborhood grocery, traditionally a launching pad for ethnic politicians in nineteenth-century America. He reached still other blacks as newspaper editor, powerful orator, and inveterate writer of letters to the editor. And he was constantly visible to blacks as a city councilman and state legislator.

No doubt Thompson benefited from the sponsorship of white men like Thomas Glasscock, Paul Strobach, and George Spencer. He attracted their attention, however, because of his personal qualities and, even more important, because of the bloc of black voters he commanded. Throughout the South there were black leaders who were mere puppets manipulated by white masters, but this was not the case with Thompson or the more numerous men like him. After Thompson's victory and that of his black running mate in the city's first Reconstruction council election, a local paper reported, "The white rads . . . [were] awful mad because the black rads nominated . . . [them]." Neither was he, as some Democrats claimed, the force behind the throne, controlling white colleagues in a city that had been "Africanized." Rather, like Atlanta city councilman William Finch and his Raleigh counterpart James H. Harris, Thompson was a skillful politician who, despite the desires of white Republicans and Democrats, insisted on putting his own advancement and the advancement of his people ahead of injunctions to keep a low profile and stay in his place. He took stronger stands than did Bruce but in a less abrasive way than Elliott, so that at least one staunch Democrat could call him "a very respectable negro." But unlike Mississippi or South Carolina, Alabama did not have a black majority and secure Republican rule. Without the compromising skills of Bruce or the solid base and talent of Elliott, Thompson could go only so far up the political ladder.

214

In the end, both the black masses and the white leaders kept Thompson from rising to greater heights. His momentary loss of power within the church (it was never fully regained), along with the attractiveness to rural blacks and white Republicans of James T. Rapier (a Bruce-like figure), denied him any real chance to gain the congressional nomination he sought. The abuses of Redemption and the misfortunes of his personal life subsequently left him a political has-been at a remarkably young age. But Thompson was not unique, for a surprising number of black southern leaders, including Robert Brown Elliott, whether because of death, disillusionment, poor health, emigration, or other interests, ended their political careers prematurely, depriving other blacks of much needed leadership.

In assessing the first generation of black officeholders, as represented by Bruce, Elliott, and Thompson, few scholars today would give much credence to the original Dunning-ite indictment. Even the corruption charge loses much of its significance when viewed in the context of Gilded Age society and the greater involvement of whites, both Republican and Democrat. Besides, black political participation per se, not corruption, was always the real issue for critics. Yet no single view has emerged to replace the old stereotypes. There is agreement on who these people were, what kind of qualifications they had, and what actions they took, but there are divergent assessments of their performance and legacy. Some historians, liberally inclined and explicitly reacting to the Dunning attack, have produced complimentary studies of these men which seek to rehabilitate their memory. While valuable in the effort to set the record straight, such works often gloss over the faults of their subjects in order to have them conform to what might be expected of race leaders today. Increasingly, however, other historians more radical in orientation have been more critical of these leaders, taking them to task for doing too little to help their race. Disparagingly referred to as "representative colored men" by Nell Painter, they are seen as having been out of touch with the black masses and more interested in their own careers and in white approval than in helping their people. Thomas Holt, in his study of South Carolina, argues that bitter infighting based on class and color differences led black legislators to ignore the land issue and other matters of importance to the masses and helped produce the divided party that proved no match for the Democratic counterrevolution. Still other historians view black politics as irrelevant and call instead for concentration on nonpolitical figures more firmly grounded in local communities.

Black leaders of the Reconstruction need to be studied on their own terms and viewed within the context of the times rather than judged by the greater commitment to racial progress and stronger means of implementation present in the late twentieth century. As typified by Bruce, Elliott, and Thompson, these politicians used a variety of strategies, drew on diverse constituencies that included white and black elements often at odds over objectives, and focused on different issues. Of the three, Thompson was the most representative black politician, not only because he rose no higher than the state legislature, but because of his personal characteristics, political positions, and roots in the black community. Lacking the brilliance of the combative Elliott and the tactical skill of the more accommodating Bruce, Thompson sought out the middle ground of protest *and* accommodation in an effort to appeal to both his black base and his white sponsors. On less secure political turf and with less talent than Bruce or Elliott, he proved more vulnerable to the vicissitudes of Reconstruction politics.

On some levels black leaders were clearly inadequate. Bruce was not the only black who seemingly put his own interest and ambition before the needs of his race. Many, like Elliott, could have been more honest. They might have done more to help the poor and might have pressed harder for integration, or at least truly equal separate treatment. Some were too easily manipulated by whites. But these were men of their times, imbued with its values and attitudes. They were also politicans. The great majority of officeholders make no mark in office, produce no important legislation, and often act first to further their own careers and get reelected. They frequently engage in internecine combat based on both rational and irrational considerations. Why should these black politicians be judged by a different standard? Must there be only heroes or villains?

Even if a different standard is used, however, there is much that was positive about these men and ample reason to continue to emphasize their role in Reconstruction. They often functioned as the nation's conscience, and to a greater degree than any other component of the Republican coalition. To demand universal male suffrage, equal access to public accommodations, schools, and welfare facilities, and federal guarantees for such rights was to take a radical positon in the mid-nineteenth century. Yet these men also delivered. The careers of Bruce, Elliott, and Thompson, for example, suggest they brought tangible benefits not only to their race but to their states and localities, particularly in the area of education. By doing so in an often eloquent, well-reasoned manner against white opposition, they themselves made

216

a forceful case for racial equality. Such men, in fact, served as symbols for blacks and nonracist whites of what America might mean to the oppressed and of what blacks deserved. That these black leaders did not accomplish more was due in part to their own inadequacies but more to the opposition they faced from whites, Republicans and Democrats alike. That they were able, in the face of overwhelming odds, to help provide the foundation for the twentieth-century's Second Reconstruction was testimony to their courage, political skills, and persistent faith in the American ideals of freedom and equal opportunity.

Eric Foner   **11**

Black Reconstruction Leaders
at the Grass Roots

In NOVEMBER 1869, in Greene County, Georgia, disguised Klansmen forced Abram Colby into the woods "and there stripped and beat him in the most cruel manner, for nearly three hours." Born a slave and freed in 1851, Colby earned his living as a minister and barber. Since the end of the Civil War he had taken an active part in black political life, organizing "one of the largest and most enthusiastic" branches of Georgia's Equal Rights Association in 1866 and winning election to the state legislature two years later. According to the local agent of the American Missionary Association, Colby was whipped because he had recently appealed to Governor Rufus Bullock to protect the county's black population, and his assailants "had besides as they said, many old scores against him, as a leader of his people in the county." Eighteen months later South Carolina Klansmen whipped Samuel Bonner, an unassuming black sharecropper, along with his mother and sister. Before the assault Bonner was asked if he were a Republican. "I told them," he later recalled, "I was that, and I thought it was right."

Minor episodes in the history of Reconstruction, these incidents nonetheless illuminate larger themes of its political culture and the nature of grass-roots black leadership. Colby exemplifies the humble social status of local black leaders; although free before the Civil War, he was illiterate and, according to the 1870 census, owned no property. His experience in the legislature reveals the fragility of black-white cooperation in Reconstruction politics, for white Republicans were among those who voted to expel Colby and other blacks. Bonner's willingness to assert his convictions in the face of violence epitomizes the depth of commitment that animated the Reconstruction black community. These small dramas guide us into the world of local black politics, its organization, ideology, and leadership during Reconstruction.

Southern black politics, of course, did not begin with the Recon-

---

This essay, originally titled "Black Politics in Reconstruction: A Reassessment," was first presented at the annual meeting of the Organization of American Historians, April 1984.

struction Act of 1867, as Abram Colby's career illustrates. Before the end of the Civil War, black political organizations had appeared in such Union-occupied areas as New Orleans. And in 1865 and 1866, in black conventions throughout the southern states, future Reconstruction leaders like James T. Rapier and William H. Grey first came into prominence. By and large, however, the tone of these early conventions was moderate. Throughout the South, 1865 was a year of labor conflict, with freedpeople refusing to sign contracts and some seizing plantations and staking a claim to the soil. But the free-born mulattoes, ministers, and northern blacks who dominated the conventions all but ignored the land question.

Whatever the accomplishments of these conventions (and one delegate told the 1866 gathering in Tennessee that his constituents believed "we do nothing but meet, pass resolutions, publish pamphlets, and incur expenses"), the process of selecting delegates politicized black communities. Some delegates were elected by local mass meetings; others were sent by churches, clubs, and black army units stationed in the South. In the fall of 1866, two black men held "a regular canvass" in Greene County, North Carolina; an organized election followed to choose a delegate to the state's second black convention. The local chapters of the Georgia Educational Association, established at the state's January 1866 black convention, became "schools in which the colored citizens learn their rights." Nonetheless, this first phase of political organization was spotty and uneven—large areas of the black belt remained untouched by organized political activity.

It was in 1867, the *annus mirabilis* of Reconstruction, that a wave of political activism swept across the black belt. Itinerant lecturers, black and white, brought their message into the heart of the rural South. A black Baptist minister calling himself Professor J. W. Toer toured parts of Georgia and Florida "with a magic lantern to exhibit what he calls the progress of reconstruction. . . . He has a scene, which he calls 'before the proclamation,' another 'after the proclamation' and then "22nd Regt. U.S.C.T. Duncan's Brigade." Voting registrars held public meetings to instruct blacks on the nature of American government and "the individual benefits of citizenship in the nation and in the state." In Monroe County, Alabama, where no black political meetings had occurred before 1867, freedpeople crowded around the registrar shouting "God bless you," "Bless God for this." Throughout the South there were complaints of blacks neglecting plantation labor: "they stop at any time and go off to Greensboro or any other place to attend a political meeting" complained a white Alabamian.

220

So great was the enthusiasm for politics that, as one former slave minister later wrote, "politics got in our midst and our revival or religious work for a while began to wane." Although suffrage was restricted to men, black women and even children often played a vocal part in political gatherings. One plantation manager summed up the situation: "You never saw a people more excited on the subject of politics than are the negroes of the south. They are perfectly wild."

The meteoric rise of black political activity was reflected in the growth of the Union League. Few developments of this period are more tinged with irony than the metamorphosis of a loyalist club, developed among the respectable middle classes of the Civil War North, into the political expression of impoverished freedpeople. An earlier generation of historians tended to dismiss the Union League by portraying it as a vehicle through which carpetbaggers manipulated the votes of gullible blacks, who were attracted to its meetings by secret passwords and colorful initiation rites. In fact, its purposes were far more complex: the league served simultaneously as "a political school for the people," as a North Carolina teacher described it, a vehicle for the emergence of a greatly expanded class of black political leaders, and an institutional structure blacks could utilize for their own purposes and through which they could articulate their own aspirations.

Even before 1867, local Union League branches had sprung up among blacks in some parts of the South, and the order had spread rapidly among Unionist whites in the Alabama, Georgia, and Tennessee hill country. In 1867, as blacks poured into the league, many white members either withdrew or formed segregated local chapters. Many local leagues were all-black or all-white, but integrated leagues also existed, in which black and white Republicans achieved a remarkable degree of interracial harmony. In Union County, North Carolina, a racially mixed league met "in old fields, or in some out of the way house, and elected[ed] candidates to be received into their body."

By the end of 1867 it seemed that virtually every black voter in the South had enrolled in the Union League, the Loyal League, or some equivalent local political organization. Meetings were generally held in a black church or school, or at the home of some prominent black individual, or, if necessary, secretly in woods or fields. In Paulding, Mississippi, a hundred or more blacks, along with a few whites, met monthly at the home of Jim Cruise, a black house carpenter. Usually, a Bible and a copy of the Declaration of Independence and the Constitution lay on a table, a minister opened the meeting with a prayer, new members took an initiation oath, and there were pledges to support the Republican party and uphold the principle of equal rights.

The main function of these meetings, however, was political education. "We just went there," related Henry Holt, an illiterate black league member from North Carolina, "and we talked a little; made speeches on one question and another." Republican newspapers were read aloud, candidates were nominated for office, and political issues were debated. One racially mixed league discussed at various meetings the organization of a July 4 celebration, cooperation between the league and the Heroes of America (a secret white Unionist organization dating from the Civil War), and issues like disfranchisement, debt relief, and public education which were likely to arise at the forthcoming constitutional conventions. In Maryville, Tennessee, the Union League held weekly discussions on the issues of the day—the impeachment of President Johnson, the national debt, and such broader questions as, Is the education of the female as important as that of the male? Should students pay corporation tax? Should East Tennessee be a separate state? Although mostly white in membership in a county only one-tenth black, this league called for Tennessee to send at least one black to Congress. In 1868 its members elected a black justice of the peace and four blacks to the seven-member city commission.

It would be an error, however, to assume that the Union leagues were "political" only in the sense of electoral politics. Their multifaceted activities reflected what might be called the politicization of everyday life during Reconstruction. Colleton County, South Carolina, league members (led by a freedman with the venerable Palmetto State name Wade Hampton) marched in a body to the local magistrate demanding the arrest of a white man who had injured a black with a slingshot. A local North Carolina league official—a minister describing himself as "a poor Colord man"—proposed to Governor Holden that the league "stand as gardians" for blacks who "don't know how to make a bargain . . . and see that they get the money." In Alabama's black belt, league organizer George W. Cox was besieged by freedpeople requesting information about suing their employers, avoiding fines for attending political meetings, and ensuring a fair division of crops at harvest time. Two of the most militant collective actions by blacks during Georgia Reconstruction, the Ogeechee uprising of 1869 and Cudjo Fye's "rebellion" of 1870, were sparked by the arrest of league members by white authorities.

In 1867 and 1868 Union League activity reached its zenith. By 1869 it had begun to decline in many parts of the South, disrupted by Klan violence or absorbed into the burgeoning apparatus of the Republican party. "It is all broke up," said one black member from Graham, North Carolina, an area of rampant Klan activity. In Texas, Republican chieftain James Tracy moved to assimilate the leagues into a more disciplined party structure, evoking strong protests from militant black leaders like the legislator Matthew Gaines. But in wide areas of the black belt, the tradition of local political organization embodied in the leagues persisted throughout Reconstruction. Sometimes the names changed, but the structure and purposes remained the same. In Abbeville County, South Carolina, the Union League was succeeded by The Brotherhood, the United Brethren, and finally, in 1875, the Laboring Union; as former slave A. J. Titus explained, "they was all laboring men, you see." In the Vicksburg region a successor to the Union League, called the "council" by blacks, met until 1874 to discuss self-protection and Republican politics. Its members, armed with pistols and shotguns, unsuccessfully resisted white efforts to oust black sheriff Peter Crosby in the Vicksburg crisis of December 1874.

In this hothouse atmosphere of political mobilization, the Union leagues generated a new class of local black political leaders. Local leaders in the black belt, where few free blacks had lived before the Civil War, and especially outside Louisiana and South Carolina, with their large and politically active freeborn communities, tended to be former slaves of very modest circumstances. Many were teachers and preachers or other individuals who possessed a skill of use to the community. Former slave Thomas Allen, a Union League organizer elected to the Georgia legislature, was a propertyless Baptist preacher, shoemaker, and farmer. But what established him as a leader was literacy: "In my county the colored people came to me for instructions, and I gave them the best instructions I could. I took the New York Tribune and other papers, and in that way I found out a great deal, and I told them whatever I thought was right." In occupation, the largest number of local black leaders appear to have been artisans, men whose skill and independence marked them as leaders but who were still deeply embedded in the life of the black community. There were others, apparently lacking in distinctive attributes of status, respected for personal qualities—oratorical ability, a reputation for moral standing, or simply good sense, honesty, or a concern for the welfare of their neighbors. Calvin Rogers, a black constable murdered by the Florida Klan, was described by another freedman as "a thorough-going man; he was a stump speaker, and tried to excite the colored people to do the right thing. . . . He would work for a man and make him pay him." Others were men who had achieved prominence as slaves before emancipation, like Louisiana justice of the peace Hamilton Gibson, a "conjurer."

In his study of social and political organizations among Memphis blacks, Armstead Robinson has identified a fairly sharp distinction between political leaders, who tended to be prosperous and light of skin, and religious/benevolent leaders, who were generally unskilled former slaves. In the less-stratified rural black belt, however, lines of occupation and social function frequently overlapped: preachers and teachers earned their living in part as artisans or laborers, politicians helped establish churches, meetings of fraternal organizations discussed political events, and Union leagues raised money for black schools. This was a world suffused with politics, in which local leaders gave articulate expression to the multiplicity of grievances and the timeless aspirations of their humble constituents.

In Union leagues, Republican gatherings, and impromptu local meetings, black and white Republicans in these years debated the basic question of the polity—What was the meaning of freedom and citizenship in republican America? Black leaders drew upon a broad range of experiences and ideas, some derived from slavery itself and others grounded in the traditions of the larger society, in defining the bounds of black politics. The language of American republicanism suffused black political culture. As Rev. J. M. Hood put it at the North Carolina Constitutional Convention of 1868, "the colored people had read . . . the Declaration [of Independence] until it had become part of their natures." A petition of eleven Alabama blacks complaining in 1865 of contract frauds, injustice before the courts, the refusal of whites to rent land to freedpeople, and other abuses, concluded with a revealing masterpiece of understatement: "this is not the pursuit of happiness." And ten years later, a group of Louisiana freedpeople felt it appropriate to open their petition for the removal of a hostile local official with these well-known words: "We the people of Louisiana in order to establish justice, insure domestic tranquility, promote the general welfare . . . do ordain and establish this Constitution."

There was much more here than simply accustomed language; blacks, freeborn and slave, were staking their claim to equal citizenship in the American republic. To them the republican inheritance implied the rights to vote and to education, the free exercise of religion, access to the courts, and equal opportunity in all the avenues of economic enterprise—every right already enjoyed by whites. As one black delegate to the Virginia Constitutional Convention put it, no civil right "ever enjoyed by citizens prior to the year 1861" could now justifiably be denied to blacks. Anything less would be a violation of the principles upon which the nation had been founded. As Louisiana's Oscar J. Dunn insisted, "it is the boast and glory of the

American republic that there is no discrimination among men, no privileges founded upon birth-right. There are no hereditary distinctions." Continued proscription of blacks, Dunn warned, would undermine the republic and "open the door for the institution of aristocracy, nobility, and even monarchy."

At their most utopian, blacks in Reconstruction envisioned a society purged of all racial distinctions. This did not mean the abandonment of race consciousness—there is abundant evidence that blacks preferred black teachers for their children as well as black churches and ministers. But in the polity, blacks, who had so long been proscribed because of their color, defined equal citizenship as color-blind. Thomas Bayne told the Virginia Constitutional Convention that his constituents expected him to help draft a constitution "that should not have the word black or white anywhere in it." Politicians seeking to arouse a sense of racial self-consciousness sometimes found black audiences unreceptive to their message. Martin Delany, the "father of black nationalism," discovered in South Carolina that it was "dangerous to go into the country and speak of color in any manner whatever, without the angry rejoinder, 'we don't want to hear that; we are all one color now.' " He was astonished to find that the freedpeople did not share his belief in the necessity of electing blacks (particularly Martin Delany) to office. Rather, they believed "that the Constitution had been purged of color by a Radical Congress."

The black claim to equal citizenship was grounded in more than a restatement of republican principles, however. Repeatedly in Reconstruction it was linked as well to black participation in the Civil War. Indeed, while blacks revered Lincoln as the Great Emancipator, it was also an article of faith that they had helped emancipate themselves. "They say," an Alabama planter reported in 1867, "the Yankees never could have whipped the south without the aid of the negroes." At the same time, the secular claim to citizenship was underpinned by a religious messianism deeply rooted in the black experience. As slaves, blacks had come to think of themselves as analogous to the Jews in Egypt, an oppressed people whom God, in the fullness of time, would deliver from bondage. They viewed the Civil War as God's instrument of deliverance, and Reconstruction as another step in a divinely ordained process. Black religion reinforced black republicanism, for, as Rev. J. M. P. Williams, a Mississippi legislator, put it in an address to his constituents in 1871, "my dear friends, remember this, of one blood God did make all men to dwell upon the face of the whole earth . . . hence, their common origin, destiny and equal rights." Even among nonclerics, secular and religious modes of political discourse were virtually interchangeable. One example is a speech by North Carolina black Edwin Jones, as reported by a justice of the peace in 1867: "He said it was not now like it used to be, that . . . the negro was about to get his equal rights. . . . That the negroes owed their freedom to the courage of the negro soldiers and to God. . . . He made frequent references to the II and IV chapters of Joshua for a full accomplishment of the principles and destiny of the race. It was concluded that the race have a destiny in view similar to the Children of Israel."

Republicanism, religious messianism, and historical experience combined to produce in black political Reconstruction culture a profound sense of identification with the American polity. The very abundance of letters and petitions addressed by ordinary freedpeople to officials of the army, the Freedmen's Bureau, and state and federal authorities revealed a belief that the political order was open to black participation and persuasion. Blacks enthusiastically embraced that hallmark of the Civil War era, the rise of an activist state. With wealth, political experience, and tradition all mobilized against them in the South, blacks saw in political authority a countervailing power. On the local and state level, black officials pressed for the expansion of such public institutions as schools and hospitals. And in proposing measures (generally not enacted) for free medical care and legal assistance for the poor, government regulation of private markets, restrictions on the sale of liquor, and the outlawing of fairs and hunting on Sunday, they revealed a vision of the democratic state actively promoting the social and moral well-being of its citizenry.

It was the national government, however, that blacks ultimately viewed as the guarantor of their rights. Those whose freedom had come through the unprecedented exercise of federal authority were utterly hostile to theories of state rights and local autonomy. As Frederick Douglass put it, until Americans abandoned the idea of "the right of each State to control its own local affairs, . . . no general assertion of human rights can be of any practical value." Blacks did not share fears of "centralism" common even in the Republican party; like white Radical Republicans, black leaders found in the guarantee of republican government—the "most pregnant clause" of the Constitution, Robert B. Elliott called it—a grant of federal power ample enough to promote the welfare and protect the rights of individual citizens. Throughout Reconstruction, black political leaders supported proposals for such vast expansions of federal authority as James T. Rapier's plan for a national educational system, complete with federally mandated textbooks.

226

The course of events during Reconstruction reinforced this tendency to look to the national government for protection. The inability of state and local authorities to control violence prompted demands for federal intervention. "We are more slave today in the hand of the wicked than we were before," read a desperate plea from five Alabama blacks. "We need protection . . . only a standing army in this place can give us our right and life." Blacks enthusiastically supported the Enforcement Acts of 1870 and 1871 and the expansion of the powers of the federal judiciary. One black convention went so far as to insist that virtually all civil and criminal cases involving blacks be removable from state to federal courts, a mind-boggling enhancement of federal judicial authority. To constitutional objections, most blacks would agree with Congressman Joseph Rainey: "Tell me nothing of a constitution which fails to shelter beneath its rightful power the people of a country."

Republican citizenship implied more than political equality overseen by an active state, however. It helped legitimize the desire for land so pervasive among the freedpeople, for a society based upon a landed aristocracy and a large propertyless lower class could not be considered truly republican. "Small estates are the real element of democracy," wrote the *New Orleans Tribune.* "Let the land go into the hands of the actual laborers."

In 1865 and 1866 the claim to land found little expression at statewide black conventions. In 1867, however, the situation was very different. At the grass roots, demands for land among blacks and, in some areas, poor whites animated early Republican politics. The advent of suffrage and Thaddeus Stevens's introduction of a confiscation bill in the House rekindled expectations that had, in most areas, subsided after January 1866. A northern correspondent reported that "Thad Stevens' speech has been circulated among those of them who can read and fully expounded to those of them who cannot." As southern Republican parties were organized in the spring of 1867, virtually every convention found itself divided between "confiscation radicals" and more moderate elements. In Mississippi, a black delegate proposed that the party commit itself to the confiscation of Confederate estates and their distribution to freedpeople. At a black mass meeting in Richmond, a freedman announced that large holdings belonging to rebels should be confiscated for the benefit of poor, loyal blacks. The issue was most divisive in North Carolina, where local demands for land were voiced by both black Union leagues and loyalist whites in the Heroes of America. One delegate told the state Republican convention, "the people of this State have a hope in confiscation, and if that is taken away the Republican party [will] give away the power they have gained."

The outcome of the confiscation debate reveals a great deal about the limits within which black politics could operate during Reconstruction. No state convention endorsed the idea, although a few called for planters voluntarily to sell land to impoverished freedmen. The obstacles to confiscation were indeed immense. National Republican leaders, including long-time Radicals like Henry Wilson, publicly condemned Stevens's initiative. "Let confiscation be, as it should be, an unspoken word in your state," Wilson advised North Carolina black leader James H. Harris. Democratic victories in the 1867 northern elections reinforced the conviction that Reconstruction had gone far enough; more radical policies would jeopordize Republican electoral chances in 1868 and beyond.

Even among southern Republicans there was strong opposition to the confiscation idea. Most white Republican leaders were committed to what Mark Summers calls the "Gospel of Prosperity," believing that their party's prospects hinged on a program of regional economic development and diversification. While envisioning the eventual demise of the plantation system, this "gospel" called for respect for individual enterprise and desired to encourage northern investment in the South, both seemingly incompatible with confiscation. Then, too, most white Republicans fully embraced the free labor ideology, insisting that while possession of land was unquestionably desirable, the freedpeople, like all Americans, would have to acquire it through hard work. Alabama carpetbagger C. W. Dustan solemnly announced that lands "cannot be owned without being earned, they cannot be earned without labor. . . . " (Dustan did not exactly follow this free labor prescription in his own life: he acquired a sizable holding by marrying the daughter of a Demopolis planter.)

Of course, as Thomas Holt has demonstrated, the black community itself was divided on the land question. The free labor ideology, with its respect for private property and individual initiative, was most fully embraced by two sets of black leaders—those from the North and the better-off southern free Negroes. Prominent northern blacks like Jonathan Gibbs and James Lynch would insist during Reconstruction that the interests of labor and capital were identical. Among "black carpetbaggers" only Aaron A. Bradley became actively involved in the land struggles of the freedpeople. So, too, the free black leadership of Charleston and New Orleans rejected confiscation. At Louisiana's Republican state convention, "all the freedmen, *save one,* were in favor of confiscation, and the measure would have been

228

adopted . . . had it not been for the energetic exertions of the white and free born colored members." Their own experience convinced successful free blacks that freedpeople required not government largesse but only an equal chance.

I have dwelt at length on the years 1867 and 1868, not only because of the remarkable political mobilization of the black community, but because many of the dilemmas that would confront black political leaders were by then already fully evident. In utopian aspirations for a New South with a restructured racial and economic order, these years revealed the radical potential inherent in Reconstruction. But the fate of the confiscation debate presaged the rapid waning of the radical impulse, both nationally and in the South. Increasingly, black politics took on a defensive cast; in place of demands for a fundamental restructuring of southern society, politics came to revolve around preserving what gains had been achieved and making the existing order operate fairly (a difficult task at best in a plantation society).

Comprising the vast majority of Republican voters, blacks would remain junior partners within the party. Even in Louisiana they would be barred from the most important positions; as one prominent black there complained in 1874, "we share, neither . . . in the control of the government which we have created, nor participate in the patronage resulting from political victories we have won." Only in Mississippi and South Carolina would blacks come to play a dominant role in shaping Reconstruction policy. But even there, politics never escaped a "colonial" pattern—the interests of the national Republican party always took precedence over the needs of the localities. Unable to establish their own legitimacy in the eyes of their powerful opponents, the survival of the new southern governments ultimately rested on federal support. Thus, the boundaries of Reconstruction were determined in Washington. As Albert T. Morgan observed of Mississippi, "three-fourths of the republican members of the Legislature regard themselves as still under the control and dominion of *Congress* as the supreme government. They can hardly settle our per diem without the feeling of *subserviency to Congress.*"

As Reconstruction wore on, black political leaders were caught in a web of seemingly insoluble dilemmas. The few black congressmen had to choose between supporting national economic policies like a deflationary monetary program, arguably detrimental to the interests of their constituents, and joining Democrats in opposition, which would further alienate northern Republican support. Their broad conception of federal authority was increasingly out of step with a national party described by U.S. Attorney General Amos T. Akerman as "anxious for an end of Southern troubles" and convinced that "Southern Republicans must cease to look for special support to Congressional action." By the mid-1870s it was well understood in the South that the remaining Republican states could expect no help from federal authorities. Former slave Jerry Thornton Moore, president of a local Republican club in Aiken County, South Carolina, was told by his white landlord that Democrats planned to carry the 1876 elections "if we have to wade in blood knee-deep." "Mind what you are doing," Moore responded; "the United States is mighty strong." Replied the white man, "but, Thornton, . . . the northern people is on our side."

Increasingly abandoned by the national party, black politicians had nowhere to turn. Democrats offered even less than Republicans, and at any rate, black voters refused to countenance independent politics. When Alabama legislator C. S. Smith proposed to the 1876 national black convention that blacks declare their political autonomy, he won hearty applause inside the hall, but "colored men on street corners" spoke of cutting his throat. Blanche K. Bruce earned a grass-roots reputation as a "conservative negro" for a Senate speech condemning Republican indifference to the plight of southern freedpeople. When Edward Shaw, a prominent Memphis black leader, ran for Congress in 1870 against the white Republican incumbent, he received only 165 votes. The 1870s did witness a rise in black political assertiveness and an increase (where Reconstruction survived) in the number of blacks holding office, but this could only take place within the context of the Republican party.

At the local level, numerous enclaves of genuine black political power existed during Reconstruction. Reporter Edward King, traveling across the South in 1873 and 1874, encountered many examples of black officeholding—black aldermen and city councilmen in Petersburg, Houston, and Little Rock; parish jury members in Louisiana; black magistrates in the South Carolina low country. Hundreds, perhaps thousands of blacks held positions ranging from constable to school board official, tax assessor, and sheriff. Their numbers were fewest in states like Georgia and Florida, where conservative Republicans had drafted constitutions centralizing appointive power in the hands of the governor, and most extensive in South Carolina and Mississippi. About a third of Mississippi's black population lived in one of the thirteen counties that elected a black sheriff, the official who collected taxes, appointed registrars, and controlled selection of juries.

The existence of black and sympathetic white local officials often made a real difference in the day-to-day lives of the freedpeople, ensuring that those accused of crimes would be tried before juries of their peers (who, whites complained, often refused to convict in cases of vagrancy or theft) and enforcing fairness in such prosaic aspects of local government as road repair, public employment, and poor relief. In Louisiana, blacks, whites, and Chinese were employed to repair the levees, and, in a startling departure from traditional practice, all received the same wages. As the chief engineer reported, "our 'Cadian friends were a little disgusted at not being allowed double (colored) wages, and the Chinamen were astonished at being allowed as much and the American citizens of African descent were delighted at being '*par.*'" Any doubt as to the importance of sympathetic local officials is quickly dispelled by a glance at the conduct of local government in counties remaining under Democratic control (as well as some localities dominated by conservative white Republicans.) In such areas blacks persistently complained of exclusion from juries, discrimination in tax assessment and collection, and an inability to obtain justice before the courts. In one Democratic Alabama county in 1870, a black woman brutally beaten by a group of white men was forced to raise $16.45 for court costs before the judge released the offenders and instructed the injured woman to drop the matter or face a jail sentence. This state of affairs harked back to the mockery of justice practiced in southern courts during Presidential Reconstruction and looked ahead to the situation that would obtain under the Redeemers.

For some black politicos, as for many whites in nineteenth-century America, official positions became a means of social advancement. Politics was one of the few areas of dignified work open to black men of talent and ambition, and compared with other employment opportunities, the rewards of even minor office could seem dazzlingly high. The thirteen dollars per diem earned by members of the Louisiana Constitutional Convention, or the seven dollars per day plus mileage paid to North Carolina legislators, far outstripped the wages most blacks could ordinarily command. More important offices garnered far higher rewards—sheriffs could earn thousands of dollars in commissions and fees, and state officeholders were handsomely paid during Reconstruction. Blacks consistently opposed attempts to reduce the pay of officials. As one black put it at the Virginia Constitutional Convention, "the salary is none too great. Many of us have no incomes." And, at any rate, as another black delegate observed, "all our troubles have arisen from not paying people for their services."

Some black politicians translated official positions into significant personal gain. Josiah Walls, a Florida congressman, was able to acquire a large estate formerly owned by Confederate general James H.

Harrison, and Senator Blanche K. Bruce accumulated a fortune in real estate. Louisiana lieutenant governor C. C. Antoine owned an expensive racehorse whose earnings were considerable. On a less-exalted level, about one-third of the forty-six blacks who served in the Virginia legislature used their salaries to purchase land. Like white politicos, some black officials were less than scrupulous in the pursuit of wealth. P. B. S. Pinchback, who lived in luxury in New Orleans, told a reporter that his wealth derived from "speculation upon warrants, bonds and stocks." Pinchback forthrightly admitted that inside information enabled his speculations to succeed: "I belonged to the General Assembly, and knew about what it would do. . . . My investments were made accordingly."

For most black leaders, however, politics brought little personal wealth. Even the most prominent found it difficult to translate political standing into a real share in the economic resources of their states. A Charleston streetcar company formed by leading black politicians and chartered by the state failed, as did the Mississippi River Packet Company organized by Pinchback, Antoine, and others. The black community was too poor to subscribe capital to such endeavors, and whites shunned them entirely.

Far from being a vehicle for social mobility, politics in many cases entailed devastating financial loss. Former slave Henry Johnson, a South Carolina Union League and militia leader, was a bricklayer and plasterer by trade. "I always had plenty of work before I went into politics," he remarked, "but I have never got a job since. I suppose they do it merely because they think they will break me down and keep me from interfering with politics." Jefferson Long, a Macon tailor, had commanded "much of the fine custom of the city" before embarking upon a career that would take him briefly to Congress. However, "his stand in politics ruined his business with the whites who had been his patrons chiefly." Robert Reed, a black Alabama legislator, was told by local whites "that there is not a white man in the State that can beat me farming, and if I kept out of politics I would be the richest man in the State." Reed did not stop political organizing, but the costs of such commitment could be high. When North Carolina black leader A. H. Galloway, a former soldier, brick mason, and state legislator, passed away in 1870, a black newspaper commented, "He died poor, very poor."

Loss of livelihood was not the most serious danger black political leaders had to face. Political violence, so pervasive in large portions of the Reconstruction South, was often directed precisely at local leaders—black officeholders, Union League organizers, and militia captains. As Emanuel Fortune, himself driven from Jackson County, Florida, by the Klan, explained, "the object of it is to kill out the leading men of the republican party.... They have never attacked any one but those who have been somewhat prominent in the party, men who have taken prominent stands." At least 10 percent of the black delegates to the 1867–68 constitutional conventions were victims of violence, including six actually murdered. Other assassination victims included men like Richard Burke, an Alabama preacher, schoolteacher, legislator, and Union League officer, and Wyatt Outlaw, Republican organizer in Alamance county, North Carolina. During the mid-1870s Redemption campaigns, political violence claimed the lives of black constables and justices of the peace in Issaquena County, Mississippi, and black militiamen and local officials in Hamburg, South Carolina, among many others. For every leader murdered, many more were driven from their homes. To remain politically active in such circumstances required a rare degree of personal courage and the kind of integrity epitomized by former slave David Graham, a deputy U.S. marshal in South Carolina, who told a congressional committee: "The white people liked me very well until I got into politics, and they have hated me ever since.... I heap rather farm than be in politics; politics is the most disgusting thing I was ever in in my life. I can't sleep in my house only part of the time. I want to get out of politics, but here I is; these other leading fellows can't get along without me."

Violence devastated the Republican party in many a local community. After a series of outrages in Union County, South Carolina, one black commented, "the Republican party, I may say, is scattered and beaten and run out.... They have no leaders up there—no leaders." The reign of terror in Yazoo County, Mississippi, in 1875, according to one black official, "got the republicans so demoralized that we did not know what to do. We had no leaders. Every leader had been run out of the town and out of the county. They did not know what to do, so they just 'hung up.' "

Indeed, it might be argued that the black community was more dependent on its political leadership, more vulnerable to the destruction of its political infrastructure by violence, than the white community. Local black leaders played such a variety of roles in schools, churches, and fraternal organizations, as well as politics, that the killing or exiling of one man affected a multiplicity of areas. For a largely illiterate constituency, local leaders were bridges to the larger world of politics, indispensable sources of political information and guidance. They were also looked to for assistance in contract disputes, advice about the marketing of crops, and all sorts of other issues. John R. Lynch later recalled how, when he served as a Mississippi justice of the peace, free blacks "magnified" his office "far beyond its importance," bringing him complaints ranging from disputes with their employers to family squabbles. Black officials epitomized the revolution that seemed to have put the bottom rail on top, the openness of the new political order to black influence. Their murder or exile inevitably had a demoralizing impact upon their communities.

Alone among the nations that abolished slavery in this hemisphere, the United States accorded its former slaves legal and political equality within a few years after emancipation. The unprecedented character of this development, the sense among blacks that their newly won rights were constantly at risk, the refusal of large numbers of Democrats to acknowledge freed blacks as part of the "political nation," helps explain the abnormal aspects of Reconstruction politics—the high degree of political mobilization in the black community, the burdens placed upon black leaders by their constituents, and the widespread use of violence and economic coercion as political weapons.

In the spring of 1868 a northern correspondent, reporting on election day in Alabama, captured the sense of hope with which Reconstruction opened, the conviction among the enfranchised black voters that politics could indeed change their lives. "In defiance of fatigue, hardship, hunger, the threats of employers," blacks had flocked to the polls. Not one in fifty wore an "unpatched garment," few possessed a pair of shoes, yet they stood for hours in line in a "pitiless storm." Why? "The hunger to have the same chances as the white men they feel and comprehend. . . . That is what brings them here" to vote. With the overthrow of Reconstruction, politics could no longer serve as an effective vehicle for expressing such aspirations. The emerging black political class was devastated by Redemption—murdered or driven from their communities by violence or deprived of the opportunity to hold office, except in a few exceptional areas of the South. Black politicians ceased to exercise real power, apart from a handful of men dependent on federal patronage and on prominent politicos who advised Republican presidents on token appointments for blacks. Men of ambition in the black community now found other outlets for their talents, whether in education, business, the church, or the professions. Nearly a century would pass before the southern black community was again as fully galvanized at the grass roots by political activity.

Alfred Moss   **12**

Alexander Crummell: Black Nationalist
and Apostle of Western Civilization

ALEXANDER CRUMMELL was one of the most complex and significant figures in the nineteenth-century Afro-American community.
His claim to this distinction—despite his elitism, association with a
church of limited influence among blacks, lengthy absence from the
United States, and negligible influence on the black masses—attests
to his unique personal and intellectual abilities. In a period when
whites generally denied that the terms "intellectual," "leader," "exemplar
Christian," and "gentleman" could be used to describe any black,
Crummell embodied all of these traits. From the 1840s until his death
in 1898, he was a major figure among the small group of educated
blacks who articulated ideas about the meaning of black existence
and appropriate strategies for future black development. His thoughtful and persuasive arguments for Christianity, Western culture, and,
paradoxically, for black nationalism as the indispensable tools for
black empowerment had a significant impact on the tiny cadre of
black leaders who sought to protect, motivate, and lead the masses
of their race. Throughout his life he sought, by the creation and
strengthening of black institutions, to translate his beliefs into practice.

One of the few black clergy in the predominantly white Episcopal
church, Crummell was a committed Christian for whom racial
leadership, personal piety, and the Victorian code of respectability
were intimately intertwined. His piety, coupled with a judgmental
nature, made him a typical Victorian Evangelical Christian. Perhaps
less typical was the fact that his pristine moral character made it
impossible for his enemies to attack his personal life. Crummell's
religious and intellectual convictions led him to feel perfectly justified in dealing with individuals, institutions, and even races in a very
judgmental, directive, and authoritarian manner.

Crummell was a scholar. Whether preaching, delivering an address
on a secular topic, or communicating through his various published
works, his creative use of ideas, comprehensive understanding of the
thought and writings of other intellectuals, and intelligent use of
statistics made this unmistakably clear. Those who heard him speak
or preach were almost invariably impressed by the eloquent and

scholarly nature of his discourse. He used his verbal skills to articulate with impressive clarity his opinions about almost every issue that confronted a community of which he felt a part.

Although a Victorian in almost every way, Crummell was not a sentimentalist in his speaking and preaching. As he made clear to his fellow Protestant clergy of both races, he detested and felt free to denounce "ignorant and merely strong-languaged preachers." Knowing the power and influence of ministers in the black community, he frequently assailed unprepared preachers, charging that they "repulsed thinking men and degraded the people."

Crummell's origins and early experiences differed from those of most blacks in the antebellum United States. He was born in 1819 in New York City to Boston and Charity Hicks Crummell. On his mother's side he was a member of a New York family that had been free for several generations. His father, who described himself as the kidnapped son of a West African prince, had, on arrival in America and by means that are not clear, secured his freedom and eventually established himself as a successful businessman and leader in the New York black community. The elder Crummell provided a secure and comfortable home for his family. He also used his resources to secure for his son the best possible education in a society where most schools, public and private, refused blacks admittance. Beyond this Boston Crummell, by example and through his interpretation of the world, nurtured in his son a strong sense of self-worth. There are many indications in Alexander Crummell's writings that his father and other family members interpreted their physical blackness and absence of Caucasian features as a sign of racial purity and freedom from the "stain of bastardy." At a time when some members of the Afro-American community, as well as a number of influential whites, argued that mulattoes were superior to "pure blacks," the views of Crummell's father served as both a source of protection and affirmation.

Many of Crummell's adult ideas on race and community were shaped by the fact that his early life was spent in New York as a member of one of the most dynamic black communities in antebellum America. The blacks of New York were actively involved in abolitionist activities, agitation for greater political rights, and efforts to arrest the pattern of social segregation that excluded them from public schools and places of public accommodation. In these and a variety of other ways they attempted to secure greater respect from whites and increased political, social, and economic opportunities for themselves. One of the most important expressions of this drive for betterment was the time, energy, and resources that went into the creation of social institutions to provide needed services for a segregated and disadvantaged community. Crummell was a direct beneficiary of these activities, both emotionally and practically. He grew up witnessing all around him blacks—his family prominent among them—individually and mutually promoting self-worth, independence, and community.

Crummell's education began at the African Free School in New York City and later continued at a high school for blacks established in 1831 through the efforts of Peter Williams, the black Episcopal priest who was rector of Crummell's church. When Crummell exhausted the resources of these institutions, Williams located a suitable place for him to continue his studies—Hayes Academy, a school opened in 1835 by abolitionists in Canaan, New Hampshire. However, Crummell spent only a brief time there, for less than a year after his arrival Hayes Academy was destroyed by a mob of New Hampshire men hostile to black education. Later that year Crummell entered the Oneida Institute in Whitesboro, New York, an institution headed by Beriah Green, a radical white abolitionist and pious Evangelical. Crummell, one of three black youths who integrated the student body, found the setting emotionally supportive and a respite from racial hostility. During his first year he had a conversion experience and "made a profession of religion."

From an early age Crummell expressed a desire to enter the Episcopal ministry. His attraction to this largely white and socially conservative denomination can be traced directly to the examples and influence of his father, of Peter Williams, and of other members of the black elite who were Episcopalians. The appeal was reinforced by a belief that the liturgy, theology, and history of the Episcopal church had played a large role, throughout the English-speaking world, in creating and refining a class of pious, cultured, public-spirited, often wealthy individuals who were models of the best types of social leaders and reformers. Crummell identified with such whites. He also hoped, as an Episcopal priest, to stimulate greater missionary work among blacks, not only for religious purposes, but in order to employ his church as a cultural agency capable of helping to expand the size, quality, and material success of the black elite.

By the time Crummell left the Oneida Institute these inclinations had matured into a firm resolve. Under the direction of Peter Williams, he sought to become a postulant or candidate for Holy Orders in the Diocese of New York. Largely because of Williams's entreaties, Benjamin T. Onderdonk, the Episcopal bishop of New York, accepted him but cautioned Crummell at the same time not to seek admission to the Episcopal church's General Theological Seminary. Crummell disregarded this advice because he wished the same training as the best-prepared white clergy, and in 1839 he applied for admission. He was rejected on account of his race, with the explanation that his acceptance would be an insult to students from southern dioceses. He was also dismissed as a postulant by Bishop Onderdonk, who considered his application an act of insubordination.

Fortunately, several prominent white members of the Episcopal church, moved by Crummell's piety and their belief in his potential as a black leader, rallied to his cause. These men helped him make arrangements to study for ordination in Boston. The same white friends persuaded Alexander Griswold, Episcopal bishop of New England, to accept him as a postulant. While a theological student, Crummell served as lay missionary to a small black congregation in Providence, Rhode Island. In 1844 he was ordained a priest by the Episcopal bishop of Delaware.

Despite strenuous efforts Crummell's missionary endeavors, both before and after his elevation to the priesthood, were only minimally successful. In 1844 he decided his situation in Providence was hopeless and moved to Philadelphia, where he established a small mission. Any possibility of more successful work was aborted, however, by an immediate conflict with Henry Ustick Onderdonk, the Episcopal bishop of Pennsylvania and the brother of Crummell's earlier adversary. When Crummell refused to submit to the bishop's request that he exclude himself from any bodies responsible for church governance, he was dismissed from the diocese. Discouraged, he accepted a curacy in his home parish in New York City. The discouragement was compounded by negative reactions to his preaching in the congregations he served. The black laborers and their families who formed the bulk of the parishioners in his mission stations usually found his sermons unintelligible and dry.

Nevertheless, Crummell continued his ministry, supplementing it with more gratifying involvements, which moved him into broader spheres of racial leadership. These included participation in the struggle for equal suffrage in Rhode Island and New York, abolitionist activities, the Negro convention movement, and efforts to expand and improve black education. Such activities drew him into debates on major issues facing the free black community and brought him into contact with individuals and audiences who did appreciate the thoughtful, intelligent, and restrained way in which he expressed himself. All of these experiences stimulated Crummell to begin to systematize many of the ideas that later became important components of his black nationalist and Pan-African ideologies. Eventually the meager return from an ungratifying ministry convinced him that it was part of his mission to find a solution to the major problems of black people. These he conceived as moral weakness, self-hatred, and industrial primitiveness. Seeking to secure financial resources for a more effective ministry, Crummell, accompanied by his wife and four children, went to England in 1847.

Although the intent of Crummell's trip was to raise funds for a ministry in the United States, once in England he found more promising opportunities. The decision to pursue them would ultimately delay his permanent return to the United States for twenty-six years. Through sermons and lectures Crummell acquainted English audiences with the plight of free and enslaved American blacks, in the process raising funds that were eventually contributed to the endowment of St. Philip's in New York.

Upon arrival in England, Crummell was struck by what he perceived as the absence of racism. The six years he resided in that country made him a lifelong Anglophile who constantly praised the excellence of English institutions, particularly Christianity as embodied in the Church of England. These feelings were stimulated, in part, by the gracious and supportive responses of the individuals who befriended him. Certainly, compared to the constant humiliations that characterized black life in America and his mistreatment at the hands of the Episcopal church, Crummell's reception and treatment, crowned by the receipt of an A.B. degree from Queen's College, Cambridge, in 1853, must have seemed unmistakable evidence of enlightenment and civility.

After Crummell earned the degree he chose neither to return to the United States nor to remain in England. Instead, presenting health considerations as the main reason, he went as a missionary-educator to Liberia, a small West African country. This decision was determined by desires to find a setting in which he could fulfill his mission as a leader and uplifter of his people, to escape from the racist restrictions of the antebellum United States, and to bring Western culture and religion to his brethren in Africa.

The decision also represented a significant shift in his views on colonization. Early in his public career, Crummell had shown some ambivalence regarding the emigration of blacks from the United States. At an 1840 meeting of New York blacks he opposed a resolution deploring emigration as a route to black improvement. Nevertheless, during his early career in the United States he worked to secure equal opportunities for Afro-Americans. By 1844 he had become a vigorous opponent of colonization efforts, arguing that blacks in the United States had been brought there by God, with the result that they had become "citizens of this land, integral portions of this republic." No doubt this intense opposition was largely directed at the American Colonization Society. Moreover, during the early part of his stay in England, Crummell was a consistent opponent of the ACS. After 1850, however, he established relations with the society, whose support helped make possible his emigration to Liberia in 1853.

Difficult as it is to trace the exact influences and concerns that led to Crummell's reconsideration of his views on the ACS and colonization, it is clear that once in England, and perhaps partly as a result of greater interaction with blacks outside the United States, he became convinced of the immense potential for black development in a setting controlled by Christian, Westernized blacks. His struggle between 1850 and 1853 to place himself and his family in such a setting made it clear that access to Liberia and financial support for his work while there would best be ensured by alliance with the ACS and other largely white procolonization groups. Thus, Crummell turned from a position of disinterest in various black colonization schemes and active opposition to the ACS to one in which, for the next twenty years, he not only encouraged groups interested in black repatriation but actively supported and, on occasion, was a spokesman for the American Colonization Society. In taking this position, he separated himself from the bulk of black leaders in the United States.

Liberia, a small nation dominated by former slaves and free blacks from the United States, became the focus of Crummell's vision of the regeneration of the black race. Once there he found a tenuous settlement of poorly equipped, Westernized blacks attempting to cope with problems that threatened the very existence of the country. The Americo-Liberian elite had difficulty effectively governing and developing the territories they claimed. They faced the constant hostility and resistance of indigenous African tribes who saw them as foreign oppressors. In addition, the unity of the Americo-Liberians was fractured by a sharp political and social division between "pure blacks" and mulattoes. Given Crummell's strong beliefs as to the worth of "unmixed blacks" and his hostility to the pretensions of mulattoes, his sympathies were drawn to the "pure black" faction. Nevertheless, despite Liberia's many problems, he clung to the hope that this country could achieve what seemed impossible for black Americans.

The keys to Liberia's success in nation building, as Crummell constantly reiterated to his new compatriots lay in the development of a strong national identity, in concert with strenuous efforts to bring Christianity, trade, and Western culture to the entire continent. These marks of a superior social order were to be passed on to indigenous Africans, whether they wanted them or not. Such work was the responsibility of a capable black elite, whose traits had to include "character," a commitment to Christian beliefs and practices, economic aggressiveness, and a concern for the moral and practical uplift of the masses. Crummell was convinced that a united and economically self-sufficient black community, led by individuals of this sort, would disseminate to the world the unique cultural and spiritual gifts of black people. It was to this end that God had allowed the "children of Africa" to be brought into slavery and in the process come to know and be a part of a superior civilization. This belief added another dimension to Crummell's enthusiasm for colonization, for it cast all blacks of the diaspora into the role of potential "civilizers" of indigenous Africans.

During the American Civil War, Crummell devoted himself to persuading skilled and educated Afro-Americans to resettle in Africa. Through writings and two speaking tours of the United States, he offered arguments based on Christian sentiment, economic self-interest, and race consciousness to support his calls for a return to the "Fatherland." In comments designed to awaken American blacks from the fantasy of achieving racial equality in the United States, Crummell prophesied that legal proscription and caste would always set limits on their aspirations, whereas in Africa preferment, honor, and wealth were open to any black of ability and drive. But beyond all this, no child of Africa, Crummell stressed repeatedly, no matter how Westernized, could ever forsake or forget the "Fatherland."

Crummell was caught up in a whirlwind of activity for all of the twenty years he spent in Liberia, earning, at various times, salaries from missionary agencies, colonization groups, and Liberian educational institutions. During this period he wore alternately, and sometimes simultaneously, a variety of hats: missionary, educator, institution builder, propagandist for his adopted nation, recruiter of immigrants, and, through a series of sermons and public addresses delivered on important occasions, analyst and critic of the Liberian community.

Although he initially sought to avoid direct involvement in the political power struggle between the "pure black" and mulatto factions, Crummell's black nationalist and Pan-Africanist views automatically aligned him with the black faction. When, for example, he supported the building of Liberia College in the interior of the country rather

243

than in the capital so that the youth of the indigenous tribes would be drawn to the school, he was expressing agreement with the position of the black faction among the settler elite. The rejection of this proposal and the establishment of the college in Monrovia were defeats for both Crummell and the black political faction.

The same black-mulatto conflict made Crummell's years on the faculty of Liberia College among his unhappiest in the country. Despite the opposition of Crummell and several other faculty members, Joseph J. Roberts, the mulatto who headed the institution, succeeded in ensuring that the bulk of the students were mulattoes and that they also were the recipients of most of the institution's scholarship funds. Roberts made life as difficult as possible for the professors who opposed him, apparently in the hope that they would resign. The protests and demonstrations Crummell and some other professors directed against Roberts's tyranny and racism provided the college president with pretexts for the dismissal of his opponents. Crummell resigned in 1866 to forestall this final humiliation.

Crummell's spirits began to show the effects of his many struggles and disappointments after his resignation from Liberia College. In an address delivered in 1870, he actually went so far as to propose that the United States assume control of Liberia by making it a protectorate. This was not only a declaration of Crummell's disillusionment with the Liberian leadership but with colonization. He chided the culturally Westernized leaders of his adopted nation for doing so little to either effectively "civilize" the indigenous Africans or to stimulate trade. Privately he expressed the belief that the Americo-Liberian elite was devoid of any vital spiritual or intellectual force that would give significant purpose to their and their country's existence.

In 1872 Crummell decided his situation was untenable: the racism of the mulattoes and white missionaries continued unabated; he lacked adequate funds for his missionary and educational work; and, always a victim of various physical ailments, he began to experience severe health problems that probably resulted as much from depression as from fatigue and overwork. That same year, as Liberian political disorder turned to civil war, his son was imprisoned by the mulatto faction. There were clear indications that a similar fate, or possibly even assassination, awaited Crummell.

Early in 1873 Crummell left Liberia and returned with his family to the United States. Departure under such circumstances was a crushing defeat for him, yet it did not cause him to yield his belief in black nationalism or the importance of Christianity, commerce, and Western civilization in regenerating his race. Indeed, Crummell would always speak hopefully of Liberia someday fulfilling her potential greatness. After reestablishing himself in his native country, however, Crummell invested his hopes for the upbuilding and vindication of his race in the Afro-American community of the United States, employing the last years of his life to promote among American blacks the same kind of racial solidarity and many of the same strategies for racial uplift he had espoused in Africa.

Shortly after his return, Crummell was appointed "Missionary-at-Large to the colored people of Washington, D.C." by the Episcopal bishop of Maryland. This appointment represented an attempt to expand the Episcopal church's very limited ministry to the black community in the nation's capital. For his part Crummell was extremely pleased to be placed in a city he considered the "mecca of the colored race." The number of blacks holding minor political offices and government clerkships gave the Washington black community the appearance of prosperity. Educational opportunities existed for the most able and aggressive blacks, the community had spawned a number of institutions in response to its isolation from the white community, and it contained a sizable percentage of the few blacks who held college and university degrees. Howard University, the country's major black educational institution, was situated there; and the city was, for a good part of the year, the residence of those blacks who represented various parts of the South in Congress. In addition, its residents included such racial statesmen as Frederick Douglass, the prominent A.M.E. bishop Daniel A. Payne, and John Mercer Langston. Few, if any, blacks in Washington or elsewhere were able to affect public policy, but the utterances of such "race leaders" as Douglass, Payne, and Langston frequently shaped the terms of public discourse in the Afro-American community. Washington was a setting in which Crummell believed that his "gifts" as a teacher, thinker, and institution builder could make a major impact on the racial thought and behavior of blacks.

Crummell also believed that the Episcopal church would have the greatest success in attracting blacks if it concentrated on the establishment of strong parishes in urban communities. Such parishes would not only be houses of intelligent and orderly worship, but also social service centers. He was certain that if the Episcopal church presented itself to the black community in this form, numerous blacks of intelligence, ability, and moral sensitivity would be drawn into association with a religious community that met practical needs while offering a more enlightened religious experience. Such parishes would also appeal

245

to elite Afro-Americans because they provided a perspective and setting that affirmed them as racial leaders and as role models for the ignorant, illiterate, confused, and hopeless of the race. After a brief period of service in several small, weak black congregations, Crummell established just such a parish at St. Luke's Church in 1880. By the 1890s this congregation had become self-supporting, with a membership that included some of the best-educated, most prosperous, and most race-conscious members of the Washington black community. Crummell's establishment of St. Luke's and his broader ministry made a strong, positive impression on younger black Protestant clergy, particularly those in the Episcopal, Congregational, and Presbyterian churches, many of whom sought to emulate his achievements in their own ministries.

At the same time he was building St. Luke's, Crummell continued to involve himself with larger concerns and to propagate his ideas through public addresses and publications, as well as sermons. Shortly after settling in Washington, he was recognized as the moving force in the formation of the interdenominational Union of Colored Ministers in the city. As a result of his efforts, in 1883 a national caucus of black Episcopal clergy and laity was organized to fight racism in the Episcopal church. In 1892, as white Washingtonians increasingly divorced themselves from the social concerns of their black fellow citizens, Crummell strongly urged the black clergy of the city to take the lead in establishing charitable institutions for the race. Keeping his distance from politicians and political organizations, Crummell sought, through words and example, to influence prominent black politicians and journalists. He also sought, in every possible way, to encourage younger blacks of promise and demonstrated ability, such as the Harvard-educated scholar W. E. B. Du Bois, the poet Paul Laurence Dunbar, the journalist John E. Bruce, Presbyterian cleric Francis J. Grimké, and educator and feminist Anna J. Cooper.

Crummell promoted as well the formation of institutions that brought educated blacks into formal association with each other, hoping these organizations would assist their efforts to secure voice and influence in both the black and white communities. The high point of his work in this regard came in 1897, when he was the central figure in the establishment of the American Negro Academy, a national organization that contained some of the best-educated and most prominent of the black elite. His great hope was that these "trained and scholarly men" would take the lead in shaping and directing "the opinions and habits of the crude masses," while at the same time defending Afro-Americans from the assaults of those who despised them. In keeping with his lifelong efforts to promote racial pride, Crummell excluded from the academy blacks who were devoid of "race loyalty," particularly those mulattoes who, in his opinion, flaunted their whiteness as a sign of social superiority or who identified with the race only when it benefited them. Although the heavy preponderance of mulattoes among educated blacks ensured a sizable mulatto presence in the ANA, all who entered were, in Crummell's estimation, true "race men."

While the academy was always a weak organization, for thirty-one years it promoted the exchange of ideas among black intellectuals and helped perpetuate the black protest tradition in an age of accommodation and proscription. Crummell's personal and institutional efforts to encourage the expanding black professional classes helped to give them a heightened sense of community and positive self-identity at a time when educated blacks faced virulent racial hostility. It is almost certain that W. E. B. Du Bois developed his concept of the "Talented Tenth"—the idea that the small minority of blacks who had received a liberal arts education should lead, liberate, and elevate their people—within the context of the academy, directly influenced by Crummell's ideas and activities.

During the last twenty years of his life Crummell remained a spokesman for racial solidarity and the values of "Christian civilization." His understanding of racial solidarity rested on the belief that segments of the human community, especially in England, France, and Belgium, had achieved greatness because of their adherence to the "social principle." This was the term Crummell used to describe "the disposition which leads men to associate and join together for specific purposes." Repeatedly he chastised black Americans for their lack of cooperative spirit in almost every area of common endeavor, citing as evidence their desire to "forget . . . that they are colored people" and their apparent willingness to let their racial institutions die. To Crummell such behavior was subversive of the "social principle" and thus of all possibilities of black progress. In his use of arguments based on this principle, his unique and paradoxical commitment to black nationalism and Western cultural models appears with a clarity that is nowhere so evident in other aspects of his thought.

Despite Crummell's continuing ability to marshal effectively both words and logic in defense of his positions, there were signs of strain and uncertainty in his arguments. This reflected the difficulties he encountered in seeking to apply his brand of Christianity and black solidarity in an increasingly urban, industrial, secular America. Although Crummell admitted the unfairness of practices that deprived most blacks of political rights, he took the position that ultimately

247

efforts to develop the race morally and materially were vastly more important. He vigorously propounded this view at a time when southern blacks were forced to accept disfranchisement while simultaneously watching native-born whites and white ethnics successfully use politics to support their thrust for economic and social mobility. Few Afro-Americans could, as Crummell did, take satisfaction in high character and racial unity when these qualities brought them so little that was tangible in return.

Crummell not only disparaged political activity but was openly hostile to black politicians as a group. Much of this was related directly to his belief that the inability of Liberia to rise to its greatness was, in large part, due to the swarm of politicians who kept the nation divided and unable to unite on basic goals, a situation they exploited to promote their own personal power and enrichment. To his mind the situation was the same in the United States. Here, however, the negative effects were compounded by the willingness of black politicians to do the bidding of whites who essentially cared nothing for the interests of blacks. While Crummell's reservations about the utility of black "political agitation" contained certain elements of realism, his position denigrated the need many blacks felt to claim for themselves certain basic citizenship rights, whether they were attainable or not. His reservations also represented an unrealistic misjudgment regarding the crucial role of political power in supporting and sustaining black efforts to attain economic and social parity with whites.

A lifelong hostility toward mulatto pretensions combined with Crummell's recall of another aspect of the Liberian experience to add to his distaste for political activity. Still smarting from his defeats and humiliations at the hands of Liberian mulattoes, he was deeply disturbed that so many of his race's politicians in the United States were light-skinned or near-white, priding themselves on their difference in color and background from the mass of blacks. Crummell vehemently castigated these so-called leaders as a "fanatical and conceited junto, more malignant than white men," who pushed "themselves forward as leaders and autocrats of the race" while "at the same time repudiating the race." Such opinions suggest that as Crummell aged he felt a heightened need to assert the worth of "pure blacks." While some of his criticisms of Afro-American politicians were accurate, they also reflected a lingering bitterness from unhealed wounds as well as envy of more popular figures whom he considered his inferiors in intellect, racial loyalty, and leadership skills. After Crummell's return to the United States, all overt political activity on his part was restricted to ecclesiastical institutions. Despite his bitter hostility toward politicians, or perhaps because of it, this seems to have been by choice. As a consequence, his impact on the secular community was essentially as an intellectual whose ideas commanded attention within educated black circles and among a small number of whites.

Prior to the Civil War, Crummell had stressed the need for blacks to secure agricultural and mechanical training as well as classical and higher education. After returning to the United States, he reaffirmed these views as a vocal proponent of the dignity of labor, the virtues of rural life, and the great need of most blacks for education that was "solid and practical." This in no way indicated a shift in his equally firm belief that "higher education" was of the utmost importance to ensure a corps of capable race leaders. By 1890, however, Crummell had begun to be disturbed by the growing popularity of the "miserable fad of industrialism," which he described as something "a lot of white men in the land who pity the Negro but who have never learned to love him" espouse as a "pretext" for placing a "limitation on our brains and culture." He was filled with disgust for a "set of black opportunists who will jump at anything a white man says, if it will give them notoriety and help them jingle a few nickles in their pockets." This disparaging reference was directed at black promoters of industrial education such as Booker T. Washington. As Crummell saw manual training coming to dominate the thinking of whites who supported black education (and, as a consequence, the rhetoric of black educators), he placed greater emphasis on the indispensable role of college-trained blacks.

Despite Crummell's criticisms of the abuses resulting from a heightened interest in industrial education, the last two decades of the nineteenth century constituted a period when he, along with most other black leaders like the rising Booker T. Washington, put greater emphasis on the need for black moral and economic self-help. While Crummell arrived at his opinions independently, these themes, along with his negative attitude toward politics and black politicians, were all part of a broad shift, throughout the Afro-American community, away from an emphasis on political rights and mobility through higher education and toward practical goals thought achievable by moral discipline, hard work, and practical skills. Such sentiments reflected the desperate search among blacks for new strategies as white hostility, North and South, closed off many of the economic, political, and social opportunities that had previously existed. What Crummell deplored was the linkage of these strategies with the accommodationism espoused by Booker T. Washington in his famous Atlanta Exposition address in 1895.

In 1894, at the age of seventy-four, Crummell retired from the rectorship of St. Luke's. He made this decision because he was beginning to find the physical demands of the position overwhelming. However, during the four remaining years of his life he continued to be an active figure. Indeed, one of his most important efforts, the establishment of the American Negro Academy, took place a year before his death in 1898.

Throughout his long and varied career Crummell was a consistent spokesman for a form of black nationalism whose basic concepts were familiar to many Afro-Americans when he was a youth. His unique contribution was the freshness he brought to old concepts through an intelligent and scholarly restatement of these ideas. Much of his influence derived from the fact that most of the ideas to which he was so deeply committed had wide acceptance among English-speaking blacks during the nineteenth century. This is not to say that he brought nothing new to these concepts, for the vigor and creativity of his reformulations helped to sustain their force and appeal. Crummell's use of information and insights from the fields of anthropology, sociology, and statistics in his sermons and addresses marks him as more thoughtful and knowledgeable than most of his contemporaries. Without any formal acquaintance with the field of psychology, he developed a superb understanding of the dynamics of racism, particularly its negative impact on blacks' sense of self-worth. Certainly his carefully articulated beliefs in ties between all peoples of African descent and in a uniquely black understanding of world history laid the groundwork for early twentieth-century black thinkers who were more secular, less optimistic, and less in awe of Western culture than he was.

Crummell's fundamental identity was that of a Christian priest and theologian. This was the basis on which he constructed all of his ideas and strategies. Whether functioning as a clergyman in Europe, Africa, or the United States, Crummell undertook, as an integral part of his religious duties, the defense of blacks from racist ideas and practices, as well as the creation of black leaders and institutions committed to the elimination of white control. At the same time his brand of Christianity was, in its approach to non-Christian, non-Westernized peoples, deeply influenced by the paternalism as well as the cultural and religious imperialism of the predominantly white Anglo-American social order of which he was a part and by which he was so significantly shaped in mind and spirit.

Like so many nineteenth-century thinkers Crummell confused culture

250

with civilization, leading him to believe and argue that the impressive technology, political systems, economic orders, and cultures of the predominantly white nations of the North Atlantic community represented the height of civilization. His application of this belief produced the argument that the problems of blacks were as much due to personal deficiencies—which he was certain could be overcome—as to white oppression. The same perspective frequently made him a hostile and unsympathetic surveyor of African and unassimilated aspects of Afro-American culture. As a consequence, Crummell's deep commitment to Western culture and European Christianity limited his capacity to perceive many of the most damaging ways in which the religion and culture of whites contributed to the economic, political, social, and psychological debasement of blacks. Nevertheless, his efforts to affirm the unity of all black people, to improve the moral and intellectual quality of black leadership, and to promote the economic and cultural development of his race played an important role in readying blacks for the challenges of the twentieth century.

John Dittmer

13

The Education of
Henry McNeal Turner

OUTSIDE OF the African Methodist Episcopal church, where he is venerated as one of the pillars of that denomination, Henry McNeal Turner is best known today (when he is known) as a combative black nationalist who promoted ill-fated schemes to send black Americans "back to Africa." He was the "forerunner of Marcus Garvey." But important as that was, Turner's significance as a black leader rests upon much more than his impassioned advocacy of African emigration. More than any other public figure of his day, he encouraged identification with the African homeland, instilling confidence and pride among Afro-Americans "inferiorated" by centuries of slavery. Yet Turner also committed himself to the ongoing black struggle for freedom and dignity inside white America. His public life encompassed one of the most turbulent periods in Afro-American history, from the latter days of slavery to the nadir of black life at the outbreak of World War I.

Viewed in terms of individual achievement, Turner's career was a nineteenth-century American success story. Rising from humble origins, he gained national recognition as an important Reconstruction politician and, after the failure of that democratic experiment, quickly moved up through the ranks of the A.M.E. church hierarchy. Later, as senior bishop, he became one of the most influential and outspoken black churchmen. Turner believed that in the postwar South religious leaders must become involved in the secular life of the community, and thus he saw his mission as both spiritual and political. In the 1880s Turner emerged as a leader of the African emigration movement, and his unrelenting support of that cause gained him a wide audience and a major voice in the debate over the Afro-American's future. He was the preeminent black nationalist of the period, and his appeals to race consciousness and pride, coupled with his blistering attacks on white society, won him the respect of thousands of American blacks.

At the same time Turner was one of the most paradoxical public figures of his era. The champion of the inarticulate black masses, he did not effectively represent their interests during the early period of his political ascendancy after the Civil War. The same man who pleaded for black unity was unwilling to compromise with other leaders and was himself a divisive force in the black community. His criticism of white America, as it developed over the years, was more biting and incisive than that of his contemporaries, yet Turner openly consorted with racist politicians, not all of whom supported his emigrationist platform. It is difficult, even today, to reconcile many of these apparent contradictions. Turner kept his own counsel and did not leave behind memoirs or correspondence that might shed light on the complexity of his thought.

The contradictions in Turner's public life were reflected in his personality. A large, powerful man, crude and awkward of manner, Turner evoked the image of the two-fisted frontiersman. He was a spellbinding orator whose cruel irony and penetrating sarcasm withered his ideological enemies. Yet this rough facade masked a sensitive, deeply religious man whose spiritual mission was to alleviate the suffering of his people. This messianic vision at first manifested itself in the optimistic belief that white political leaders would live up to the promises made in the immediate postwar period. The collapse of Reconstruction and the subsequent failure of the federal government to safeguard black Americans' constitutional rights dashed Turner's hopes, left him profoundly cynical about the motivations of all white people, and reinforced his conviction that blacks could achieve their just destiny only by returning to the African homeland. The contrast between his youthful optimism and later bitter disillusionment tells us as much about America in the half century after Appomattox as it does about the intellectual odyssey of Henry McNeal Turner.

On Emancipation Day in 1866 a large audience of freed slaves turned out in Augusta to hear a young preacher named Henry Turner deliver the commemorative address. At thirty-two already one of the major figures in black Georgia, Turner had worked his way up from the cotton fields to a position of state leadership in the A.M.E. church. He was clearly a man to be reckoned with, and his presence in Augusta was proof of how far blacks might carry their aspirations. Emancipation itself had created an atmosphere of excitement and anticipation, and the citizens attending this meeting were expecting an oration equal to the joyous occasion. Their speaker did not disappoint them.

In his address Turner rehearsed the history of racial injustice in America, but his tone was upbeat, focusing on the contributions of Africans and Afro-Americans to the advancement of civilization. He urged his listeners to take pride in achievements won in the face of adversity. The young minister saw the Civil War as a turning point and, along with many other black activists, looked to the future with optimism. Using the American flag as his symbol, Turner observed that while in the past "every star was against us; every stripe against us," now "we can claim the protection of the stars and stripes. The glories of this faded escutcheon will ever bid us go free." He concluded with the advice that, so far as southern whites are concerned, blacks should "let by-gones be by-gones. . . . Let us show them we can be a people, respectable, virtuous, honest, and industrious, and soon their prejudice will melt away, and with God for our Father we will all be brothers."

That Turner would face the dawn of Reconstruction with such misguided optimism was due in part to his own successful rise from obscurity. Although he was born free in South Carolina in 1834, family necessity dictated that Henry be sent to work alongside slaves in the cotton fields, so he too felt the overseer's lash. Determined to escape the plantation environment, Turner saw education as a way out. With the help of several friendly whites he learned to read and write, and while still in his teens he caught the attention of officials of the white Methodist Episcopal Church-South, who enlisted him as an itinerant minister. Turner traveled freely throughout the Deep South in the mid-1850s, preaching to slaves and free blacks, and his powerful sermons attracted whites to his meetings as well. Then in 1858 he learned of the A.M.E. church, and the idea of an all-black denomination exerted strong appeal. Assigned to the A.M.E. mission in Baltimore, Turner began a rigorous program of educational training, studying Latin, Greek, Hebrew, and theology with several professors at Trinity College. Appointed deacon in 1860 and elder two years later, the young minister moved to Washington, where he pastored Union Bethel Church, the largest black congregation in the city.

In Washington, Turner developed friendships with leading antislavery congressmen such as Benjamin Wade, Thaddeus Stevens, and Charles Sumner, contacts he would cultivate during his years as an active politician. He gained national attention when Abraham Lincoln appointed him the first black army chaplain. Turner served with distinction, accompanying troops into battle while ministering to their spiritual needs. After the war he moved to Georgia to work with the Freedmen's Bureau, but racial discrimination soon led to his resignation. He then accepted Bishop Daniel A. Payne's offer to become presiding elder and superintendent of the A.M.E. missions in Georgia.

Banned from the South for over thirty years, the A.M.E. wasted no time in dispatching over seventy missionary-organizers into the states of the Old Confederacy in a massive effort to win over the former slaves who had been members of white-run denominations. Returning to Georgia in 1865, Turner found many freedpeople still prisoners of old slave habits. They exhibited little racial pride and were fearful of antagonizing their former masters. From the outset Turner realized that by necessity his mission would be political as well as religious. A largely self-educated intellectual, he retained the common touch and sought by courageous example to raise the consciousness of free blacks. Throughout his life he would speak to the condition of impoverished blacks, and they would remain his natural constituency and major base of support.

Turner threw himself into his organizational work with unsurpassed energy and enthusiasm. Of his efforts in the field one black Georgian wrote: "I never saw a man travel so much, preach and speak so much and then be up so late of nights . . . drilling his official men. Surely if he continues this way, and lives the year out . . . he has nine lives." There was some question as to whether Turner would "live the year out," for many southern whites did not take kindly to this invasion of black organizers. Tempers flared on both sides. In Macon, after white Methodists won a court victory giving them control of church property, they awoke to find the church burned to the ground. Turner received a number of death threats and welcomed protection from armed supporters as he traveled throughout the rural South. (What was at stake here was more than church property or the souls of freedpeople. For whites, the sight of black men and women organizing to take charge of their destiny did not bode well for the future of white supremacy.)

Turner saw the necessity of striking fast, while the South was off-balance, and he licensed preachers "by the cargo," declaring that "my hastily made preachers have been among the most useful." The efforts of the A.M.E. missionaries met with instant and spectacular success, as they recruited thousands of converts. Early in 1866 Turner claimed that Georgia had been secured for the A.M.E. church, stating, "I have visited every place it was safe to go, and sent preachers where it was thought I had better not venture."

A man of Turner's talents quite naturally became involved in secular matters, including the burning question of civil and political rights. When asked by the Republican Executive Committee to organize black voters in Georgia, he retraced his steps across the state, writing campaign broadsides, organizing Union leagues, and speaking at freedpeople's conventions. His message was always the same: "We want power, it can only come through organization, and organization comes through unity." Crucial to his success in mobilizing the black vote were the A.M.E. churches he had founded the previous year. In these often isolated communities the minister, in addition to preaching the gospel, educated and politicized parishioners. The church was the only institution capable of providing secular leadership, and it quickly became the focal point of black political life as well.

Describing himself as "a minister of the gospel and a kind of politician—both," Turner could look back with satisfaction on the two years since the war's end. He had established the A.M.E. church in Georgia on a solid footing and laid the groundwork for his future leadership of that denomination. While his claim that he "organized the Republican Party in this state" was somewhat exaggerated, his grass-roots organizing campaign was unprecedented; indeed Georgia would not again see anything like it until the civil rights movement a century later. At thirty-three Turner was the most influential black religious and political leader in Georgia, the state with the largest black population. As an elected member of the state constitutional convention in late 1867, he looked forward to working with white men of good will to shape a new government responsive to the needs of all its citizens.

Like many grass-roots organizers who would follow him, Turner proved more effective in the field than in the legislative halls. Throughout the long deliberations leading to Georgia's Reconstruction constitution, his stance was both conservative and accommodationist. Consistently supporting planter interests, he introduced a resolution to prevent the sale of property of those owners unable to pay their taxes, and he supported a petition to Congress to grant $30,000,000 for planter relief. He also introduced a resolution providing financial assistance for banks, supported poll tax and education requirements for suffrage, and even attempted to persuade the convention to take up a petition for the pardon of Jefferson Davis. Perhaps Turner summed up his convention performance best when he later ruefully observed that "no man in Georgia has been more conservative than I. 'Anything to please the white folks' has been my motto. . . ."

Aside from his key convention role in establishing a public school system, Turner did not address the concerns of his black constituents. He avoided the issue of land reform, despite widespread interest among freedpeople for "forty acres and a mule." Indeed, by protecting planter property he helped reduce the amount of land for purchase at reasonable prices. His stand for suffrage restrictions would have drastically reduced the potential black electorate, and his failure to push for a constitutional amendment making absolutely clear the right of blacks to hold public office contributed to the expulsion of all black members of the state legislature.

The accommodationist position taken by Turner and the other black delegates rested in part on political expediency. Over three-fourths of the nearly 170 convention delegates were conservative white southerners. Blacks, who made up no more than 20 percent of the total, felt the need to compromise to maintain any political influence. But such assumptions also stemmed from the rather naive faith of Turner and most other blacks at the convention that white Georgians would agree to meaningful black participation in government. As members of the educated black elite they assumed to know what was best for the illiterate black masses, and they were confident of their ability to deal with seasoned and powerful white politicians. They were wrong on both counts.

After satisfying the requirements of the Congressional Reconstruction Acts of 1867, Georgia was readmitted to the Union and in April 1868 held elections for governor and state legislators. Conservative white Democrats and Republicans dominated the new General Assembly, but thirty-two blacks did win election, including Henry Turner. During his brief tenure in the legislature, Turner served with greater distinction than he had at the constitutional convention. Now openly suspicious of the agenda of white lawmakers, he increasingly saw his role as that of defender of the rights of freedpeople. Along with other black legislators he introduced bills to provide state subsidies for black higher education, to charter black cooperative stock companies, and to create a black militia to offer some protection against Klan violence. Aware of the nature of economic exploitation against blacks, Turner was among the first to make effective use of the term "peonage" to describe the widespread practice by which many landlords held on to unwilling tenants. He offered legislation to protect sharecroppers, to enact an eight-hour work day, and to abolish the convict lease system.

As he moved away from his accommodationist stance, Turner's relationship with white politicians became confrontational. The state's most articulate black leader, he was singled out for abuse. Angered by slanderous attacks on his character, and upset by the failure of white Republicans to support problack legislation, Turner lashed back at his critics. His speech during the debate that led to expulsion of all black legislators, the most powerful of his career, was a manifesto for human rights: "I am here to demand my rights and to hurl thunderbolts at the man who would dare to cross the threshold of my manhood. . . . Never, in the history of the world has a man been arraigned before a body clothed with legislative, judicial, or executive functions, charged with the offense of being of a darker hue than his fellow-men.... The great question, sir, is this: Am I a man?" Turner went on to defend the Negro against charges of inferiority ("I hold that we are a very great people") and to voice contempt for the "treachery" of the white race. At the close of his address he led the black delegation out of the chamber, turned to face his colleagues one last time, and contemptuously scraped the mud off his shoes.

This would not be Turner's legislative swan song. Under protection of federal bayonet the black representatives would gain readmission, and Turner would serve during the 1870 General Assembly session. But by the time he returned, Radical Reconstruction in Georgia had been so effectively undermined that there was little chance for the black delegation to have any impact. The Democrats quickly consolidated their power. After lobbying unsuccessfully for further federal intervention, Turner called upon his old friends in Congress to secure him appointive office. These efforts to obtain federal patronage met such intense white resistance—as when President Grant appointed him postmaster of Macon—that Turner retired from active political life in the early 1870s. Deprived of his political power base, disillusioned by federal indifference to white violence and voter fraud, Turner returned full-time to his religious duties.

Except for church historians, scholars have given Turner's religious career and beliefs short shrift. For over a half century the church was the central concern in his life, providing him with his livelihood and a strong base of operations in the black community. Moreover, his theological interpretation of history laid the foundation for his early political optimism, his evolving black nationalism, and his ultimate obsession with African emigration.

Bishop Turner's theology was grounded in the Bible, particularly in the teachings of the Hebrew prophets and in the gospel of Jesus. A firm believer in the omnipotence and sovereignty of God, Turner said: "There is a God that runs this universe: and a nation and people are no exception." Given this fundamentalist view of the relationship between God and humanity, Turner had to come to terms with the tragic history of the African peoples since the diaspora. In so doing he developed a messianic vision which had as its keystone the concept of God's providential design for people of African descent. Throughout his ministerial career Turner insisted that slavery was a "Providential institution." God was "not asleep or oblivious to passing events" but knew that the slave regime "was the most rapid transit from barbarism to Christian civilization for the Negro." Thus God permitted the enslavement of Africans and placed them under the trusteeship of white Americans. It was whites' brutal treatment of slaves that subverted divine will and purpose and was "an insult to God." It would take the Civil War to "satisfy the divine justice and make slavery despicable in the eyes of a country which loved it so dearly and nurtured it so long." This logic led Turner at first to see Reconstruction as a conversion experience for whites in which they would undergo a change of heart. Convinced that "all great convulsive courses have been succeeded with liberative consequences," he held out the olive branch to southern whites, hopeful that together they would build the new Jerusalem.

The bitter experience of Reconstruction soured Turner on elective politics but did not shake his faith in God's providential design. The bishop simply adapted the model to fit new circumstances. His experience with the evils of slavery, the racism of northern troops, and the perfidy of both South and North after the war convinced Turner that God's plan for the Negro did not include a positive role for whites. From the outset of his ministry he had believed the church must develop racial pride and consciousness among millions of blacks beaten down by centuries of oppression. Now, beginning in the late 1880s, Turner viewed this mission with a great sense of urgency and began to develop a black theology of liberation grounded in the basic tenets of Christianity.

To achieve this end, Turner realized, blacks must reject all teachings of the white church that confirmed their inferior status. He was particularly sensitive to the symbolic significance of "whiteness" in Christian teachings and discouraged singing of such verses as, "Now wash me and I shall be whiter than snow," explaining that the purpose of washing was to make one clean, not white. More dramatic was his assertion, often repeated, that "God is a Negro." When this statement drew criticism from whites—and from a few blacks—Turner patiently pointed out that historically every race of people had portrayed God in its own image; but he also lashed out at those whites and "all of the fool Negroes" who "believe that God is a white-skinned, blue-eyed, projecting-nosed, compressed-lipped and finely-robed *white* gentleman, sitting upon a throne somewhere in the heavens." Turner was deeply disturbed by the negative influence of white Christianity upon the black psyche: he knew that "Christianity" reflected the values of the greater society, and he despaired of any significant improvement in the self-image of Afro-Americans so long as they were subjected to daily indoctrination by the dominant culture. "As long as we remain among the whites," he wrote in 1898, "the Negro will believe that the devil is black . . . and that he [the Negro] was the devil . . . and the

260

effect of such sentiment is contemptuous and degrading." This is one of the reasons, Turner concluded, "why we favor African emigration."

The black exodus was both the culmination and the cornerstone of Turner's theology. It linked his messianic vision of the A.M.E. Christian mission and his African dream of a strong and proud black nation, free from the corrupting influence of white society. He had always believed that God's providential plan was to Christianize Africa. As early as 1866 the young minister expressed interest in emigration, and after Reconstruction it became his consuming passion. Contrary to critics' charges, Turner never contended that all Afro-Americans would choose to return to the land of their ancestors. But "millions of the Negro race" would emigrate, bringing with them the message of Christ crucified and (paradoxically) the benefits of Western civilization. To comprehend Turner's black nationalism and the depth of his dedication to Africa, then, one must examine both within the context of his strong religious beliefs.

Turner's election to the bishopric in 1880 culminated twenty-two years of active service for the A.M.E. church in a variety of positions. After five years of religious and political organizing in Georgia, he resigned as elder to become pastor of a large Savannah congregation. In 1876 the Methodist hierarchy called him to Philadelphia to become business manager of the nearly bankrupt A.M.E. Book Concern. Turner impressed his superiors with his administrative skills and made good use of the opportunity to write for publications, edit the *Christian Recorder,* revise the church hymnal, and compile the *Catechism of the A.M.E. Church.* He also used his position to political advantage, traveling from conference to conference to meet influential black Methodists.

Turner became bishop over the objections of his former patron, Bishop Daniel A. Payne, and other northern-based church leaders. The pious and idealistic Payne was uncomfortable with this crude, awkward preacher-politician from the South. Turner's support came from the southern rank-and-file A.M.E. members and their pastors, many of whom he himself recruited into the ministry. In charge of the Georgia Conference, the denomination's largest, Turner and his followers became a powerful voice for the A.M.E. church's southern majority.

Church leadership gave Turner a forum denied him in the 1870s. He enjoyed the rough-and-tumble ecclesiastical politics. One of his contemporaries remembers him as "always looking for a fight." Another recalled that he "was no kid glove leader, and no hat box bishop. There was nothing of the smell of the parlor and drawing room about him." Turner saw himself as the leader of the masses but not one of them. He wielded power autocratically, eschewing familiarity. One minister who addressed Turner as "brother" at a convention got a sharp reprimand, as Turner stopped the proceedings with an explosive, "I want you to understand, I am the BISHOP."

Turner's private life centered around his spacious home at 30 Younge Street in Atlanta. Even here the outside world intruded, for amid a mountain of books, journals, and manuscripts, a clerical staff was on hand to do the bishop's bidding. Married four times, Turner survived three wives and all but two of his children. He did not normally refer to his personal tragedies, but in 1893 he did inform newspaper readers that in the ten-year period just ended he had lost his mother, his eldest daughter, his first wife, his youngest daughter, and his second wife. His final marriage at age seventy-three to his private secretary, Laura Pearl Lemon, a divorcee, evoked a storm of criticism in the A.M.E. bishopric, but Turner survived the attempts to remove him from office. A firm believer in the institution of marriage, he once wrote to his son John that "bachelors are a public nuisance."

Although his attitude toward husband-wife relations appears to have reflected the mores of the Victorian age, Turner was ahead of his time in advocating an expanded public role for women. While serving in the Georgia legislature he introduced a bill giving women the vote, and in 1888 he ordained a woman as deacon in the A.M.E. church. (The Council of Bishops immediately rescinded the appointment, claiming that the Scriptures did not authorize such action and grumbling that it was an act "without a precedent in any other body of Christians in the known world.") Turner persisted in involving women in the activities of the church, founding the Women's Home and Foreign Mission Society, praising black women because they "intend to make a fight for their rights," and opening the columns of his newspapers to women writers. Turner received strong support and little criticism from women in the A.M.E. church; he in turn was proud to recognize their contribution and worth.

As senior bishop for twenty of his thirty-five years in the episcopacy, Turner put his stamp on the church in numerous ways. An iconoclast at the head of a vast bureaucracy, he scorned regulations that did not serve his purposes. Thus, when faced with the need for strong local leadership in the new A.M.E. mission in South Africa, he created the post of vicar-bishop—an office unknown to Methodism. Turner's pragmatism continually caused conflict with his fellow bishops. He also ruffled feathers on the congregational level with attacks on emotionalism in the pulpit and insistence on rituals and use of clerical vestments to promote formality and dignity in worship services. But

262

his major contributions to the church lay in the fields of education and foreign missions.

Like most black leaders Turner saw education as the key to progress, and from the beginning of his ministry he stressed the need for well-trained ministers and teachers. Moreover, since he believed that education could be either a means of social control or a potent weapon for liberation, he insisted that schools be organized and run only by blacks, without interference from white teachers or trustees. Under Turner's leadership the A.M.E. transferred most of its educational activities to the South, establishing a dozen schools and colleges during the last two decades of the nineteenth century. The centerpiece of the system was Morris Brown College in Atlanta. Turner took special interest in this institution, serving for a time as its chancellor, overseeing its expansion, and at one point mortgaging his personal property to keep the college afloat. In 1900 the college's board of trustees established Turner Theological Seminary in honor of the contributions of the senior bishop.

While not nearly so well publicized as his promotion of African emigration, Turner's missionary work on the continent produced tangible results for the A.M.E. church and facilitated the rise of black consciousness in South Africa. The conviction that the A.M.E. church had an obligation to Christianize Africa was not original with Turner, but early efforts to do so had failed because of the church's meager economic resources and the more immediate task of evangelizing the freedpeople in the South. The crusade to convert Africans began in earnest in the late 1880s, when Bishop Turner became president of the A.M.E. Missionary Department and expanded its jurisdiction to include Africa. Late in 1891 he made his first trip to Africa, drawing upon his considerable organizational skills to establish annual conferences in Sierra Leone and Liberia. Then, and in two subsequent visits in 1893 and 1895, Turner ordained preachers, elders, and deacons, established schools and churches, and won over hundreds of converts to African Methodism. Welcomed by large crowds wherever he went, Turner responded enthusiastically and in a series of widely read letters promoted both African missions and emigration.

The A.M.E. church's major gains came in South Africa, where Turner became involved in the racial politics of that strife-torn region on the eve of the Boer War. A.M.E. church interest stemmed directly from establishment of the South African Ethiopian church in 1892 by African religious leaders upset by the color bar in white churches and stirred by nationalistic feelings of "Africa for Africans." The two religious bodies had so much in common that in 1896 the Ethiopian church sent a delegation to Atlanta to arrange a merger. Turner appointed Reverend James W. Dwane, leader of the Ethiopian group, as superintendent of the newly created A.M.E. church in South Africa and authorized his return to Africa to work on the transition of the clergy and members of the Ethiopian mission into the A.M.E. denomination.

Two years later Turner made a five-week triumphal tour through South Africa, traveling over a thousand miles from Cape Town to Pretoria, meeting with Paul Kruger, the president of the Orange Free State, and organizing the Transvaal and Cape Colony conferences. Although he received a polite reception from government officials, they became suspicious that he and American A.M.E. missionaries were pursuing goals more political than religious. The "race solidarity" and "race regeneration" messages brought by these missionaries alarmed colonial administrators, who began placing restrictions on the ministers. Turner was specifically accused of arousing nationalist passions among the Zulus, and after the Zulu revolt failed in 1906, A.M.E. missionaries were barred from most of Natal and Transvaal.

Turner's South African campaign also got him into trouble with his fellow bishops back home. The controversy erupted with the appointment of Dwane as vicar-bishop. Turner argued that the position was not inconsistent with Methodist tradition, but the A.M.E. episcopacy repudiated his action. The Dwane affair was but one of a series of issues that had been dividing Turner and the more traditional bishops (the majority of them did not share his enthusiasm for African emigration), and in the 1890s his power in the church began to decline. But by then Turner had once again reimmersed himself in the secular world, promoting and organizing black migration to Africa, renewing his interest in state and national politics, and making his bid to fill the leadership void left by Frederick Douglass.

For Afro-Americans the decade of the 1890s was the low point of their post–Civil War experience. Acts of racial violence had reached a new high, the courts were continuing their retreat from the constitutional guarantees afforded American citizens, and the depression of 1893 further tightened the chains of crop lien and peonage. Traditional black leaders appeared unable to come to terms with these catastrophic developments. Douglass was now an old man (he would die in 1895), and his assimilationist ideology, based on black political empowerment, had failed to anticipate the depth and virulence of white racist sentiment. The time was ripe for new leadership, and Henry McNeal Turner was ready to make his move.

Save for Douglass, Turner was as well known and as well respected as any black leader. His appeals to black pride and his famous denunciation of the U.S. Supreme Court for its decision in the 1883 civil rights cases had won him a large audience. Turner understood better than most the implications of that ruling, which declared unconstitutional the Civil Rights Act of 1875. That "barbarous" decision should be "branded, battle-axed, sawed, cut and carved with the most bitter epithets and blistering denunciations that words can express. . . . It absolves the allegiance of the Negro to the United States." His position as senior bishop provided a strong power base in the black community, and his organizing skills and oratorical prowess would serve him well in a bid for national leadership. Turner also had a program, one based on the realities of the past three decades of American history: the Afro-American dream of assimilation had failed; it was time for blacks to found their own nation in Africa.

Although he continued to demand equal rights for blacks in America, African emigration was the heart and soul of Bishop Turner's program. His first trip to Africa in 1891 was an emotional and exhilarating experience, one that confirmed his feelings about Africa as the homeland. Upon his return he persuaded the A.M.E. church to establish a monthly newspaper, the *Voice of Missions,* which quickly became the personal voice of Henry Turner. Under his editorship the *Voice* achieved a wide circulation. The monthly devoted its columns to attacks on racial discrimination, essays on black history and achievement, and, above all, articles promoting African colonization. Turner soon began receiving hundreds of letters from poor southern blacks, eagerly requesting information on passage to Africa. Convinced by this outpouring of interest that his idea was one whose time had come, he pushed forward with plans to settle colonies in Liberia, where the black government would welcome Afro-Americans. Middle-class blacks here remained either lukewarm or hostile to emigration, with their spokespeople usually unequivocal in their opposition.

To rally middle-class support for his crusade, Turner sent out a call for a national convention of Afro-Americans, to meet in Cincinnati in November 1893. With the Democrats back in the White House, the decline of Douglass, and the failure of organizations such as the Afro-American League to unify and galvanize black leadership, a political vacuum now existed that Turner purported to fill. Though the call specifically stated that the convention would "have no application to party politics," he made it clear that "the Negro cannot remain here in his present condition and be a man . . . for at the present rate his extermination is only a question of time."

The response to the convention call was gratifying. Turner's emphasis on the need to rally against racial injustice struck a common chord, and many prominent blacks responded. When the bishop rose to make the keynote address, nearly 800 delegates and a large group of local blacks were in the audience. The occasion afforded Turner a unique opportunity, yet he opened the meeting with a curious speech. He began by reiterating his concept of slavery as a providential institution and then went on to observe that during the Civil War the "Negro was as loyal to the Confederate flag as he was to the federal." Turner devoted much of his talk to the increase in lynching and, more specifically, the question of rape as its primary cause. Though he attacked the "rape defense," Turner did argue that blacks must assume responsibility for dealing with rapists in their midst. Only at the end of his speech did he address the issue of emigration, coupling it with an eloquent plea for the development of a "consciousness that I am somebody, that I am a man . . . that I have rights . . . that I am entitled to respect, that every avenue to distinction is mine."

The audience received Turner's speech warmly, but his somewhat muted emigrationist appeal failed to sway convention delegates, who rejected a committee report recommending that black Americans "turn their attention to the civilization of Africa as the only hope of the Negro race." To avoid a showdown vote he would have lost, Turner sent the report back to committee for revision. Bishop Turner's efforts to unify the delegates around a nationalist and emigrationist program had failed. While he adamantly denied having called the convention to promote his program, the black press was correct in labeling the outcome as a personal defeat for the bishop. Turner was never comfortable in the role of conciliator, and his rebuff by representatives of the black elite in Cincinnati affected him in much the same way as his earlier humiliation at the hands of white Georgia Reconstructionists. Never at home in bourgeois society, Turner reverted after Cincinnati to his familiar polemical style to answer his black critics.

African emigration was the major issue preventing Bishop Turner from achieving widespread influence in the black community. Opposition to African emigration was by no means unanimous among black leaders, but many agreed with Frederick Douglass's oft-quoted remark that "Africa's glory is in her palm trees, not in her people." Turner was restrained in his criticism of legendary figures such as Douglass and Alexander Crummell, a former missionary to Liberia and an early emigrationist who later reversed his position. Booker T. Washington also consistently opposed emigration, at one point dismissing the movement by saying, "A return to Africa for the Negro is out of the question, even providing that a majority of the Negroes wished to go back, which they do not."

Turner was circumspect in his public stance toward Washington, the well-known accommodationist. He did not single out the Tuskegean for attack on the emigration question, and while he was at times critical of Washington's leadership, Turner never joined the anti-Bookerite camp and often went out of his way to pay compliments to Tuskegee Institute and its founder. The bishop was no friend of industrial education, and ideologically he and Washington were far from compatible. Political factors account in part for Turner's reluctance to turn against Washington. After his Atlanta Compromise speech in 1895, Washington quickly emerged as the most influential black leader, and while this was a role Turner coveted, the bishop may well have decided that he had his hands full with lesser political foes without taking on the powerful Tuskegean. Both men, moreover, had huge egos, and each bitterly resented attacks directed at him personally. While opposing African emigration, Washington never made Bishop Turner the issue, and for the most part Turner returned the favor. Washington also did not wish to alienate Turner. He invited the bishop to visit Tuskegee and suggested to Edgar Gardner Murphy that Turner be invited to a 1900 conference on race relations in the South. Turner and Washington never became allies; theirs was a modus vivendi based on mutual wariness, if not respect.

Turner reserved his strongest invectives for less prestigious opponents. High on the list was editor T. Thomas Fortune of the *New York Age.* The two men had little regard for each other, and when in 1899 a group of 104 would-be African colonists became stranded in New Jersey, Fortune characterized them as "the dupes of Bishop Turner." The bishop's reply to his fellow editor included the following suggestion: "We are fast reaching the conclusion that . . . the best thing that could be done for the race would be to hang a lot of these so-called Negroes to silence their tongues."

A source of heavy criticism was Turner's association with southern white supremacists who advocated black deportation as a solution to the region's "Negro problem." Turner championed the schemes of Senator John T. Morgan of Alabama and Senator Matthew C. Butler of South Carolina and once praised the racist editor John Temple Graves as "the greatest statesman and philosopher in the land" after the latter's call for separation of the races. Turner also came under fire for serving as honorary vice-president of the American Colonization Society, an organization advanced by early nineteenth-century slaveholders to rid the South of its potentially dangerous free black population. Turner responded pragmatically to criticism of his political ties to southern racists: "If I am hungry or thirsty and my enemy brings me bread or water I shall satisfy my anxiety." Like Marcus Garvey, who would also do business with segregationists, Turner had so little regard for white people that he expressed both amusement and contempt for blacks who believed some whites capable of honestly championing the cause of racial equality in America.

What angered Turner most about the attacks of black opponents was their exaggeration and distortion of his position on emigration and Africa. As early as 1883 he lamented, "Every solitary writer who has been trying to excoriate me for my African sentiments has done so under the hidden idea, 'He wants us all to go to Africa.'" Simply stated, Turner's goal was that a significant minority (his numbers varied) of blacks should "found and establish a country or a government somewhere upon the continent of Africa." Beyond that Turner was vague in his statements concerning the form of government and the nature of the economic system in his proposed African state. There was more truth to the charges that the bishop exaggerated the appeal of Africa to attract emigrants ("And gold dust can be switched up by women and children in marvelous quantities along the shores of rivers and creeks after heavy rains . . . "); yet he did make a point of telling prospective settlers of the difficulties they would initially face and insisted that blacks should not emigrate without sufficient funds to maintain themselves until they found employment.

In the end the most persuasive arguments against African colonization came from the emigrants themselves. In the mid-1890s two boatloads of colonists left the United States for Liberia amid much fanfare and press coverage. Months later reports of disease, malnutrition, and death started filtering back. As the first colonists returned to America with horror stories of life in Liberia, the newspapers reported every tragic detail. Black opponents of emigration seized upon these reports to discredit both the movement and its chief promoter, Bishop Turner. Not all colonists had bad experiences in Africa, however; a few stayed and prospered. But returnees reinforced stereotypes of the "dark continent," and Turner could not dispel that image. His assertions that those who came back had selfish motives, exaggerating their plight to justify their defection and win sympathy back home, were undermined when he labeled them as "shiftless no-account Negroes . . . accustomed to being fed and driven around by white men. . . . " It appeared that Turner, to repair the damage of unfavorable publicity, had resorted to blaming the victim.

Although he continued to press for African emigration, the failures of the early expeditions, along with the solid opposition of most black leaders, prevented the bishop from rekindling the spirit of the early 1890s, when thousands of poor southern black sharecroppers shared his African dream of a homeland free from the tyranny of white supremacist rule.

In addition to his work with African missions and for colonization, Turner found time to become active once again in state and national politics. His retirement from active political life in the 1870s had not been total: occasional comments on national affairs and his widely read denunciation of the U.S. Supreme Court in 1883 had won him a large audience. While he never regained his early zeal for party politics (almost all of his later political pronouncements included the disclaimer that the Afro-American's stay in this country was "a temporary one"), in the 1890s he began to speak out more frequently on issues facing black Georgians. As the decade ended he was vehemently denouncing the new United States imperialism in Cuba and in the Philippines.

For the last quarter century of his life Henry McNeal Turner was a political maverick. The most important black member of the small Prohibition party, he agreed to be a delegate to the party's 1888 national convention. In Georgia, Turner was not alone among black leaders in supporting Democrat William J. Northen for governor in 1892, for Northen was a southern moderate who promised increased funds for black schools and a state antilynching law. The bishop joined most black spokespeople in resisting the appeals of Tom Watson's Populists. More comfortable with powerful Democrats than white insurgents, Turner also questioned the Populist commitment to interracial politics. Ideologically, the Populists had little to offer him, for the bishop never concerned himself much with economic alternatives to corporate capitalism.

Turner received much notoriety—and a degree of political influence —for his support of Democratic candidates running for national office. The bishop was almost alone among blacks in his support of Grover Cleveland's 1892 bid for the presidency. Turner wrote to Cleveland endorsing Georgia editor Hoke Smith for secretary of the interior and was rewarded by having three of his relatives appointed to jobs in the interior secretary's office. (This information surfaced in the 1906 Georgia gubernatorial campaign, embarrassing candidate Smith, by this time one of the state's champion race-baiters.) When Turner actively supported Democrat William Jennings Bryan in his unsuccessful presidential campaigns, the bishop drew fire from black Georgia's political establishment. Republican to the core, leaders such as William A. Pledger, editor of the *Atlanta Age* and the first black Republican state chairman in Georgia, and attorney Judson Lyons, who, as register of the United States Treasury, was the nation's highest black appointee, viewed Turner's actions as heresy, and the black press excoriated him for his crimes.

The bishop's alliance with stand-pat conservative Democrats in Georgia and in Washington does not lend itself to easy explanation, for unlike Senators Morgan and Butler, the Northens and Smiths did not support Turner's plans for African emigration. They were, at best, racial paternalists and had no program for addressing the range of problems facing black Americans. Turner never attempted to reconcile his vehement attacks on American "democracy" with his support of politicians who embraced the status quo in race relations. His endorsement of Democratic candidates enabled him to settle some scores with white and black political foes, provided him with a forum for his emigrationist views in the white press, and gained him some access to important politicians. But in the long run Bishop Turner did not look upon his political activity as preparing the way for meaningful and lasting black participation in the American system. Events at the turn of the century only strengthened his conviction that white America was on a collision course with people of color, both at home and abroad.

Although well into his sixties and in failing health, Turner seemed to grow angrier and more militant with age. Enraged by escalating white violence against defenseless blacks, the bishop responded with a *Voice of Missions* editorial titled, "Negro, Get Guns": "Let every Negro in this country who has a spark of manhood in him supply his house with one, two, or three guns ... and when your domicile is invaded by the bloody lynchers or any mob ... turn loose your missiles of death and blow the fiendish wretches into a thousand giblets. ... " This was too much for the white press, which accused him of fomenting race war. Although he backed off some here, Turner's nationalistic message remained clear and strong. He carried his analysis a step further when the United States, acting upon its imperialistic impulses, declared war on Spain in 1898.

Turner had opposed American intervention in Cuba, but when the McKinley administration moved to crush the Aguinaldo independence movement in the Philippines, the bishop's rage knew no bounds. Labeling the war there the "crime of the century," Turner castigated blacks who volunteered to help put down the insurrection: "I boil over with disgust when I remember that colored men from this country ... are there fighting to subjugate a people of their own color. . . . I can scarcely keep from saying that I hope the Filipinos will wipe such soldiers from the face of the earth. . . . to go down there and shoot innocent men and take the country away from them, is too much for me to think about, and I will write no more, for I cannot stand it."

His increasingly outspoken behavior further eroded Turner's support in the church hierarchy, and while he successfully resisted efforts to "encourage" his retirement as senior bishop, he did lose control of the *Voice of Missions* in 1901. Unabashed, he founded his own personal journal, the *Voice of the People,* and continued to put forward a broad black nationalist platform with African emigration as its centerpiece. But circulation of the new monthly remained small, and Turner's fiery appeals now met more apathy than hostility. Still, Bishop Turner remained a commanding presence. When black Georgia's political and intellectual leaders met in Macon in 1906 to form the Georgia Equal Rights Association, Turner was selected to head the group, which included such strident activists as Augusta editor William J. White and Atlanta University's W. E. B. Du Bois.

The Georgia Equal Rights Convention was something of a last hurrah for Bishop Turner. He would live on for nearly a decade, and his name would surface from time to time, usually at the center of some minor controversy. But age and infirmity—as well as American history—had taken their toll. A once herculean frame had grown portly, and his broad shoulders were drooped. Yet as he rose to address his colleagues assembled in Macon, he was again the Turner of old. In his deep booming voice he thundered his most famous lines: "I used to love what I thought was the grand old flag, and sing with ecstasy about the Stars and Stripes, but to the Negro in this country the American flag is a dirty and contemptible rag. Not a star in it can the colored man claim, for it is no longer the symbol of our manhood rights and liberty. . . . Without multiplying words, I wish to say that hell is an improvement on the United States where the Negro is concerned." For Henry McNeal Turner the flag had always stood as a metaphor for the American dream. His remarks at Macon represented a final judgment upon a nation that had consistently disappointed him, along with millions of other black Americans.

Turner remained active in the church until the end. He died in Ontario, Canada, on April 8, 1915, at the age of eighty-one, after suffering a heart attack. He had gone there against the advice of his physician to preside over the Quarterly Conference of the A.M.E. church.

The estimated 25,000 mourners who attended Bishop Turner's

funeral in Atlanta represented a cross-section of black America, with a number of prominent figures leading the procession. The eulogies praised his church and missionary work, along with his contributions to black education, but made only passing reference to his early political career and his emigrationist activities. Most of those paying their respects were poor blacks. They were not asked to make speeches, but they recognized in Turner's life the embodiment of their spirit. Whether or not they shared in his African dream, they endorsed his appeals to racial pride and applauded his bold, incisive attacks on American society. Bishop Turner was, in Du Bois's words, a "charging bull," the "last of his clan: mighty men, physically and mentally, who started at the bottom and hammered their way to the top by brute strength."

Henry McNeal Turner was a leader who defies easy categorization. A deeply religious man with the political instincts of a street fighter, an intellectual whose natural constituency existed in the shacks of unlettered sharecroppers, Turner could be maddeningly inconsistent in his political behavior, but he was unswerving in his advocacy of black nationalism and African emigration as the only righteous road to freedom and dignity. He was an agitator and a prophet, who articulated the hopes and frustrations of three generations of Afro-Americans trapped along the color line.

George C. Wright   **14**

William Henry Steward: Moderate
Approach to Black Leadership

THOUGH LITTLE KNOWN in modern times, William H. Steward was a Kentucky leader of local and national influence who played an active role in numerous protest movements by Afro-Americans. His story is important because it illuminates the strategies and philosophies of cautious, diplomatic black leaders during a period of deteriorating race relations. Steward understood well the complexities of his situation, of trying to champion the rights of blacks while maintaining the goodwill of whites. During his civil rights career he was involved in movements against Jim Crow housing, segregated railroads, and the ousting of blacks from Berea College. But, acting out of a sincere belief in a moderate approach to racial problems and wanting to maintain white support, Steward endorsed the accommodationist stance of Booker T. Washington, worked with conservative whites in and out of interracial organizations, and strongly denounced militant blacks for attempting to move too fast. He knew that in Kentucky established white leaders were determined that they—and not the Negrophobes with their violent methods of suppressing blacks—would handle the "Negro problem," and he therefore tried to adopt tactics that would aid blacks in their quest for racial improvement while also being acceptable to moderate whites.

Several factors contributed to Steward's successful fifty-year career as a black leader. Like many accomplished black leaders in his day, he turned to the Negro church as a base of power. Indeed, his association with the church transformed him from a local to a state leader and then a national leader. Furthermore, throughout his long career Steward remained active in the secular world by being involved in civic activities, working in the Republican party, and serving as a leader in the Grand Lodge of the Kentucky Masons. Also, because of the prestigious jobs he held in Louisville, he was accorded respect and a position of leadership in the Afro-American community.

Perhaps the overriding factor in Steward's assumption of leadership was his close ties with influential whites. Throughout the nation many black leaders of the period, especially in the South from Reconstruction to the early 1900s, were so designated by whites. From the 1870s on, Louisville's white leaders sought out and made leaders of "sensible Negroes" who realized that black advancement would be a long process and that racial and social equality was unobtainable. They assured Steward and other black leaders that cooperation with whites in Louisville would eliminate the racial problems found elsewhere. As Steward's daughter once explained, her father was selected as a black leader because he had the trust of the white establishment. "Whites only know their servants. They respected my father and honored him. They came to him whenever they had racial problems."

Steward was born in 1847 of free, light-skinned parents in Brandenburg, a rural farming community located on the Kentucky River thirty miles west of Louisville. Nothing is known about the Steward family except that they, like many other blacks in the area, moved to Louisville at the outbreak of the Civil War. Once settled in the city, Steward acquired the rudiments of an education at the school run by the First African Baptist Church. Through the efforts of an uncle who was already established in Louisville, he found employment as a laborer. He quickly gained the confidence of his employer and was promoted to messenger, a job that afforded him the opportunity to meet several prominent businessmen.

Equally important was Steward's decision to join the First African Baptist Church. Established in 1829, the First African Baptist was the leading black church in the state. In addition to its school, the church had several social programs that were beneficial to the entire community. Steward was greatly influenced by its pastor, Henry Adams, and by Horace Morris, the church's leading member. Adams, who was born a free black in Georgia in 1802, pastored the church for more than forty years and almost single-handedly directed its school. Morris, a native of Louisville, was respected by local whites and would become the first black cashier of the Freedmen's Savings Bank in Louisville. In the years immediately after 1865, Adams and Morris led the black quest for racial justice in Louisville. For the race to survive they stressed the need to make few demands on whites while attempting to cultivate their friendship. At the close of the war, Adams disappointed many free blacks by urging them to return to the farms where they had been enslaved. His call for a Negro Baptist convention was in keeping with his belief that blacks would have to strive to uplift themselves. By the late 1860s Morris was Kentucky's leading black Republican and was appointed to the Colored Board of Visitors for the Louisville public schools, a position that allowed him to help select the city's first black teachers. Like his pastor, Morris reminded blacks of the importance of maintaining alliances with whites. In the mid-1870s, after the death of Adams and the departure of Morris to a federal job in Washington, whites would look to Steward as the local black leader.

Without a doubt a key to Steward's early career was his association with Adams and Morris, black leaders whose accommodating approach was acceptable to white leaders. Moreover, Steward's jobs in the early 1870s required his being well-thought-of by whites. For example, in 1872 Steward was hired to teach at the Negro school, which offered a certain amount of security and prestige. Not surprisingly, there was much competition for these teaching positions, and right from the start, local black leaders used their influence with white officials to win such jobs for themselves, their children, and their friends. Steward's association with Morris helped him secure a teaching job, which he held for three years, at the Eastern Colored School.

Each new employment opportunity enhanced Steward's reputation in the white community. In 1875, when he was hired as a messenger and purchasing agent for the Louisville and Nashville Railroad Company, a local white newspaper explained that his new job was an exclusive one: the only blacks hired for such positions were personally known by influential whites. Several years later he was hired as a letter carrier for the Post Office, becoming the first Kentucky black named to this position. Like the school system, employment at the Post Office offered job security, a liveable wage, and respect in the Afro-American community. Also, as an indication of the respect and trust Steward had with local whites, he was chosen to deliver the mail in Louisville's most exclusive white area, instead of being relegated to the black district.

By the late 1870s Steward was involved in practically every civic activity undertaken by local blacks. Others turned to him for assistance in their racial uplift efforts because his involvement often led to generous contributions from Negro churches and wealthy whites. For their part local whites willingly contributed to the organizations and institutions directed by black leaders who took moderate positions on racial issues and who were quick to blame blacks themselves for most of their problems. In other words, whites aided those institutions that posed no threat to the existing racial order. They also contributed to black institutions in part to ensure that blacks would not demand access to white institutions.

A group of black leaders, well aware that civic leaders were doing nothing for the homeless black children in the community, joined forces in 1877 and began raising money for an orphanage. Steward was named to the Orphan Home Committee, and his efforts led to the leasing of an abandoned army hospital and the opening of the Colored Orphan Home. Steward's church was especially generous to the orphanage. The Fifth Street Baptist (the church had changed its name in the 1870s) gave an annual contribution, purchased a carpet for the home, and appropriated funds for a new roof. For more than three decades Steward served on the home's board of directors.

Steward and other leaders repeatedly denounced the "dens of sin" found in black neighborhoods. In 1885 these concerned citizens launched a campaign for a black YMCA as an alternative to idleness and the evils of street life. The group selected Steward as chairman, and he successfully solicited local white YMCA officials for financial assistance to purchase an old building as the site of the Negro branch. Steward and school principal Albert E. Meyzeek formed a Christian training program, organized recreational activities, and purchased books and equipment for a reading room. Over the years the group moved to several larger quarters, with funds for the new accommodations being raised primarily through the efforts of Meyzeek and Steward. On one occasion they mortgaged their own homes to secure a loan for the black YMCA.

Considering that Steward was well known by white leaders and was on intimate terms with Horace Morris, it is not surprising that he became influential with the school board after the departure of Morris. Steward was selected to serve because of his racial philosophy. On more than one occasion he had denounced Kentucky's more militant black leaders for calling for school desegregation. For his part Steward talked about education making blacks useful. He realized that the very idea of blacks being admitted to most white hotels and restaurants, areas of entertainment, and private facilities was offensive to whites, and he therefore strictly avoided calling for any changes that suggested social equality between the races. He did argue, however, and would throughout his career, that as citizens and taxpayers Negroes had a right to decent public schools, adequate city services in their neighborhoods, and equal treatment on the streetcars and railroads. Unlike dining out or attending the theater, riding the streetcars was a necessity, and discrimination in public transportation created an unreasonable burden for blacks. In a tone that whites found acceptable, Steward consistently told blacks that abstinence, honesty, and hard work would lead to black advancement. At a time when the status of Kentucky's black population was steadily declining, Steward said, "I am proud to tell you boys that you have a bright future right here in the South. Your color will not keep you back in this age if you are qualified for in this age fitness and character must win. You boys and girls must not think that you can go to the North and find social equality for that does not exist anywhere; you must build your own social circles and lift up your own girls."

When forming public schools for blacks in 1870 the board of education had organized the Committee on Colored Schools and the Colored Board of Visitors to "exercise a general supervision over said schools" and to "ascertain the moral character of all applicants for teaching positions." On the surface the existence of the two committees was a positive step; but in reality their major function was to report on the conduct of the teachers, a prime consideration for employment and retention. The board of education adopted a policy of writing morality clauses into the contracts of black teachers while refusing to interfere in the private lives of white teachers. Not surprisingly, black teachers were disciplined for denouncing white racism or challenging the established black leaders. On several occasions Steward served on both committees, but even when not officially on either committee he was allowed by the board of education to make recommendations relating to school personnel.

The case of William T. Peyton illustrates how the Steward faction used the threat of "immorality" to maintain control over black school personnel. Peyton was an ambitious man who sought both the principalship of the black high school and political patronage. To accomplish his goals he denounced the Republican party and joined the Democrats, a move that greatly angered Steward, who consistently urged blacks to remain loyal to the GOP. When Peyton was hired as an elementary school principal, Steward leveled a number of unsubstantiated charges against him in a series of newspaper articles, even hinting at sex scandals involving Peyton and his female teachers. Steward's opposition prevented Peyton from being named principal of Central High School in 1893, though he was unsuccessful in his attempt to get Peyton dismissed entirely from the school system. Three years later, however, Steward's repeated attacks led to Peyton's firing.

As one of his contemporaries stated, "No colored man in the city of Louisville has secured more appointments for colored teachers than William H. Steward." From the dismissal of Peyton in 1896 until 1910, when a new board of education was created (which disbanded the Board of Visitors and the Committee on the Colored Schools), Steward played the leading role in selecting the teachers and principals of the Negro schools. Also, despite the fact that he was not a school employee, he was a regular speaker at the Teacher's Saturday Forum, where he warned teachers to lead upstanding lives and remain free of controversy.

The church played a key role in practically all of Steward's civic activities. Afro-Americans of his day saw the church as being involved in the total life needs of its members, not just their spiritual needs. Steward's influence in the Negro church was unique because he was not a minister but was closely associated with the Fifth Street Baptist Church, the leading black church in the state, and had contacts with influential whites. Indeed, Steward was so effectively involved in the affairs of the black church that he was often called the "pioneer of Colored Baptist in Kentucky" and was mistakenly referred to as "Reverend." He was perhaps the leading Negro layman in Baptist church affairs in the United States during the late nineteenth century.

The General Association of Negro Baptists in Kentucky was founded in Louisville in August 1865, at a convention that had been called by Reverend Henry Adams. The ministers attending the convention agreed that their primary goals were to spread the gospel and educate former slaves. A resolution was passed calling for the establishment of a school to train young men and women in Christian work. The ministers agreed to ask their respective church members to contribute five cents a month toward the start of the school, and Reverend Adams promised to seek white patrons for the school.

It is unclear whether Steward had any involvement in the first convention, but in 1867 he was named secretary of the general association. Under his leadership the Baptist organization obtained a charter and purchased property in Louisville as the site for a school. It took the general association another ten years to raise the needed capital and develop an education program, but finally, on November 25, 1879, Kentucky Normal and Theological Institute opened. (The name of the school was changed to State University in the mid-1880s and to Simmons University in 1918). At its inception the school offered industrial training, which the founders justified by stating that Kentucky had a shortage of skilled black workers. This was, of course, also a way of attracting donations from white businessmen. For his leading role in developing the school, Steward was selected chairman of the board of trustees, a position he would hold for the remainder of his life.

Steward started a Baptist newspaper to raise funds for the school and to inform the public about State University's progress and activities. The *American Baptist* was adopted as the official organ of the general association and all of the small district associations in the state. During a day when black newspapers sprang up quickly and disappeared just as fast, the *American Baptist* became a rock of stability: it was published every week for the remaining fifty-six years of Steward's life and is still in existence, now over a hundred years old. In the paper

Steward printed news of church affairs but devoted considerable space, especially on the editorial page, to politics and other secular concerns. Widely read by the black clergy, the paper increased Steward's reputation within the Baptist denomination and, by the 1890s, helped him secure the presidency of the National Afro-American Press Association.

Though more comfortable when working with Baptist organizations and doing community work, the ambitious Steward was almost inevitably drawn into the area of civil rights. Throughout his career, he sought to champion black rights without offending his white supporters. This proved to be very difficult because Louisville whites were often inconsistent in their attitude toward black access to public accommodations and participation in politics. For example, after a boycott by blacks over their mistreatment on the streetcars in 1870–71, whites reluctantly agreed that blacks could ride and sit wherever they desired. Yet several months after this agreement, those blacks who rode on certain lines were once again being relegated to seats in the back and forcibly removed if they sat elsewhere. Some whites called for a streetcar ordinance on several occasions, but it failed every time. In the years immediately after the Civil War, the city's amusement places and restaurants often extended their services to Afro-Americans, but at the same time the internationally known Galt House and other hotels denied all service to blacks.

Louisville whites, however, were united in 1875 in their opposition to the federal Civil Rights Act, which forbade discrimination in hotels, restaurants, and amusement places, as well as on public conveyances. Henry Watterson, editor of the *Courier-Journal,* called the Civil Rights Act "an insult to the white people of the southern states." Local white businessmen resolved that blacks had better refrain from entering places where they were not welcomed. Louisville Republican leaders, who had been trying since the end of the war to broaden their base of support, found the new law a source of embarrassment. They assured blacks of their continued commitment to their uplift but quickly added, "our objection to the bill has been based on our doubts of the Constitutional right of Congress to pass a bill relating to such subjects." The Republicans advised blacks to ignore the bill and continue improving themselves. Surely, they hoped, no blacks would foolishly hurry "to exercise their new privileges in an offensive way."

Most local blacks were unsure how best to respond to the new law. A small group headed by Dr. Henry Fitzbutler, the state's first black physician, maintained that the Civil Rights Act was the culmination of their drive to secure all of their rights as citizens, and though blacks should not throw themselves on whites, they did have the right to enter places of public accommodation. This group called upon the entire Afro-American community to participate in a celebration on March 25 in honor of the bill's passage. But led by Steward, a second group explained that instead of a celebration, which could lead to a riot, the black community should hold a quiet church service. Furthermore, Steward bitterly denounced the actions of Fitzbutler's group, referring to them as troublemakers. Nathaniel R. Harper, the first black admitted to the bar in Kentucky and a loyal Republican, concurred with the view expressed by Steward. He took part in planning the church service and announced that his singing group would provide the entertainment.

On March 25 the more outspoken leaders cancelled their celebration, leaving the church service as planned by Steward and Harper as the only black expression in honor of the Civil Rights Act. Steward opened the program with a speech on the merits of black uplift through hard work and unity. After his group finished singing, Harper gave a long speech urging blacks to go slow and to educate themselves to "a higher morality than exists at present within the race." For the most part the "go slow" approach advocated by Steward and Harper was adhered to by Louisville blacks. On one occasion two unidentified blacks asked to be seated in a hotel dining room, and the proprietor grudgingly served the men. But upon leaving the hotel the two were attacked and beaten by a white mob. No records exist of local blacks filing suit after being denied their rights under the new law, which probably indicates that few if any challenged the white establishment by venturing into hotels and restaurants—and if they did and were refused services, they felt too powerless to press the matter in court. Few blacks, in any event, could afford such luxuries as dining out, staying in hotels, or attending the theater; and those who could were rightfully fearful of violence. To make sure that local blacks understood that the Civil Rights Act had not changed the racial status quo, the local white press detailed the incident about the beating of the two men and unsuccessful attempts by blacks throughout the nation to press their rights under the new law. The overturning of the act by the United States Supreme Court in 1883 barely caused comment in Louisville. Interestingly, on this occasion the city's black leaders met and issued a statement urging whites to live up to the American creed and voluntarily to admit respectable blacks to their establishments. In an attempt to put the best light on the status of the race, these men concluded that if blacks could somehow acquire wealth, then they would be acceptable to whites.

The overturning of the Civil Rights Act occurred during a time of increasing racial discrimination. In Louisville, by the mid-1880s, blacks were totally excluded from several white establishments and welfare institutions to which they had previously been admitted. By 1885 the four theaters no longer admitted blacks at all, and the annual fair was closed to them as well. A law enacted in 1884 segregated the races at the Louisville School for the Blind, and blacks were denied the right to use most of the free public bathhouses scattered throughout the city. Despite an ever-increasing black population, the public hospitals refused to increase the number of rooms available to blacks. Finally, racial segregation reached a peak in Kentucky in 1892 when the state legislature passed a separate coach law pertaining to railroad travel.

As Steward consistently pointed out, the Democrats were responsible for enacting Jim Crow laws in Kentucky, which only reinforced his actions on behalf of the Republican party. Like so many black leaders of his day, Steward never forgot the initial commitment of the Republican party to black freedom or the racist tirades of the state's Democrats and their strong opposition to the Thirteenth, Fourteenth, and Fifteenth amendments. Steward and the vast majority of Louisville blacks voted for Republicans during the 1870s and 1880s, even though the party was not in office and had virtually no influence or patronage positions. In an attempt to garner more broad-based support, however, Republican leaders began to project an image of being primarily concerned with the white business community and only secondarily with blacks. This strategy, coupled with the public's growing concern over corruption under a succession of Democratic administrations, led to the Republicans winning for the first time in 1894, when a coalition of party regulars, dissident Democrats, and members of the American Protective Association, a nativist organization, elected a Republican to Congress.

Immediately after the successful congressional race, a group of blacks led by Dr. Fitzbutler called upon the Republican party "to elect men to office in the Republican party who are willing to accord colored Republicans every political right as citizens." Fitzbutler's group realized that the Republicans stood a good chance of capturing the city government for the first time and that party officials had refused to make commitments to blacks. Steward and Harper denounced the statements made by Fitzbutler and noted that the militant blacks might cost the party the election.

The Republican party finally gained control of the city council in November 1895. Two months later the mayor died and the Republican-controlled city council chose their leader, George Todd, as the city's first Republican mayor. With their party firmly in control, black leaders urged the mayor to hire blacks as policemen and firemen and to give high-level political patronage jobs to a number of Negro Republican workers. Todd refused to consider their request, saying that during his administration "Negroes will have to stay in their place." He kept his word, relegating them to janitorships, just like the Democrats had traditionally done.

As the November 1897 election approached, Todd realized that a solid black vote was essential for the Republicans to retain control of city hall. Being out of office had united Democrats, and they were using the police and fire departments as power bases to get out the white ethnic vote. Though not directly in control of city government for several years, the Democratic machine, under political boss John Whallen, had remained a force behind the scenes. Mayor Todd had failed to dismantle the Whallen machine in city government largely because the police and fire departments remained loyal to Whallen and were willing to do his bidding. To make sure of black support, Todd met in late August with a group of black leaders at Steward's home. After assuring the mayor of black support, Steward voiced his concern about blacks being appointed to patronage positions. Within a matter of days after the political meeting (a session that Todd informed the press "was just a social gathering"), the Republicans appointed Steward as judge of registration and election for the Fifteenth Precinct of the Ninth Ward, the first black to hold such a position.

Steward campaigned vigorously for the party, but it was not enough to offset the apathy of Fitzbutler's group, which did not actively campaign, or the determination of the Democrats to regain control of local government. The election was marked by voter fraud and police abuse of blacks. According to the *Commercial,* a Republican newspaper, black voters in wards all over town were intimidated by the police and often prevented from voting. Even the Democratic *Courier-Journal* acknowledged that the election had been corrupt and that polling places had opened late in black areas. But the same newspaper charged blacks with provoking disturbances that led to their arrest. "The police never acted with more effect," Watterson's paper concluded. The Democratic challenger, George Weaver, won over the incumbent mayor Todd by only 2,728 votes out of 40,000 cast. This election set the pattern for the future, with the Democrats winning several elections by arousing the racist fears of white workers.

Steward's political involvement did reap some rewards for blacks, and Republican leaders consistently sought his advice on racial matters. But even more significant, with their control over local government and their claim as the "white man's party," the Democratic leaders were willing to listen respectfully to Steward's concerns about education, health care, and the need for recreational facilities in the black community. As his daughter would later recall, by having the ear of white politicians of both parties, Steward helped to minimize racial violence in Louisville.

As president of the National Afro-American Press Association in 1896, Steward became active in Republican politics on the national level. Leaders of this organization endorsed the candidacy of William McKinley and pledged "to formulate some plans to secure an honest count and proper registration of the negro votes of the Southern states." Steward's involvement in the election led to one of the personal high points of his career—a private conversation with the president-elect, in which Steward expressed his hope that blacks would receive a fair number of appointments. The discussion also touched on lynchings and mob rule in the South. Though ultimately unsuccessful, Steward urged McKinley to speak out forcefully against lynchings.

His position as a racial leader, both in Kentucky and on the national level, naturally led to Steward's association with Booker T. Washington, the noted accommodator who became the preeminent black leader at the end of the century. No doubt any black leader of Steward's stature knew Washington and had become aligned with either the pro- or anti-Washington factions. Steward was among those leaders who quite naturally supported Washington, having expressed a philosophy of racial self-help and working with paternalistic whites similar to the Tuskegean's, long before the latter became a national figure.

Steward was so circumspect in his activities on behalf of the civil and political rights of Louisville blacks during Washington's ascendancy in the early years of the twentieth century that evidence about them is virtually nonexistent. Like Washington he seems to have operated clandestinely, behind the scenes, in the rearguard effort to preserve what he could of the race's rights. He kept Washington informed of the efforts against both disfranchisement and Jim Crow in Kentucky. In 1904, for example, Steward wrote to Washington that a bill providing for the disfranchisement of black voters had failed in the Kentucky legislature. He credited a committee he headed "that has been working quietly on the matter for some time" as being responsible for the defeat of the measure.

Though some of Steward's actions were unknown to his white supporters, he did work openly to prevent the passage of a Jim Crow streetcar ordinance in Louisville. In the early 1900s, in nearly a score of southern states, streetcar segregation laws were enacted. Blacks responded with protests and in some cases boycotts, all of which failed. In Louisville, during these years, a number of whites called for the segregation or total exclusion of blacks from streetcars. They claimed that blacks were boisterous and that black men offended white women. In January 1910, after repeated white complaints, Steward, school principal Albert E. Meyzeek, and Reverend Charles H. Parrish met with streetcar officials and white civic leaders. Steward's group assured whites that the behavior of blacks would improve and that Negro men would avoid sitting next to white women. The black leaders then organized a meeting to enlighten the Afro-American community about the informal policy agreed upon with streetcar officials. As Meyzeek explained to the large gathering, "We have in measure succeeded in placing the negroes of the city on probation, and one overt act will cause us to lose all the grounds we have gained." Also, for several weeks in the local black newspaper Steward and the others reminded blacks how they should act on the streetcars. Their efforts succeeded: all attempts (there would be three between 1910 and 1918) to obtain a formal streetcar ordinance in Louisville failed, even when backed by politicians. Indeed, it is significant that in a border state like Kentucky, Steward's contacts with influential whites produced greater success than anything Washington and other black leaders could do further South.

Paradoxically, though loyal to Washington, Steward became actively involved in the Louisville branch of the NAACP. Founded in 1909 to address the growing problems of lynchings, mob rule, disfranchisement, and Jim Crow laws, the NAACP, with its headquarters in New York, was viewed as an anti-Washington organization whose very existence revealed the failure of the Tuskegean's accommodationist views to resolve the race problem. In 1914 Steward, Parrish, and several other ministers took the lead in forming a local NAACP affiliate after their pleas to civic leaders had failed to prevent the passage of the Louisville Residential Segregation Ordinance, which was similar to ordinances being enacted in several cities across the country. Steward's involvement in the NAACP was a logical continuation of his leadership in the fight against disfranchisement and Jim Crow streetcar measures in the preceding decade. He also realized that even without Washington's blessing, many of the nation's moderate black leaders were joining the NAACP. The organization had become recognized as the most effective vehicle yet established for efforts to protect the rights of the black race. Conceivably, Steward felt compelled to join the NAACP so as to remain *the* black leader of Louisville and to prevent racial activities from taking a direction he thought might be undesirable. Moreover, though the membership in the Louisville branch was comprised totally of blacks, a number of the city's white civic leaders approved of the organization and gave financial contributions that greatly aided the fledging branch. In the case developed to challenge the Louisville ordinance, the NAACP was able to secure the services of Clayton Blakey, a partner in the city's most prestigious law firm, as legal counsel. This was in keeping with the NAACP's belief, in the context of that time, that highly respected white lawyers were essential in the drive for black equality. As a leader of the local branch, Steward readily agreed with this strategy, since it was consistent with his long-held belief of working with whites for black advancement.

With the assistance of the national office, the Louisville NAACP successfully challenged the residential segregation ordinance, which rested on the idea of excluding equally whites and blacks from each others' neighborhoods. As expected, both the local and state courts upheld the law as a proper exercise of the police power of Louisville's city legislators. But in November 1917 the U.S. Supreme Court, in a unanimous decision, overturned the ordinance, which led to more housing becoming available to Afro-Americans in Louisville, as the decade after 1917 saw blacks move steadily westward in the city. The decision also provided the national association and the Louisville branch of the NAACP with the momentum to continue fighting racial injustices on a number of different fronts.

The movement that led to the overturning of the residential segregation ordinance proved to be the high point of a united black Louisville. Thereafter, the leadership was bitterly divided, with separate factions pitting older, established blacks against younger, more aggressive blacks. Unlike the group led by Steward, most of the new leaders had very few white allies because they had concluded that whites were interested only in very limited gains for Negroes. The split was apparent in the case of the city's bond proposal in 1920 to upgrade the University of Louisville. Steward and the established ministers supported the bond proposal even though blacks would gain no tangible benefits from its passage: "We note that generally speaking, the white people who have in the past been our best friends, sympathizing with us in our struggles, helping in our churches and in our schools and lending a helping hand along all lines are the promoters in the bond issue. . . . It would not be to our advantage to break with these white friends." However, young black leaders, led by Wilson Lovett, a businessman who had been in Louisville for less than a decade and was on the verge of opening the first black-owned bank in Kentucky, were unmoved by this argument and called for the black community to vote against the bond proposal. Their effort succeeded and the proposal was rejected by 4,000 votes, with blacks supplying the crucial margin as their precincts returned a plurality of 12,000 votes against the measure.

After the successful defeat of the bond proposal, Lovett used that issue to have Steward and Parrish removed from the executive board of the NAACP at the branch's election in late November 1920. This was a bitter blow, since the two men had founded the branch and had served continuously on the executive board. Both promptly resigned from the NAACP and began working on the Commission on Interracial Cooperation (CIC). That organization had been founded in 1919 for the purpose of preventing postwar racial conflicts in the South. W. D. Weatherford, Will W. Alexander, and other forward-looking southern whites wanted to work at the grass-roots level with blacks who "had shown a realistic attitude and achieved something—not all—that they hoped for but more than [they] or any other [Negroes] could have done alone." Those Louisville whites who joined the CIC believed that conditions should be improved for blacks but that segregation maintained peace between the races. They also agreed that education should train blacks for menial jobs and help them accept the reality of being black in the white South. Black board members did not challenge such positions. W. E. B. Du Bois had men like Steward and Parrish in mind when he told a white commission member that his "greatest objection to the Interracial Commission is the kind of Negro you pick to go on it. . . . You have favored too much the sort of Colored men that we call 'WHITE FOLKS' NIGGERS." Du Bois's statement was probably too strong an indictment of a number of the CIC's black leaders. But on far too many occasions black CIC members in Louisville and elsewhere remained silent about racial injustices while white members proclaimed that there were numerous improvements in race relations.

A case in point was the ousting of Afro-Americans from the public parks in June 1924. At various times in the early 1900s, blacks had met white resentment when picnicking in the public parks near white residential areas, though no official ordinance had been enacted to segregate the parks. A minor disagreement between two Negro teachers and some white security guards in Iroquois Park led the board of park commissioners, with the complete backing of Republican mayor Huston

Quin (whose law partner had worked with the NAACP in the residential segregation case of 1914), to adopt a resolution excluding blacks from all but two of the city's parks. Instead of joining the NAACP in denouncing Jim Crow parks, Steward and the local CIC called for the opening of parks in Negro neighborhoods. City officials immediately granted $40,000 for a new park which would include a playground and a swimming pool. The CIC responded by praising the mayor and park commissioners for their actions. In reality, except for the newest park, the black parks were, as several NAACP spokespeople pointed out, little more than vacant fields, lacking in even such basic facilities as water fountains and restrooms. Steward and his allies justified their actions as having benefited the race; unlike the more militant blacks who had come up empty-handed, they proclaimed that their efforts had resulted in concessions from the white establishment. His effort in helping to resolve the park controversy, Steward added, was consistent with the work he had been doing for blacks for over fifty years.

The moderate approach Steward assumed on the park issue and other racial problems was understandable given the reality of life in America around the turn of the century. He was a leader at a time when southern blacks were being disfranchised and lynched and northern blacks were being segregated and victimized by rioting whites. Conditions in Louisville were deteriorating, though not as much as further south. Yet local blacks knew what awaited them if they dared move too quickly. All along Steward was aware that there were some whites who were willing to keep racial violence under control. From a pragmatic position he urged blacks to make their community a desirable place to live and stressed the importance of education, frugality, and morality for the race's advancement. His efforts to prevent both black disfranchisement and an increase in Jim Crow ordinances were also notable. In fact, he was able to do more to preserve the race's rights than a powerful black leader like Booker T. Washington could in the Deep South. In summary, Steward should be viewed as an example of what diplomatic and cautious leadership could achieve in a border city during the late nineteenth and early twentieth centuries.

William Steward died on January 3, 1935, at the age of eighty-eight. Surprisingly, the local white and black press had very little to say about his passing or his life-long activities in the Afro-American community. Steward did contribute significantly to black Louisville, especially in the founding of State University, the active role he played in the various Baptist associations, the time and money he gave to the black YMCA and orphan home, and his consistent efforts for racial uplift.

15

Isaiah T. Montgomery's
Balancing Act

"**I** HAVE STOOD BY, consenting and assisting in striking down the rights and liberties of 123,000 freemen," admitted Isaiah T. Montgomery, the only black delegate at the 1890 state constitutional convention in Mississippi. His seemingly irrational action was just one step on the dangerous tightrope of race relations that black leaders were forced to negotiate in the late nineteenth-century South. In a lengthy speech announcing his cooperation in the scheme to guarantee white supremacy by disfranchising black voters, Montgomery justified his sacrifice as the only means "to bridge a chasm [between the races] that has been widening and deepening for a generation . . . that threatens destruction to you and yours, while it promises no enduring prosperity to me and mine." He conceded that the former slaves lacked political experience but told the whites, "You have suffered your prejudice to set bounds and limits to our progress." He agreed to the new restrictive law in order to eliminate the "blood-shed, bribery, ballot-box stuffing, corruption, and perjury" that had characterized Mississippi elections. In return he asserted that whites owed his people "peace and mutual assistance toward progress." The Mississippi constitution quickly approved by the white Democratic delegates provided for a test that could legally bar all illiterate voters, but in practice only blacks were declared ineligible to vote. This system was soon adopted in one form or another throughout most of the South as the rights freedpeople had won during Reconstruction were gradually nullified by the restored Democratic governments.

For the rest of Montgomery's life white politicians in Mississippi continued to praise what they termed his enlightened and courageous stand. The Democratic press throughout the nation lauded the speech, which seemed to provide black endorsement for legally eliminating their rights to the franchise. However, black spokesmen in the North, beyond the reach of former Confederates, reported a very different response. Henry F. Downing, president of the United States African News Agency in New York, circulated Montgomery's speech to black leaders claiming, "His surrender of the rights of 123,000 Negroes upon the altar of expediency is an act unprecedented either for its heroism or its audacity. Which?" The majority of replies printed by T. Thomas Fortune in his *New York Age* were harshly critical of Montgomery's action. The aged Frederick Douglass paused on his way to assume the ambassadorship of Haiti to note that the speech showed the Mississippian to be a man of "keen observation and deep reflection" who was "not to be dismissed by calling him a traitor or self-seeking hypocrite." He felt that Montgomery had been tricked into making disastrous concessions with no reciprocal benefit for his race: "He has made peace with the lion by allowing himself to be swallowed." Douglass feared that the measure supported by Montgomery would effectively nullify the Fourteenth and Fifteenth amendments to the United States Constitution and concluded, "No thoughtless, flippant fool could have inflicted such a wound upon our cause as Mr. Montgomery has done in this address."

T. McCants Stewart, a prominent black lawyer in New York, pointed out that by requiring voters to interpret the Constitution, Mississippi would "make it possible for the judges of election to enfranchise every illiterate white man and to disfranchise every illiterate colored man." He deplored Montgomery's advocacy of such discrimination. John R. Lynch, Republican politician from Mississippi then enjoying a federal appointment in Washington, quoted at length from both Democratic and Republican newspapers in the state, attacking the understanding clause as a mere ruse more dishonest than the former "shot-gun and ballot box stuffing methods." He insisted that "the entire scheme is a fraud, a sham and a swindle, the sole purpose of which is to perpetuate the ascendancy of the Democratic party in the state." Lynch concluded that this act of Montgomery's was a disappointment, "although no one who knows the man will impute to him other than honest and sincere purposes."

Only one black commentator seemed to understand Isaiah Montgomery's motives for acquiescing in the disfranchisement of free blacks in Mississippi. Frederick Douglass, Jr., suggested, "He is ready to make sacrifices to conciliate his white brother in order that he may have that peace and security which are so necessary to prosperity and good government." Montgomery was, indeed, seeking "peace and security" from his white neighbors for the infant black community of Mound Bayou, Mississippi, which he had founded just three years before. His major goal was to help it become a haven where blacks could enjoy "prosperity and good government" without white interference. As an experienced black leader, Montgomery knew that the success of the project was dependent upon winning the approval of important whites in the county and in the state. He hoped the literacy test would be applied fairly to both whites and blacks, and he expected that as blacks became more educated and prosperous they would gradually be accepted into the white polity. However unrealistic his hopes now seem, in 1890 he believed he had little choice but to go along with the plan assuring white supremacy.

Although black people had been free for a generation, it had become evident that white southerners were determined to keep them from achieving any position approaching equality in southern society. Attempts at economic and intellectual progress were discouraged because whites intended to keep the former slaves as subservient agricultural laborers. The return of state government to local control encouraged white determination to abrogate the political gains made by blacks in the reforms of Reconstruction. These trends reenforced Isaiah Montgomery's belief that only in a segregated community could blacks hope to achieve peace and prosperity.

The all-Negro town of Mound Bayou was still a tiny settlement in 1890. Only three years earlier Montgomery had led a small band of pioneers to this fertile but undeveloped land in the Yazoo Delta, bordering the new rail line midway between Memphis and Vicksburg. Having arranged to purchase small plots from the railroad company on favorable terms, Montgomery persuaded the colonists "that they might as well buy land and own it and do for themselves what they had been doing for other folks for two hundred and fifty years." With great difficulty these impoverished settlers managed to support their families by selling the timber they cleared from their fields. They survived the rigorous early years and by 1890 had earned a total of $8,780 from timber sales, in addition to producing some 379 bales of cotton and 3,045 bushels of corn on the 655 acres they had reclaimed from the dense forest. Montgomery opened a branch of the U.S. Post Office, in the hall of his log house, using a partitioned soapbox for the mailboxes. One of his sisters, a former student at Oberlin College, set up a school for the few children whose parents could spare them from field work. New settlers were arriving faster now, and Mound Bayou was well on its way to becoming an independent Negro community. This was the promising project that Isaiah Montgomery sought to safeguard by placating white politicians at the Mississippi constitutional convention.

Montgomery's dream of a segregated colony had evolved through years of experience as a black leader in the postwar South, during which he had become skilled at pleasing white folks. His contacts with them began during his childhood as one of some 350 slaves at Hurricane, a large plantation on the Mississippi River below Vicksburg that belonged to Joseph Davis, elder brother of Confederate president Jefferson Davis. Montgomery's father, Benjamin, a brilliant, self-educated slave, was the plantation business manager. He bought supplies and sold the crops for the entire plantation, served as the engineer in charge of gin repairs and levees, and in addition operated a very profitable retail store. Isaiah spent his early years in the family home above the store, learning to read and write from his literate parents and various tutors they hired. When he was ten his master took him into the big house as his valet and clerk. While continuing his education in Joseph Davis's office and fine library, Isaiah learned to humor the vagaries of the white family. Among his playmates in his leisure time were two white boys near his own age who were wards of his master so whites were no mystery to him. An extremely intelligent lad, Montgomery must have recognized quite early the limitations of his status as well as the best ways to ameliorate that handicap.

Isaiah was more fortunate than most slaves. Joseph Davis was a benevolent master who respected his bondsmen and bondswomen as people and provided them with opportunities to develop skills from which they could profit. He ruled that each slave might keep anything he or she earned beyond the value of his or her labor in the field. Under this arrangement Benjamin Montgomery paid Davis so that his wife could remain at home caring for their four children while he devoted most of his time to managing his store and marketing the crops. As a result, young Isaiah received far more parental attention and enjoyed more family cohesion than most slave children. In addition to generous allotments of food and clothing and comfortable housing, other Davis innovations in slave management included a court system under which no slaves were punished except upon conviction by a jury of their peers.

Under this comparatively benign form of slavery Isaiah Montgomery revealed his qualities of leadership at an early age. For example, three times a week he and several other black youngsters were sent down and across the river to collect the mail for the plantation. As the only fluent reader in the group, Isaiah assigned the others the strenuous task of rowing home while he read aloud the latest news from the papers. Occasionally he masterminded escapades for which his playmates, both black and white, took the blame. However, his master liked the bright lad and encouraged his education in many directions. Although Montgomery undoubtedly wished for the freedom enjoyed by his white comrades, he learned to make the best of his bondage.

During the Civil War, Montgomery demonstrated his ability to win the patronage of influential whites from the North as well as those in the South. In 1863 Admiral David D. Porter, commander of Union naval operations on the Mississippi, was so charmed by the sixteen-year-old that he enlisted Montgomery as his cabin boy on various ships engaged in helping General Grant capture Vicksburg and free the Mississippi from Confederate control. When Montgomery became very ill with dysentery after six months' service, the admiral sent him to join his family, then living in Cincinnati under the patronage of the wife of a Union officer. The entire family was adept at winning white support.

After the war the Montgomerys returned to Hurricane, reopened their store as Montgomery & Sons, and vied with northern officials of the Freedmen's Bureau for control of the enlarged black community there. Benjamin Montgomery seems to have had a personality clash with Samuel Thomas, who headed the bureau in Mississippi, so he and his two sons enlisted the aid of their former master, Joseph Davis, who used his considerable influence to have Thomas removed. Here young Isaiah Montgomery witnessed again the benefits of white friendship.

When the plantations at Davis Bend were restored to Joseph Davis in 1866, he promptly sold them to Benjamin Montgomery and his sons, who proposed to set up a cooperative community of freedpeople. By the time he was twenty-five Isaiah Montgomery was recognized as an important leader there. He was in full charge of Hurricane, the largest plantation, surveying and leasing plots of land and supervising the crops, as well as approving credit at the store for his lessees and overseeing bookkeeping operations for the three plantations then owned by their firm. While serving as informal counselor to many black residents, Montgomery used all his diplomatic skills to maintain good relations with whites, including agents and suppliers in New Orleans, Vicksburg, Cincinnati, and St. Louis; white neighbors on Davis Bend; the executors of Joseph Davis's estate; and white politicians who came to the plantations courting black votes. He already understood that no black community in the South could succeed without white approval.

Although remarkably successful for a time, by 1879 the Montgomery enterprises had fallen victim to external forces, including the declining price of cotton and land, repeated floods and insect pests, and worsening political conditions. After his father's death, Isaiah Montgomery looked around for a good location for a new black community where former Davis slaves and other remnants of the Davis Bend colony might find the prosperity they sought with a minimum of white interference. Since many blacks were migrating to Kansas, he made a tour of possible sites in that state, consulting with the governor and winning the support of the Kansas Freedmen's Relief Association, a charitable group of Topeka citizens concerned about the plight of the migrants. Although he secured land with their help and was scheduled to lead a group of Mississippians there, Montgomery ultimately decided that was not a viable plan and returned to Davis Bend. Seven years later another white man, Major George W. McGinnis, manager of the land office of the new Memphis-to-Vicksburg railroad, contacted Montgomery and offered him favorable terms for property along the right-of-way.

After years of experience as a southern black leader, Isaiah Montgomery expected white people of "the better class" to be trustworthy and cooperative as long as he meticulously followed racial etiquette. Within a decade and a half after his noted sacrifice at the 1890 state convention, the village of Mound Bayou, with its surrounding agricultural region, seemed to enjoy many of the advantages he had sought. Under Montgomery's leadership most of the colonists were working their own farms and struggling to pay for them. They could finance each year's crops with loans from the black-owned Bank of Mound Bayou and buy their necessities at any of several general stores there. Locally owned gins processed their cotton; and the saw mill prepared their logs for housebuilding and also sold the surplus lumber. The telephone operator and all local government officials were their black neighbors. As nearly as possible Mound Bayou was a self-contained, black-owned and black-operated community, where white interference seemed negligible. At a time when racial tensions were rising and the number of lynchings in Mississippi and throughout the South had reached appalling heights, Montgomery, now the mayor of the incorporated village, could take considerable pride in having provided a sort of haven for free blacks, where they could begin to prosper.

The blacks of Mound Bayou were never entirely free from the handicap of racial discrimination, however. The founder of the community was not only concerned with the economic well-being of the colonists but was equally determined to provide opportunities for their intellectual growth. Like his late father and his former master, Isaiah Montgomery believed that education was the key to the long-term improvement of any group of people. Shortly after the founding of the settlement, he donated a tract of land in the village for the establishment of the Mound Bayou Normal and Industrial Institute. Montgomery persuaded the American Missionary Association to supply the school with teachers from the North and to provide part of its support. A few years later the Colored Baptist Church of Bolivar County opened another private school that also drew from the surrounding colony pupils who sought a better education than the county schools offered blacks. The mayor and citizens were helplessly indignant about the inequitable distribution of public education funds drawn primarily from the poll tax. Although white taxes supplied less than one-fifth of the total budget, the 1,300 white children received the same educational allotment as the 12,000 black pupils. As a result, colored schools were open only four months of the year and paid their teachers as little as fifteen dollars per month, while white teachers received fifty-five dollars per month for a six-month term. The only solution that Montgomery could devise in that racially tense state was to solicit additional funds from northern philanthropists to assist Mound Bayou's private schools.

Always an optimist, Montgomery asserted that in their own private schools black parents could establish the sort of practical curriculum he believed would prove most useful. Echoing ideas he had heard from Benjamin Montgomery and Joseph Davis long before they were popularized by his friend Booker T. Washington, the mayor of Mound Bayou advocated technical training that emphasized the latest methods of scientific agriculture. Girls were to be taught homemaking skills so they could provide better care for their families. Advocacy of these vocational programs did not mean that Montgomery opposed college training for those blacks who had the intellectual and financial capacity for it; in earlier years he had helped to send his sisters to Oberlin College, and he encouraged his children and grandchildren to seek higher education. Montgomery had a great deal of respect for students of history or philosophy, but he was convinced that if the Negro race was going to improve its lot en masse, the vast majority must begin at a more practical level.

Believing that the conduct of community members must be above reproach, the mayor strove to enforce accepted standards of moral behavior. Within twenty years of its founding, Mound Bayou boasted six churches in the village and four more in the surrounding township, "by far too many" for proper support, one preacher insisted. The churches served as centers for social as well as spiritual activities, and Montgomery, who, unlike most black leaders, lacked a power base in the church, still did not hesitate to enlist their aid to enforce his strict moral code. When he became concerned about "loose family relations" among the citizens, he called a town meeting and suggested formation of a committee made up of one representative from each church to investigate the situation. A house-to-house canvass revealed some forty unmarried couples living together; when they were ordered to legalize their relationship or leave the colony most agreed to get married. The same sort of pressure forced the prostitutes who frequented the town on Saturdays to move elsewhere.

Aware of the powerful temperance drive among whites, Montgomery was strictly opposed to local sale of alcoholic beverages. Not personally averse to a glass of wine now and then, he felt that abuse of alcohol was one legacy of slavery his people could overcome more easily if the temptation were removed, so he did his best to prevent the sale of liquor in Mound Bayou. Bolivar County prohibited such sales, but whites who were interested in repealing the law tried from time to time to enlist the support of Mound Bayouans. In one case the liquor interests promised, in exchange for local cooperation, to establish a saloon within the village with one of the citizens as proprietor. Montgomery quickly called another public meeting and, in his own words, "I simply said to the people that experience in our own town had taught us that a saloon was a bad thing to have in the community. . . . We voted the law down and there has been no serious attempt to open the county to the liquor traffic since."

Montgomery was proud of the fact that there was very little crime within the settlement. During the first twenty years of its existence only three persons were sent from the mayor's court to the white circuit court for trial. There were two homicides, both, the mayor was quick to note, committed by strangers. The majority of cases in Montgomery's court involved minor infractions such as failure to pay the annual three-dollar tax for road maintenance. Occasionally someone was suspected of operating a crap game on Saturday night. If that person persisted even after warnings, the town marshal and "some of the more substantial citizens" would raid the game and arrest the participants. If convicted, gamblers and illicit sellers of liquor were usually admonished to return to the farm and become "useful members of the community." When asked to explain the high level of order and public morality in Mound Bayou, Montgomery attributed it to public opinion: "The regulations that we enforce have public sentiment behind them. The people recognize that the laws, when they are enforced, represent the sentiment of the community and are imposed for their own good. It is not so easy for them to realize that where the government is entirely in the hands of white men." Thus he underscored one of the advantages of life in a small, segregated colony.

Despite his efforts to meet white expectations, Isaiah Montgomery was acutely concerned by the turn of the century with increasing evidence of racial hostility. His public statements continued to be optimistic about the opportunities for industrious blacks to improve their condition and achieve acceptance in society at large. In the

Outlook, a national Progressive weekly, Montgomery published an article, "The Negro in Business," in which he asserted that "with proper qualifications and reliability, a colored man may successfully conduct almost any kind of business in an average town"; he hastened to add, "he must, however, have tact, grit, and sufficient backing to hold on till his business is well understood." Montgomery believed that "the South, notwithstanding its tirade of abuse and slander against [the black man], is his land of promise." He concluded that "despite the political circumstances which render the lives and property of colored people insecure all over the South, . . . as they adapt themselves to sound business principles, more and more will come to them the recognition that is due to every useful and upright citizen." To encourage black business development Montgomery joined with Booker T. Washington and other black leaders to form the National Negro Business League, which held its first meeting in Boston in August 1900. At the next annual meeting, held in Chicago, the mayor of Mound Bayou delivered a speech on "The Founding of a Negro City" which presented the town's advantages so persuasively that several energetic new citizens joined the colony.

Soon after this a series of events shook Montgomery's faith in the trustworthiness of southern whites, even of "the better class." In 1902 he reluctantly accepted a federal appointment as receiver of public moneys for Mississippi, and his ensuing experience demonstrates the tremendous difficulties faced by any black who held public office in the South in that racist era. As Montgomery said at the time, he was extremely busy building his colony and "loath to turn aside for political preferment." Through his friendship with Booker T. Washington, he had already begun to see the possibility of tapping northern philanthropy to launch more ambitious enterprises in Mound Bayou. It was difficult to leave his fledgling experiment, but since his appointment was authorized by President Theodore Roosevelt himself and endorsed by the newly powerful Washington, he dared not refuse. From the time he arrived in Jackson, most of his white office staff was hostile toward him, and when his very able assistant was transferred to another office, Montgomery had difficulty keeping up with the work.

Although he seemed unaware of it, there was a powerful faction of Mississippi Republicans who wanted to purge all black officeholders, and Montgomery became their target. He had been in office just over a year and was out of town on leave when an inspector claimed to have found irregularities in his accounts. That weekend a special agent arrived from New Orleans and ransacked the receiver's desk, safe, and private papers and tried to gain access to his private bank account. When the surprised Montgomery returned, he quickly explained his financial affairs, which apparently contained a technical violation of rules but no shortage of funds. The racist special agent, while leading Montgomery to believe he had cleared up the misunderstanding, recommended to his superiors that the collector be forced to resign for depositing "moneys of a semi-official character in an unauthorized bank." Anything less, the agent insisted, "would result in an attack on the administration for shielding and whitewashing a nigger."

When Montgomery was summoned to New Orleans for a secret meeting with Booker T. Washington's secretary, he was shocked to be told he must resign. Suddenly his friends in high places wanted nothing to do with him. He was left to defend himself as best he could, although, as his brother said, he was "not a combative man." He remained in office for several months but eventually accepted the inevitable and resigned, returning to Mound Bayou. This bitter experience must have forced the fifty-six-year-old leader to question his faith in the trustworthiness of the white elite in Mississippi. Within a few months he was restored to the good graces of Booker T. Washington, and a few years later President Roosevelt had forgiven him enough to honor his request that the presidential train pause briefly on its way through Mound Bayou so that the chief executive could greet the citizens. Soon after, probably at Roosevelt's suggestion, Montgomery was invited to join him on the platform in Kentucky at the dedication of a memorial building on the hundredth anniversary of Abraham Lincoln's birth. Before depositing a copy of the Emancipation Proclamation in the cornerstone, Montgomery praised the Great Emancipator and other white friends of his race, though he had come to realize the severe limits to be expected from white helpfulness.

Shortly after the turn of the century, as unpunished acts of terrorism against the most successful members of the Negro race increased, the mayor of Mound Bayou began to express doubts about the effectiveness of his accommodationist policies. It is true that when the extreme racist James K. Vardaman won the nomination for governor of Mississippi, Montgomery wrote such a reassuring letter to a worried black farmer that the *Memphis Commercial Appeal* published it in full. Explaining that the race issue had been introduced in a contest between two white factions, he admitted that "the good people of Mississippi faltered" temporarily. But, he continued, " . . . you will find white friends still ready to utter words of encouragement, and extend a helping hand to those of us who strive to live a deserving life." He reiterated that "only trustworthiness and the solid virtues of an upright character will win for us a creditable and lasting place among our fellow-citizens." Not long afterward, in a letter to a Republican committeeman in Washington, Montgomery admitted his disappointment at "the persistent opposition" to black advancement in his state. In large areas of Mississippi, he reported, "white caps [disguised terrorists] have driven out sober, industrious, and reliable people, many of them home owners . . . because they prospered, and their example was likely to be helpful to others." But that same day he wrote to a white northerner of his opposition to a plan to encourage black migration to an agricultural colony in Mexico, and he enlisted Booker T. Washington's aid in attracting northern white capital to keep financial control of Mound Bayou and its environs in black hands.

Montgomery's genuine concern for the colony of Mound Bayou did not interfere with his efforts to better his own fortunes; he believed that he and the community would prosper together. He not only profited from Mound Bayou enterprises, such as a large retail store, a cotton gin, and a lumber yard, but also made considerable money as the agent for the railroad from which the colonists bought their land. His financial success allowed him to spend his later years comfortably established as the patriarch in a twenty-one-room red brick mansion which dominated the village scene. When he or his family traveled, railroad officials provided them with passes to staterooms which allowed them to avoid the Jim Crow cars. Perhaps the private benefits of his accommodation to whites helped console Montgomery for his acute disappointment with their treatment of his race in general. At any rate, his personal success earned him the respect of his fellow citizens, who realized that his acceptance was never won at their expense.

Montgomery had to be constantly vigilant in walking the racial tightrope. In the summer of 1904 he served as a delegate from Mississippi at the Republican National Convention. On his way home he granted an interview to the *St. Louis Globe-Democrat,* in which he unwisely said he thought the Democrats would be "very much disappointed with the result" if they made the race question an issue in the presidential campaign. The *Vicksburg Herald* reprinted his remark, noting that it read "a little like a threat. . . . " The editor commented that the statement did not illustrate "his characteristic good sense," for no one knew better than he "what it would mean to himself and the colony he has so creditably built up and cared for, if he incurred the reputation of a race agitator." Such menacing comments reminded the Mound Bayou leader of the importance of preserving his good standing. When Booker T. Washington asked him to reply to a request from a Massachusetts editor for particulars about outrages against successful blacks in Mississippi, Montgomery refused, saying, "For reasons which you well understand, I cannot afford any special notoriety in connection with these matters."

As one terrorist episode followed another, Isaiah Montgomery was forced to acknowledge "the depths to which Mississippi has fallen." In letters to his friend Washington, he chronicled cases such as that of Rev. C. A. Buchanan, a prosperous printer of Baptist publications in Clay County. He had "a decent home and a Piano" and kept a horse and buggy to take his daughter to and from the shop where she served as his cashier and bookkeeper. One day, while he was in Natchez on business, "a mass meeting of whites decided that the mode of living practiced by the Buchanan family had a bad effect on the cooks and washerwomen, who aspired to do likewise, and became less disposed to work for whites." The family was ordered to leave town within three days, and Buchanan was threatened with death if he returned. At the time of his letter to Montgomery, Buchanan was negotiating with the sheriff and the banker for the sale of his property. Similar stories came from other towns: a small grocer was forced to abandon his business and flee because he was considered too prosperous; a successful merchant was forced to sell his carriage and walk, while a black man who ran two hacks from the depot was ordered to sell one of them; and another successful businessman "was ordered to close up and don overalls for manual labor." Montgomery wanted the Mississippi Republican Committee to gather facts on these incidents and bring them to public attention by petitioning the governor, although he acknowledged it would probably do little good. A few months later Montgomery reported that claimed reforms in the white-cap counties were illusory and that black leaders should not deceive themselves "as to the extent of the conflict."

As conditions worsened Isaiah Montgomery came to question the wisdom of his sacrifice of the franchise at the 1890 constitutional convention. The beneficial results he had predicted had failed to materialize. Whites not only refused to enfranchise those blacks who achieved wealth and education, but they used every means, both legal and illegal, to keep them from advancing beyond their positions as impoverished peasant laborers. Montgomery spelled out his disillusionment in an unusually candid series of letters to a Michigan college student who inquired about the practical application of the franchise restrictions and their effect on the racial situation in Mississippi. Admitting that he had expected the law "to very largely eliminate the coloured vote" in the state, Montgomery asserted that he assumed the blacks would be reenfranchised gradually and peacefully as they

302

gained education and wealth. Meanwhile, he expected that with no black threat to unify them, whites would divide on many questions and the few black voters could then use their balance of power to protect their own interests. In practice, he reported, none of these benefits had occurred. Montgomery had not foreseen the creation of the white primary, which removed all black political influence since the general election became a mere ratification of decisions made by the white elite in the closed primary. As he noted, "the operation of the primary election effectively saps the essence of [the black's] ballot," and his sacrifice had been in vain.

In fact, in less than two decades after 1890 the question of black voting seemed trivial compared with the other rights that were being violated. Montgomery's policy of success through personal effort as the road to white acceptance was frustrated at every turn. He told the Michigan student many of the horror stories from the white-cap districts and added that they seemed to have the approval of high government officials. He reported that Governor Vardaman, speaking in a nearby town, pointed at some well-dressed blacks in the audience and said the race problem "could soon be settled by getting rid of their saddle colored leaders, the Preachers, Lawyers, Physicians and professional men, after which the common Negro would give no trouble." What good would accommodation do if there was to be no opportunity for advancement and if success was to be punished by terrorists? In a final burst of pessimism, Montgomery predicted that "the dominant spirit of the south will be satisfied with nothing less than a retrogression of the Negro back towards serfdom and slavery."

Skillfully balancing on the tightrope, Isaiah Montgomery had tried to further the interests of his people by winning the support of his white neighbors, relying on the appeal of the "self-made man" then so popular in white America. From the beginning he strove to improve himself and his colony so that both would be accepted as assets to American society—and he had to admit that the policy had failed. But what were his alternatives? Could he have accomplished more by challenging the white power structure? On the contrary, there would have been no Mound Bayou with its limited success as a haven for persecuted blacks had the leader been seen as a disturbing agitator. In 1907 Montgomery was asked, "Are you not afraid that some day the whites will be moved to wipe out Mound Bayou by violence?" He replied that he was not afraid of that threat because "the Negroes who have shaped and controlled the destiny of Mound Bayou understand conditions too' well to allow any radical or indiscreet policy to prevail here." Furthermore, he added, "there are too many white men around us . . . who are our friends and willing to see that no . . . undue advantage is taken of us by irresponsible parties." In fact, Mound Bayou was not destroyed suddenly by white violence, but it was allowed to decay slowly, like most southern villages, as a result of economic strangulation. This protection was the only benefit of all the sacrifices Isaiah Montgomery had made to whites in his long years as a black leader in Mississippi.

Several years after Montgomery's death, a white Mississippi politician, in eulogizing him, said, "His outstanding life's work, in my opinion, was his courageous stand as a member of the Mississippi Constitutional Convention of 1890." Although the results fell far short of his hopes, it is sad to note that Isaiah Montgomery would probably not have disputed State Senator Roberts's statement. Such were the limited possibilities for a black leader in the South at the turn of the century.

Sharon Harley

16

Mary Church Terrell: Genteel Militant

B Y THE CLOSE of the nineteenth century, Mary Eliza Church Terrell had established a national reputation as a black women's club leader, a women's suffrage activist, and a gifted public speaker. Not quite thirty years old, in 1892 she helped to organize one of the first black women's secular groups in the United States. Four years later she became the first president of the newly formed National Association of Colored Women. In addition to assuming major positions in the black women's club movement, Terrell was involved in predominantly white women's suffrage and reform circles. To both black and white women's reform movements she brought a firm belief in racial justice and women's equality, well-tuned leadership skills, a brilliant mind, and a talent as a public speaker for articulating the goals and beliefs of the movements. Her success on various fronts in the closing decades of the nineteenth century would assure her a prominent place in the twentieth-century American public arena, especially as the opportunities for women leaders expanded.

Mary Eliza Church, the first of two children of Robert Reed Church and Louisa Ayers Church, was born on September 23, 1863, in Memphis, Tennessee. Robert Church, a self-educated former slave, initially worked as a boatman on his white father's steamboat. By the close of the nineteenth century Church's financial success as a saloonkeeper, banker, and real estate dealer in Memphis made him one of the wealthiest black men in the United States. Likewise, Mary's mother, a property owner and a popular dressmaker, as well as the owner of one of the most fashionable hair salons in Memphis, was a successful businesswoman. As a consequence of her parents' financial success, Mary Church, affectionately called "Mollie" by family members and friends, had an especially privileged life by nineteenth-century standards, regardless of race.

This article was completed while I was a postdoctoral fellow in the Division of Political History, National Museum of American History at the Smithsonian Institution. Financial assistance was provided by the Smithsonian Institution, the National Endowment for the Humanities, and the General Research Board of the University of Maryland, College Park.

As a child Mary accompanied her father on a number of business and political trips throughout the South. It was on a trip from Memphis to Cincinnati that she had her first personal encounter with Jim Crow practices in the postbellum South, when a train conductor attempted to remove her from the coach reserved for whites. Somewhat baffled as to why this incident had occurred, the young Mary Church responded, "I could think of nothing that I had done wrong. I could get no satisfaction from Father, however, for he refused to talk about the affair and forbade me to do so." This train incident, however, was not the first time she had felt the pain and humiliation of being a member of the despised, "darker" race. In her autobiography she recalls her earlier grief upon learning that her grandmother and her parents were former slaves, a fact her parents had attempted to conceal from her. Although she eventually recovered from her feelings of bitterness and embarrassment over these early revelations and experiences, she never wavered from her belief that racial injustice was evil and that it and all forms of injustice must be fought.

The limited education available to black youth and the segregated school system in Memphis prompted Mary Church's parents to send her, when she was six years old, to a model school associated with Antioch College in Yellow Springs, Ohio. Upon completing her work there she moved to Oberlin, where she attended the public high school and later the preparatory school at Oberlin College, eventually enrolling in the classical course at the college. As a member of both the debating team and the Aeolian Literary Society at Oberlin College, Mary Church perfected her oratorical skills and developed an understanding of parliamentary procedures which later proved valuable in public life. She launched her writing career as the Aeolian representative on the editorial board of the *Oberlin Review,* the school's newspaper.

Many of the ideas about racial justice and women's equality that Mary Church Terrell expressed on the lecture circuit, in published papers, and at meetings of women and reform associations appear to be revisions of basic ideas she developed while a student at Oberlin. In one college paper she urged women to devote some time to their own self-culture and study rather than permit "household cares" to absorb their minds. This line of thinking, popular among late-nineteenth-century women reformers, was the basis for the formation of hundreds of women's self-culture and reading clubs. In the fall of 1879, a decade prior to her first public address on the suffrage issue, Mary Church, only sixteen years old, expressed prosuffrage views in her senior preparatory paper, entitled "Should an Amendment to the Constitution Allowing Women the Ballot Be Adopted." She urged those who argued that voting was outside the "woman's sphere" to be consistent: "farmers wives often dig potatoes in a busy time, and mothers are obliged frequently to bring refractory corporal punishment, both of which are tasks of men, yet there has never been a sermon nor a speech in congress against either as we have heard." The issue of women's proper sphere never arose, she also observed, when females provided the financial support for their brothers' college education. Most of the paper, however, using arguments that she would employ as a prosuffrage publicist in the late nineteenth and early twentieth centuries, focused on the injustices of denying approximately 50 percent of the American citizenry the ballot and tied the struggle of women for the ballot to the struggle blacks waged for emancipation and justice.

Although she denounced all forms of oppression, Mary Church Terrell conformed largely to conventional middle-class thinking, particularly in her views of the poor and the role of the middle class. For instance, in one college essay on "The Poor in Our Cities," she not only made a distinction between the "deserving" and "undeserving" poor but embraced the prevailing view of the poor as a dangerous class. Yet it was probably just as difficult for the young Mary Church, a member of one of the black community's most socially prominent families, to escape the influence of middle-class reformist thinking as it was for her to ignore the opposition to injustice that was so much a part of the Oberlin tradition. After all, although she expressed sympathy for the poor, she had clearly led a privileged life. During her freshman year at Oberlin, for example, she attended the inauguration of President James A. Garfield as the guest of former Mississippi Reconstruction senator Blanche K. Bruce and his family, where she met Frederick Douglass.

Following her graduation from Oberlin in 1884, Mary Church was committed to doing more than leading the purposeless existence of a real Southern lady. As she wrote in her autobiography, "All during my college course I had dreamed of the day when I could promote the welfare of my race." Accordingly, over her father's objections she accepted a teaching post at Wilberforce, Ohio, in the fall of 1885. Two years later she joined the faculty of the Preparatory School for Colored Youth in Washington, D.C., where she taught in the foreign language department, headed by Robert Heberton Terrell, her future husband. A year later, financed by her father, she took a leave of absence for travel and study of foreign languages in Europe. Abroad in 1888–90 she met a number of distinguished people; the experience also proved beneficial to her later public life as a paid lecturer and an activist in the women's movement. Indeed, as she assumed a more active role in the women's club movement and in the reform campaigns in the last decade of the nineteenth century, newspaper reports about her in the black and white press seldom failed to mention that she had spent two years abroad. Clearly, it was something that distinguished her from most black and, for that matter, most white American women of the period.

After her return to the United States, Mary Church taught only one year before resigning her position to marry Robert H. Terrell. Their marriage in October 1891 brought together two of the most prominent members of Washington's black social elite. If it had been the intention of those who developed the school regulation forbidding married women from teaching to encourage these women to remain at home and raise a family, it did not have that effect on Mary Church Terrell. With the encouragement of her husband she embarked upon a full-time career as a paid lecturer, suffrage activist, civic worker, organizer, and leader in the early black women's club movement.

Despite the demands of his own career, which included serving successively as chief of the division in the Fourth Auditor's Office of the United States Treasury Department (a position traditionally reserved for black men), as principal of the M Street High School in Washington, D.C., and, finally, at Booker T. Washington's recommendation as a municipal judge in the District of Columbia, Robert H. Terrell never openly complained about his wife's frequent absences from home. Nor did he object to her public statements, which occasionally put him at odds with other members of Washington's camp. The personal correspondence between the two suggests a loving and mutually supportive relationship. She attributed her success as a club woman and a professional lecturer in part to her husband's encouragement. Robert Terrell, for his part, fully supported the causes his wife advocated. Expressing his views about black males who opposed female suffrage, he wrote in 1915, "I have contempt I cannot name for the man who would demand rights for himself that he is not willing to grant everyone else."

Robert Terrell did not raise their two daughters, Phillis and Mary, alone, nor did he assume most of the household responsibilities. During most of their married life Mary Church Terrell's mother and a series of live-in domestics and cooks provided child care and domestic assistance. Although apparently devoted to her husband and daughters, Mary Church Terrell was at least equally committed to her professional work as a lecturer and writer, as well as to her organizational work. Viewing her lectures and organizational work as part of a personal commitment to advance her race and her sex, she was no different from a growing number of educated, middle-class women of the late nineteenth century who, as "mothers of the world," assumed the responsibility of aiding the nation's needy and weak.

During the closing decades of the nineteenth century, increasing numbers of middle- and upper-class women reacted to a society they perceived as threatened by the effects of urbanization and industrialization. In the 1880s white women reformers and suffragists had begun forming national associations to more effectively address the problems caused by urbanization and to increase networking among women reformers, suffragists, and club women. In 1891 the General Federation of Women's Clubs was formed.

In addition to the goals that black female reformers shared with their white counterparts, the secular reform organizations of black women had unique goals because of the burdens that black women carried as members of both a despised race and a despised sex. Black female reformers needed to take on the added responsibility of racial uplift among the "less fortunate" members of their race as well as their sex, at a time when all blacks were increasingly the victims of segregationist practices and racial hostility. In Terrell's view, educated black women especially became active in uplifting their race because "they know that they cannot escape altogether the consequences of the acts of their most depraved sisters. They see that even if they were wicked enough to turn a deaf ear to the call of duty, both policy and self-preservation demand that they go down among the lowly, the illiterate and even the vicious, to whom they are bound by the ties of race and sex, and put forth every possible effort to reclaim them."

When in 1892 Mary Church Terrell joined seven other educated black Washington women, primarily teachers, to form the Colored Women's League, she and they were fully aware of the black woman's double burden. In addition to their efforts to inform the public about the moral and social progress of the black race, the members of this pioneering women's group initiated a number of practical measures to benefit the Washington black community, ranging from an evening school for adults to mothers' meetings and day nurseries for the children of working mothers. Although one of the founders and incorporators of the league in 1894 and a principal speaker at its first national convention in July 1896, Terrell did not assume a major leadership role, perhaps because of other demands on her time. She was the first woman president of the prestigious Bethel Literary and

Historical Association in Washington, founded in 1881, whose members discussed major issues and intellectual questions of the day. Although the initial reaction to her as the first female president was negative in some quarters, after she had been at the helm for a short while, it was the general consensus that "she could preside with ease and grace, plan with foresight, and execute with vigor."

From April 1895 until 1901 Terrell also was involved in the formulation of educational policy for the District of Columbia public schools as a member of the board of trustees. Her appointment marked the first time a black woman was so honored by the district commissioners, who previously had appointed only males as black board members. As the only board member who had had any teaching experience in the district's public school system, her opinion was frequently sought by her colleagues. She introduced a resolution to have February 14 —Frederick Douglass's birthday—honored in the school system, which was unanimously adopted by the board. Although as a black woman Terrell was generally considered the board's "colored representative," white teachers in the system appealed to her for assistance and support in a number of school matters. She resigned in 1901 to avoid a possible conflict of interest when her husband was being considered for the position of principal of M Street High School, but she was reappointed in 1906 and remained on the newly formed board of education until 1911.

Meanwhile, a predominantly elite black group in Boston, led by Josephine St. Pierre Ruffin, had formed in 1893 the New Era Club, whose activities paralleled those of black club women in Washington, D.C., and in urban communities throughout the United States. In 1894 Terrell was appointed by Ruffin, president of Boston's New Era Club and editor, along with her daughter, Florida Ruffin Ridley, of its official organ, *Women's Era,* head of the publication's "Washington" department. Terrell was responsible for providing news about Washington women and their club activities. By the mid-1890s she was juggling her time between various local black women's secular organizations, meetings of the school board, limited domestic responsibilities, public speaking engagements, and meetings of predominantly white women's national organizations.

In the absence of a national body of black club women, blacks could not become affiliates of the National Council of Women, the General Federation of Women's Clubs, or most other national organizations, nor could they, as they discovered in 1893, participate in the Women's Exhibit at the World's Fair. Affiliation with the General Federation of Women's Clubs was not an issue for black club women since the federation did not welcome "clubs composed of women with a racial origin different from white." Nevertheless, impressed with the ability of national bodies to tackle major social and moral problems, black women were encouraged to organize along similar lines. The Colored Women's League established branches in various cities, including Richmond and Norfolk, Virginia, Baltimore, Maryland, and Newport, Rhode Island, and began calling itself a national body. In 1895 the league was invited by the National Council of Women to bring greetings at its annual meeting, which was held in Washington, D.C., even though the various league clubs had never met as a single national group.

Like Terrell black women believed that through the formation of a national body whose leadership included their "most representative" women, more whites and publicly active black men would come to recognize that black women compared favorably to white women in moral refinement, culture, and alertness to the issues of the day. In the midst of the general rising sentiment among black club women for a single national body, an insulting attack on the moral character of all black women by the president of the Missouri Press Editors Association prompted Ruffin to call a national meeting of Afro-American women in Boston for July 1895. She invited all interested black women to attend this conference. Terrell was unable to be present at this important gathering, which established the National Federation of Afro-American Women under the presidency of Margaret Murray Washington, wife of Tuskegee Institute's principal.

After the formation of the national federation, black club women and the black press began to question the validity of having two national bodies of colored women—the Colored Women's League and the National Federation of Afro-American Women. Quite possibly the idea of merging with the league, in light of the limited resources and time of black women, prompted Margaret Murray Washington to schedule a second national meeting in Washington, D.C., just a few days after the National Colored Women's League conference ended. A committee of seven members from each group met and formed a joint committee for the purpose of establishing a single national organization of black women. As a committee member Mary Church Terrell, ironically, did not represent the league, which she had helped to found, but the rival national federation. Possibly because she, unlike the other committee representatives, had personal ties with both organizations and therefore was less likely to show favoritism to either of the merging groups, Terrell was elected to chair the joint committee. After several rounds of voting the committee elected her the first national president of the newly formed

National Association of Colored Women (NACW). Members of the joint committee indicated on more than one occasion that Terrell was the "Compromise Leader" whose "fairness" in the position of chair persuaded them to cast their votes for her.

By all accounts the initial selection of Terrell proved a good omen for the first truly national body of black women. One of a handful of black women to graduate from a four-year liberal arts college, she was repeatedly characterized by her contemporaries as one of the most brilliant women in late-nineteenth-century America. The honors already bestowed upon her as the first female president of the Bethel Literary and Historical Association and as the first black female appointee to the District of Columbia's school board provide a clear indication of how prominent members of Washington's black and white community viewed her. Her elite social status in the black community, her exceptional oratorical ability, and her fine physical features only added to the already favorable public opinion of Mary Church Terrell. By virtue of her election as NACW president, she became, in the closing years of the nineteenth century, the principal voice and representative of the black women's club movement and one of the most visible blacks of her sex in the United States.

Just over one year following her initial election as president of the first major national organization of black women, Terrell traveled to Nashville, Tennessee, to preside over its first annual convention; over sixty delegates attended, representing twenty-six clubs. After discussing issues ranging from lynching and Jim Crow to suffrage and the plight of rural women, the delegates ratified the NACW constitution and elected Terrell to a two-year term as national president. In a series of presidential addresses at this meeting and at subsequent national meetings, Terrell revealed her views on a variety of women's and racial issues, especially the role of black women's clubs in general and NACW in particular.

In her first presidential address at Nashville, Terrell appealed to the women to work arduously on behalf of the poor, especially women and children. She opened her speech with an explanation of why black women had formed the National Association of Colored Women:

> We call ourselves an Association to signify that we have joined hands one with the other to work together in a common cause: to proclaim to the world that the women of our race have become partners in the great firm of progress and reform. We denominate ourselves colored, not because we are narrow, and wish to

lay special emphasis on the color of the skin. . . . But we refer to the fact that this is an association of colored women, because our peculiar status in this country at the present time seems to demand that we stand by ourselves in the special work for which we have been organized.

Employing the maternal rhetoric so popular among late-nineteenth-century women reformers, Terrell then beseeched NACW members, "Listen to the cry of the children, my sisters. Upon you they depend for the light of knowledge, and the blessing of a good example."

Terrell's leadership would be tested at the second biennial meeting of the NACW in Chicago in the summer of 1899. The first battle was over the issue of seating delegates who failed to bring their official credentials with them, which Terrell opposed as a violation of the NACW constitution. Efforts by Josephine St. Pierre Ruffin, Terrell's chief rival for control of the organization, to have the body ignore this ruling were rejected by Terrell, who ruled Ruffin out of order. While these two prominent black club women had worked together in the past, their friendship had soured in light of Ruffin's unsuccessful attempts to be elected president of the National Association of Colored Women. Indeed, the second major crisis of the Chicago convention centered on the election of officers, primarily the office of president and recording secretary.

The main issue regarding the presidential election was whether Terrell was interested in running for president again and, more important, whether she was eligible for reelection. Initially, the delegates decided that Terrell and other current officers were ineligible because the NACW constitution, ratified in 1897, limited officers to two terms. After a closed-door session the executive committee ruled in Terrell's favor, maintaining that she had only served one term since the NACW constitution had gone into effect and that the two-term limit could not be applied retroactively. Aware of Terrell's popularity, the principal contenders, including Ruffin and Washington, recognized that their chances for being elected were minimal. The final count proved them correct: Terrell received 106 votes and the remaining four candidates amassed a combined total of 37 votes.

Clearly, envy and jealousy motivated some of the attacks against Terrell as individual NACW women, outstanding in their own right, vied for leadership positions. Yet it was Terrell's leadership ability, "good breeding," and social prominence that contributed to her popularity in black women's reform circles. As a black woman Mary Church Terrell was revered, especially in middle-class and aspiring middle-class black communities, because she embodied all that black women hoped to achieve for themselves and the image that they hoped to project to the larger society. Despite criticisms from a small but well-known group within the NACW, the second biennial meeting was declared a success by a number of observers, including W. E. B. Du Bois and members of the local black and white press. Du Bois concluded that the meeting's success was largely the result of the able leadership of its president, Mary Church Terrell.

In her third speech as NACW president in 1901 at Buffalo (where the local club leader Josephine Silone-Yates was elected her successor), Terrell admitted that the organization had not achieved all of its goals. She maintained, nevertheless, that it was due less to a lack of effort on her part or the organization's part and more to "conditions peculiar to the race" and "the lack of experience and lack of means" of colored women less than four decades out of slavery.

Despite internal criticisms Terrell had successfully spearheaded the early development of the National Association of Colored Women. To improve the status of black women as mothers, wives, and workers, the NACW, under her tutelage, established kindergarten programs (in many cases before they became part of local public school systems), day nurseries, training schools, orphanages, and mothers' clubs. During her reign as president she was invited to a number of leading white women's suffrage and reform meetings, and the NACW was accepted in 1900 as an affiliate member of the largely white National Council of Women. When Terrell's presidency ended the NACW was firmly established as the premier black women's self-help organization, in which black women could engage in various social welfare reform activities and discuss issues of concern to blacks, especially black women and children. For the next fifty years Terrell, as "Honorary President," remained a committed and active member of the National Association of Colored Women, speaking at biennial conventions, presiding over various committees, and participating in public forums as an NACW representative.

During the opening decades of the twentieth century the bulk of Terrell's time was consumed by her continuing responsibilities as a paid lecturer and writer, as a suffrage activist, and as a member of the newly reorganized District of Columbia Board of Education. In conjunction with her pioneering work in and outside the NACW, Terrell was an active participant in the predominantly white women's suffrage and reform movements during the 1890s. She began to establish her national reputation as a lecturer primarily on the basis of addresses she delivered at the meetings of the National American Women's

Suffrage Association (NAWSA), the National Congress of Mothers, and other national reform organizations

A life member of the NAWSA and, later on, of the more militant National Women's party, Terrell was probably the most eminent black female advocate of women's suffrage in the 1890s and in the opening decades of the twentieth century. She attended suffrage meetings, joined suffrage picket lines, and lectured on the subject before white and black audiences. As one of the few black women to address predominantly white audiences, she appeared as a speaker at the national meeting of the NAWSA in 1898. Her address on "The Progress of Colored Women" was enthusiastically received and was later published.

Susan B. Anthony, NAWSA president from 1892 to 1900, indicated that Terrell's unanimous selection as one of nine principal speakers and as the only black speaker at the 1900 NAWSA national meeting in Washington, D.C., had less to do with her racial identity than with her diligent work "in that broad arena of common purpose—the moral and intellectual elevation of our sex." With verve and force Terrell brilliantly argued on this occasion and others that the denial of suffrage to women, many of whom were intelligent and cultured, violated the democratic principles upon which the United States was founded.

As a result of her active role at NAWSA national conventions and at national reform meetings, including temperance, peace, and social purity meetings at the turn of the twentieth century, primarily as a speaker, Mary Church Terrell was widely known in many white reform and white women's suffrage circles. Despite her popularity as a speaker and her reputation as a club leader, she was never elected an officer in any of the white women's groups, however. The failure of prominent black club women to assume leadership positions within the national suffrage and reform organizations reflected far more than the desire to devote their full time and energy to the developing black women's club movement. The prevailing racial climate in the United States and the efforts of white suffrage leaders to gain white support in the South dictated against welcoming black suffragists as active members and leaders of the movement. Despite Terrell's commitment to women's causes, the favorable reception she was accorded at national meetings, and her friendship with leading white suffragists and reformers, she was fully aware that not all of these organizations, even those that welcomed her as a speaker, welcomed women of color as members; nor did she actively seek membership in such organizations. "Under no circumstances," she remarked, "would I force myself into a club whose members would object to my presence because I am a colored woman. I have too much self-respect for that. . . . Knowing that I am barred from them on account of my race, I bow to the inevitable as philosophically as I can."

As white suffragists sought southern support for a federal amendment giving women the right to vote, opposition to black female participation in the suffrage campaign increased in the opening decades of the twentieth century. Yet Terrell's commitment to the suffrage movement and her loyalty to the suffrage leadership remained generally strong, probably because she believed that "however much the white women of the country need suffrage, for many reasons which will immediately occur to us, colored women need it more."

In 1919, one year prior to the ratification of the Nineteenth Amendment, Terrell defended the predominantly white National Women's party (NWP) against charges of racism leveled by the National Association for the Advancement of Colored People (NAACP). She claimed that the NWP, headed by Alice Paul, welcomed blacks as members and invited them to participate on an equal basis with white suffragists, in their parades, meetings, and social activities. Even so she deeply regretted the refusal of the party to support a campaign to make certain that black women were not denied the vote on racial grounds. In the end Terrell accepted the party's explanation that it "wanted to continue to work on discriminations that were common to all women, and not on discriminations that were based on race only, rather than sex."

By focusing exclusively on forms of discrimination that all women faced, the NWP leadership effectively excluded the black woman's cause from their agenda. After all, the pervasiveness of institutional racial segregation and discrimination at the turn of the century sharply limited the forms and level of discrimination that black and white women shared. Despite Terrell's support for the suffrage cause and her statements in support of the NWP, she knew that racial prejudice and expediency motivated many white suffragists, especially as they courted southern support for their cause. At the major women's suffrage parade held in Washington, D.C., in the summer of 1913, for example, the suffrage organizers attempted to persuade black participants to march separately, at the rear of the parade, rather than by their home state or their profession, as was customary. As Walter White, assistant executive secretary of the NAACP, wrote Terrell in 1919, "Just as you say, all of them are mortally afraid of the South and if they could get the suffrage amendment through without enfranchising colored women, they would do it in a moment." After the ratification of the suffrage amendment, Terrell, as president of the Colored

Women's Republican League and director of work among colored women voters, took up the special cause of these women on behalf of the Republican party.

Throughout the late nineteenth century and the early decades of the twentieth century, Terrell combined her political and women's club work with her professional work as a paid lecturer. She described herself as an optimist: although she did not overlook the negative impact of segregation and racial violence on black lives, she chose to focus on positive rather than negative aspects of their experience in her lectures. This certainly was the thrust of one of her most popular talks, "A Bright Side of a Dark Subject." Tactical considerations alone suggested the need to avoid the ugly and negative experiences of blacks, especially incidents of racial violence. Terrell recognized that people, especially whites, would probably not pay to hear horror stories about black-white relations. Besides, she naively thought that the more whites knew about black progress, the quicker they would embrace blacks as equals.

In fact, because whites were so woefully uninformed when it came to understanding blacks, Terrell felt that one of her major responsibilities as a lecturer was to interpret the black experience for her white audiences. Her general optimism, however, did not lead her to overlook such burning issues of the day as lynching and the convict lease system. For example, she contributed an article in 1904 to the influential *North American Review,* in which she attributed lynching to race hatred and lawlessness in the South, not to rape or to the desire for social equality on the part of blacks. In this article and in her public lectures she criticized both the North and the South for failing to respect the rights of blacks.

At the turn of the twentieth century, a significant battle was being waged within the black community between the W. E. B. Du Bois and the Booker T. Washington camps which centered on the best approach to advance the black race. In this struggle the Terrells attempted to remain centrists, identifying with both groups. Despite Mary Terrell's expressed repugnance for the accommodationist philosophy traditionally identified with Washington, she believed, like Washington, in the "dignity of labor," that industrial training should have a place, alongside classical education, in the public school system, and that blacks should remain in the South. She even went so far as to oppose Du Bois's appointment as assistant superintendent of the District of Columbia public schools in favor of Roscoe Conkling Bruce, the nephew of Margaret Murray Washington, who was considered a "Bookerite." At the same time, however, Terrell spoke out publicly against many of the ideas associated with the Washington school of thought and was a member of various organizations, including the Constitution League and the NAACP, which were generally considered hotbeds of anti-Washington sentiment. Mary Church Terrell was also a founding member of and active leader in the Washington branch of the NAACP, established in 1913. With the apparent support of her husband, she insisted on working with the Du Bois–NAACP group, even though it put her husband's judicial career and his backing from the Washington camp at risk. Still, she continued to consider herself a friend of Washington's and regularly invited him and his family to stay at her home whenever they were in the nation's capital.

Terrell's political shrewdness and her fierce independence probably contributed to the difficulty of characterizing her as either pro-Washington or pro–Du Bois. Consequently, some journalists referred to her as the "Mrs. Booker T. Washington," "whose ideas of the elevation of her people conform to the practical theories of Booker Washington," while others maintained that she was a "firm believer in every principle enunciated by the platform of the Niagara Movement." Through her actions and her public rhetoric, Terrell revealed that she did not identify exclusively with either the Du Bois camp or the Washington camp, much as she refused to confine herself exclusively to either women's causes or racial causes. All in all, she and her husband were able to successfully straddle the fence between the opposing camps throughout this period.

Despite the progressive views expressed throughout her active public life, Terrell epitomized black upper-middle-class leadership and seldom appeared among the black masses, except in church gatherings. Her actions and her ideology tended to benefit mostly the educated middle-class and educated blacks with middle-class aspirations. Although she expressed a desire, like most middle-class blacks and whites, to "enlighten" and "uplift" the masses, not many uneducated, low-income residents of the Washington black community recognized her as a leader or even knew who she was. Some of the poor benefited from the day-care programs and kindergarten programs established by various self-help women's groups with which she was affiliated. But her efforts on behalf of the masses were limited largely to an occasional comment about the need for a training school for black domestics and talks on the subject of "Colored Domestics," although she personally donated money and clothing from time to time to needy members of her neighborhood.

The middle-class orientation of Terrell's leadership should not, however, detract from her overall importance as a brilliant late-nineteenth-century club woman and public speaker. While her leadership style represented the traditional educated, middle-class tendency to effect racial equality and justice through personal persuasion and by educating whites (and blacks) about the progress of the black race, she was courageously outspoken and unrelenting in her fight to end racial and gender proscriptions in late-nineteenth-century American society.

On July 24, 1954, at the age of ninety, Mary Church Terrell died in Annapolis, Maryland, where she kept a summer home next to the house that the late Frederick Douglass had occupied. Her death brought to an end the life of a black woman whose active public career spanned two centuries and encompassed a myriad of causes. The people who benefited most from her life were the early black club women whom she organized and inspired, the black and white men and women whom she impressed with her brilliant oratory, and the white female suffragists and reformers to whom she willingly lent a helping hand.

Bibliographical Essay

Every history has produced its share of heroes, legends, and myths. For every eulogistic book written about black heroes and leaders, one might find scores of comparable works on white Americans. Few of the authors of such books have felt any need to conceal their essential purpose—to instill racial and national pride in their people. Among the earliest studies of prominent black Americans is *Men of Mark: Eminent, Progressive and Rising,* published in 1887. The 1,400-page volume consists of 177 biographical sketches of blacks who had achieved distinction as "lawyers, doctors, authors, editors, divines, lecturers, linguists, scientists, college presidents, and such." The author, the Rev. William J. Simmons, president of the State University at Louisville, Kentucky, catalogued the achievements of his race. He included slave rebels (Denmark Vesey and Nat Turner), but he focused on those blacks who had enjoyed success—almost any kind of success. The sketches range from Crispus Attucks, who achieved martyrdom in the Boston Massacre, to Booker T. Washington; from Wiley Jones of Pine Bluff, Arkansas, who owned a streetcar railroad, a race track, and a park, to Troy Porter, an Illinois plumber and gas fitter. It is clearly a eulogistic volume, calculated to celebrate the progress of the race: "to show to the world—to our oppressors and even our friends—that the race is still alive, and must possess more intellectual vigor than any other section of the human family, or else how could they be crushed as slaves in all these years since 1620, and yet to-day stand side by side with the best blood in America." Of the nineteenth-century black leaders selected for this volume, the only ones not included in *Men of Mark* are Isaiah T. Montgomery

This essay is intended as an introduction to the published literature concerning the individuals treated in this volume. It is intended for the general reader and student, as well as professional historians, and is deliberately selective rather than comprehensive. We have not included references to unpublished manuscript and archival sources. The essay is in large part based on bibliographical materials submitted by the authors of the essays.

and, significantly, the three women— Harriet Tubman, Mary Ann Shadd, and Mary Church Terrell.

Some ninety-five years after Simmons's tome, Rayford W. Logan and Michael R. Winston edited the *Dictionary of American Negro Biography* (1982), an authoritative undertaking that reflects the impressive advances in historical scholarship in Afro-American history since World War II. It complements *The Dictionary of American Biography* (20 vols., 1936) and its four supplements, which treat some 120 Afro-Americans, and *Notable American Women* (4 vols., 1971–80), which examines the lives of 41 black women. See also Howard N. Rabinowitz (ed.), *Southern Black Leaders of the Reconstruction Era* (1982), and John Hope Franklin and August Meier (eds.), *Black Leaders of the Twentieth Century* (1982), which treats important leaders like Booker T. Washington whose careers spanned both centuries. Many of the individuals in this volume are also represented in Carter G. Woodson (ed.), *Negro Orators and Their Orations* (1925), and Howard Brotz (ed.), *Negro Social and Political Thought, 1850–1920* (1966).

Richard Bardolph, *The Negro Vanguard* (1959), is "not a compilation of success stories" but an attempt to identify and examine the social origins of "the most celebrated Negro Americans in the country's past." Nathan I. Huggins discusses the issues, strategies, and styles that have characterized Afro-American leadership in John Higham (ed.), *Ethnic Leadership in America* (1978). Sterling Stuckey, in *Slave Culture: Nationalist Theory and the Foundations of Black America* (1987), focuses on David Walker, Henry Highland Garnet, W. E. B. Du Bois, and Paul Robeson. The internal history or psychobiography of four prominent blacks—Frederick Douglass, W. E. B. Du Bois, Richard Wright, and Martin Luther King, Jr.—are explored in Allison Davis, *Leadership, Love, and Aggression* (1983). For a study of black thought and ideology focusing on institutions and leaders, see August Meier, *Negro Thought in America, 1880–1915* (1963). For a study of black thought focusing on the oral expressive tradition of Afro-Americans, see Lawrence W. Levine, *Black Culture and Black Consciousness: Afro-American Folk Thought from Slavery to Freedom* (1977).

RICHARD ALLEN. His personal memoir, discovered after his death, has been reprinted with an introduction by George A. Singleton as *The Life Experience and Gospel Labors of the Rt. Rev. Richard Allen (1960)*. Two important biographies are Charles H. Wesley, *Richard Allen: Apostle of Freedom* (1935), and Carol V. R. George, *Segregated Sabbaths: Richard Allen and the Rise of Independent Black Churches, 1760–1840* (1973). For the foundation of Bethel A.M.E. church, see

324

C. M. Tanner, *Reprint of the First Edition of the Discipline of the African Methodist Episcopal Church with Historical Preface and Notes* (1916), and Benjamin T. Tanner, *An Outline of Our History and Government for African Methodist Churchmen* (1884). Daniel A. Payne, *History of the African Methodist Episcopal Church* (1891), remains a valuable account by a leading black churchman. For new perspectives on Allen and his times, see Will B. Gravely, "The Rise of African Churches in America, 1768-1822," *The Journal of Religious Thought,* 41 (Spring–Summer, 1984), and Dee Andrews, "Notes and Documents: The African Methodists of Philadelphia, 1794-1802," *Pennsylvania Magazine of History and Biography,* 108 (Oct. 1984).

NAT TURNER. The best source of information on the Nat Turner insurrection is Henry Irving Tragle (ed.), *The Southampton Slave Revolt of 1821* (1971), an extensive compilation that includes newspaper reports, trial records, and official correspondence, as well as generations of historical accounts. It includes the original *Confessions of Nat Turner* by Thomas R. Gray. For a shorter compilation of documents, see Eric Foner (ed.), *Nat Turner* (1971). William Sidney Drewry focused on the revolt in his doctoral dissertation (Johns Hopkins University), published as *The Southampton Insurrection* (1900). Although the bias is proslavery, the book contains valuable photographs of the area and material drawn from interviews with local residents.

Modern scholarship on Nat Turner and slave revolts begins with Herbert Aptheker, *American Negro Slave Revolts* (1943), which includes a chapter on "The Turner Cataclysm." Aptheker's master's thesis, completed in 1937 under Allan Nevins at Columbia University, was published three decades later as *Nat Turner's Slave Rebellion* (1966). Among more recent works, Stephen B. Oates, *The Fires of Jubilee: Nat Turner's Fierce Rebellion* (1975), is a readable and dramatic study. Thomas C. Parramore, *Southampton County, Virginia* (1978), offers new research on Thomas R. Gray. See also Vincent Harding, *There Is a River: The Black Struggle for Freedom in America* (1981), in which he compares Turner and David Walker. Finally, an eloquent and moving reflection on the Turner legend, "Remembering Nat Turner," can be found in Michael S. Harper (ed.), *The Collected Poems of Sterling A. Brown* (1980).

HARRIET TUBMAN. Having left no papers, and cautious in revealing her unlawful, secretive work on behalf of runaway slaves, Harriet Tubman posed a problem for later biographers. Sarah H. Bradford, her first biographer, acknowledged that *Scenes in the Life of Harriet Tubman* and *Harriet Tubman: The Moses of Her People* (1886, reprinted in 1961 with an introduction by Butler A. Jones), were based in large part upon material "related to me by my heroic friend." Earl Conrad's biography, *Harriet Tubman* (1943), made an exhaustive effort to unearth material on Tubman both as a private person and a public figure. See also Dorothy Sterling, *Freedom Train: The Story of Harriet Tubman* (1954).

Tubman's role in slave rescue operations is discussed in William Still, *The Underground Railroad* (1872); Wilbur H. Siebert, *The Underground Railroad from Slavery to Freedom* (1898); James A. McGowan, *Station Master of the Underground Railroad: The Life and Letters of Thomas Garrett* (1977); and Charles L. Blockson, *The Underground Railroad in Pennsylvania* (1981). Her relationships with the Zion Methodists are described in William J. Walls, *The African Methodist Zion Church* (1974).

FREDERICK DOUGLASS. The place to begin is Douglass's own account of his life: *Narrative of the Life of Frederick Douglass, an American Slave, Written by Himself* (1845); *My Bondage and My Freedom* (1855); and *Life and Times of Frederick Douglass* (1892). Philip S. Foner's collection, *The Life and Writings of Frederick Douglass* (5 vols., 1950–75), remains useful, though several of the documents are misdated. A comprehensive, though selective, collection of Douglass's work is underway by John W. Blassingame (ed.), *The Frederick Douglass Papers;* three of the projected fourteen volumes have appeared (1979, 1982, 1985), consisting of Douglass's speeches, debates, and interviews through 1863.

Benjamin Quarles, *Frederick Douglass* (1948), is a full-length scholarly biography. Waldo Martin, *The Mind of Frederick Douglass* (1984), is an intellectual study. See also Nathan Huggins, *Slave and Citizen: The Life of Frederick Douglass* (1980), a short interpretive biography; and August Meier, "Frederick Douglass' Vision for America: A Case Study in Nineteenth-Century Protest," in Harold H. Hyman and Leonard W. Levy (eds.), *Freedom and Reform: Essays in Honor of Henry Steele Commager* (1967). Dickson J. Preston, *Young Frederick Douglass: The Maryland Years* (1980), focuses on Douglass's "family life" as a slave.

Douglass was the most distinguished and influential of the black abolitionists; others are the subjects of several essays in this volume. For more general studies of black participation in the antislavery movement, see Benjamin Quarles, *Black Abolitionists* (1967), and

Jane H. and William H. Pease, *They Who Would Be Free: Blacks' Search for Freedom, 1830–1861* (1974).

MARY ANN SHADD. The only biographical study is Jim Barden and Linda Jean Butler, *Shadd: The Life and Times of Mary Ann Shadd* (1977), designed primarily for younger readers. Her work in Canada is examined in Jason H. Silverman, *Unwelcome Guests: Canada West's Response to American Fugitive Slaves, 1800–1865* (1985), and in Robin W. Winks, *The Blacks in Canada: A History* (1971). See also Alexander L. Murray, "*The Provincial Freeman:* A New Source for the History of the Negro in Canada and the United States," *Journal of Negro History,* 44 (Apr. 1959), and Harold B. Hancock, "Mary Ann Shadd: Negro Editor, Educator, and Lawyer," *Delaware History,* 15 (Apr. 1973).

JOHN MERCER LANGSTON. The most important source on his life and thought remains his autobiography, *From the Virginia Plantation to the National Capitol* (1894), and a collection of speeches together with an introductory sketch by his white friend, the Rev. J. E. Rankin, *Freedom and Citizenship* (1883). See also William Cheek, "A Negro Runs for Congress: John Mercer Langston and the Virginia Campaign of 1888," *Journal of Negro History,* 52 (Jan. 1967), and "John Mercer Langston: Black Protest Leader and Abolitionist," *Civil War History,* 16 (Mar. 1970).

HENRY HIGHLAND GARNET. The most important contemporary sources are Alexander Crummell, "Eulogy on Rev. Henry Highland Garnet, D.D.," in *Africa and America* (1891); James McCune Smith, *A Memorial Discourse by Rev. Henry Highland Garnet with an Introduction by James McCune Smith* (1965); Garnet, *Walker's Appeal, with a Brief Sketch of His Life* (1848) and *The Past and Present Condition, and the Destiny of the Colored Races: A Discourse* (1848); and Howard H. Bell (ed.), *Proceedings of the National Negro Convention Movement* (1969). Modern studies include Earl Ofari, *Let Your Motto Be Resistance* (1972), and Joel Schor, *Henry Highland Garnet: A Voice of Black Radicalism in the Nineteenth Century* (1977). For some of the themes developed in this essay readers should also consult Sterling Stuckey, *The Ideological Origins of Black Nationalism* (1972) and "Henry Highland Garnet: Nationalism, Class Analysis, and Revolution," in *Slave Culture: Nationalist Theory and the Foundations of Black America* (1987).

MARTIN R. DELANY. The most revealing source on his life is Frank A. Rollin [Frances Rollins Whipper], *Life and Public Services of Martin R. Delany* (1883). The book was written in collaboration with Delany and includes extensive interviews with him, but it neglects the emigration movement and fails to deal with his last years. For Delany's own writings, see his emigrationist accounts: *The Condition, Elevation, Emigration and Destiny of the Colored People of the United States* (1852) and *Official Report of the Niger Valley Exploring Party* (1860), reprinted as Howard Bell (ed.), *Search for a Place: Black Separatism and Africa* (1969). See also Sterling Stuckey (ed.), *The Ideological Origins of Black Nationalism* (1972).

Modern scholarship on Delany includes a biography by Victor Ullman, *Martin R. Delany: The Beginnings of Black Nationalism* (1971). For a more critical approach that places him within the traditions of Pan-Africanism and black nationalism, see Cyril E. Griffith, *The African Dream: Martin R. Delany and the Emergence of Pan-African Thought* (1975), and Floyd J. Miller, *The Search for a Black Nationality: Black Emigration and Colonization, 1787-1863* (1975). For an examination of Delany within the Afro-American intellectual tradition, see Wilson J. Moses, *The Golden Age of Black Nationalism, 1850-1925* (1978). See also Richard J. M. Blackett, "In Search of International Support for African Colonization: Martin R. Delany's Visit to England," in *Canadian Journal of History,* 10 (1975), and "Martin R. Delany and Robert Campbell: Black Americans in Search of an African Colony," in *Journal of Negro History,* 62 (1977). Dorothy Sterling, *The Making of an Afro-American: Martin Robison Delany, 1812-1888* (1971), is intended largely for young readers.

PETER H. CLARK. His only published work, *The Black Brigade of Cincinnati: Being a Report of Its Labors and a Muster-Roll of Its Members; Together with Various Orders, Speeches, and Etc., Relating to It* (1864), chronicles the labors of Cincinnati blacks impressed into service, building fortifications when the city was believed to be threatened by a Confederate invasion. Herbert G. Gutman, "Peter H. Clark: Pioneer Negro Socialist, 1877," in *Journal of Negro Education,* 34 (Fall 1965), includes the full text of his speech to the Cincinnati railroad workers during the 1877 strike. There is no biography of Clark. For additional insights into his life and work, see Philip S. Foner, "Peter H. Clark: Pioneer Negro Socialist," *Journal of Ethnic Studies,* 5 (1977), and Lawrence Grossman, "In His Veins Coursed No Bootlicking Blood: The Career of Peter H. Clark," *Ohio History,* 83 (1977).

Studies of black Ohio also illuminate Clark's life. See Wendell P. Dabney, *Cincinnati's Colored Citizens: Historical, Sociological, and Biographical* (1976); David A. Gerber, *Black Ohio and the Color Line, 1860–1915* (1976); Richard C. Wade, "The Negro in Cincinnati, 1800–1830," *Journal of Negro History,* 39 (Jan. 1954); and David L. Calkins, "Black Education in Nineteenth Century Cincinnati," Cincinnati Historical Society *Bulletin,* 38 (1980), 115–28.

THREE RECONSTRUCTION LEADERS. The best sources are the black conventions in the aftermath of emancipation and the state constitutional conventions of 1867–68 in which blacks played a critical role. The black conventions have been published in Philip S. Foner and George Walker (eds.), *Proceedings of the Black State Conventions, 1840–1865* (2 vols., 1980). The most important state convention that has been reprinted is *Proceedings of the Constitutional Convention of South Carolina . . . 1868* (1868; rpt., 1968). Of equal importance, especially in the study of local black political leadership, is *Report of the Joint Select Committee to Inquire into the Condition of Affairs in the Late Insurrectionary States* (13 vols., 1872), known as the Ku Klux Klan hearings. John Franklin (ed.), *Reminiscences of an Active Life: The Autobiography of John Roy Lynch* (1970), is a unique recollection by a black officeholder.

Howard N. Rabinowitz (ed.), *Southern Black Leaders of the Reconstruction Era* (1982), includes essays on Blanche K. Bruce and John Roy Lynch (Mississippi), Josiah T. Walls (Florida), James T. Rapier (Alabama), and James O'Hara (North Carolina); collective studies of black delegates to the state constitutional conventions, black leadership in New Orleans, black councilmen in Richmond, and state legislators in South Carolina; and studies of local leaders Holland Thompson (Montgomery), Aaron A. Bradley (Georgia low country), William Finch (Atlanta), Dr. Benjamin A. Boseman, Jr. (Charleston), and George T. Ruby (Texas). In addition, Rabinowitz assesses the changing image of black reconstructionists, and August Meier examines new perspectives on black political leadership in the Reconstruction era. For a critical discussion of black leadership in this period, see Nell I. Painter, *Exodusters: Black Migration to Kansas after Reconstruction* (1976).

Numerous studies of prominent black Reconstruction leaders have been published, including Melvyn I. Urofsky, "Blanche K. Bruce, United States Senator, 1875–1881," *Journal of Mississippi History,* 29 (May 1967); Russell Duncan, *Freedom's Shore: Tunis Campbell and the Georgia Freedmen* (1986); Euline W. Brock, "Thomas W. Cardozo:

Fallible Black Reconstruction Leader," *Journal of Southern History,* 47 (May 1981); Peggy Lamson, *The Glorious Failure: Black Congressman Robert Brown Elliott and Reconstruction in South Carolina* (1973); William C. Harris, "James Lynch: Black Leader in Southern Reconstruction," *The Historian,* 34 (Nov. 1971); Okon Edet Uya, *From Slavery to Public Service: Robert Smalls 1839–1915* (1971); Loren Schweninger, *James T. Rapier and Reconstruction* (1978); and Peter D. Klingman, *Josiah Walls* (1976).

Although ignored by historians when it first appeared, W. E. B. Du Bois, *Black Reconstruction in America 1860–1880* (1935), remains a classic by a leading black intellectual. Studies of Reconstruction in individual states and localities illuminate black political leadership. See in particular Peter Kolchin, *First Freedom: The Response of Alabama's Blacks to Emancipation and Reconstruction* (1972); Edmund L. Drago, *Black Politicians and Reconstruction in Georgia: A Splendid Failure* (1983); Charles Vincent, *Black Legislators in Louisiana during Reconstruction* (1976); Vernon L. Wharton, *The Negro in Mississippi, 1865–1890* (1947); Joel Williamson, *After Slavery: The Negro in South Carolina during Reconstruction, 1861–1877* (1965); Thomas C. Holt, *Black Over White: Negro Political Leadership in South Carolina during Reconstruction* (1977); William C. Hine, "Black Politicians in Reconstruction Charleston, South Carolina: A Collective Study," *Journal of Southern History,* 49 (Nov. 1984); Armstead Robinson, "Plans Dat Comed from God: Institution Building and the Emergence of Black Leadership in Reconstruction Memphis," in Orville B. Burton and Robert G. McMath, Jr. (eds.), *Towards a New South?* (1982); Barry A. Crouch, "Self-Determination and Local Black Leaders in Texas," *Phylon,* 39 (Dec. 1978); and Luther P. Jackson, *Negro Office Holders in Virginia, 1865–1895* (1945).

ALEXANDER CRUMMELL. The place to begin is with his own writings. The four published collections are: *The Duty of a Rising Christian State* (1856), *The Future of Africa* (1862), *The Greatness of Christ, and Other Sermons* (1882), and *Africa and America* (1891). A classic tribute to Crummell can be found in W. E. B. Du Bois, "Of Alexander Crummell," in *The Souls of Black Folk* (1903). In the absence of a full-length biography readers should consult Otey M. Scruggs, *We the Children of Africa in This Land: Alexander Crummell* (1972); Gregory U. Grigsby, *Alexander Crummell: Pioneer in Ninteenth-Century Pan-African Thought* (1987); Wilson J. Moses, "Civilizing Missionary: A Study of Alexander Crummell," *Journal of Negro History,* 60 (Apr. 1975); and Monday B. Akpan, "Alexander Crummell and His African 'Race

Work': An Assessment of His Contribution in Liberia to Africa's 'Redemption,' 1853–1873," *Historical Magazine of the Protestant Episcopal Church,* 46 (June 1977). Studies of black thought that illuminate Crummell's career include August Meier, *Negro Thought in America, 1880–1915* (1963); Wilson J. Moses, *The Golden Age of Black Nationalism* (1978); William Toll, *The Resurgence of Race* (1979); and Alfred Moss, *The American Negro Academy: Voice of the Talented Tenth* (1981).

HENRY MCNEAL TURNER. The most important source is Edwin S. Redkey (ed.), *The Writings and Speeches of Henry McNeal Turner* (1971). There is no scholarly biography. M. M. Ponton, *Life and Times of Henry M. Turner* (1917), is a brief eulogistic biography by an admirer. Joseph R. Coan's Heritage Lecture Series addresses, "Bishop Henry McNeal Turner Speaks to This Generation" (AME Church, 1981, 1982), assess Turner's significance for the 1980s. See also Gayraud S. Wilmore, *Black Religion and Black Radicalism: An Interpretation of the Religious History of Afro-American People* (1983).

On Turner's early work as a Union chaplain, an A.M.E. organizer, and a Republican activist, see Leon F. Litwack, *Been in the Storm So Long: The Aftermath of Slavery* (1979); Clarence E. Walker, *A Rock in a Weary Land: The African Methodist Church during the Civil War and Reconstruction* (1982); Edmund L. Drago, *Black Politicians and Reconstruction in Georgia: A Splendid Failure* (1982); and Henry J. Young, *Major Black Religious Leaders, 1755–1940* (1977). On Turner's emigrationist activities, and for some valuable insights into his personality, philosophy, and historical significance, see Edwin S. Redkey, *Black Exodus: Black Nationalist and Back-to-Africa Movements, 1890–1910* (1959). For his significance within black intellectual life, see August Meier, *Negro Thought in America, 1880–1915* (1963). The final years of activism are described in John Dittmer, *Black Georgia in the Progressive Era, 1900–1920* (1977).

WILLIAM HENRY STEWARD. The most important sources are Henry Clay Weeden, *Weeden's History of the Colored People of Louisville* (1897); William H. Gibson, *Historical Sketch of the Progress of the Colored Race in Louisville* (1897); and W. D. Johnson, *Biographical Sketches of Prominent Negro Men and Women of Kentucky* (1897). Several autobiographies illuminate the growth of Kentucky Negro Baptist and black leaders, including Elijah P. Marrs, *Life of Reverend Elijah P. Marrs* (1885), and Elisha W. Green, *Life of Rev. Elisha W. Green, One of the Founders of the Kentucky Normal and Theological*

Institute (1888). For accounts of the black Baptist churches in Kentucky, sketches of church leaders, and the growth of State University, see Charles H. Parris (ed.), *Golden Jubilee, General Association of Colored Baptists in Kentucky* (1915). The modern study of black Louisville is George C. Wright, *Life behind a Veil: Blacks in Louisville, Kentucky, 1865–1930* (1985).

ISAIAH T. MONTGOMERY. A short article by Montgomery, "The Negro in Business," *Outlook,* 69 (Nov. 16, 1901), is a representative statement of his optimistic philosophy. The early history of Mound Bayou, including much about Montgomery, is described in Booker T. Washington, "A Town Owned by Negroes, Mound Bayou, Miss.: An Example of Thrift and Self-Government," *World's Work,* 14 (July 1907), and reprinted in Louis R. Harlan and Raymond W. Smock (eds.), *The Booker T. Washington Papers* (13 vols., 1972–84), 9, 307–20. See also the correspondence between Montgomery and Washington in Louis R. Harlan (ed.), *The Booker T. Washington Papers,* especially the revealing and despondent letter sent by Montgomery on September 6, 1904 (8, 61–63), describing the work of white terrorism and intimidation and its implications for the success ethic.

There is no biography of Montgomery. The most complete account of the family is Janet Sharp Hermann, *The Pursuit of a Dream* (1981). On Mound Bayou and Montgomery, see also August Meier, "Booker T. Washington and the Town of Mound Bayou," *Phylon,* 15 (Winter 1954); Norman L. Crockett, *The Black Towns* (1979); and Louis R. Harlan, *Booker T. Washington: The Wizard of Tuskegee* (1983).

MARY CHURCH TERRELL. The place to begin is her autobiography, *A Colored Woman in a White World* (1940). On the black women's club movement, see Terrell, "The Club Work of Colored Women," *The Southern Workman,* 30 (Aug. 1901), and "The History of the Club Women's Movement," *The Aframerican Woman's Journal,* 1 (Summer/Fall 1940). See also Fannie B. Williams, "The Club Movement among Colored Women of America," in Booker T. Washington, *A New Negro for a New Century* (1900); Elizabeth L. Davis, *Lifting as They Climb* (1933); Gerda Lerner, "Early Community Work of Black Club Women," *Journal of Negro History,* 59 (Apr. 1974); and Sharon Harley, "Beyond the Classroom: Organized Lives of Black Female Educators, 1890–1930," *Journal of Negro Education,* 51 (Summer 1982).

LEON LITWACK

Notes on Contributors

WILLIAM CHEEK and AIMEE LEE CHEEK are the authors of a forthcoming study of John Mercer Langston and the antebellum northern free black community. William Cheek teaches at San Diego State University.

JOHN DITTMER teaches at DePauw University. He is the author of *Black Georgia in the Progressive Era, 1900–1920* (1977).

ERIC FONER teaches at Columbia University. His publications include *Free Soil, Free Labor, Free Men: The Ideology of the Republican Party before the Civil War* (1970), *Nothing But Freedom: Emancipation and Its Legacy* (1983), and a forthcoming volume in the New American Nation series on Reconstruction.

DAVID A. GERBER teaches at the State University of New York at Buffalo. He is the author of *Black Ohio and the Color Line, 1860–1915* (1970) and editor of *Anti-Semitism in American History* (1986).

SHARON HARLEY teaches at the University of Maryland at College Park. She is co-editor (with Rosalyn Terborg-Penn) of *The Afro-American Woman: Struggles and Images* (1978).

JANET SHARP HERMANN is the author of *The Pursuit of a Dream* (1981).

LEON LITWACK teaches at the University of California at Berkeley. He is the author of *North of Slavery: The Negro in the Free States, 1790–1860* (1961) and *Been in the Storm So Long: The Aftermath of Slavery* (1979).

WALDO E. MARTIN, JR. teaches at the University of Virginia. He is the author of *The Mind of Frederick Douglass* (1984).

AUGUST MEIER teaches at Kent State University. He is the author of a number of monographs, including *Negro Thought in America, 1880–1915* (1963); and with Elliott Rudwick, *From Plantation to Ghetto* (1966), *Core: A Study in the Civil Rights Movement, 1942–1968* (1973), and *Black History and the Historical Profession, 1915–1980* (1986).

ALFRED MOSS teaches at the University of Maryland at College Park. He is the author of *The American Negro Academy: Voice of the Talented Tenth* (1981).

NELL IRVIN PAINTER teaches at the University of North Carolina. She is the author of *Exodusters: Black Migration to Kansas after Reconstruction* (1977).

BENJAMIN QUARLES is retired after teaching for many years at Morgan State College. He is the author of numerous volumes, including *Frederick Douglass* (1948), *The Negro in the Civil War* (1953), *The Negro in the American Revolution* (1961), *Lincoln and the Negro* (1962), and *Black Abolitionists* (1969).

HOWARD N. RABINOWITZ teaches at the University of New Mexico. He is the author of *Race Relations in the Urban South, 1865-1890* (1978) and the editor of *Southern Black Leaders of the Reconstruction Era* (1982).

ALBERT J. RABOTEAU teaches at Princeton University. He is the author of *Slave Religion: The "Invisible Institution" in the Antebellum South* (1978).

JASON H. SILVERMAN teaches at Winthrop College. He is the author of *Unwelcome Guests: Canada West's Response to American Fugitive Slaves, 1800-1865* (1985).

STERLING STUCKEY teaches at Northwestern University. He is the author of *The Intellectual Origins of Black Nationalism* (1972) and *Slave Culture: Nationalist Theory and the Foundations of Black America* (1987).

PETER H. WOOD teaches at Duke University. He is the author of *Black Majority: Negroes in Colonial South Carolina from 1670 through the Stono Rebellion* (1974).

GEORGE C. WRIGHT teaches at the University of Texas. He is the author of *Life behind a Veil: Blacks in Louisville, Kentucky, 1865-1930* (1985).

Index

Father Divine and the Struggle for Racial Equality
Robert Weisbrot

Communists in Harlem during the Depression
Mark Naison

Down from Equality: Black Chicagoans and the Public Schools, 1920-41
Michael W. Homel

Race and Kinship in a Midwestern Town: The Black Experience
in Monroe, Michigan, 1900-1915
James E. DeVries

Down by the Riverside: A South Carolina Slave Community
Charles Joyner

Black Milwaukee: The Making of an Industrial Proletariat, 1915-45
Edited by Joe William Trotter, Jr.

Religious Philanthropy and Colonial Slavery: The American
Correspondence of the Associates of Dr. Bray, 1717-1777
Edited by John C. Van Horne

Black History and the Historical Profession, 1915-80
August Meier and Elliott Rudwick

Rise to Be a People: A Biography of Paul Cuffe
Lamont D. Thomas

Making Their Own Way: Southern Blacks' Migration to Pittsburgh, 1916-30
Peter Gottlieb

My Bondage and My Freedom
Frederick Douglass, edited by William L. Andrews

Black Leaders of the Nineteenth Century
Edited by Leon Litwack and August Meier

Reprint Editions

King: A Biography
David Levering Lewis
Second Edition

The Death and Life of Malcolm X
Peter Goldman
Second Edition

Race Relations in the Urban South, 1865-1890
Howard N. Rabinowitz, with a Foreword by C. Vann Woodward

Race Riot at East St. Louis, July 2, 1917
Elliott Rudwick

W. E. B. Du Bois: Voice of the Black Protest Movement
Elliott Rudwick

The Negro's Civil War: How American Negroes Felt and Acted
during the War for the Union
James M. McPherson

Lincoln and Black Freedom: A Study in Presidential Leadership
LaWanda Cox

Slavery and Freedom in the Age of the American Revolution
Edited by Ira Berlin and Ronald Hoffman